Chinese Art

Chinese Art

Bronzes * Jade * Sculpture * Ceramics

By Daisy Lion-Goldschmidt

MUSÉE GUIMET PARIS

*

Jean-Claude Moreau-Gobard

WITH A FOREWORD BY GEORGE SAVAGE

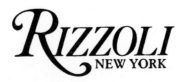

RIZZOLI
NEW YORK

Translated from the French, *Arts de la Chine*
by DIANA IMBER

French-language edition:
© 1966 by Office du Livre, Fribourg, Switzerland

English revised edition published 1980
in the United States of America by:

RIZZOLI INTERNATIONAL PUBLICATIONS, INC.
712 Fifth Avenue/New York 10019

Library of Congress Catalog Card Number: 79-92811
ISBN: 0-8478-0302-3

Printed and bound in Switzerland

CONTENTS

FOREWORD

Chinese civilization is remarkable for its continuity. Throughout its long history China has been invaded many times by alien peoples and creeds, but the invaders have always been absorbed into the traditional way of life. This emerges from the pages which follow. The work of the Ch'ing dynasty, which ended with the foundation of the Republic in 1911, constantly echoes that of the Shang peoples more than three thousand years before.

The origin of the Chinese people is controversial. Some would see in the Neolithic funerary vases of Kansu Province, China's gateway to Central Asia, signs of immigration from Mesopotamia and the West. Certainly there is an apparent affinity between these vases and those which have been found in the Black Earth region of Southern Russia. There is also an undoubted relationship between Chinese decorative motifs and the general body of Pacific art, which includes that of Central and Southern America. Support for a theory that these cultures had a common origin, independently of those of the West, is growing. It is an attractive supposition on which little work has hitherto been done.

The Chinese language, which belongs to the Sino-Tibetan group, is now monosyllabic, and this, and its grammatical structure which is simple in the extreme, imposes upon it a remarkable economy and brevity of expression. In its written form the characters are largely pictographic – that is, they represent objects, ideas, and words, instead of sounds. They are extremely decorative, especially when written with a brush, and, somewhat naturally, calligraphy in China has been elevated to the status of an art. Ideograms occur frequently in decoration of all kinds.

It is hardly surprising that a culture exhibiting so many points of difference from that of the West should have been the focus of undiminished interest throughout the centuries. The authors of the present volume, however, have provided a viewpoint which is new by emphasizing the earlier and more important work. For the most part this is hardly known to any but a few specialists, but the critical and scholarly commentary, as well as the detailed descriptions of the objects themselves, will be invaluable to the general reader, and stimulating and thought-provoking to those who are on more familiar territory.

The strangeness of the art of China is largely a myth. It is no more difficult to understand and appreciate than the arts of the early civilizations of Europe and the Middle East once the essential facts have been grasped. In its later phases it is often more remarkable for humorous observation than for spiritual exaltation, which always came hardly to the Chinese. The history of art elsewhere has contained far too little of the first, and a surfeit of the second.

The Chinese have simply adopted a different scale of values which is, in some ways, more civilized and sophisticated than our own, and reveals a sympathetic sense of unity with life and its realities. To our own certainties of right and wrong they oppose the Confucian Doctrine of the Golden Mean, admirably crystallized by Lin Yu-tang in the phrase: A is right, and B is not wrong either.

It is for this reason that any events in China ought to be regarded as a passing phase in its long and eventful history. Like those which have gone before, alien creeds will be assimilated into the Chinese perception of life and the urbane civilization in which it has always excelled.

George Savage

PREFACE TO THE SECOND EDITION

An introduction to Chinese Art, based on a study of a representative selection of masterpieces, is the type of book that ages well. Now, twenty years after its initial publication, the Chinese Art *series is being republished, and the only revisions necessary have proved to be minor.*

China is of growing interest to the Western world today. The ease of travelling, books and articles on trips to China and scholarly works on recent discoveries have captured the public's imagination; so this is a particularly propitious moment for a second edition of this series in a new and less expensive format that should enable a wider audience to become acquainted with China's many-sided art.

Although China is opening her doors to the West, she has not forgotten her past traditions – the works of exceptional quality born of her ancient civilization. These works of art constitute the best bridge to foreigners trying to understand China, and the Chinese, who conserve and restore the remains of their fabulous past with infinite care, are well aware of this. Archaeological excavations have been started throughout China, specialist publications abound, and many museums have been established. In the light of recent discoveries, it has been especially interesting to note the development in our knowledge of Chinese art over the last twenty years.

Surprisingly, none of the observations made previously in this book have had to be revised. Although work carried out in China has added an enormous quantity of new facts – partially divulged in exhibitions that travelled throughout the world in 1973 and 1974 – the masterpieces selected two decades ago have remained masterpieces, of as much value and interest today as then, despite the new finds that have come to light.

Even the old attributions of objects in the book are still *valid, except for some minor details that have been rectified in this edition. The only major revisions concerned objects in private collections, which have been dispersed in the meantime. Many such collections have been lent or bequeathed to museums, for instance the collection of the late King of Sweden, Gustave VI Adolphe, which was left to the Östasiatiska Museet, Stockholm, or the Michel Calmann Collection, which is now one of the prize possessions of the Musée Guimet, Paris. These changes have been taken into account here as far as possible.*

Daisy Lion-Goldschmidt
March 1980

INTRODUCTION

The works of art illustrated in this book have been selected for the most part from private collections. It has been possible to reproduce objects which are unknown to the general reader, and which have only been seen very rarely in specialist exhibitions. Many of them have never been published previously; others only in specialist reviews or catalogues. We have thus been able to base our study of the essentials of the history of Chinese art on very interesting documentary examples.

We have confined ourselves to four aspects of art, leaving to one side painting, which would require a much more detailed study than has been possible here, as well as the more episodal techniques, such as lacquer, cloisonné enamels, textiles, and silver. The arts discussed here cover a period of history extending over four millennia. These are bronzes, jades, sculpture, and ceramics. The bronzes, mysterious and technically unequalled, at first bear witness to an austere religious ritual prevailing in the earliest times, gradually to become an art of ornament and decoration. The jades, almost sacred in Chinese eyes, are remarkable also for the hours of patience and skill needed to produce them. Sculpture is really inseparable from the bronzes and jades, since many sculptural masterpieces are in these materials, although, in general, the art of sculpture is manifested in stone. However, here we arrive at a perplexing problem. Although it may not be difficult to find landmarks of technical development in bronze and jade in Western collections, it is really impossible to outline a history of Chinese sculpture without mentioning the enormous monumental carvings which exist in that country. We have been able partly to surmount this difficulty by reproducing some famous pieces now in museums. The great public collections have also come to our aid with many archaic bronzes, enabling us to achieve continuity. The last part of the book is devoted to a rapid survey of the principal aspects of Chinese ceramics. We have been purposely brief on this subject, since Professor Fujio Koyama's important work on the ceramic art of Asia has recently appeared in this series.

The choice of plates and commentaries is the result of the combined research of M. Jean-Claude Moreau-Gobard and myself. M. Moreau-Gobard has been responsible for choosing the pieces from his vast knowledge of the important collections of Europe. He has done much research on many of the objects, and has collected the material for the greater number of the captions. He has also supervised the difficulties of colored illustrations, involving, as it often does, careful comparison with the original.

This book is primarily intended to be a collection of plates illustrating the important stages in the history of Chinese art. It is difficult to express adequately our thanks to the many private collectors and curators of museums who have allowed us to reproduce their treasures. It would be impossible to mention them all, but we owe a special debt of gratitude to those among them who have so kindly provided interesting documentary information on the objects, and who have helped us with invaluable advice.

Daisy Lion-Goldschmidt

BRONZES

W HEN THEY were first confronted, early in this century, with the archaic Chinese bronzes, European scholars were nonplused. Perplexed by such astonishing *tours de force* they were reluctant to fix their origin at such an early period. In fact, the technical perfection, originality of form, and the esoteric character of their ornament is the sublime expression of one of the greatest moments in man's history. This is particularly true of the ritual vessels. Nothing in any other civilization compares with them. Classical Greek or Italian Renaissance art approaches them in quality, but their import is quite different. One is immediately struck by the strangeness, the clarity of line, by the interweaving patterns – now baroque and threatening, now infinitely delicate – heavy with symbolism and magic, which make them mysterious and vital.

The finest period of the Chinese bronzes can be dated somewhere between the 14th century B. C. and the beginning of our era. They are essentially a rich and varied collection of ceremonial vessels and weapons. At first a solely religious art, it developed over the centuries, and gradually lost its hieratic, majestic quality to become a decorative art of great virtuosity, unique and unequaled elsewhere.

From the end of the Chou dynasty (1122–249 B.C.) the ancient bronzes were revered and studied in China. The accidental discovery of one during the Han period (206 B.C. to A.D. 220) was an event of national importance. Great collections were made during the Sung dynasty, especially by the Emperors whose artists described and catalogued them for us. They remained, however, unknown to the Western world until the end of the 19th and the beginning of the 20th centuries. They made an immediate impact, but nothing was known, and it was impossible to date them, or to establish their historical context.

The archaeological work undertaken by the Peking Academy since 1928 has brought much information to light. We know now that the earliest bronzes date from the Shang dynasty. The Shang ruled from 1500 to 1028 B. C. over the Northern plains, and especially the Central Plain – the fertile region at the mouth of the Yellow River. The main finds were made at the site of the last of the Shang capitals, where they settled about 1300, namely An-Yang in the north of Honan Province, a town henceforth destined to be famous in the world of archaeology.

The Shang or Yin* civilization which succeeded previous Neolithic stages of development emerges as a highly organized, hierarchic, and urbane society, enjoying much material prosperity. The Emperor was the center of an official class of priests, soothsayers, and scribes, and also, doubtless, of the warlike nobility. Rich royal tombs have been found in An-Yang; also the remains of palaces and dwellings,

---

* The term, Yin, often used to indicate the first historical dynasty in China and sometimes in conjunction with Shang ("Shang-Yin"), does not appear before the Chou era. We prefer the more traditional *Shang*.

built on raised terraces of beaten earth, still showing the wooden pillars which supported the roof; remains of the bronze foundries, the jade cutters' and potters' workshops. The tombs of the emperors and the aristocracy contained arms and vessels of bronze, marble figures, jade, and pieces of silk, together with objects in carved ivory, bone, or pottery. Many bones engraved with occult signs or writing of ritual significance in the daily life of the Emperor, as well as incised inscriptions on bronze, show that writing was known and already well advanced, but the truth is that, beyond the names and succession of the Emperors, we know almost nothing of the history of Shang society, nor of its religion. This, however, seems to have been based on a cult of the elements and natural forces, a logical point of view for an agricultural people whose lives were subject to the unremitting seasons. Sky, earth, and mountains, rivers, light and shade, death and rebirth, seem to have played a primitive role in their beliefs. In the Imperial House and noble families, ancestor worship was an essential part of religious life. The souls of the dead had to be kept "alive" to protect their descendants, who held annual feasts at which the finest dishes were solemnly offered as a gift to the dead ancestors before being shared among the living.

The bronzes, rare and precious objects, reserved only for the great, were the ceremonial instruments of these complex rites which required many different vessels.

Of the Chou dynasty, which supplanted the Shang in 1028, we know more. They came from the Western Province of Shensi, and had probably been subjects of the Shang emperors. Their culture was not so highly developed, but they respected and continued the tradition of ancestor worship, clinging to the artistic heritage of their predecessors. China became a vast agglomeration of more or less powerful principalities. The chronicles of the Chou describe the smallest events in their history, the organization of vassal states, warlike expeditions, and political differences.

Little by little, however, the fiefs became fewer and larger. Four rival powers ruled China between them, and the role played by the emperor became purely religious. This state of affairs gave the period its name – that of "The Warring States." It lasted from 481 to 221 B.C., and is remarkable for an amazing artistic renaissance. The accession to power of the Ch'in, who established a central government for the first time, put an end to these troubled years. The reign of Shih Huang-ti is the beginning of the Chinese Empire, which was to reach its widest influence in times of the Han dynasty.

The evolution of the ancient Chinese bronzes is bounded by this historical frame. It is a remarkable fact that this art reached its highest point as early as the An-Yang period (1300–1028 B.C.). The perfection of these bronzes is such that even today, with all the advantages available in the modern foundry, it is scarcely possible to surpass them technically. An even more surprising fact is that, until recently, nothing was known of any forerunners to these masterpieces. Yet it is impossible to accept their sudden appearance, perfect as they were, without assuming the passage of many years of groping experiment beforehand. However, some of the present researches conducted by the Archaeological Institute of the People's Republic are helping to clarify this problem. Shang sites, older than An-Yang, and mostly situated in Honan Province, have been discovered, among them the ancient city of Ao, where Chêng

Chou now stands. Tomb furnishings uncovered there include bronze vases, and objects of stone, pottery, horn, and bone. Traces of bronze foundries have been found with molds and crucibles, which confirm the existence of a more primitive industry than that of An-Yang. The alloys are less refined, the material weak, and the shapes heavier and not so perfectly proportioned. Undoubtedly present research will unearth new discoveries, and throw more light on those stages in development which must have preceded the final perfect achievement of the bronzes.

Problems of dating have given rise to much important work; notably and primarily among these the researches of the Swedish scholar, Bernhard Karlgren. Some inscribed pieces can be dated exactly. In Shang times these inscriptions consisted in two or three characters representing the name of the ancestor in whose honor the vase was made. Not more than a dozen among them, those with an Emperor's name, can be dated with authority. Chou inscriptions, however, became more important, and sometimes contain hundreds of characters. Besides the name of the honored ancestor, these give the name of the donor, and also describe the important occasion of its casting – an occasion provided, perhaps, by an audience of the Emperor or Prince on the granting of land concessions, an appointment, or a reward. The date and place of the ceremony are shown. The vassal showed his gratitude by casting the piece; the inscription expresses his loyalty to the sovereign and contains the pious wish that "his sons and grandsons will preserve and use this sacred vessel for all time." The few landmarks provided by the inscriptions are not enough, though, to make a coherent chronological picture of Chinese bronzes of the period. Scholars relying on the study of form and decoration have been able to determine successive stylistic epochs.

The classification usually adopted is as follows:

1. Shang epoch, before An-Yang (c. 1500–c. 1300);
2. Shang epoch (An-Yang period)–beginning of the Chou epoch;
3. Middle period of Chou (c. 950–600);
4. End of Chou, embracing the Warring States (c. 600–221).

This chronology is much simplified. I have deliberately avoided the literary divisions (e.g. the Period of the Spring and Autumn Annals – 722–481) and the political classification (Western Chou – 1027–771, Eastern Chou – 771–256) which are encountered in some texts, and which have nothing to do with the development of style. On the other hand, the suggested dates are by no means absolute and can only give a general indication, since successive styles frequently overlap. In general, however, each of these four phases is represented by shapes and treatment of decoration which are characteristic.

The oldest Chinese traditional beliefs credited the bronze founder and his forge with supernatural powers. To the legendary Emperors, Huang Ti, one of the Five Sovereigns, and to Yü the Great, founder of the Hsia dynasty, was attributed the casting of tripod cauldrons, talismans of the half-mythical Hsia kings. These vague memories explain the precious, almost sacred aura surrounding the metal. Again, legend tells that bronze "came from a far country." In fact, we do not know how the technique of bronze casting originated in China. It is possible that it came from the West, where Syria and Mesopotamia had known and practiced this art since the third millennium. The oldest pieces found in Honan Province at Hui Hsien, at Ch'êng Chou, or at Hsiao-t'un on the An-Yang site, are fragile, and of a very primitive alloy, in every way far less expert than those of the classical An-Yang period (1300–1028). Analysis of the bronzes of An-Yang shows average proportions of about 83 per cent of copper and 17 per cent of tin. At least six different alloys were used, according to the purpose for which the piece was intended, be it vase, bell, or weapon. The large proportion of tin explains the silver effect of many of the archaic bronzes.

Casting was done directly by means of founder's sand or plaster molds, and also by the "lost wax" (*cire perdue*) method.

Straightforward molds in two pieces were used to make weapons, arrowheads, and other flat objects. Molds in several pieces, held together with tenon and mortice joints, were used for the more complicated objects. At An-Yang, and on other sites too, clay molds, crucibles, and cores have been found in the remains of the founders' workshops. It seems probable, although there is no absolute proof, that the "lost wax" process was used for the finely chiseled bronzes; without this assumption it is impossible to see how the workers could have achieved the decoration to be seen on some of them.

It is certain, though, that after the Shang, the Chinese had completely mastered this very difficult technique. The perfect finish, sharp detail of the ornament, homogeneity of the metal, and the surface quality have never been surpassed. One must also appreciate the enormous value attached to the ancient bronzes, and remember that they were reserved, like treasure, for the emperors and a privileged caste.

Today, we see the Chinese bronzes in a condition very different from the original. Their long period underground has covered them with a patina, sometimes rough with incrustations penetrating the metal, and sometimes smooth and soft to the touch, like jade. Thus, they take on all the shades of green, from the warm somber tones to the bright delicate tints. Often, there are russet, purple, or blue patches depending on the chemical changes which have affected the metal. Certain green tones are produced by the presence of hydrous copper carbonate, the formula for malachite. Another copper carbonate produces the blue of azurite, and a pure oxide, cuprite, is responsible for the reddish tones. Western connoisseurs hold that these colors, with their manifold shades and tones, greatly enhance the beauty of the archaic bronzes.

Were it possible to collect together all the ritual vessels at present known, the total would easily surpass the astonishing figure of twelve thousand. Although there are many different shapes, they can be
reduced to a few essential types used for the ritual of ancestor worship. This consisted in offerings of
food and drink. Vessels were required in which to cook and serve the dishes (meat, rice, and millet),
to preserve and hold the wine for drinking, and to contain and pour water. Food was cooked in the
vessels known as *li*, *ting*, and *hsien*, and served in the *kuei* and the *tou*. Wine was heated and mixed
with water in the *kuang* and the *huo*; it was stored in a *tsun*, *yu*, or *hu*. The chalices, cups, and goblets
(*ku*, *chüeh*, *chih*, and *chia*) were used for libation. There were also water bowls, called *p'an* and *chien*,
ewers known as *yi*, and ladles (*shao*).

These names originated in different ways: some are found engraved on the vessels themselves, and
can be read from the inscriptions. Others have been attributed to them by literary sages of the Chou
dynasty, and some only by latter-day interpretation of ancient texts. After the ritual vessels, bells
(*chung*) are among the most imposing of ancient Chinese bronzes (Plate 40). They continued, with
variations, from the Shang to the Han dynasties. But many different weapons have also been found in
tombs, among them daggers, axes, and knives. Some of the finest of these seem to have been ceremonial
in purpose, turquoise encrusted, and, by the end of the Chou dynasty, inlaid with jade, gold, and silver.
There was also harness, and chariot and furniture ornament. Belt hooks and mirrors are to be seen after
the period of the Warring States.

The names of the ritual vessels given here by no means exhaust the known forms, and besides, each
name indicates a group of shapes rather than a single type. Even if the form of a certain type stays
more or less the same, its proportions and attachments (handles, feet, covers, and so forth) may vary,
depending on the period and the place where it was made. There are, in fact, great local differences,
born of the vastness of China. For instance, the Chou princedoms evolved independently up to a certain
point, in spite of the unifying religious traditions. However, without much more scientific excavation
and research it is not yet possible to be exact about these charateristics. We should, therefore, examine
the bronzes and their decoration as a whole, taking their origin into account only in the later periods.

The *li* is the earliest of all the ritual vessels, and perhaps the most characteristically Chinese in its
striking originality (Plate 20). It is a large cauldron with a wide uncovered mouth, always recognizable by its three hollow legs meeting and spreading at the top to form the body of the vase (cf. the
huo, Plate 3, and the lower part of the *hsien*, Plate 10). The prototype of the *li* is to be seen in the
neolithic pottery of Honan and Shantung. It seems to disappear about the middle of the Chou period.

The *ting*, a tripod with solid, more or less cylindrical legs, and a general hemispherical body surmounted by two vertical rounded handles (Plate 21, 7 and 8), is nearly as old as the *li*, and has also
very early Neolithic forbears. It continues until and beyond the Han dynasty. In the Chou period it
becomes shallower and sometimes has legs in the shape of dragons or birds. About the end of this

period it sometimes has a cover, the feet are curved, and the incurving handles are attached to the body of the vase instead of to the upper rim.

Between *li* and *ting* there is an intermediate class, known as the *li-ting*. It is recognizable by its hollow legs, less spreading than those of the *li*, and clearly separated one from the other (Plate 17). The *hsien* (Plate 10) is a composite vessel with two different and superimposed elements, one a tripod similar to the *li* and the other a hollow container, with a grille at the base to serve as a cauldron for steaming food. Its form scarcely varies, although it continues for a very long time.

The *kuei* has its origin in the Yang-Shao painted pottery. At first it is a large bowl supported by a circular base (Plate 26). Later, the base develops into a massive plinth of cubic form. It has two or (rarely) four large handles. These are decorated with masks in relief, from the underside of which hangs a kind of pendant. The *tou* derives its characteristic form from the black neolithic pottery, many pieces of which have been found in Honan and Shantung, notably at Ch'êng Tzŭ Yai. A hemispherical cup on a flared base, it always has a cover which, when reversed, forms a separate cup (Plate 42). The *tou* does not arise before the third period of the Chou dynasty, and continues in use under the rule of the Han.

No pottery seems to correspond to the *kuang*. It is a strange, complex type, resembling a sauce-boat. It has a convex lid shaped like an animal's back which terminates in the well-modeled head of a tiger, buffalo, or elephant (Plate 22). A handle like those on the *kuei* adorns the opposite side. *Kuang* are often found together with long-handled ladles called *shao* (Plate 25). Both these forms disappear after the period embracing – stylistically speaking – the Shang and the beginning of the Chou epochs. The *huo* is a pouring vessel, a kind of kettle with a closed spout, a handle, and a cover (Plate 3). It has three or four legs reminiscent of the *li* and the *ting*. This type is present through all the phases of Shang and Chou.

The term *tsun* is applied to many different forms. Indeed the relevant Chinese character, without defining a specific type, means a ritual wine vessel. In one of its meanings it comprises the tall vase with a wide central band and a flaring mouth which much resembles the *ku*, though it is more massive (Plates 9, 13 and 23). Grouped in the same family are the vessels in the form of animals (*niao shou tsun* and *hsi tsun*). There was a wide variety of these during the Shang era – elephants, the buffalo, the rhinoceros, rams, and birds. These have an opening in the back. The style of these animals, modeled in the round, sometimes back to back, combines a striking realism with extreme stylization. This conjunction of widely differing elements – ritual ornament and animal force – gives them a fantastic appearance.

Finally, the vases now called *fang i* are really a kind of *tsun*. These are powerful architectural constructions of rectangular section, resembling primitive dwellings. The cover represents the roof (Plate 2). *Fang i* have been found at Hsaio T'un, a village in the middle of the ancient site of An-Yang, and showing by its stratification that it dates from one of the earliest stages of Shang culture. This type of vase is not seen after the end of the Shang dynasty.

The *yu* were used for storing and carrying wine. They are covered vessels of a general elliptical section, with low-slung belly and characteristic handles. These have a relief mask of an animal at the point of attachment (Plate 27). The general impression is striking in a rather baroque way, and all known specimens date from Shang or early Chou times. The *hu* was used in the same way as the *yu*, and is shaped rather like a bottle. It, too, has a low-slung belly, and a tall neck which often has rings or tubular "ears" to carry a chain (Plate 37). They are rare in the First Phase, but common during the period of the Warring States and under the Han. They are frequently monumental in their proportions, and specimens of square section are to be seen occasionally.

Lithe, elegant, and pure in form, it is the *ku* which holds pride of place among the ritual bronzes (Plate 6). These vessels belong exclusively to the First Phase – to the Shang dynasty. It is in the form of a tall goblet or libation chalice, flaring at the mouth and foot, and with a broad band in the center. It has four vertical flanges, indented to a varying degree, which complete the rhythmic design with wonderful *finesse*. The *ku*, sometimes of square section, was much copied in jade and porcelain after the Sung dynasty.

The very elaborate form of the goblets, *chia* and *chüeh* (Plates 18 and 19), might seem at first sight to be a rather late development in the art of bronze. They are, on the contrary, among the earliest finds before An-Yang, notably at Ch'êng Chou (15th–14th centuries?). At that period they are cruder, and their components less perfectly balanced. After An-Yang (c. 1300–1028) they have the characteristic shape which distinguishes them from all other Chinese bronzes.

They are a kind of goblet mounted on three lancet shaped feet. They have, also, a handle, and two uprights with conical caps. The *chüeh* has a large pouring lip balanced by an extension to the rear of the vessel. It is possible that this shape derives from the prehistoric pottery shape, *li-ting* (Plate 17). The uprights are not so easily explained, though many theories have been advanced. Of these, the most likely seems to be that of Professor Yetts, who thought they were used to enable the vessel to be withdrawn from the fire by means of pincers passed under the caps. The *chia* and the *chüeh* disappeared sometime in the 10th century B.C. There are some *chia* which have four feet, and are square. These are often monumental (even as large as 73 cm in height), whereas the *chüeh* is always reasonably small. Mention must finally be made of another type of *chüeh*, the *chiao*, to be distinguished by a cover embracing both extensions, and without the uprights.

The drinking vessel, *chih*, is much less elaborate. It is at once reminiscent of the *hu* and the *yu*, but it has neither the slender neck of the first of these, nor the handle of the second (Plates 4 and 5). It is generally small and ovoid, originally with a cover which has often disappeared.

The *p'an* is a wider shallow bowl for washing, or perhaps for serving fruit, and is mounted on a circular foot (Plates 29 and 36). No pottery prototype is known, but recent researches have unearthed some examples belonging to the early Bronze Age. Before these were discovered this shape had been thought to be fairly late, all previously known examples being of the early Chou period. The *p'an* continues until the middle of the Han dynasty. It usually has semi-circular handles surmounted by dragons' heads rearing above the rim of the vessel. The interior is almost always decorated with vividly naturalistic animals incised or in light relief, and these are sometimes accompanied by large dragons with coiled tails. Inscriptions are also found, often long. One of these has no less than 357 characters.

The *chien* may be distinguished from the *p'an* by its greater size and depth. It is often extremely large. A kind of basin, it does not appear before the middle of the Chou period, and was still in use under the Han. The ideogram suggests that it may have been used as a mirror, perhaps in a magical sense to reflect the rays of the sun or moon. Texts of the Chou period, however, say that it was used to hold ice.

Finally, there are the less well known vessels, such as the *p'ou*, a kind of urn, which derives from the earliest period (Plate 1); the *lei*, a large covered receptacle with handles, tall and often square; also the *tui* (Plate 41) which developed from the *ting* of the late Chou dynasty, and like the *ting* has three feet, although it is generally round or ovoid with the simplicity of line which is typical of the period. The upper part of the *tui* is a cover with three handles so arranged that it may be reversed to form a cup. Large flat bottles, called *pien-hu*, were rather late, as were the *lien*, which were cylindrical cosmetic boxes. With these two classes we come into the realm of everyday objects. The bronze has already lost its ritual character, and, in doing so, breaks away finally from the traditional forms. This may be seen in the incense burners (Plate 55), oil-lamps (Plate 46), and many purely ornamental pieces for furniture, chariots, staves, or harness.

There remain still two important groups representative of the classical Bronze Age. These are the bells and the weapons. The bells, used in religious ceremonial, appear first in the Shang period. They were made in series, each identical except in size, and thus they produced different notes. They are elliptical, and have no clapper, the sound being produced by striking the bell with a wooden mallet. The archaic bells had a long tubular "sleeve" on which they were placed, as it were "upside down," and in this way their decoration – large *t'ao t'ieh* masks – appears in the correct position. Later bells were furnished with thirty-six nodules, in four groups of nine. These were to be struck; and, at this period, the bells were hung from handles. The finest, both in the quality of the bronze and the decoration, are undoubtedly the famous series made in the period of the Warring States (Plate 40). They are considered to be some of the finest examples of the art of bronze.

Another musical instrument was the wide cylindrical drum, but early examples are extemely rare. Recently some have been unearthed in Royal tombs in the Southern Province of Yünnan. They are immense, and date from the 2nd century B.C. These drums have an amazing decoration sculptured in the round on their upper platform, representing a large crowd of people in front of a house, or perhaps attending some ceremony. They are related to those, far more widely known and made in the Han period, which were found in large quantities at Doug-sou in Vietnam, and which have beautiful incised decoration. About the same time, in China, bells were made in the form of drums – hollow, tall, and wide at the top. These pieces were quite undecorated, except on the handle, which is frequently a piece of animal sculpture (Plate 53).

The finest weapons were made during the Shang dynasty. They are often richly decorated and complex, and must have been ceremonial objects. Of these the most important are the axes made to fit into a wooden socket (Plate 24), the halberds, and the daggers (*ko*), which often had sumptuously inlaid hilts (Plate 14). Knives have been found in the royal tombs at An-Yang with curving blades, surmounted by realistic heads of ibexes. The discovery raises the question of naturalistic animal decoration in China. This was previously thought to have originated in Central Asia, but now it seems that a realistic tradition may have existed at the same time as the hieratic style of the Shang, and it was this style which spread towards Siberia long before Western ideas returned in due course to inspire and influence the art of the Warring States.

The most important and representative objects of art of the Warring States period are the mirrors and belt hooks. Mirrors have had a long history in China. At first, it seems, they were thought to have magic properties. About 600 B.C. they were square, but later developed into a round disk, polished on one side and decorated on the back with a design centered on a pierced knob which was to enable the mirror to be hung from the belt. During the period of the Warring States mirrors were small and thin. A delicately incised design of flowers, dragons, stylized birds, or perhaps geometrical *motifs* (lozenges, broken lines, and zigzags) was imposed on a ground of spirals, commas, and granulations executed with the greatest skill (Plates 50 and 51). The principal centers of manufacture were in the regions of Lo-Yang, in Honan, and in the Huai valley, near Shou Chou in Anhui Province. Han mirrors are at once thicker and more important, the knob becomes larger, and the rigid linear decoration is based on geometric *motifs* expressing a complex symbolism. The composition grows heavier about the 3rd century B.C., representing legendary members of the Taoist hagiology in light relief (Plate 57). It is on mirrors of this period that one encounters the first representations of the Buddha in China.

Belt hooks were treasured pieces for personal adornment, and combined the jeweler's art with that of the bronze worker. At first, about the 5th century B.C. (Plate 47), they were small, but under the Han they were often quite large (Plates 48 and 49). They consist of a flat piece of metal, one end of which is fined down and turned back to form a hook, often in the shape of a bird's or a dragon's head. On the back of the broader part, which is in the shape of a mask, spatulate, or feather-like, is a flat button which served to attach the ornament to the clothes. Shape and decoration are varied, and often fantastic. Many pieces are inlaid with gold and silver which blend brilliantly with the turquoise, malachite, crystal, or jade often used also to enhance the objects. Under the Han, people are sometimes figured on the belt hooks, although animals are more usual, single or entwined, and sometimes in combat, which was a favorite theme among the artists of the steppes. It is all very vivid and spirited, and its dashing, dynamic style is typical of the art of the Han.

With the Han dynasty the finest period of the bronzes came to an end. It was not only that the metal seemed to disappear, but it lost all its vigor and symbolism. Only the T'ang mirrors remain important. They were usually round, or lobed like a flower, and decorated in high relief with animals floating among waves or vine leaves. The vessels are no longer sacred, and are inspired by ceramic shapes, or by Sassanian jewelry which was very popular at the time. (Plates 58 and 59). In the Sung and Ming dynasties bronze is used almost solely for the reproduction of archaic vessels. These were copied in careful detail, even to the inlays of gold and silver. But they are not convincing. The alloys are much heavier, and the *motifs* crudely drawn, their religious significance having been long forgotten.

Finally, we must touch on the bronzes of the 4th century, after the Wei dynasty. The whole idiom changes, and a type of small sculpture of very fine quality emerges. It is gilded, and reminiscent in miniature of the grandeur of Buddhist stone sculpture. The development of this art will, however, be discussed in the chapter on Chinese sculpture.

THE DECORATIVE STYLES OF THE BRONZES

The decoration of the archaic bronzes is essentially Chinese. It is a definite, integrated system of design in which nothing is left to chance, which is also to be seen on contemporary work in other materials – jade, ivory, marble, and even, to some extent, pottery. It is probable that this kind of decoration was first used on wood carving.

Our immediate reaction when first confronted with these brooding, often monstrous, *motifs* is to experience a weird feeling of uneasiness in face of the secret power emanating from them. This is dispelled on closer acquaintance with this strange unknown world. It is impossible not to apprehend their beauty and amazing virtuosity once the initial difficulty of deciphering their content has been overcome.

The Chinese used a most complex symbolism of mythology and spiritual belief in the decoration of the archaic bronzes. Abstract designs, sometimes partly realistic in conception, were used to express spiritual ideas, the cult of cosmic powers, awe in the face of the forces of Nature and the problem of death and afterlife. These symbols, strictly reserved for ceremonial vessels, conferred on the bronzes their ritual character and occult power. It would be impossible to try to explain the meaning of each *motif*, though some authorities have attempted it, notably Carl Hentze who gives closely detailed explanations. But although their conclusions seem valid in many cases, they are not founded on contemporary texts, or any definite archaeological fact. The dark mystery of this imaginary world remains still veiled.

It was by no means a static art. It changed several centuries after its first appearance, by which time its original significance was already completely lost. The essential themes remain, but they are now, in a sense, degenerate, disintegrated, and often unrecognizable. Bronze decoration gradually loses its mythological potency and ritual meaning, to become a purely decorative art with a completely different outlook.

The repertory of themes is, to use Karlgren's happy expression, a real "grammar" of decorative symbols. It employs mostly animal themes, almost always accompanied by geometric *motifs*. The shapes are very diverse, sometimes realistic and natural, but more often stylized to the point of being difficult to identify. Not stylization only, however, but also a surprising combination of heterogeneous elements, together give birth to a kingdom of fabulous beasts. These are certainly imaginary, but they have a potent vitality which gives them a life of their own. Surprisingly, some of the more familiar domestic animals – the dog, the pig, and the horse, for instance – are nowhere represented. We find, however, the tiger, buffalo, and ram; the snake, cicada, and owl, and many other beasts besides. The elephant and the rhinoceros, which lived in Southern China, are rarely to be seen. Some of these animals appear regularly, others only infrequently.

The most important of all early decoration is the *t'ao t'ieh* mask (sometimes called the glutton) which is found almost everywhere. Its fearful aspect moved the Han peoples to give it this name, though it was certainly a benevolent, protective spirit, guardian against the evil spirits so dreaded by the Chinese. The details of the masks vary widely, but the main feature is two large globular eyes enabling it to be picked out easily. Usually, there is no lower jaw. It has a powerful muzzle, nostrils, fangs, sometimes claws, and huge horns of varying shape (Plate 21.) It is nearly always a composite design of two dragons face to face, drawn in silhouette so that each forms half of the mask. Sometimes certain parts, the jaw or the forehead, join the two sides (Plate 20), but these are more usually separated by a vertical division – a sort of nasal rib (Plate 7 and 22). The skillful combination of lines and masses, forming two separate designs at once, is a familiar Chinese trick, but it bears witness to a high degree of development, and shows us an art in which all available techniques have been mastered.

It would be easy to see the head of a tiger, the earth "demon," in the *t'ao t'ieh*, but this cat-like creature is very often crowned with a ram's or a buffalo's horns. A precise definition is probably unwise.

The same could be said of the dragon, rain god and symbol of fertility, always associated with water. The term is ambiguous, and describes a hybrid creature, offspring of a lizard or a snake, but also of the tiger and buffalo, and even depicted sometimes with a trunk or a hooked beak. The *k'uei*, an archaic dragon with a single clawed foot, is one of the recurring figures of the early period (Plate 23). Dragons have a more or less elongated body, and are sometimes covered with scales, have ears, horns, and crests, feathers standing erect on the back, and lifted or pendant tails. They are easily confused with birds, of which there are many species, with beaks, crests, and wings of different shapes (Plate 5 and 12). Among these, the owl is recognizable by its large round eyes.

Alongside these, we find the cicada, a creature whose metamorphoses are symbols of death and rebirth. It is almost always stylized in the shape of a triangle (Plate 25), and this *motif* can often be seen repeated round the frieze on the neck of certain vessels (Plate 5). These triangles often developed into what Karlgren describes as "rising blades and hanging blades," where the cicada is barely recognizable, and is itself decorated with *t'ao t'ieh* masks (Plates 6 and 23).

The snakes, twining angular creatures, have a triangular head which is always full face. The ram and the buffalo are easily recognized by the horns, which are rolled and curving, or turn up into a point (Plates 10, 4 and 33). Their heads, and more rarely that of the deer, are more individual when they are cast in the round in a decorative frieze, or as part of the handle or foot of a vase (Plates 27 and 37). Much rarer are elephants, hares (Plate 22), silkworms, fish (Plate 22), and tortoises. Very often in the Han dynasty small crouching bears form the feet of some vessels.

Representation of humans is rare. There are some exceptional pieces, as, for instance, the two similar *yu* in the Cernuschi Museum in Paris and in the Sumitomo Collection in Japan, which show a man seated before a monster which is either protecting him, or is, perhaps, on the point of devouring him. Sometimes only the head is shown (Plate 30), at others, the human being becomes a demon with tail, wings, and claws (Plate 28). However, towards the end of the Chou dynasty, and also under the Han, *djinn* and men are depicted with realism, merging into the diabolic movement which animates the scenes of sorcery and the hunt (Plate 41).

In the decorative style of the early period the plant world is not represented; except for one *motif* which is difficult to define, plants only appear in the later period. This *motif* is perhaps derived from a four-petaled flower, but Karlgren describes it more accurately as a square with crescents. A nodule at the center of four commas, described as "whorl circles," is another fairly frequent *motif* which may have a similar origin (Plate 10 and 26).

The spiral is the most important of all the geometric *motifs* to be found on the zoomorphic shapes. In the Sung texts they are called the *lei-wên* fret (cloud and thunder fret) by analogy with the archaic ideogram for thunder (*lei*), but the two things have no other connection. It is reminiscent of the Greek key fret, and is found on all shapes. It is most frequently square or rectangular, elongated or condensed, to fill the space between the main *motifs* (Plate 18 and 23). Sometimes the animals as well as the ground are entirely covered with this round or angular tracing (Plate 22). Another *motif*, the lozenge, is used, each one fitting into another, or in lines forming a kind of tapestry on the surface of the vessels (Plate 26). A similar part is played by meanders, a kind of interlaced capital *T* (Plate 27). These rather formal decorative shapes often encircle knobs in relief (Plate 26) which are, themselves, frequently grouped in squares or rectangles (Plate 8).

From the middle of the Chou period a whole new range of decoration is introduced – horizontal fluting (Plate 35) or vertical gadroons, scales and waves (Plate 36), plaits and scrolls, hooks and triangles (Plate 41), commas and granulations. Given these different basic themes, the Chinese artists combined them together in an infinite number of variations.

Among others, Bernhard Karlgren, the great Swedish archaeologist, has made a very closely detailed study of the stylistic *motifs*, their appearance and disappearance, evolution, and relation to the forms, and this work is the foundation of the chronology universally adopted today.

During the Shang and early Chou periods, Karlgren makes a distinction between two co-existent styles, which he calls A and B. The first of these can be recognized by its typically high raised relief design on a ground of spirals, by the clarity and realism of the masks and profiles, and, finally, by the fact that the design covers the whole surface. Projecting ribs extend up the sides of certain vessels (Plates 2, 7 and 21), and these give the pieces their stiff and often monumental aspect.

In style B the reliefs are less clearly defined, and their main characteristics are already blurred. The eyes of the *t'ao t'ieh* masks vanish in a tangle of spirals; birds and their tails are often separated. Geometric *motifs* multiply (gadroons, lozenges, imbricated *T*s, etc.), and the decoration is arranged in bands and friezes. On some of these points archaeologists do not agree, and particularly Max Loehr, who holds that the less extravagant treatment – incised and hollowed *motifs*, or rather flatly molded reliefs (Plate 1 and 17) – can be shown to be earlier than style A. These are the first very simple linear, or, as it were, embossed, designs, which were to be gradually developed into the vigorous *motifs* of style A. Apparently this theory has been justified by the latest finds in China – pre-An-Yang bronzes dug from the deepest strata on the same site. Often crude both in shape and casting technique, these pieces have an incised decoration with no relief work, and this is restricted to certain parts of the vessels where the *t'ao t'ieh* and the dragons are not always easy to define. However, this is not the place to enter into such a discussion, and apart from this one particular point, Karlgren's classification is still the most satisfactory.

The same archaeologist, studying the period which he calls "Middle Chou," surveys the whole development and decay of the decoration between the 10th and 6th centuries B.C. The principal themes are now on an undecorated ground (Plate 36). The *t'ao t'ieh* no longer plays the leading role. The decoration is sinuous, ribbonlike, or in friezes of scales and waves, whilst large parts are adorned with horizontal flutings (Plates 35 and 38). Except for a few heads sculptured in the round on handles or feet, or in relief on broad meanders (Plate 34), all animal decoration has disappeared. The large kingdom of symbolic monsters has given way to a semi-abstract decoration, very much simplified and "attenuated" to use the words of Karlgren.

During the Chou period from the 6th to the 3rd century B.C. a renaissance took place, which made the period of the Warring States one of the most vivid ages of the history of art in China. Finds which permit the definition of the art of this period have been made over a wide area. The Huai valley has afforded the greatest number, however, which led Karlgren to call the decoration of the period "the Huai style." These discoveries, in spite of long distances, from Shansi to Anhui, which separate them, manifest an extraordinary unity in their esthetic appearance, while still retaining immense diversity of subject. The *t'ao t'ieh* and the dragon reappear, also the spirals and the triangular blades, but now the interpretation is freer, and with a rich flexibility quite alien to the early hieratic bronzes. Once again, the decoration spreads over the entire surface (Plate 16 and 41). The forms, simple and more regular, accord well with the smooth decoration – unrelieved swarming repetitions, which sometimes become rather monotonous, with their intertwining scrolls, curves, countercurves, and coils (*p'an chih*). Although still the outlines of masks and dragons, these lines now become inextricably interwoven in a swirling movement (Plate 40).

This ornament is wonderfully skillful, and is proof, if it be needed, of the astonishingly inventive genius of the period. The casting technique was never more perfect, and allowed of remarkable feats of chiseling. The surface is covered with commas, spirals, and granulations, all attracting and reflecting the light.

Mirrors are among the most richly decorated of all bronze objects – *T motifs*, broken lines (Plate 50), birds, and dragons represented in large spirals (Plate 52), stand out against a background of super-fine chiseling. The period of the Warring States has two special characteristics – a leaning towards realism, and a marked taste for sumptuous materials. The naturalistic treatment is applied not only to the sculptured beasts on certain vessels (e.g. the bullocks and ducks of the *ting* and *li-yu* in the Guimet Museum, Paris), or only to the animal battles pictured on hooks or decorative plaques, but also to the imaginary creatures, such as the arched dragons coiled as though to spring (Plate 44). Though in part stylized, this dynamic art bears some relation to the art of the central Asian nomads, China's bellicose northern neighbors).

A large number of bronzes have damascened decoration in gold, silver, or copper (Plate 16 and 42), and this is often enriched with turquoise inlay, malachite, or other precious materials. This is undoubtedly an unconscious return to an old Shang technique (cf. Plate 14). The decoration accords with the taste of a period which substituted finery for the exigent demands of past ritual, a taste which was to continue, even under the Han dynasty (Plate 47, 48 and 49).

With this period the decorative repertory loses much of its variety. Relief disappears, and on most of the bronzes the surface is smooth, or decorated only with masks. In place of handles, they have rings, but these are really only conventional grotesques.

The taste for inlay persists, but it is much more rigid and geometrical than in the previous period. Mirrors are decorated with thread-like *motifs* and irregular indentations. The animation and dash, characteristic of Han sculpture, the sharp hooks and triangle *motifs* to be seen in textiles and lacquer, are also to be found in the inlaid bronzes. *Djinn* and animals wander in mountainous landscapes, or swirl amid waves and clouds. Some of the bronzes are painted, and have an elegant decoration of birds enmeshed in a tangle of fine spirals.

This rapid survey of an art extending over thousands of years, and that an art of a grandeur which ranks it among the finest, can only be a slender thread to guide the reader through the labyrinth of its complicated productions. It is necessary to study the ancient Chinese bronzes closely over a long period if one is to learn something of their secret, something of their astonishing richness in shape and decoration. Only in this way is it possible to see how the artists handled their themes; how they treated the contrast of decoration with the naked bronze, the reliefs with the plane surfaces; how they have framed a decoration, outlined it lightly, or shown it up in sudden contrast; how the strange rhythms and balance of the pieces are obtained.

Every period provides its own answer to these problems. To the student they will seem like the revelation of an art which, already in the 13th century B.C., to quote René Grousset, "is not only technically perfect, but stands, effortlessly, at the height of its esthetic achievement." *D. L.-G.*

1. RITUAL VESSEL. *P'ou.* SHANG DYNASTY
BEGINNING OF AN-YANG PERIOD
14TH–13TH CENTURIES B.C.

D.28.5 cm. H.22.5 cm. Guimet Museum, Paris

This squat vessel, with its round belly on a circular foot, was probably used for grain offerings. The most recent work of Max Loehr makes it feasible to say that it was made in one of the earliest stages in the history of Shang bronzes. Certainly the decoration corresponds to Loehr's "third style," which he dates from the beginning of the An-Yang period.

Apart from two undecorated areas, ornament covers the whole surface. Linear incisions only are used, and the sole relief-work is in the eyes, with their polished, hooked surrounds, and in the nasal rib.

Three large *t'ao t'ieh* masks cover the periphery of the belly. They consist of dragons, face to face, with rigid rows of parallel feathers standing up from their backs. The general design is rather indistinct, as parts of the masks and animals (the feet, ears, tail, and so on) are only differentiated by rows of dense, close spirals, which really constitute the principal *motif*. The mouth of the *t'ao t'ieh* is clearly shown by two lips which join the two halves of the mask under the nasal rib.

It will be seen that at this stage the ornament is not conceived as a whole. The frieze on the shoulder with its feathered monsters is not placed in symmetry with the masks on the body of the vase. This is also true of the lower frieze, the spirals of which all turn one way. This primitive effect was soon to be overcome as the art of An-Yang reached its full development.

The patina is very smooth and of a fine deep color.

2. RITUAL FOOD VESSEL. *Fang i*
SHANG DYNASTY. AN-YANG PERIOD
C. 1300–1028 B.C.

H.22.5 cm. Collection Frau Dr. Emma Gross, Zurich

This vessel was intended for storing food, and is a good example of the mature technique and artistry achieved by the Shang bronze founders after they had settled at An-Yang. It achieves a perfect balance of size and decoration.

Architectural in concept, and of rectangular section, it evokes an image of a house with a high-pitched roof. The central tenon, seen in profile, suggests perhaps a second roof. It has been thought that the lateral ribs may represent the ends of prominent beams such as must have been part of contemporary buildings made from rammed earth or adobe.

The decoration is in relief over a ground of re-entrant spirals (the *lei wên* fret). A big *t'ao t'ieh* mask upside down adorns each side of the cover. Both are divided by the central rib and have no lower jaw. Above them is an antler-like design which appears like crested birds when viewed from the side. The body of the vase is divided into three reserves, all decorated with masks. A very powerful *t'ao t'ieh* occupies the center. Globular eyes and open jaws displaying fangs add to its ferocity. It has ears, and, on the upper part, horns, making an autonomous design rather like an elephant's ear. Smaller *t'ao t'ieh* masks,

and of a different design, are to be seen on other parts of the vessel, but these are separate from and not athwart the central rib.

A patina, ranging in color from the tones of azurite to malachite, enhances the beauty of this vessel.

3. RITUAL VESSEL. *Huo.* SHANG DYNASTY
C. 1200–1100 B.C.

H.26 cm. Collection Frau Dr. Emma Gross, Zurich

This ritual vase, a pouring jug with a cover, is reminiscent of the *li* tripods. The shape is originally found in the pottery of the Stone Age, and it often served as inspiration for the bronze founders. The piece is immensely powerful. The handle and the spout only increase the sturdy sense of vigor.

The cover, completed by a ring and attached to the handle by a short chain, is ornamented with stylized dragons. More dragon *motifs* decorate a band below and round the mouth. Vigorous *t'ao t'ieh* masks flank the body, which swells outwards from the hollow legs. Extended horns and stylized birds complete a wonderfully harmonious design.

The patina is grayish-green, encrusted with malachite and azurite.

Exhibition: Arte Cinese, Venice, 1954, No. 1.

4. RITUAL VASE. *Chih*
END OF SHANG DYNASTY
C. 1100–1000 B.C.

H.14.5 cm. Formerly Collection Mrs. Walter Sedgwick, London

The greatly accentuated relief of the decoration on this goblet gives the striking impression that it is the mythical creature itself which forms the body of the piece. The powerful mask is that of an animal – half buffalo, half feline – with globular eyes and projecting horns. A diamond-shaped *motif* adorns the muzzle above the dilated nostrils. The neck and the base, both rhythmically divided by projecting ribs, have a frieze of dragons and birds.

The tiger and the buffalo were undoubtedly held to be earth demons. They were protective, though, rather than maleficent, and had to be propitiated according to the ceremonies sacred to Ancestor Worship.

Exhibition: Chinese Art, London, 1935–36, No. 205.

5. RITUAL VASE. *Chih*
SHANG DYNASTY. AN-YANG PERIOD
C. 1300–1028 B.C.

H.13 cm. Private Collection

This wine vessel, of the same type as the one preceding, is also elliptical, but differs in its form which is more pliant and rounded. This effect is accentuated by the sinuous line of the ribs, but primarily by the style and the finely incised deco-

ration. The flaring mouth is decorated with six stylized cicadas –
a frequent theme on ritual bronzes. One wonders, what could
have been the symbolic meaning attached to them by the
Shang peoples. Carl Hentze thinks that the metamorphosis of
the long-buried larva into an insect living in the sun so struck
them that they chose it as a symbol of the journey from dark-
ness into light, from death to resurrection.

Stylized birds on a fret ground face one another on the neck
below this design. A *t'ao t'ieh* mask in shallow relief with
prominent eyes lacking pupils covers the belly. The foot is engraved with double spirals in the form of an *S*.

The patina, a brilliant green, is enhanced with spots of cuprite
and malachite.

Exhibition: Arte Cinese, *Venice, 1954, No. 18.*

6. RITUAL WINE VESSEL. *Ku.* SHANG DYNASTY
AN-YANG PERIOD. C. 1300–1028 B.C.

H.30 cm. Collection Frau Mary Mantel, Zurich

This tall goblet was used for libations. It imposes at once by
its beauty and elegance. The slim shape soars upwards to a
wide-swept mouth in the form of a chalice. Archaeologists are
divided about the origin of this type of vessel. Andersson
believes it to have been derived from Neolithic pottery, as was
the *tou.* Kuo Pao-chün, on the other hand, holds that the
goblet was made originally from two horns bound together at
their narrowest point, and that the central band is the relic of
this ligature.

Four cicadas, stiffly triangular, decorated with *t'ao t'ieh* masks
and other *motifs* sweep up the neck. At their foot there is a
frieze of coiling dragons. A similar decoration, delicately incised, covers the central band, which is divided from above
and below by two plain bands. The lower section, widely flaring
to the foot, is divided by four fillets. These fillets, some more
prominent than others, are always found on this type of vase,
and often extend to the top of the vessel.

7. RECTANGULAR *Ting*
END OF THE SHANG DYNASTY
C. 1100–1000 B.C.

*H.27.4 cm. Art Council of Great Britain (Formerly Collection
Mrs.C.G.Seligman), London*

This ritual vessel is a variant of the circular *ting.* It has, however, preserved the two upright handles on the rim, and also
the cylindrical feet. At the corners, and in the middle of each
side, it has a fretted, notched rib. It was certainly a vessel for
cooking, as was also the round *ting.* The large handles would
enable it to be taken easily from the fire by the insertion of a
bar.

Each facet has a large *t'ao t'ieh* mask, which almost completely
covers the surface. The horns are in the form of sinuous and
fretted dragons in profile. The whole composition, modeled
in varying relief on a ground of delicate spirals, is imbued
with a sense of power and of the occult.

Exhibition: Early Chinese Bronzes, *Oriental Ceramic Society,
London, 1951, No. 16.*

8. RECTANGULAR *Ting*
END OF THE SHANG DYNASTY
C. 1100–1000 B.C.

H.21,5 cm. Private Collection

The *ting* shown here, while of a similar shape to the preceding
one, has quite different decoration. The central ribs now only
appear on the upper band, and are decorated with stylized
serpents. The body of the vessel is ornamented with projecting
nodules framing a plain rectangle. The cylindrical legs have
t'ao t'ieh masks at their juncture with the body. They are
modeled in high relief with a central nasal rib which extends
the angles of the vessel.

An earth-colored deposit, the result of long years of burial,
adheres to the metal, and in some places blurs the decoration.
Through it can be seen a fine, smooth green patina which has
large patches of cuprite.

9. RITUAL VESSEL, *Tsun*
END OF THE SHANG DYNASTY
C. 1200–1000 B.C.

H.40.5 cm. Collection Eskenazi, London

This kind of vessel, and also the one illustrated on Plate 10, is
first called *tsun* in the Sung texts. However, the Chinese ideogram for this type in its archaic form means "sacrificial vessel"
without further definition. For this reason the term has no
archaeological standing, although it has become usual.

The vase shown here is an example of a specially rare type of
bronze which was intended for storing wine. Its main features
are the sloping shoulders above a large belly, the tall, hollow
foot which has three pierced holes, and the very wide-mouthed
neck which imparts a splendidly majestic appearance.

Six prominent ribs rising from the foot to the base of the neck
divide the surface, and three of these stop short at the shoulder
to give way to a powerfully stylized buffalo head in relief.
Three large *t'ao t'ieh* masks on the belly, pivoting on the ribs,
stand out from a background of spirals, typical of the classic
period of the Shang dynasty.

10. RITUAL VESSEL. *Hsien*
END OF THE SHANG DYNASTY
C. 1100–1000 B.C.

H.39 cm. Formerly Collection of His Excellency M. Naggiara, Paris

Vessels of this class may well be described as steamers. They
are large, and made up of two sections. The upper portion, or
cauldron, has a *grille* for a base, and two twisted upright
handles on the rim. The lower part is in the form of a tripod
resembling a *li.* Sometimes it is possible to distinguish the
solder marks where the piece was assembled.

The decoration of this vessel is a single frieze on a ground of spirals – eight dragons in profile, alternating with a whorl *motif*. Three large *t'ao t'ieh* masks, with buffalo horns and sharp fangs, brood over the curved hollow legs. The pupils of the eyes are slit horizontally. These three masks blend with the tripod, covering and underlining its swelling shape. They are treated on a series of unbroken planes without incisions, and in a style which seems peculiar to this type of bronze.

The green patina has large patches of cuprite, and traces of malachite.

11. *Appliqué* IN THE FORM OF A TIGER
EARLY CHOU DYNASTY
11TH–8TH CENTURIES B.C.

L.31.7 cm. H.14.3 cm. Formerly Collection D. David-Weill, Neuilly-sur-Seine

The large crouching tiger shown here is one of a pair intended to be applied as decoration, but which have no immediately apparent purpose. This is a rare specimen in which the folded paws rest on the tail and mane in a very stylized way. The plaque itself is thin, but powerfully modeled and handled with great freedom. Its open mouth reveals two fangs and a row of teeth in a circular position, reminiscent of those on jade tigers and dragons of the same period (cf. Plates 63, 70, 73).

The tiger, the Earth Demon and symbol of strength, was one of the most frequently used *motifs* in bronze. It is often detected in *t'ao t'ieh* masks, and sometimes the zoomorphic *tsun* takes the form of a tiger.

There is no incised decoration on either of these two pieces, but some kind of woven material must have pressed against them during their long burial, for traces of a criss-cross design can be seen.

The patina is green and rough.

Two similar pieces were in the Oppenheim Collection, London.

Exhibition: Bronzes Chinois, *Orangerie Museum, Paris, 1934, No. 103.*

12. TWO PIECES OF APPLIED BRONZE
IN THE FORM OF BIRDS. EARLY CHOU
11TH–7TH CENTURIES B.C.

L.19.8 cm. H.9.1 cm. Formerly Collection D. David-Weill, Neuilly-sur-Seine

The function of these ornaments is not known. A ring can be seen on the back which must have been used for attachment, and they are obviously related to the stylized birds to be seen on the ritual vessels. The quality of the workmanship, and their size makes them objects of the greatest interest.

On the upper part of the almost square head are two long spiral hooks, one curling forward to represent the beak, and the other backwards to form the crest. The elbow and foot ends in claws and a spur, while the long tail curves downwards at a right angle to form a reversed *T*. Its outer edge is decorated with small incised hooks. All the different parts of the body are decorated with grooves.

A beautiful smooth green patina enhances the magnificence of these exceptional pieces.

Exhibition: Bronzes Chinois, *Orangerie Museum, Paris, 1934, Nos. 106–107.*

13. RITUAL VESSEL. *Tsun*
EARLY CHOU DYNASTY
10TH–8TH CENTURIES B.C.

H.25.5 cm. Private Collection

This noble vessel, of robust form, is a fine example of the early Chou bronzes, which were characterized by a very clear, simple decoration. This one consists solely of two bands framing the central bulge of the vessel, and these are decorated with stylized birds in relief on a spiral ground. *T'ao t'ieh* masks complete the composition on the upper frieze.

The patina is polished, and shaded with large patches of cuprite.

14. HILT OF A KO (CEREMONIAL DAGGER)
SHANG DYNASTY. AN-YANG PERIOD
(C. 1300–1028 B.C.)

L.14.3 cm. H.9.2 cm. Formerly Collection Louis Bataille, Paris

During the excavations at An-Yang undertaken on the site of the ancient Shang capital in the years between 1928 and 1937, a number of objects inlaid with turquoise, like this one, were found, and, among them, different kinds of ceremonial weapons. It is, therefore, possible to date them accurately.

This dagger hilt, representing a threatening *k'uei* dragon, is very vigorously treated. Its jaws are wide open, revealing two sharp fangs under a hooked muzzle.

A crest of alternating hooks runs along the back, and continues – though some pieces are lost – along the coiling tail to the terminal point. The creature's jaws, and three-clawed foot in the form of a reversed *T,* are fixed to the blade-socket. The workmanship of the bronze cells which held the turquoise inlay is very highly developed, and in spite of the missing stones, the work has a powerful and decorative effect. A similar piece is in the Guimet Museum, Paris.

15. HANDLES IN THE FORM OF *t'ao t'ieh* MASKS
END OF THE CHOU DYNASTY
PERIOD OF THE WARRING STATES
5TH–3RD CENTURIES B.C.

H.13 cm. B.10.3 cm. Collection Frau Georg Hasler, Winterthur

This pair of masks with pendant rings must have been handles, but it is difficult to decide for what kind of object they were designed – a receptacle, a box, or a piece of furniture? Except for the threatening eyes, these *t'ao t'ieh* masks bear little relation to those of earlier periods. They have ribbon *motifs,* twisting and turning in harmonious rhythm, and they are decorated with spirals and granulations. They are in a very finely chiseled relief, a manner characteristic of Karlgren's "Style Huai".

The turquoise inlays underline the purely decorative intention of the design, and enhance the fine dark green patina.

16. COVERED VESSEL. *Hu*
END OF THE CHOU DYNASTY
PERIOD OF THE WARRING STATES
5TH–3RD CENTURIES B.C.

H. 29 cm. Private Collection

The *hu* is a shape widely known under the Chou and Han dynasties. Often, as here, it has ring handles supported by masks.

This beautiful vessel is an example of the typical inlaid work which is often found on works of the Warring States period. It is more usually seen, though, on smaller objects – ornaments or belt hooks, for instance.

On the five friezes alternate dragons and birds, inlaid in copper enriched with turquoise, form a rather geometric *motif*. They are sinuous and vital, and in spite of some stylization, exhibit a naturalism which is new. Relief work has completely disappeared.

The patina is sea-green, with – here and there – touches of cuprite and azurite.

Exhibitions: Ostasiatische Kunst und Chinoiserie, *Cologne, 1952, No. 102.* – Arte Cinese, *Venice, 1954, No. 73.*

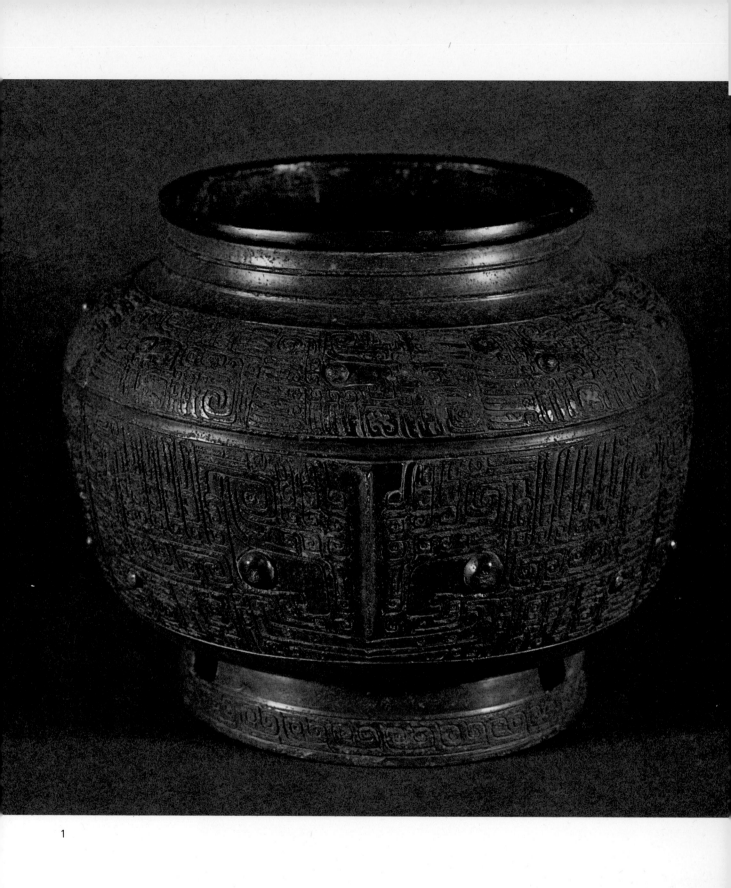

1

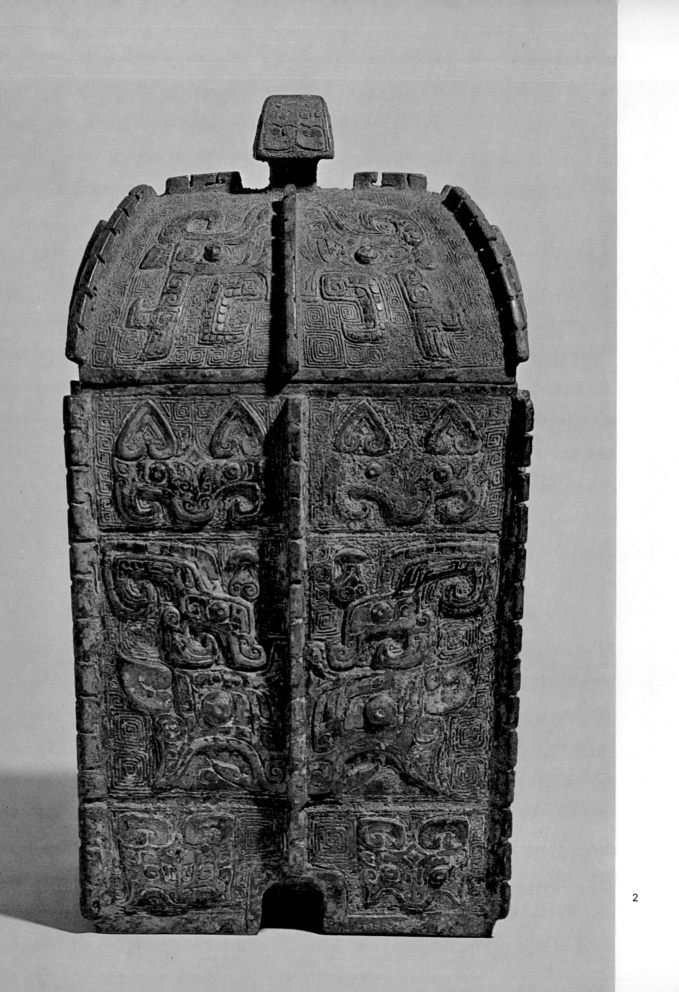

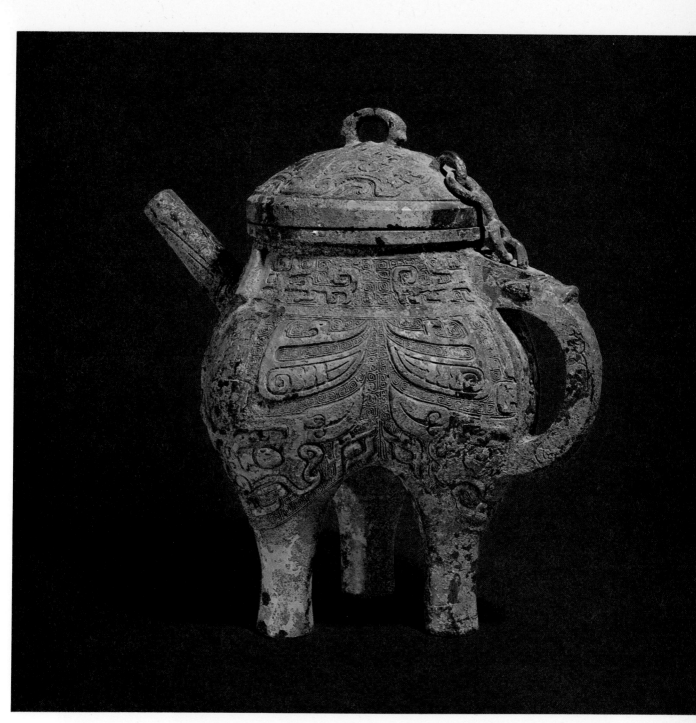

3

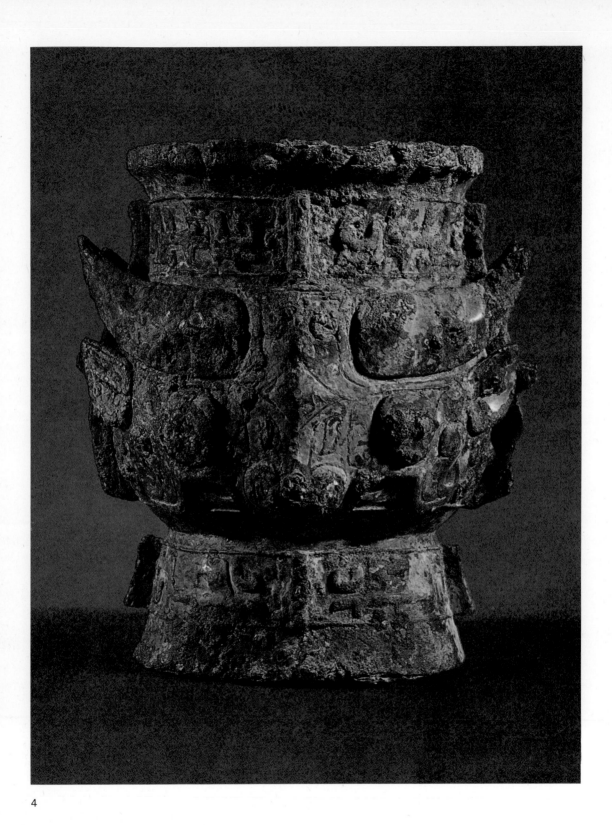

4

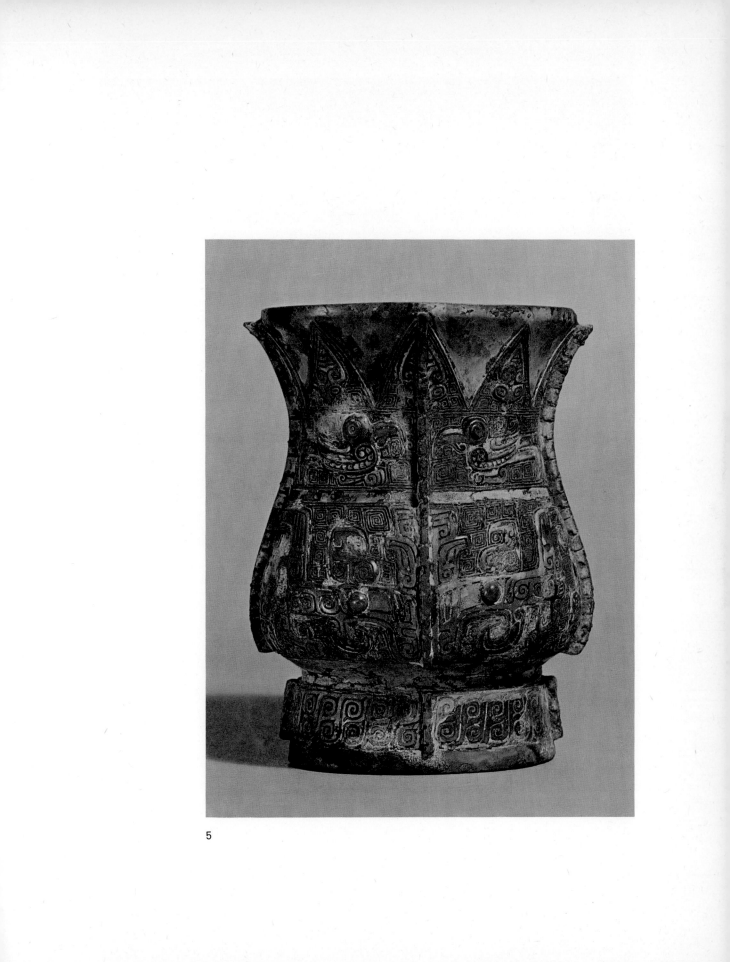

5

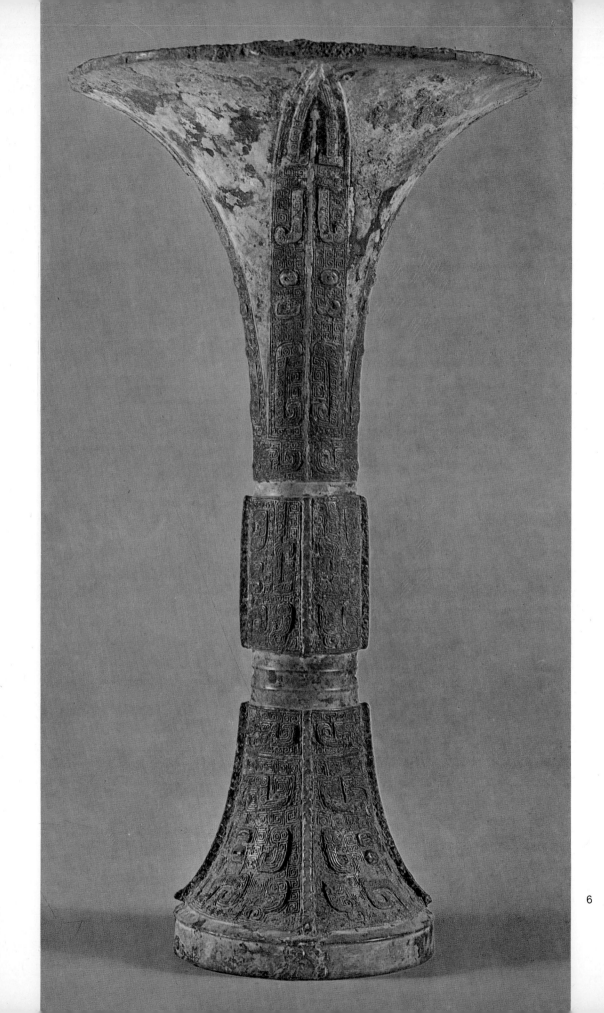

6

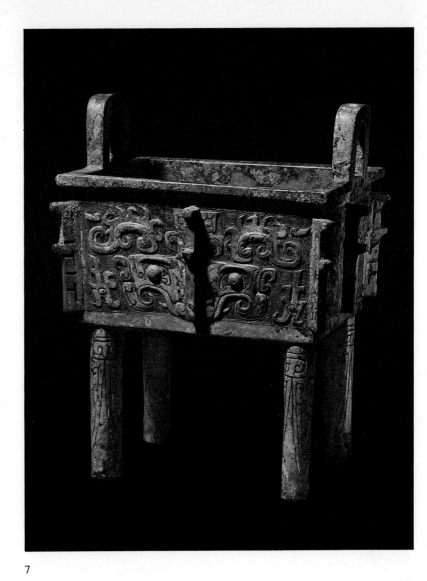

7

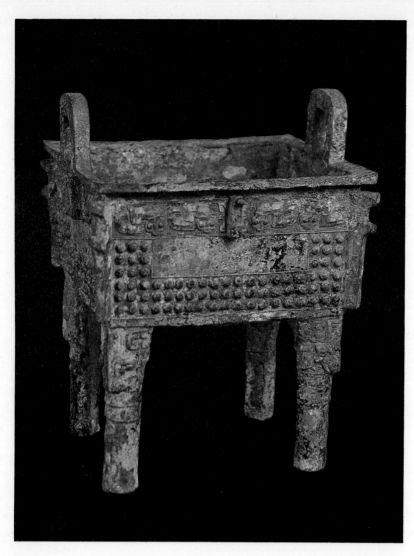

8

9 ▷

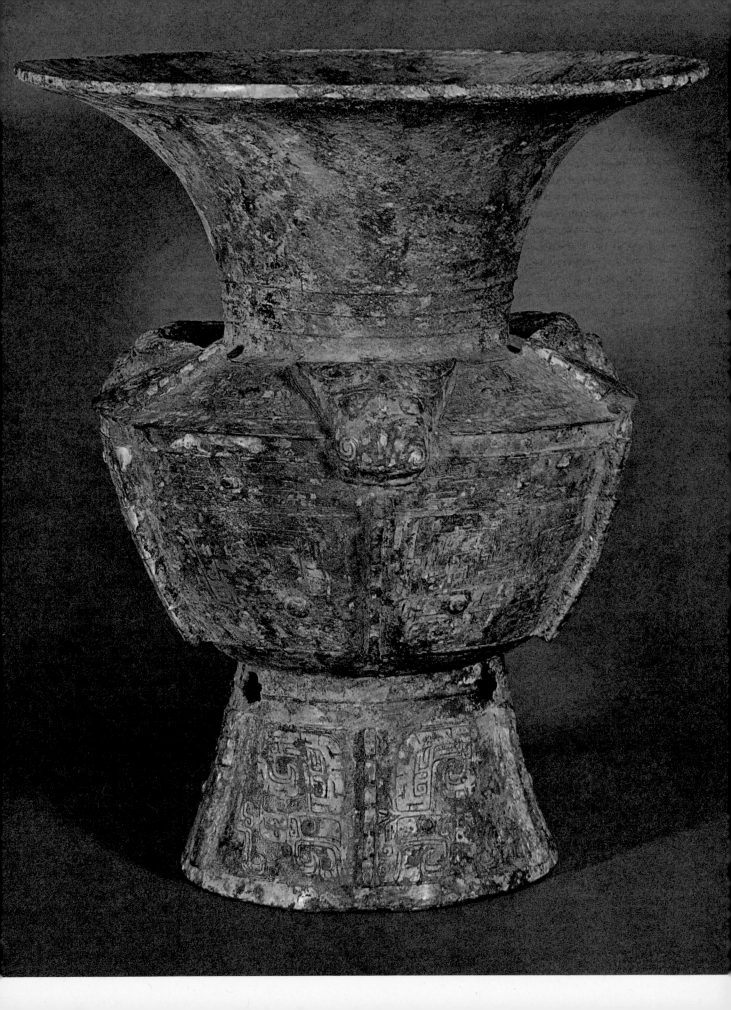

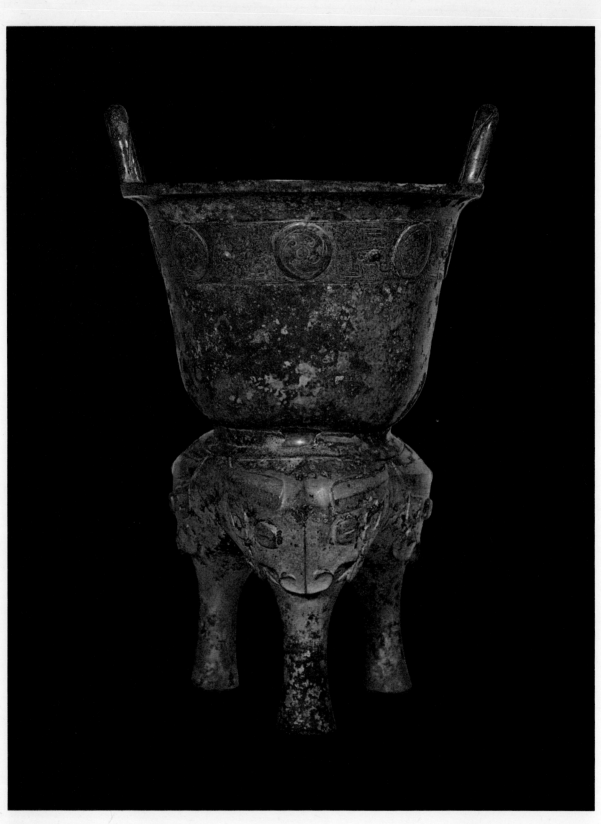

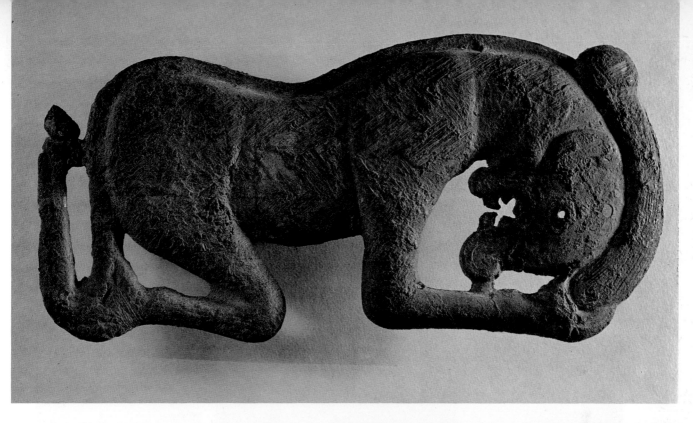

1

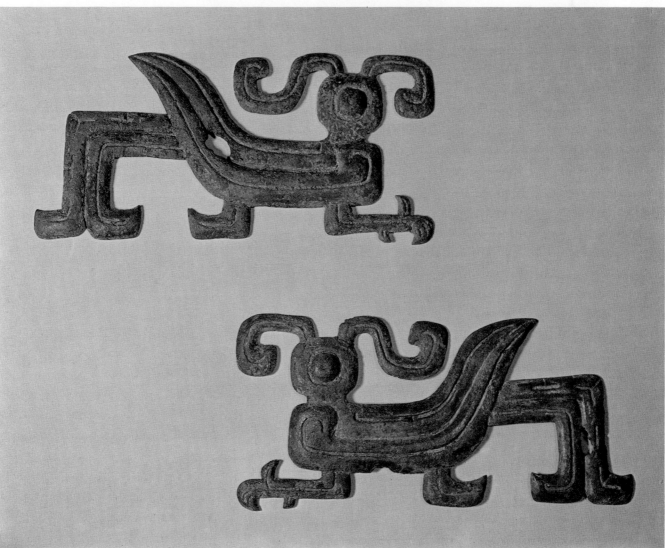

2

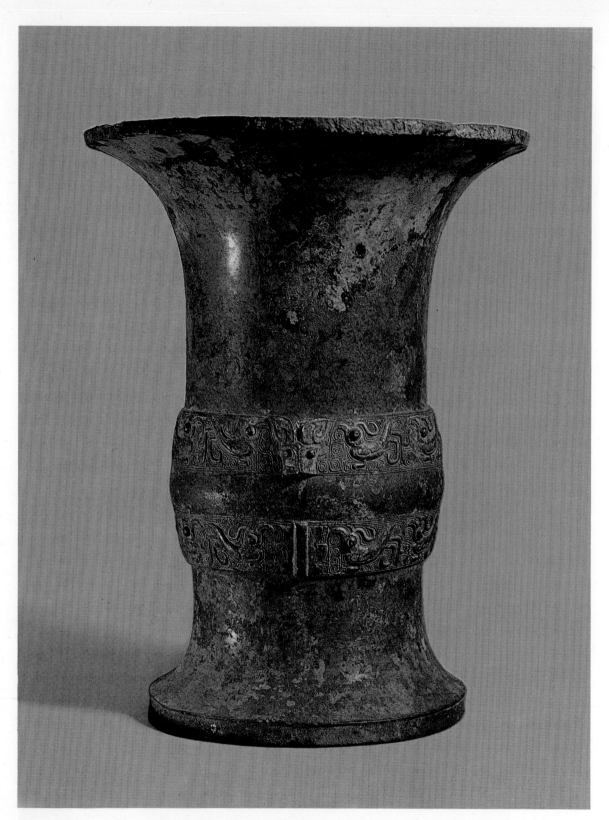

13

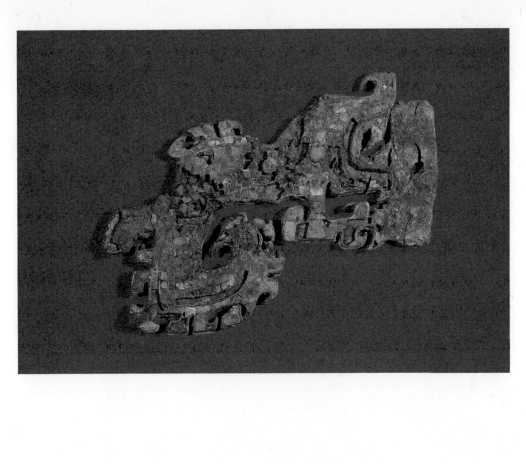

14

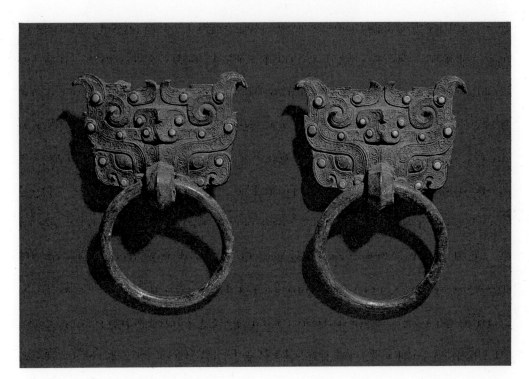

15

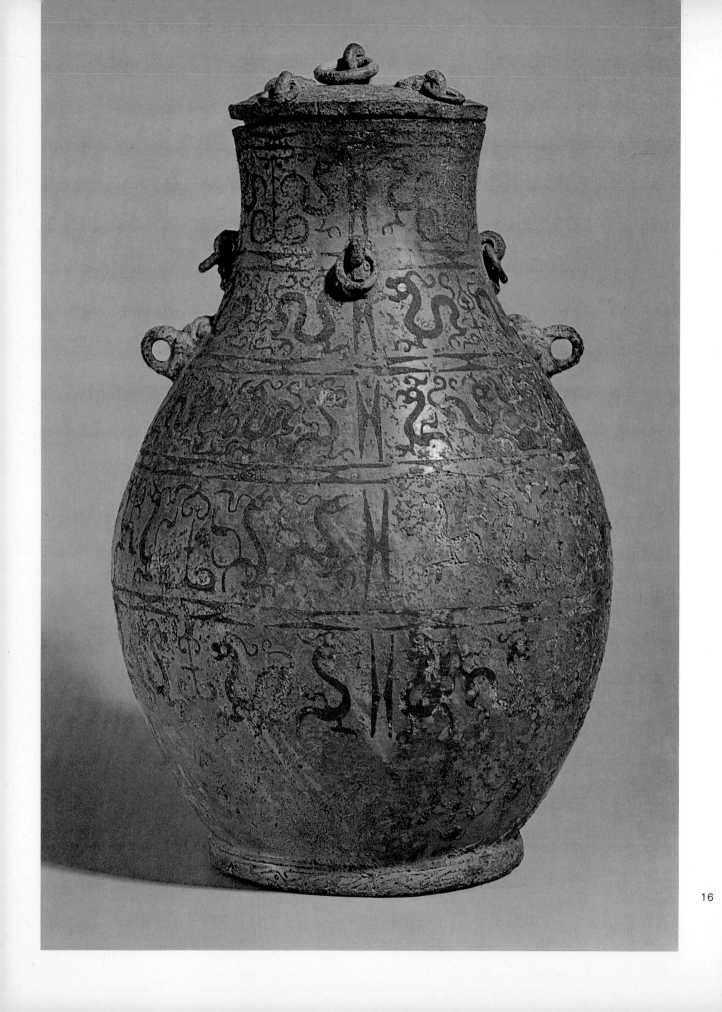

16

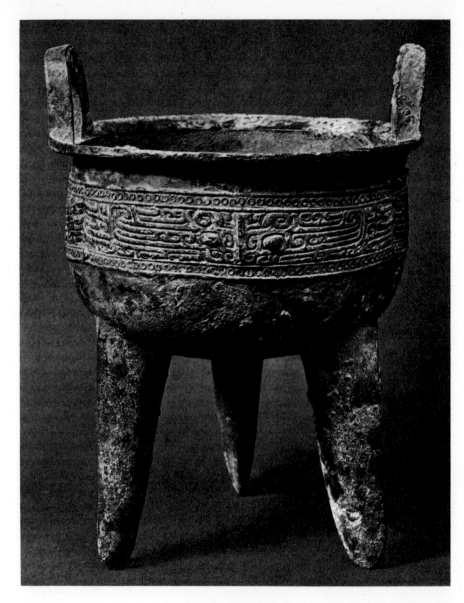

17. RITUAL FOOD VESSEL, *Li-ting*
SHANG DYNASTY. EARLY AN-YANG PERIOD
14TH–13TH CENTURIES B.C.

*H. 25 cm. Östasiatiska Museet, Stockholm (Formerly Collection
H. M. the King Gustave VI Adolphe)*

This very fine ritual vessel probably comes from An-Yang,
the last Shang capital, which they occupied from before 1300
to about 1028 B.C. It seems that at least one other similar
vessel has been found there.

The form is a mixture of *li* and *ting*. The cauldron with its upright handles is a *ting* characteristic, while the legs, though
lacking the bulbous effect, are hollow and typical of the *li*. The
long tapering legs are elegantly shaped, and this effect is enhanced by two delicate ribs on their outer and inner aspects.

The decoration is a frieze encircling the belly of the vessel, edged

with double lines and small circles. There are three masks, each
one formed by the heads of two dragons, face to face, with
extended horizontal bodies. The joints of the wax matrices, by
means of which the design was molded, can clearly be seen.

This type of relief decoration on a single plane, close and regular, corresponds to the "Second style" which Max Loehr has
proposed in his classification of primitive bronzes. The patina
is green. The hollow parts of the design were formerly filled
with some kind of black material which has, for the most part,
disappeared, revealing a pale yellow substance underneath.

An almost identical vessel belongs to the Museum of Mukden
in Manchuria; another was in the Eumorfopoulos Collection
in London (cf. Catalogue, Vol. I, Plate II).

Exhibition: La découverte de l'Asie, *Musée Cernuschi, Paris, 1954
No. 382.*

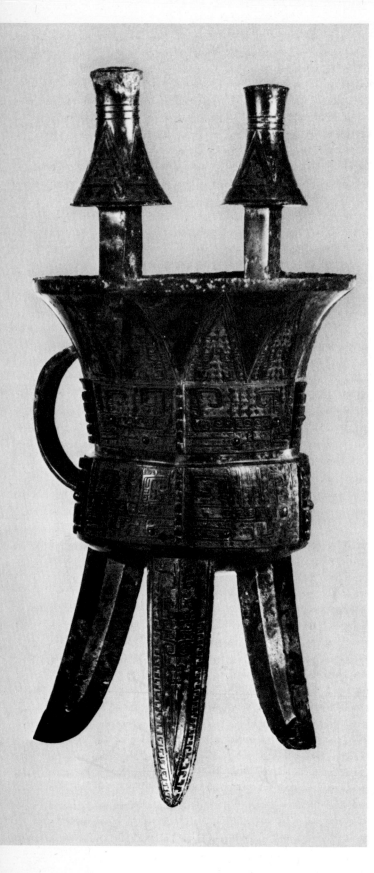

18. RITUAL WINE VESSEL. *Chia*
END OF THE SHANG DYNASTY
12TH CENTURY B.C.

*H.52.8 cm. B.30.5 cm. The Freer Gallery of Art, Washington, D.C.
(By permission of the Smithsonian Institution, The Freer Gallery of
Art)*

The beautiful *chia* illustrated here shows us this kind of vessel
at the height of its development during the 12th century B.C.
Some more primitive examples are known, dating from two or
three centuries earlier, but they are far from possessing this
grandeur, this balance, this perfect union of form and decoration. The lancet-like legs are of supreme elegance. Each of
their outer facets is covered by a triangular *motif* of stylized
cicadas, which is repeated, with variations, on the flaring neck,
and on the cap of the uprights. The body is covered by two
bands decorated with dragons in profile, not quite symmetrical, and facing one another, so as to form two *t'ao t'ieh*
masks. Apart from the denticulated ribs and prominent eyes of
the animals, the whole surface is on a single plane.
The smooth patina – a beautiful dark green – hides a metal
which has an unusually large proportion of silver in the alloy.

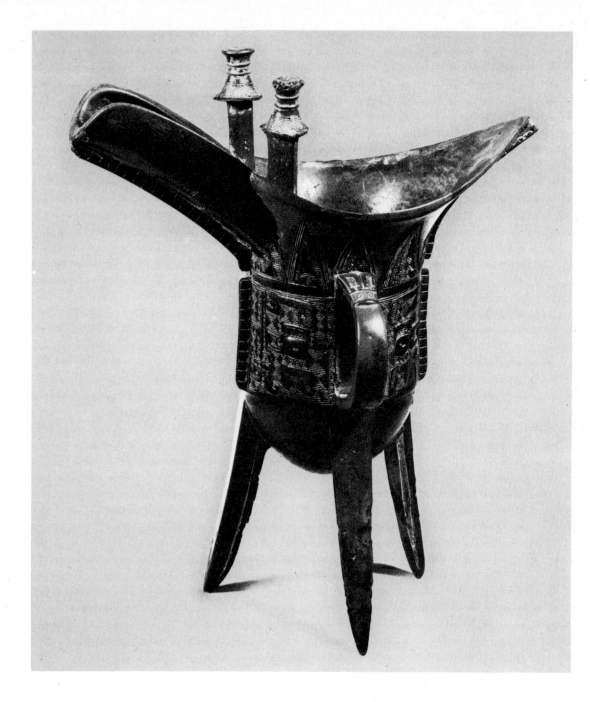

19. RITUAL WINE VESSEL. *Chüeh*
SHANG DYNASTY. AN-YANG PERIOD
C. 1300–1028 B.C.

H. 25 cm. B. 22.5 cm. The Freer Gallery of Art, Washington, D.C.
(By permission of the Smithsonian Institution, The Freer Gallery of Art)

This vessel is among the most ancient of Chinese bronzes. Recently archaeologists have found some which date from the early days of the Shang dynasty, even before its establishment at An-Yang. These, however, have a flat base, decoration of a more rudimentary kind, and sometimes only a single upright. The *chüeh* here shown is massive and firmly balanced. Round the body is a decoration of dragons in profile, very difficult to distinguish, being entirely covered with notches and spirals except for the rectangular eyes with their slit pupils. Triangular *motifs,* varied in detail, cover the swelling neck, the pouring lip, and the extension to the rear. Prominent ribs, with alternating incised lines and hooks, accentuate the shape. The handle bears a mask with square horns. The patina varies from blue to apple green, with some earth-colored incrustation.

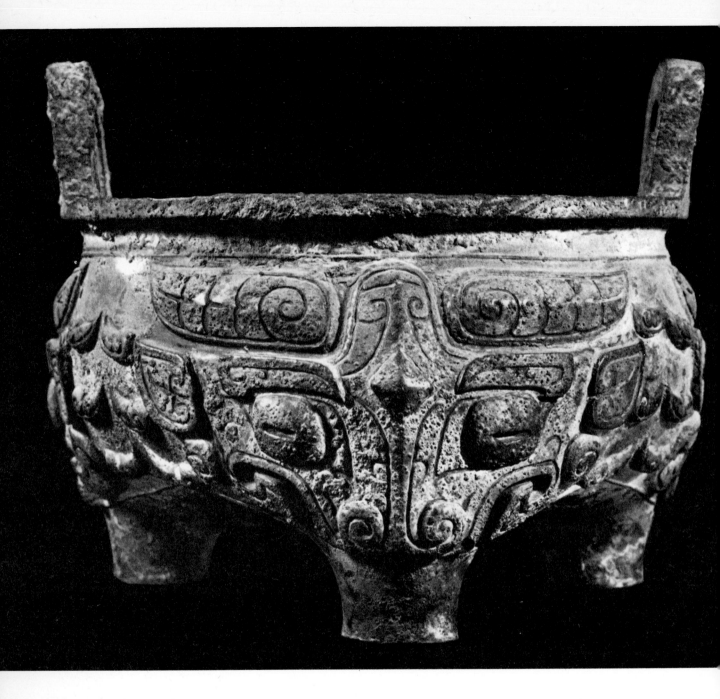

20. RITUAL FOOD VESSEL. *Li*
BEGINNING OF THE CHOU DYNASTY
C. 1000 B.C.

D.17.5 cm. H.14 cm. Private Collection

The short legs of this solid thickset vessel give it an unusual appearance. Its accentuated relief is very vigorously treated. Three *t'ao t'ieh* masks are placed over the feet of the vessel, and stand out alone from a smooth background. There is no other ornament.

Buffalo horns parallel with the eyebrows frame a prominent forehead, which is ornamented with a diamond-shaped relief pattern. The globular eyes have horizontal slits for pupils, whilst the nostrils end in converging spirals. The incised decoration is very finely drawn. The patina is dark with, here and there, touches of cuprite and malachite.

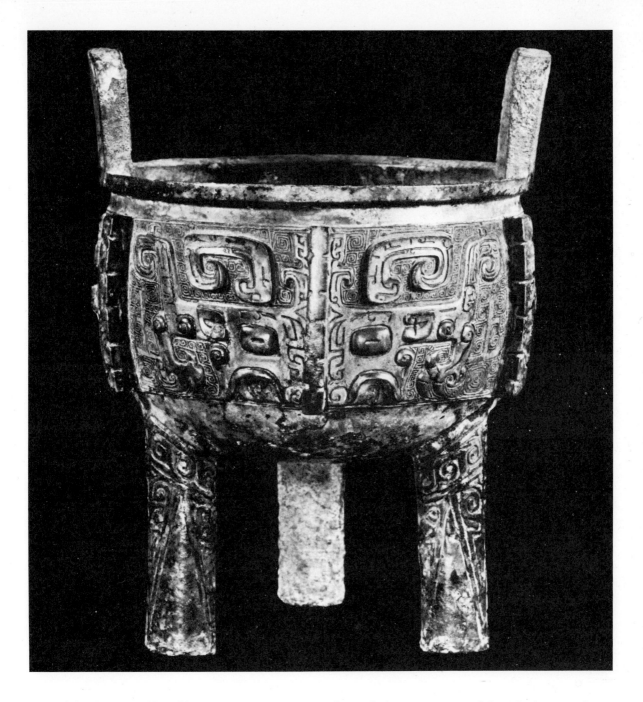

21. RITUAL FOOD VESSEL. *Ting*
SHANG DYNASTY. AN-YANG PERIOD
C. 1300–1028 B.C.

H. 25 cm. Formerly Collection Mme J. Ramet, Paris

This beautiful ritual vessel is a perfect example of a *ting* of the Shang period. A very wide decorated band covers the body of the vessel, which is divided by six vertical ribs notched in the form of a T. Three *t'ao t'ieh* masks fill the divisions thus formed. They are composed of two dragons face to face, each with a single foot, of the archaic type known as *k'uei*. The pure lines and vigorous treatment of the main theme are thrown into relief by the delicate spirals of the ground, so that the elements of the mask are easily interpreted – a large curving horn shaped like the letter C; a stiff tail, hooked at the end; a foot with its three claws clearly indicated; open, fanged mouth; and globular eyes with slits for pupils. Curls in relief on the body and foot of the beast are a rather unusual detail, and probably represent hair. The cylindrical feet of the vessel are decorated with triangular cicada *motifs*.

The patina is smooth, and of a fine green tone, with some touches of malachite and cuprite.

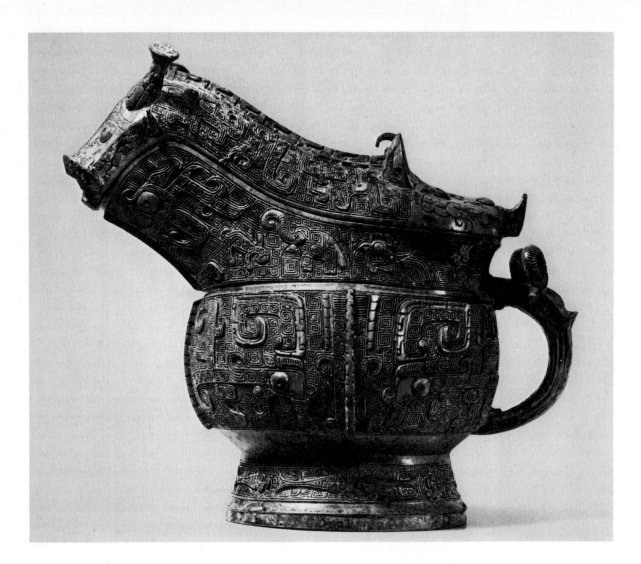

22. RITUAL WINE VESSEL, *Kuang*
END OF THE SHANG DYNASTY
(12TH–11TH CENTURIES B.C.)

*Total length 20.4 cm. H.16.7 cm. Freer Gallery of Art,
Washington, D.C.*
*(By permission of the Smithsonian Institution, The Freer Gallery of
Art)*

The striking fact about this wonderful piece is the all-over
decoration. Not only do the small square or round spirals,
triangular, hooked and parallel lines cover the background
as is usual, but here they also cover the animal *motifs,* giving
a splendid unity to the whole design. The only parts left undecorated are the two large masks on the cover, and the
handle. The precision and delicacy of the engraving is exceptional, as is the kind of animals depicted. The difference in the
horns from those of more classic dragons is noticeable at once.
The mask at the front of the cover, and those near the spout,
have truncated, bottle-shaped horns; the handle mask has long,

ringed, and curling rams' horns; while the dragons on the
body – two prominently ribbed large masks – have big horns
curving downwards.
On the neck the birds are very clearly drawn: hooked beaks,
crests, outstretched wings, and pendant tails. Around the foot
is a frieze of fish, at once realistic and stylized. Finally, on the
upper part of the vase, are some much rarer *motifs* – elephants
and hares. Their features are recorded with surprising accuracy
– the trunk, ears, tusks and heavy feet of the elephant, and the
long ears and supple pads of the hare. Most of the Shang repertory is to be found here, richly handled in a skillful combination of high and low relief, and engraving.
The whole vessel, strangely zoomorphic, and swarming with
round-eyed animal *motifs,* communicates a weird feeling of
occult power and symbolism.
The patina is a uniform gray, with slight variations in tone,
and spots of cuprite. In some places, in the interior of the
vessel, the original color remains, in conjunction with areas of
azurite.

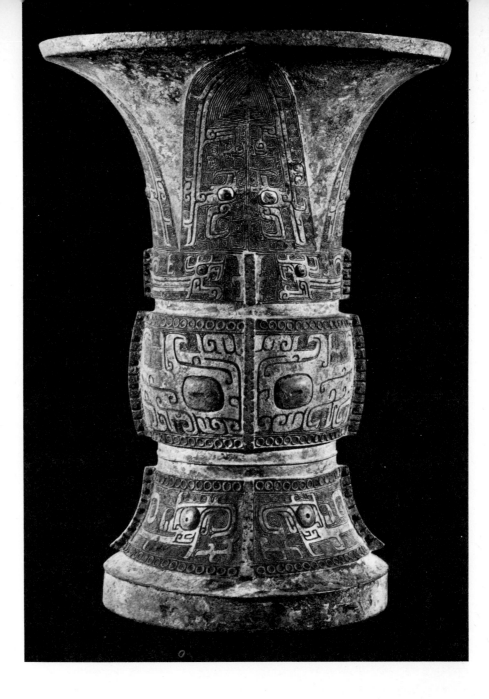

23. RITUAL VESSEL. *Tsun*
SHANG DYNASTY. AN-YANG PERIOD
1300–1028 B.C.

H. 32 cm. Collection Frau Emma Gross, Zurich

Of a more classical shape than the one illustrated on Plate 9, this *tsun* shows more clearly its relationship with the *ku:* it has the same flaring mouth, swelling central band, and projecting ribs, only they are in different proportions, giving a much more massive impression (cf. Plate 6). The decoration is divided into three, and is arranged in the same way. Almost the whole repertory of Shang decoration is employed here, giving a rigorous, oppressive effect. The design stands out against a background of sharp, regular, engraved spirals, squares, and parallel lines, which are brilliantly insinuated between the *motifs* of the main design. Four *motifs* on the neck, shaped like a triangular blade and considered by Karlgren to be a corruption of the cicada *motif,* are decorated with *t'ao t'ieh* masks. The whole central area is taken up by two large full-faced dragon masks. Below the neck, and on the foot, two *k'uei* dragons, one with a hooked beak and the other a long trunk, stand face to face. The lower division of the design is edged with small circles in relief – a typical feature of this very early period. The prominent ribs ornamented with alternate lines and hooks rise up to the flaring neck. The patina is green, enhanced with touches of cuprite.

51

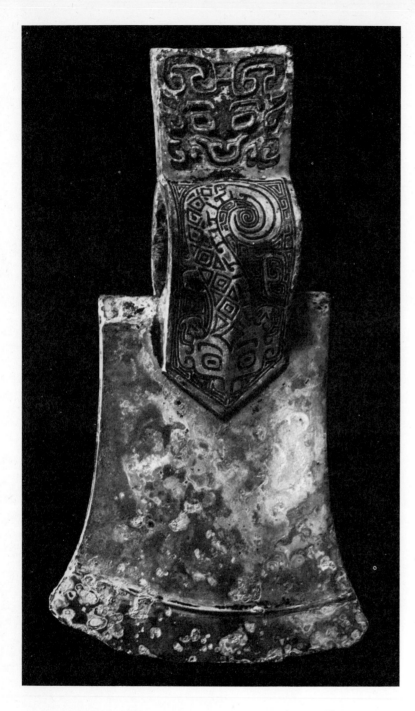

24. CEREMONIAL AXE
SHANG DYNASTY. AN-YANG PERIOD
C. 1300–1028 B.C.

L. 20 cm. Östasiatiska Museet, Stockholm (Formerly Collection of H. M. the King Gustave VI Adolphe)

This axe-head has a cylindrical socket and a curved blade. The socket which held the handle is welded over the blade, and has a flat extended rib. Decorated on both sides, the design of the socket is a clawed, full-face dragon, with its body in profile.

These creatures stand out from a flat ground engraved with spirals. They have short horns, and a lozenge on the forehead, and their body is elongated by a curling tail. The design is similar to many of the other dragons encountered on Shang bronzes.

The flange to the rear has *t'ao t'ieh* masks in linear relief, which were probably intended for inlaid decoration, perhaps turquoises.

The patina is polished, and of grayish green.

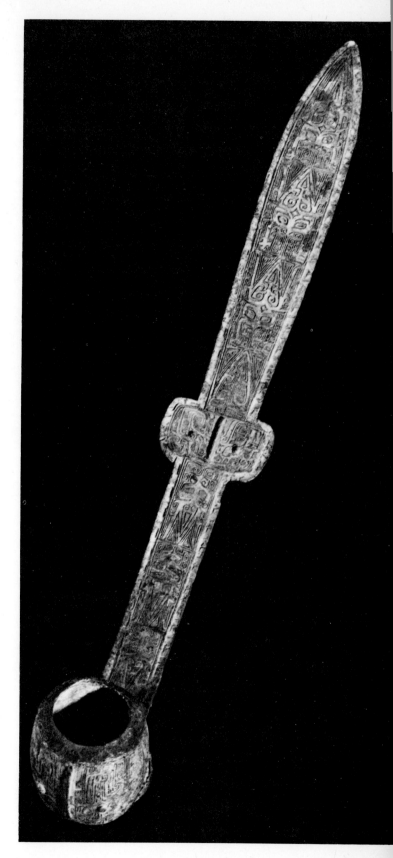

25. LIBATION SPOON. *Shao*
SHANG DYNASTY. AN-YANG PERIOD
C. 1300–1028 B.C.

L. 52 cm. Collection A. Stoclet, Brussels (Formerly the Adolphe Stoclet Collection)

This is a rare type of ritual ladle. It is both vigorous and elegant, and is a fine example of the detailed tracery achieved by some of the Shang bronze founders.

Two *t'ao t'ieh* masks adorn the bowl. The long flat handle is edged by a polished band, notched and decorated with *T* symbols. The handle spreads in the middle to form a mask, ribbed and with two projecting eyes. This is only part of the design in relief, the rest being on one plane only. Stylized cicadas decorate the remaining part. Some have feet and converge on the central *motif*. The decoration, of very fine quality, is closely designed, and of exceptional unity. Finely traced squares and triangles fill the background.

The piece has a fine unbroken green patina.

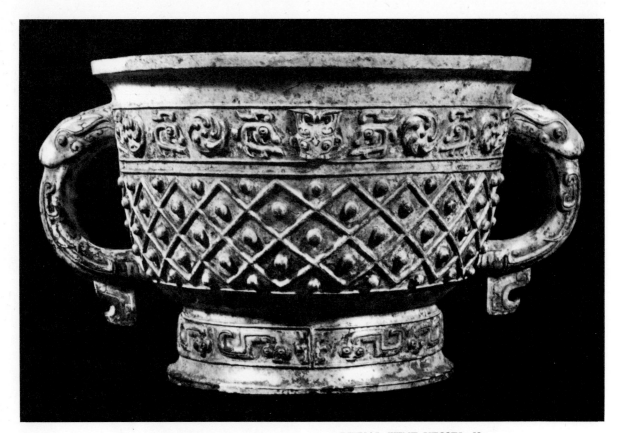

27. RITUAL WINE VESSEL. *Yu*
BEGINNING OF THE CHOU DYNASTY
C. 1000–900 B.C.

H. 31 cm. Private Collection

The *yu* are classified as vessels designed to carry the sacrificial wine. No Neolithic pottery prototype has been found, but Yetts thought that this shape may have derived from wooden pots, or dried gourds, with plaited bamboo handles. He held that the rhombic decoration on some of the handles is derived from this.

The vessel has a large and swelling belly, a slightly flaring and hollow foot, with a hemispherical cover surmounted by a rim which forms the cup when it is reversed. The handle is movable, and its points of attachment are embellished with stylized solid rams' heads. The decoration on the belly, the lid, and the handle, is composed of overlapping *T* designs, sometimes called meanders, which stand out on a ground of incised spirals, generally admitted to symbolize clouds and thunder. For this reason it is sometimes called the "cloud and thunder" fret. This treatment of the decoration is typical of Karlgren's "style B."

The neck and foot are encircled by a band of spiral decoration, and among these one can see elements of the archaic dragon, *k'uei,* and perhaps traces of a feather design. A frieze of less ornate spirals surrounds the upper part of the body, level with the ring handles.

The patina is green with splashes of cuprite.

26. RITUAL FOOD VESSEL. *Kuei*
SHANG DYNASTY. AN-YANG PERIOD
C. 1300–1028 B.C.

H. 15.5 cm. Private Collection

This vessel was probably reserved for offerings of grain. In the shape of a large bowl mounted on a hollow base, it has two crescent-shaped handles. The lower part of these has a hooked pendant *motif,* while the head of a kind of deer seems to be devouring the upper part.

The decoration is divided into three. Running round the slightly flared mouth is a frieze with two *t'ao t'ieh* masks in high relief, placed diametrically opposite. These are accompanied by alternate dragons and whorl *motifs.* The central section has a lozenge network with prominent nodules. The base has a frieze of eight stylized serpents. The whole decoration stands out from a uniform flat ground. The polished patina is an unbroken sea-green color.

An almost identical *kuei* can be seen in the Guimet Museum in Paris.

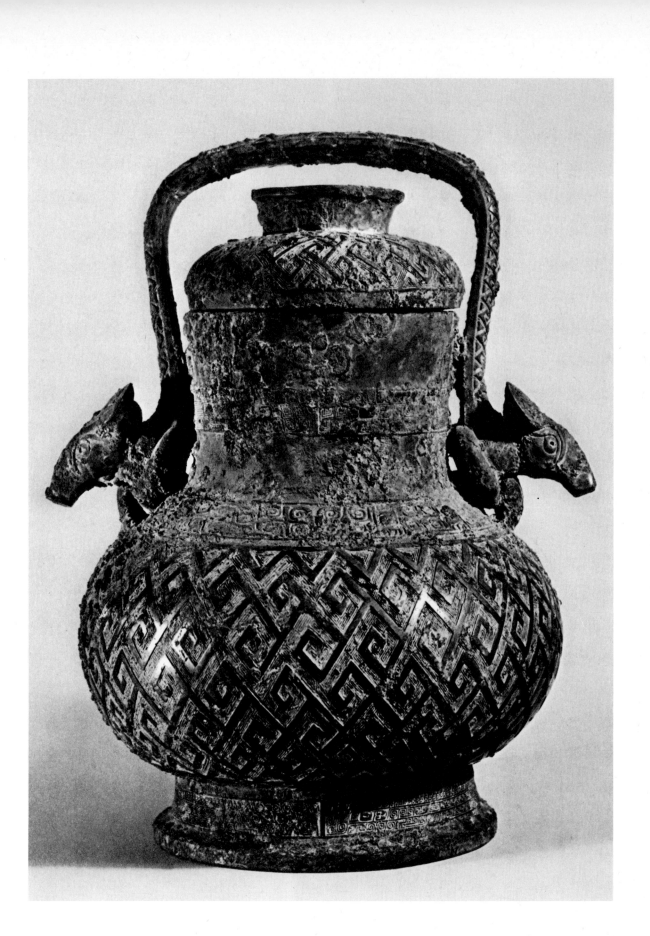

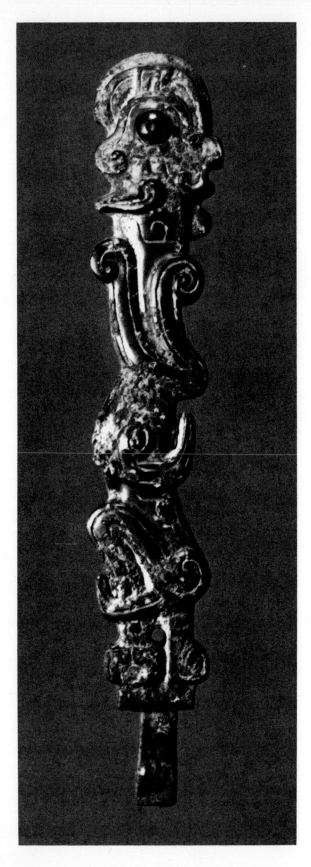

28. STAFF-FINIAL. BEGINNING OR MIDDLE OF THE CHOU DYNASTY. 9TH–7TH CENTURIES B.C.

H.16.5 cm. Östasiatiska Museet, Stockholm (Formerly Collection of H.M. the King Gustave VI Adolphe)

The complex and hybrid character of this piece strengthens the belief that it must have been a magical object. Its significance, however, escapes us. It seems to represent a creature, half-man, half-demon, with large bulbous eyes. It has a crest, a mouth revealing a duck's beak, and feet armed with talons. It is seated with legs folded inside its tail. What seem to be arms are bent, and short wings start from the belly which is decorated with a buffalo or tiger mask in light relief.

There are some other examples of this kind of work in the art of the Chou period, notably a demon on a weapon of *tao* (sword) type in the collection of the Freer Gallery of Art in Washington.

The bronze has traces of gilding. The patina is a brilliant grayish black with heavy incrustations of malachite.

Exhibition: Arte Cinese, *Venice, 1954, No. 62.*

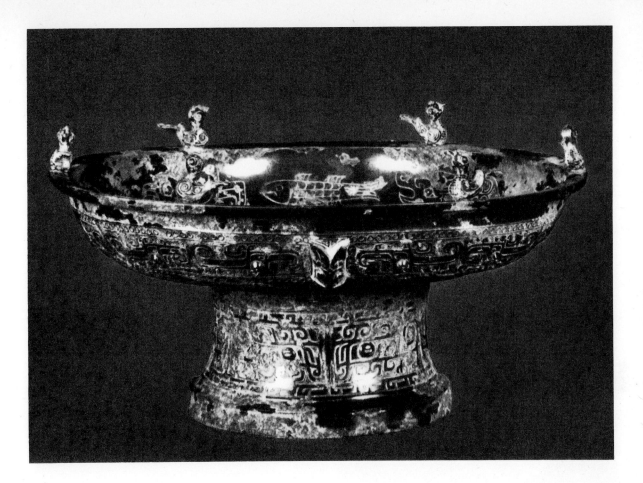

29. RITUAL WATER VESSEL. *P'an*
BEGINNING OF THE CHOU DYNASTY
10TH–8TH CENTURIES B.C.

L.35 cm. H.15 cm. Collection M. Michel Beurdeley, Paris

This *p'an* is without handles, and its foot is much taller than usual. The shape and decoration are also striking, for traditional masks and bird profiles are allied with naturalistic *motifs*.

On the outside the bowl is decorated with a frieze of birds with prominent eyes, grouped in pairs between three relief *t'ao t'ieh* masks. This decoration has, above and below, a border of small circles. The foot has three big masks, each with a projecting rib on the muzzle, and prominent elliptical eyes. These are dragons, surrounded by a network of fine incised spirals and hooked bands.

Round the edge stand six aquatic birds, treated in the round, finely chiseled and in realistic positions. Inside, the upper part of the bowl is decorated with incised ornament representing groups of creatures – a fish, a dragon, and a bird, thrice repeated, and, as it were, in pursuit. At the bottom is an engraved monster with the head of a dragon. Its round body has a series of scale-like circles, while its short tail resembles that of a tortoise. There is an inscription on either side of this fabulous creature.

The brilliant black metal harmonizes perfectly with the partial green patination.

This bronze has affinities with a *p'an* found at Lo-Yang, and now in the collection of the Hakutsura Museum, in Kobe, Japan, though the latter, perhaps dating from 1000–850 B.C., is much more elaborate, and probably earlier than the one shown here.

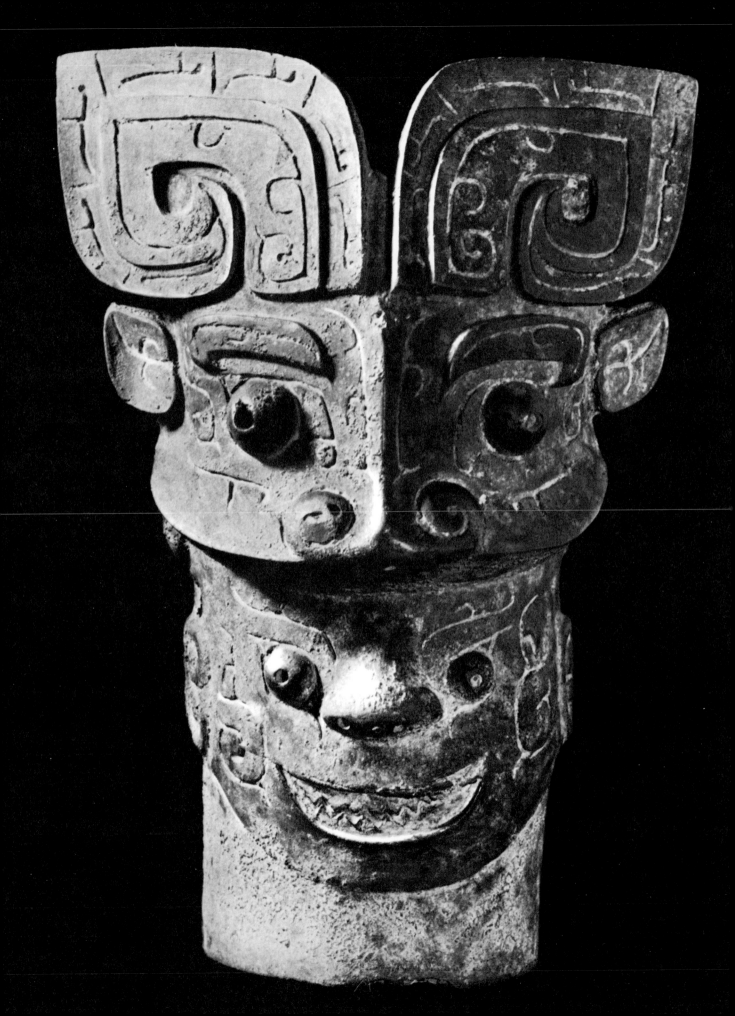

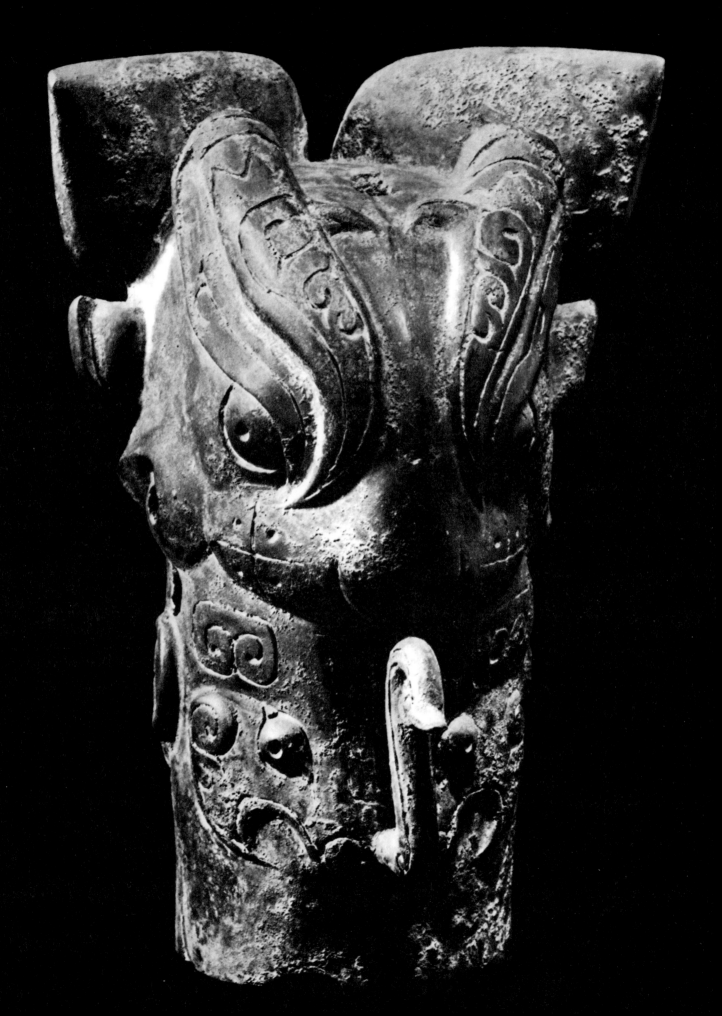

◁◁ 30. STAFF-FINIAL. SHANG OR BEGINNING
OF THE CHOU DYNASTY

*H.18 cm. (Enlarged). Formerly Collection D. David-Weill,
Neuilly-sur-Seine*

This magnificent model has two different aspects, each composed of two masks, one above the other. Its complex imagery suggests that its use was ritual or magical. The side shown on this plate illustrates a ram's mask with huge curved horns above a human face. Such representations, many different examples of which are known in jade and bronze, must have had a definite symbolic meaning for the Chinese. Interpretation, however, is still hypothetical. Several theories have been advanced. Hentze puts aside the idea that the beast is devouring the man, in favor of a Protecting Spirit. He bases his theory on the man's expression (which seems to express joy rather than fear), seeing in it mankind's harmony with, and submission to, the forces of Nature through the beneficent intervention of this protecting Spirit.

One might equally suggest the totem of a clan, or a symbol of the fight between good and evil, or perhaps moon magic. The ram's mask is handled vigorously and with great perception: all the details – horns, ears, eyebrows, and nostrils – are clearly defined. Projecting like buttons, the eyes have round pupils, in common with the other three masks. The man's face, with its short squat nose, crescent mouth, and triangular teeth, is typical of all archaic masks. It is reminiscent of the crouching figure in the grip of a monster seen on the two famous *yu* in the Sumitomo Collection at Kyōtō, and in the Cernuschi Museum in Paris.

◁ 31. STAFF-FINIAL. REVERSE OF
PREVIOUS PLATE

On this side of the piece the upper part is the mask of an ox with forward-arching horns, powerfully modeled in broad relief. It surmounts a second rather withdrawn *t'ao t'ieh* embellished with an elephant's trunk. The two upper heads are joined at the sides in a very striking way, which seems to enclose the head and the scalp of a human being.

Both facets of this piece have decoration of incisions in the forms of a C, a T, of crosses, and of long hooked lines. The patina is a greenish gray with some touches of malachite. There is a similar piece in which the symbols are reversed (i.e. the head of the buffalo surmounts that of the man) in the Pillsbury Collection, Minneapolis Museum.

32. PERHAPS A CHARIOT FITTING
BEGINNING OF THE CHOU DYNASTY
9TH–8TH CENTURIES B.C.

H.21 cm. Formerly Collection D. David-Weill, Neuilly-sur-Seine

It is probable that this magnificent object was a chariot fitting, and it may have been a socket for a wooden structural part.
Both shape and decoration divide it distinctly into two. The upper part is an elliptical socket which is decorated with an all-embracing *t'ao t'ieh* armed with large, sharp, jutting teeth. The eyes, with round pupils, are sunk deeply into their sockets. A very small second mask can be seen on the beast's forehead. The lower part is a trapezoidal plaque which must be examined upside down. It has a different type of *t'ao t'ieh* – a flat ground from which all the elements stand out in uniform relief. Above this is another mask, much less clearly defined, which may resemble a bat or an owl. It fits exactly into the horns of the lower *t'ao t'ieh*.
A beautiful green patina covers the whole surface.

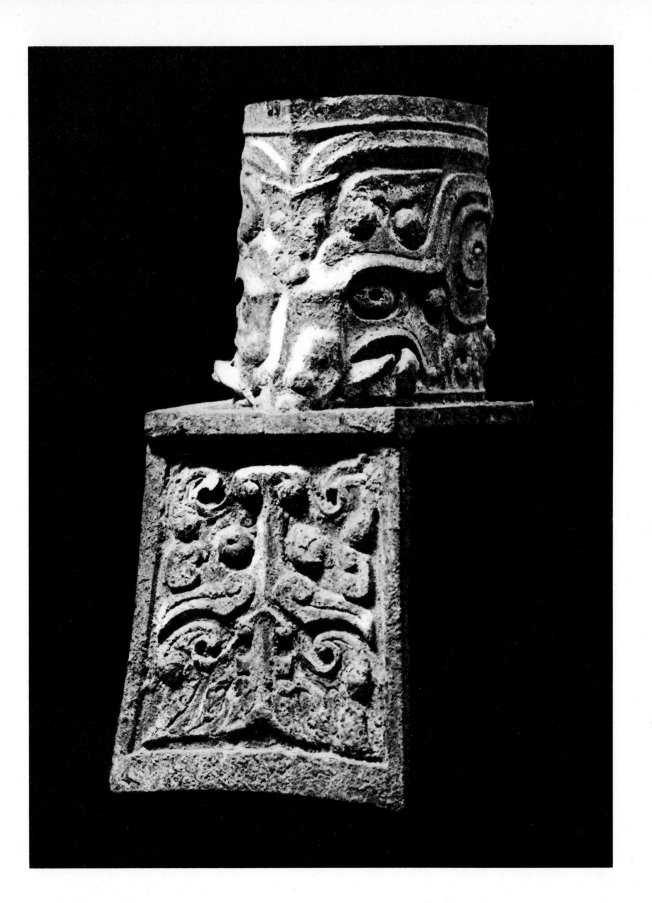

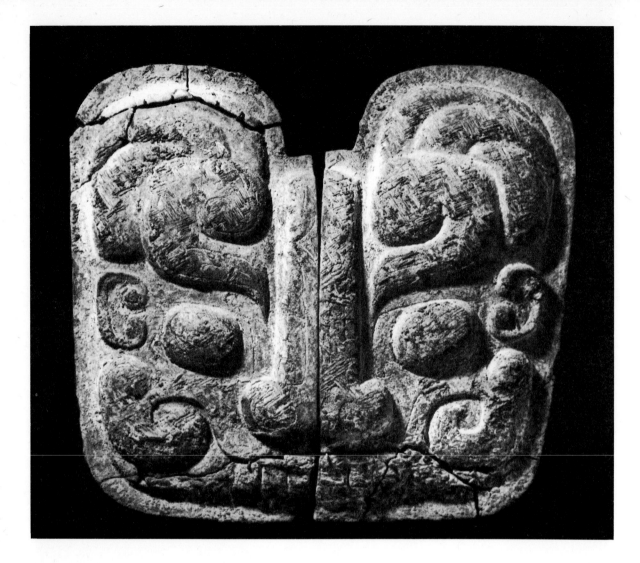

33. *T'ao t'ieh* MASK
BEGINNING OF THE CHOU DYNASTY
9TH–8TH CENTURIES B.C.

H.32 cm. B.34 cm. Private Collection, Paris

This molded mask, made in two separate parts, was probably
a piece of applied decoration. On the medial edge at the back
of each half, there are two small overlapping rings which must
have been used for fixing the two sides together. Using the
muzzle as an axis this would allow a certain freedom of movement, enabling the mask to be presented not only full face, but
also at varying angles.

Broadly and vigorously treated, this ram's horned mask bears
traces of its burial in the earth. Imprinted here and there in the
metal are the faint marks of what may have been twisted bamboo on which it must have lain, and these have taken on the
same beautiful patina as the rest.

There is a certain similarity in the technique of casting and in
the quality of the bronze which permits a comparison with the
tiger on Plate 11.

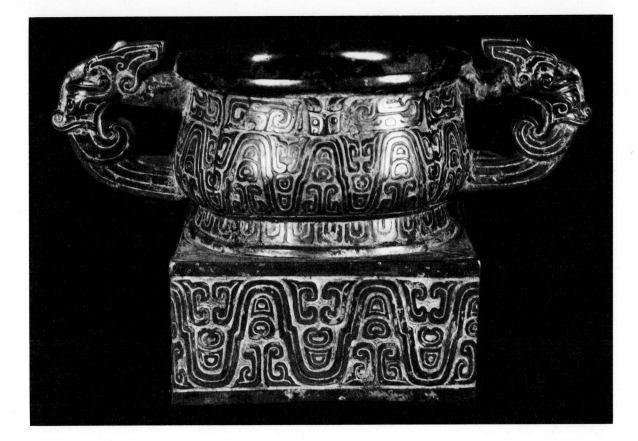

34. RITUAL FOOD VESSEL. *Kuei*
CHOU DYNASTY. 9TH–8TH CENTURIES B.C.

H.26.5 cm. Total breadth.44.5 cm. Cernuschi Museum, Paris

The ritual food vessel, *kuei,* is here seen in all the magnificence which had been developed by the middle of the Chou dynasty. The swelling shape of the cup or bowl has two immense handles spreading outwards. The base is high and square.

This decoration is typical. Continuous parallel bands of curving waves enclose alternating *motifs* which are faintly reminiscent of the earlier masks. The old Shang themes seem, somehow, to have disintegrated; their mythical character appears to have been displaced by pure ornament in flat relief on a plain ground. Only on the frieze, and on the powerful dragons' heads forming the handle, is the relief in any way accentuated. The patina is a beautiful deep green.

A comparison of this plate with the *kuei* on Plate 26 (Shang dynasty) gives a clear indication of the evolution of shape and decoration from one epoch to another.

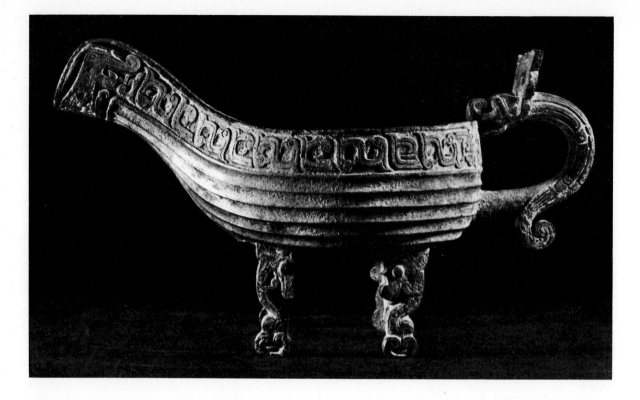

35. RITUAL WATER VESSEL. *I*
MIDDLE OF THE CHOU DYNASTY
9TH–7TH CENTURIES B.C.

L.38 cm. Formerly Collection Mrs.Walter Sedgwick, London

Towards the end of the 10th century B.C. a new style is evident in the bronzes. In the search for a purer, less angular line, different shapes emerge. Previously unknown vessels appear, and among them is the ritual water vessel resembling a sauceboat. At the same time a profound change occurs in the inspiration and handling of the decoration. The brooding sense of ancient magic vanishes as the old *motifs* give way to new, simplified, themes and intertwined flat reliefs.

The beautiful piece shown here is a good example of these new tendencies. The elongated body is decorated with horizontal fluting which accentuates the line.

A frieze of coiling, stylized birds forms a smooth border in relief. This theme seems to have only a very faint connection with the birds on earlier vessels. Now, only the design is important. The handle, large and jutting out sufficiently to balance the length of the vessel, is in the shape of a powerfully horned dragon. Its jaws are clamped to the edge of the vessel and its tail coils in a spiral.

An inscription in the interior reads as follows:

"In the first month of the Emperor, the first quarter, the day Ch'eng-wu, Hung of Ch'u made this vase…"

This inscription enables the piece to be attributed to the State of Ch'u, corresponding to the present-day Province of Hopei, which lies across the middle valley of the river Yangtze.

Exhibitions: Bronzes Chinois, *Orangerie Museum, Paris, 1934, No. 392.* – Chinese Art, *London, 1935–36, No. 147.*

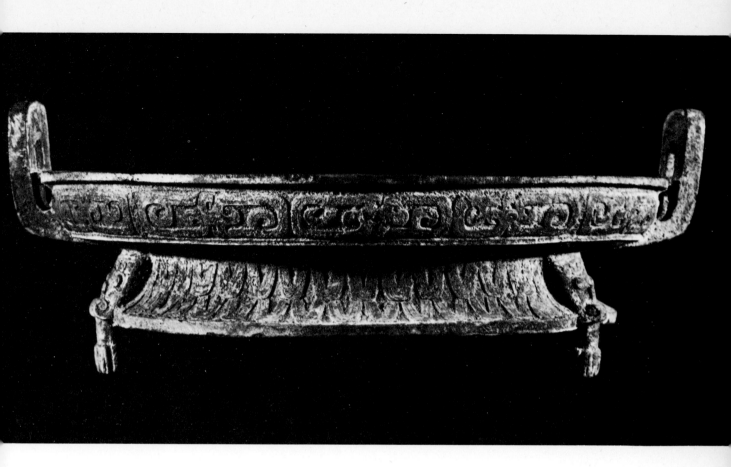

36. RITUAL WATER VESSEL. *P'an*
MIDDLE OF THE CHOU DYNASTY
9TH–7TH CENTURIES B.C.

Width overall 43.8 cm. Formerly Collection Mrs. Walter Sedgwick, London

This type of vessel is one of the most ancient of the bronzes. However, most of the known pieces date from the middle to the end of the Chou dynasty. The beautiful *p'an* here shown has all the characteristics of the style which was dominant between the 9th and the 7th century. The very shallow bowl is clearly outlined by two perfectly horizontal borders, and between these are ten repeated *motifs,* hooks and bands which are, apparently, vestigial remains of dragons. There are two undecorated vertical handles. The widening base has a double row of shell, or perhaps wave, *motifs.* Three monsters' heads are attached to it, whose jaws hold the cylindrical feet on a fluted and flaring base. The inscription is the same as the one on the preceding plate.

Exhibitions: Bronzes Chinois, *Orangerie Museum, Paris, 1934, No. 393.* – Chinese Art, *London, 1935–36, No. 147.*

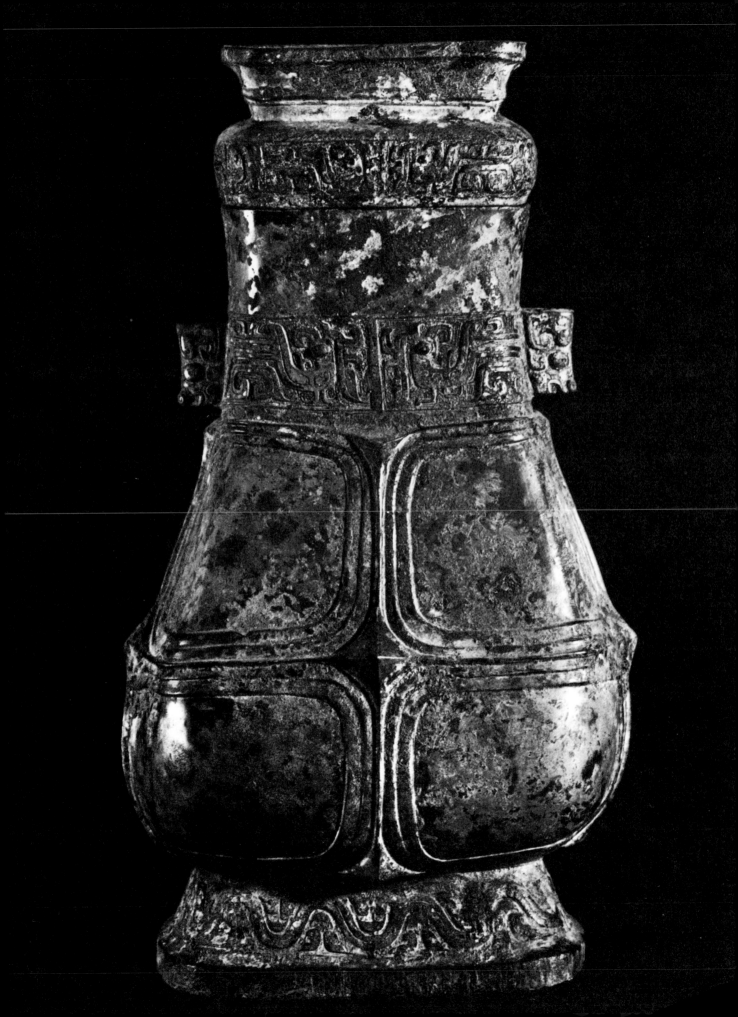

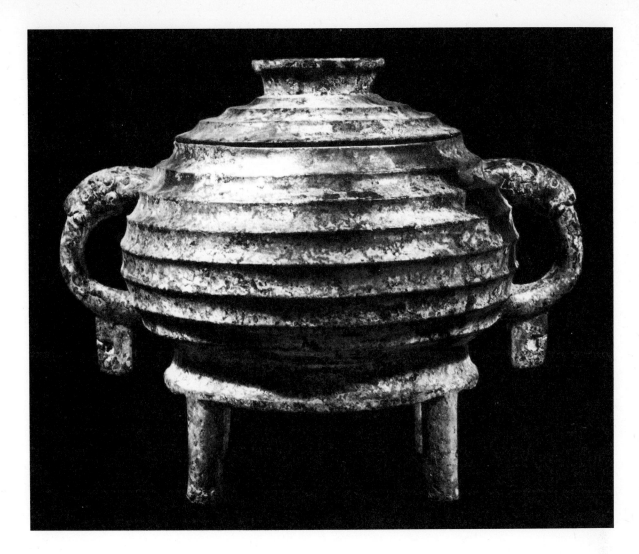

◁ 37. *Hu.* CHOU DYNASTY. C.900–800 B.C.

H. 52 cm. Collection M. and Mme Léon Velluz, Paris

The large *hu* shown here is a good example of the evolution of bronze during the Chou period. Relief handles are in the form of *t'ao t'ieh* masks which still retain the power of the more ancient prototypes. Birds with turned heads decorate the friezes of the cover and neck, and the end of their tails is separate from the main body of the *motif*. These peculiarities are typical of this period, when the archaic themes are already much altered. The decoration on the foot clearly belongs to the style known as "Middle Chou," with its serpentine band, and very degenerate masks.

The body of the vessel is divided into eight polished reserves by ribbon-like bands, recalling the thongs which were used for carrying leather vessels. These bands have a diamond in relief at the point of intersection.

The sea-green patina, which is very smooth, is enhanced by spots of cuprite and patches of azurite.

38. RITUAL FOOD VESSEL. *Kuei*
MIDDLE OF THE CHOU DYNASTY
7TH–6TH CENTURIES B.C.

H. 24 cm. Collection Dr. & Mme Uldry, Zurich

A tendency to become rounder is to be seen in the bronze forms of the middle of the Chou dynasty. Certain vessels such as the *ting* and the *kuei* now have a cover which was unknown in the earlier period. The vessel illustrated shows this development. The cover fits the profile, extending it into a dome which accentuates the quasi-spherical effect of the whole. The cover ends in a large knop which forms the base of a beautiful cup when it is reversed. The only decoration on both cup and vase is a series of horizontal flutings – a *motif* typical of the period. The pendant handles are faithful to tradition; they have lost only the vigorous clarity of earlier times. Heads of deer, softly modeled, surmount them. The circular base is supported on four cylindrical undecorated feet. This bronze has a fine sea-green patina.

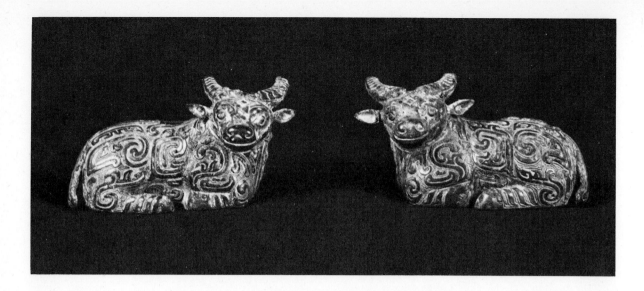

39. RECUMBENT BUFFALOS. MIDDLE OF THE
CHOU DYNASTY. 8TH–7TH CENTURIES B.C.

L.16 cm. H.8 cm. Collection M. Michel Beurdeley, Paris

Surface ornament characteristic of the Middle Chou period is
allied in these recumbent animals to close observation and a
sense of solidity. The ornament consists of incurved bands and
hooks of varying thickness which defy precise clarification.
They are accentuated by a ground of incised spirals and
parallel lines, a rather degenerate pattern surviving from the
days of the Shang and early Chou. On the other hand, the
expressive heads with large spreading ears and ridged horns,
the hooves curved beneath the body, and the detached tails are
modeled with great realism. The lozenge on the foreheads is
the sole remaining trace of the ancient stylized forms. The
realism noticeable here is a forerunner of the vivid animal
sculpture of the Warring States period, but at this time it has
no mobility.

A rectangular hole in the back of each beast seems to suggest
that they were used as supports.

The patina is a beautiful unbroken green.

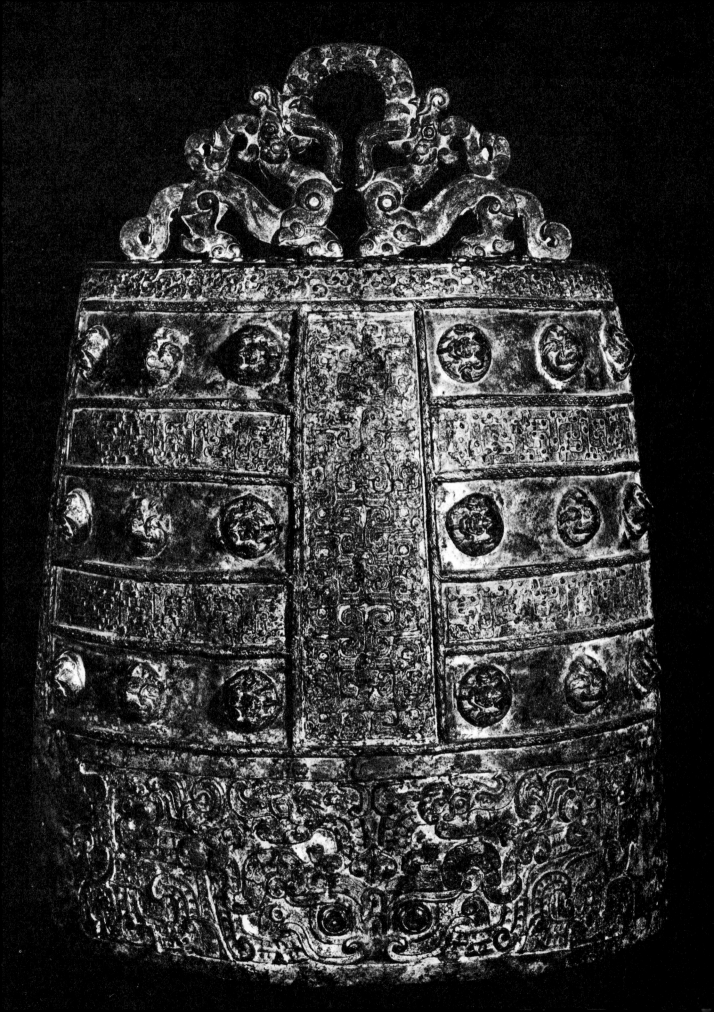

◁ 40. BELL. *Chung*. CHOU DYNASTY
PERIOD OF THE WARRING STATES
C. 480 B.C.

H. 55 cm. Formerly Collection Adolphe Stoclet, Brussels

Bronze bells were cast in a series of varying size, though very little was known about modality at the time. This accounts for the fact that there are four replicas in the same series as this magnificent bell in the Stoclet Collection – one in the Berlin Museum (H. 35.5 cm), two in the Fogg Art Museum of Cambridge, Mass. (H. 48.8 cm and 66.7 cm), and another in the Museum at Amsterdam (H. 59 cm). There must have been two more from this group to go between the one in Berlin and the smallest at Cambridge. The whole range probably had seven bells, perhaps more, to complete the scale.

While Shang or early Chou bells were fixed, as it were, upside down, fastened to a cylindrical sleeve or support, those of the later period of the Warring States were suspended by a handle. They are all without a clapper, the sound being produced by striking the ornamental nodules. They are always of elliptical section, and often have very important inscriptions.

The decoration on this series is impressively rich. Most of the artistic repertory of the Chou is displayed, and the treatment is strong, lending a certain baroque character to the decoration. Especially remarkable is the development of the *t'ao t'ieh* mask on the lower frieze. It is framed by fabulous birds, and its horns have become two separate dragons. The nodules are decorated with beasts devouring one another. On the vertical panels it is possible to distinguish four reversed masks among the interlaced designs, which also has spirals, commas, and granulations. Among the confused tangle of ribbon-like *motifs,* heads, beaks, and fangs appear.

Fine sculptural dragons, arched face to face on the top, grasp the handle in their jaws. The ends of the handle are twisted serpents' tails.

Two fine *chung,* similar in design to these but with rather less complicated decoration, are in the Freer Gallery of Art in Washington and in the Art Institute of Chicago. They are part of a different suite, and appear to be a little earlier than that in the collection of M. Stoclet for which Professor Yetts suggested a date of 480 B.C.

41. RITUAL VESSEL. *Tui.* END OF THE CHOU DYNASTY. PERIOD OF THE WARRING STATES (5TH–3RD CENTURIES B.C.)

H. 16 cm. (Enlarged.) Private Collection

Towards the end of the Chou dynasty new forms appeared, and among them was the type of *tui* shown here, which is spherical and sometimes ovoid. A popular Chinese name for it is "water melon tripod."

The decoration is typical of the style of the Warring States, notably in the renaissance of Shang styles covering the piece completely with ornament, and also in the animation of the *motifs.* These are in superimposed friezes. On the cover are repetitive scenes of men and tigers fighting, also found on certain well-known vessels of the same date known as "hunting vessels." The central part is covered with a fine *motif* of hooks and spirals which are purely decorative. It is divided from the lower panel, in which there are crested birds holding a snake in their beaks. They are to be compared with the *motif* on the contemporary *hu* on Plate 16.

The impression of relief work is gained from the background which is hollowed out, and which lifts the pattern above the surface. The lid forms a separate cup when it is turned and stood on the three rings at the top.

Exhibition: Ostasiatische Kunst und Chinoiserie, *Cologne, 1953,* *No. 103.*

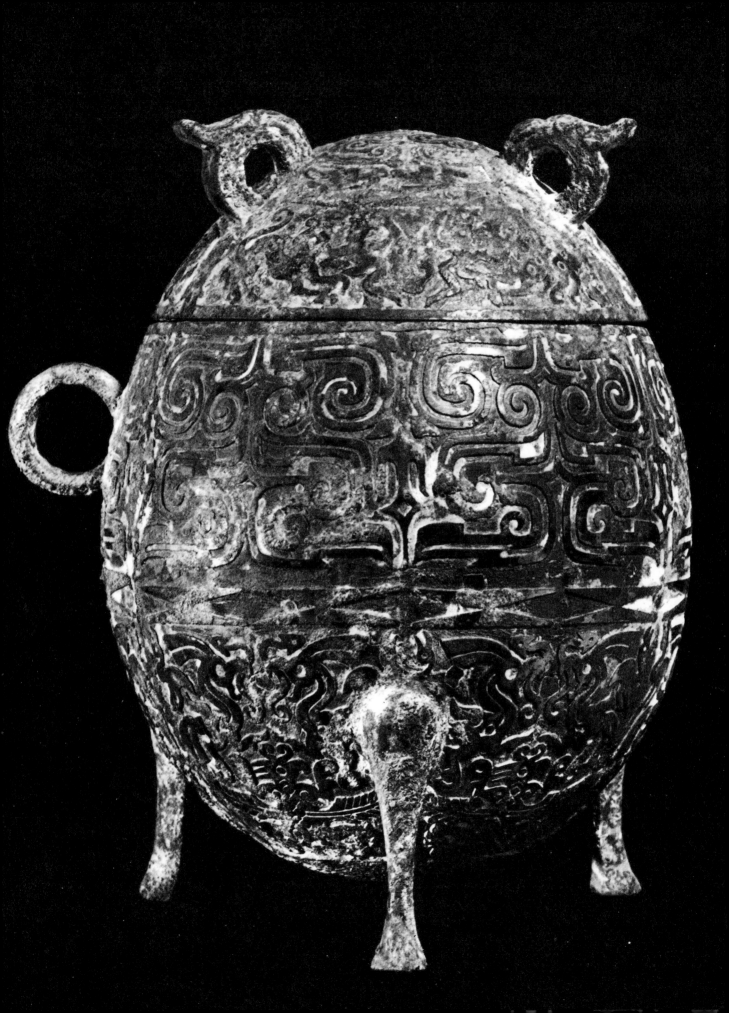

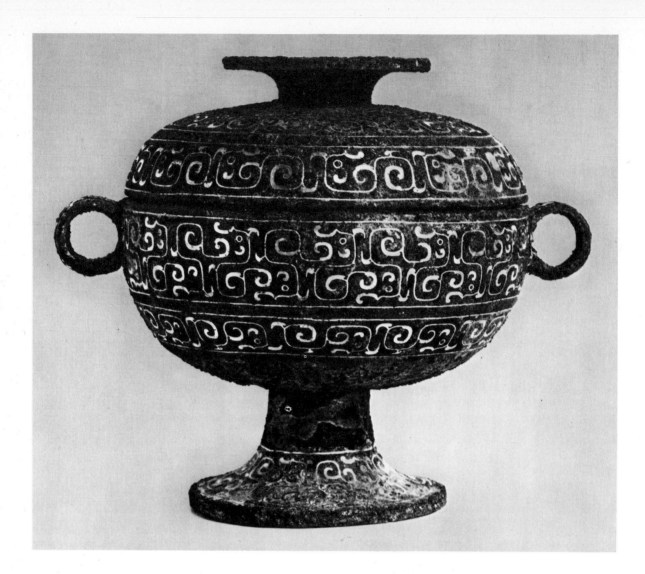

42. RITUAL CUP. *Tou.* END OF CHOU DYNASTY
PERIOD OF THE WARRING STATES
5TH–3RD CENTURIES B.C.

*H.15 cm. Total breadth 18.9 cm. The Freer Gallery of Art,
Washington D.C.*
*(By permission of the Smithsonian Institution, The Freer Gallery of
Art)*

The elegant shape of the *tou* appears rather late in the history
of bronze. In fact, no example is known which can be dated
before the period of the Warring States. It is always in the
form of a hemispherical cup on a flared base of varying height.
The cover is a second cup, reversed, with a flattened base. The
main cup has handles in the form of dragons in relief, or
vertical rings, as is the case here. Often there are four of

these. Sometimes, the cover is dome-shaped with the rings
fixed to it in such a position that the cup will rest on them
when it is reversed.

Specimens of the *tou* are generally engraved and inlaid in the
classical, rather repetitive style characteristic of the Warring
States period. There are some with turquoise inlays, but the
ornament is more usually inlaid in gold or silver. The famous
piece shown here is entirely inlaid with gold in one of the
brilliant interlaced designs which are among the finer decorative features of the period. The *motif* is a continuous design of
dragons on five friezes. They are intertwined, and face to face.
The heads are clearly visible, though the creature's body is lost
in spirals and delicately balanced hooks.

The patina is rough, and of a beautiful green, which enhances
the quality of the gold.

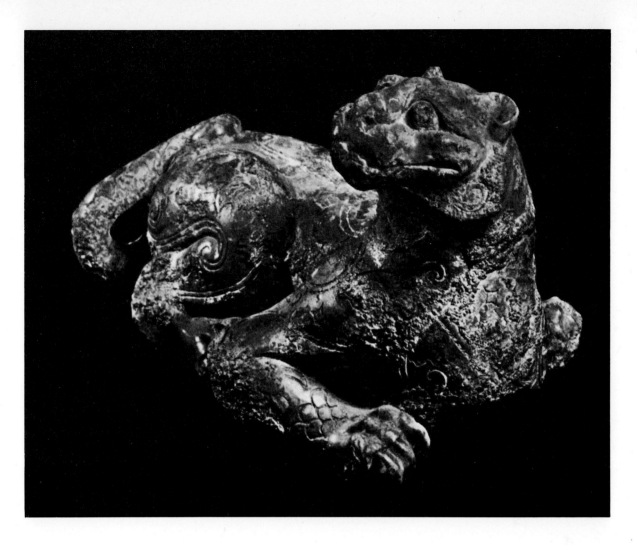

43. CROUCHING TIGER. END OF THE CHOU DYNASTY. PERIOD OF THE WARRING STATES 5TH–3RD CENTURIES B.C.

L.16.4 cm. H.10.5 cm. Private Collection

This tiger comes from the famous site at Chin Ts'un, near Loyang (Honan Province), where so many discoveries of the work of this period were made. It is possible that it decorated the cover of a very large *ting*. At this period many bronzes had three crouching animals on the cover, always closely observed and portrayed with great realism.

The vigorous natural treatment of this powerful beast gives it a monumental appearance, in spite of its small size. The engraved decoration on the body is composed of double incised scrolls and lozenges. The front part of the feet and the tail are decorated with scales.

The patina is brilliant sea green spotted with malachite. A similar piece which might, perhaps, belong to the same cover is in the Hellström Collection in Stockholm.

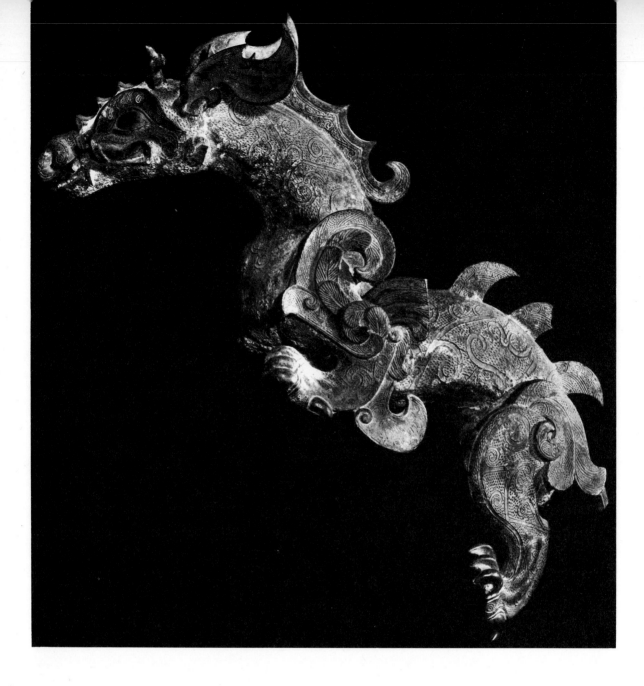

44. WINGED DRAGON. END OF THE CHOU DYNASTY. PERIOD OF THE WARRING STATES 5TH–3RD CENTURIES B.C.

L.65 cm. Collection A.Stoclet, Brussels (Formerly Collection Adolphe Stoclet)

This exceptionally fine piece was found at the bottom of a well on the site of the former capital of the State of Yen, in Hopei Province. It is possibly a piece of architectural decoration, or the handle of an immense vessel.

A thin neck surmounts an outthrust chest, and the whole body – arched over gripping claws – is tense with effort. The back feet are outstretched and muscular, the front short and recoiled. On the shoulders and thighs clusters of swirling feathers represent wings. The back has a jagged mane or crest which ends in a hook. The body has a granular appearance, perhaps intended to represent leather, and, over this, scrolls complete the decoration.

Although very different in aspect, and quite differently handled, this winged dragon does nevertheless herald the winged chimaera of the Six Dynasties, the guardian of the "Road of Spirits" which led to the places of burial.

The patina, green and bluish green, also has spots of azurite.

Exhibitions: Chinesische Kunst, *Berlin, 1929, No. 22.* – Bronzes Chinois, *Orangerie Museum, Paris, 1934, No. 413.* – Chinese Art, *London, 1935–36, No. 489.* – La découverte de l'Asie, *Cernuschi Museum, Paris, 1954, No. 401.*

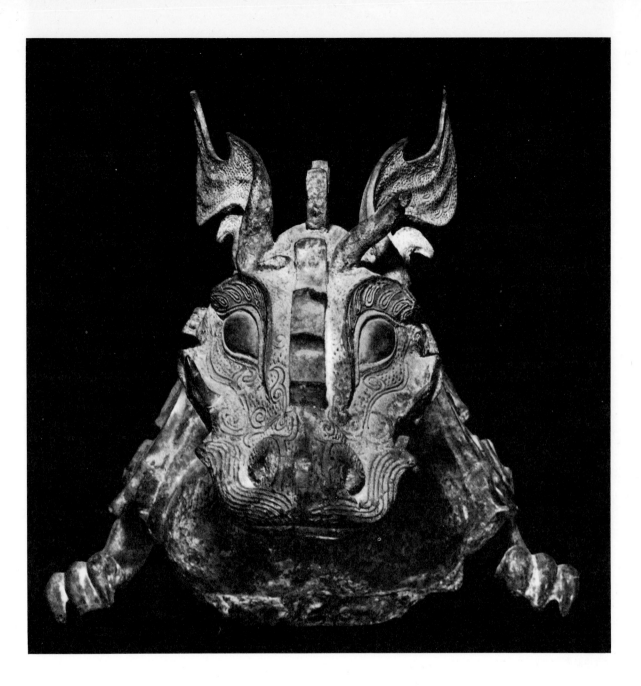

45. WINGED DRAGON. DETAIL OF THE HEAD
OF THE PRECEDING PLATE

Seen from this position the winged dragon on the foregoing
plate seems even more fantastic. The broad muzzle, jutting
fangs, and globular eyes, the jagged frontal rib, sharp horns,
and long fretted curving ears, are all essentially elements of the
t'ao t'ieh come to life. A striking evocation of the forces of
Nature, this dragon preserves all its mythical power, and is a
herald in form and appearance of all the dragons to come
throughout the long history of Chinese civilization.

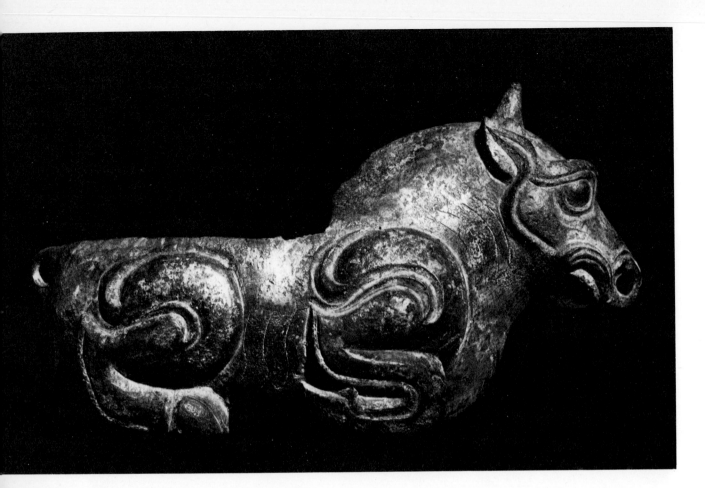

46. LAMP IN THE FORM OF A UNICORN
END OF THE CHOU DYNASTY. PERIOD OF THE
WARRING STATES. 6TH–3RD CENTURIES B.C.

L.16 cm. H.8.8 cm. Collection Frau Georg Hasler, Winterthur

Towards the end of the Chou dynasty, and under the Han, the use of bronze was extended to include useful everyday wares, and, among these, oil lamps take an important place. Very often they are made in the shape of crouching beasts, such as this recumbent unicorn.

The beast has its feet curved under it, the powerful muscles accentuated in relief. Its thick neck, and massive broad muzzled head, is very bovine. A single horn juts from its forehead. Powerful treatment is combined with stylization, for example, the sweeping curves of the arched eyebrow which joins the line of the ear and the jaw. The short tail has a ring, to which the cover, long since lost, was attached.

The patina is a beautiful dark green.

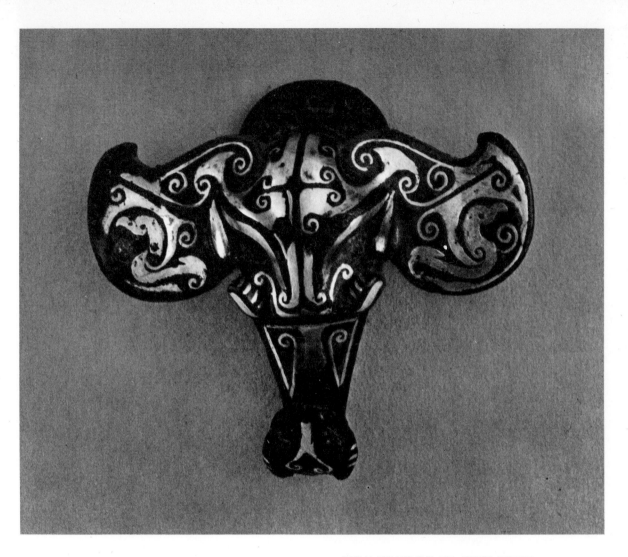

47. BELT HOOK INLAID WITH SILVER
END OF THE CHOU DYNASTY
PERIOD OF THE WARRING STATES
5TH–3RD CENTURIES B.C.

B. 5.1 cm. (Enlarged). Formerly Collection Mr. & Mrs. Desmond Gure, London

The body of this piece, which is in the shape of a broad spatula, is decorated in the center with the head of a tiger modeled in relief, which is prominent without being unduly accentuated. It extends sideways into two wide elephant's ears. The beast's tongue, curved and in the shape of a serpent's head, forms the hook.

This magnificent object is a fine example of the animal style of the period of the Warring States – a style which achieves coherent design whilst combining elements apparently disparate. The inlaid work – skillfull handling of spirals and hooks ending in silhouetted birds' heads – allows this piece to be related to the style of Chin Ts'un, the classic site of inlaid bronze. The silver outlines the whiskers, chops, and nostrils of the tiger, and also encircles its ears.

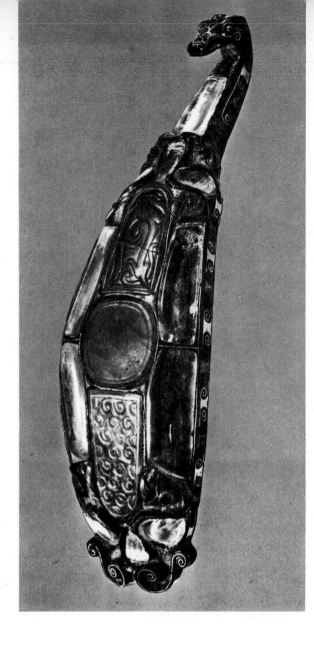

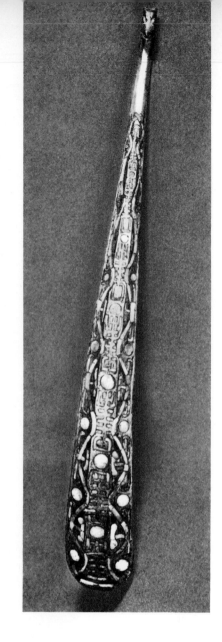

48. BELT HOOK. INLAID BRONZE. BEGINNING OF
THE HAN DYNASTY (206 B.C.–220 A.D.) OR
PERHAPS SLIGHTLY EARLIER

*L. 19.5 cm. Collection A. Stoclet, Brussels ((Formerly Collection
Adolphe Stoclet)*

The arched and swelling body of this fine belt hook has a *t'ao
t'ieh* mask at either end. The mask has curving twisted horns,
enriched with pieces of crystal. A powerfully expressive
dragon's head forms the hook, and this is enhanced by plaques
of engraved jade and crystal. The borders are decorated with
inlaid gold and silver, and the reverse side with a complex
decoration of intertwined dragons delineated with strips of inlaid silver.

Exhibitions: Chinesische Kunst, *Berlin, 1929, No. 97.* – Bronzes
Chinois, *Orangerie Museum. Paris, 1934, No. 403.* – La découverte
de l'Asie, *Cernuschi Museum, Paris, 1954, No. 429.*

49. BELT HOOK IN GILT BRONZE INLAID WITH
TURQUOISES. HAN DYNASTY (206 B.C.–220 A.D.)

L. 33.5 cm. Guimet Museum, Paris

The belt hook shown here is of exceptional size, but is characteristic of the Han dynasty by reason of its spatulate form
with three divisions. Turquoises, round or cut in fillets, decorate the three facets and richly adorn the gilt bronze. The hook
is a dragon's head, and a large flat knob is on the back.
An almost identical hook may be seen in the Pillsbury Collection in the Minneapolis Museum, U.S.A.

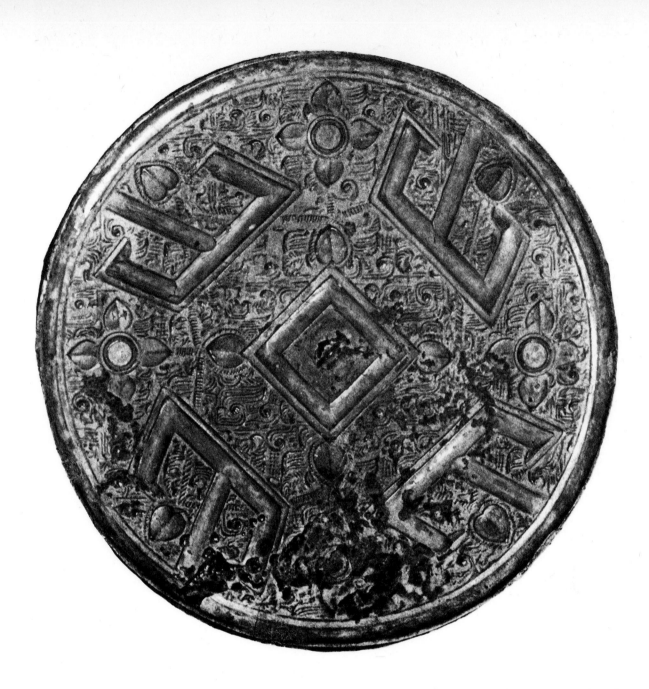

50. MIRROR WITH A DECORATION IN THE FORM OF A "T". END OF THE CHOU DYNASTY PERIOD OF THE WARRING STATES 4TH–3RD CENTURIES B.C.

D. 12.5 cm. Collection of His Excellency M. Hugues le Gallais, Venice

The appearance of bronze mirrors in China seems to date from the Chou dynasty. It is possible to distinguish two different groups in the production which precedes the Han; that of Lo-yang (Honan Province) and of Chiu-ch'ou (Anhwei Province). This piece belongs to the second group.

The mirrors of this period are in thin metal with a very small central knob. The decoration is exceptionally fine, and consists in geometric signs in conjunction with animals and flowers, the symbolic meaning of which is obscure.

The "T" decoration has been explained by some authorities as meaning *Shan,* because it resembles the Chinese ideogram for *Shan* (mountain). The example illustrated is very characteristic. A double lined square surrounds the small ring by which the mirror was suspended. Flowers and leaves extend its corners. A type of rose, or four-petaled flower, drawn on the same axis separates four large oblique "T" signs. The horizontal bars of these signs run parallel to the sides of the inside square, and, like these, have double contour lines. They are in slight relief on a ground which is finely incised with a pattern of feathers, striations, and spirals ending in a granular relief. The patina is black, with green spots.

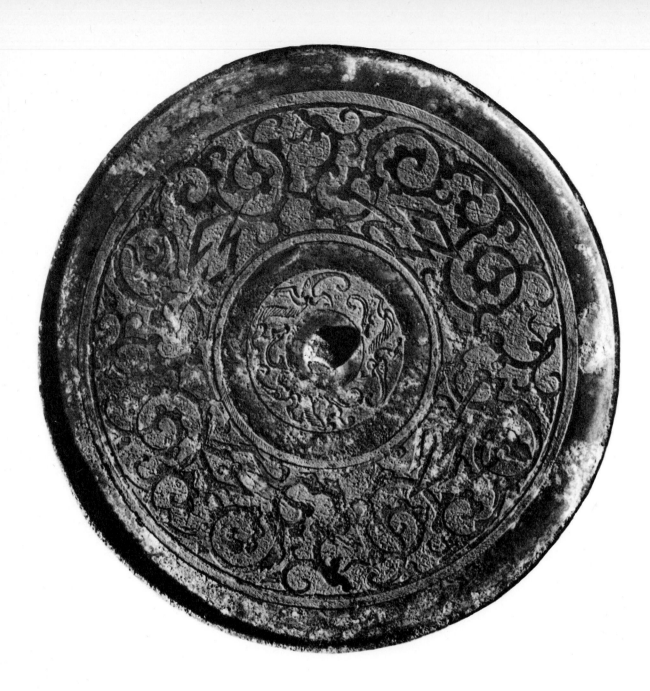

51. BRONZE MIRROR WITH SPIRAL DECORATION END OF THE CHOU DYNASTY. PERIOD OF THE WARRING STATES. 4TH–3RD CENTURIES B.C.

Private Collection

This mirror has a raised, curving rim, and corresponds in general characteristics to the one on the preceding plate. The decoration is in two concentric panels with narrow polished bands and thin corded *motifs* between.

The frieze surrounding the central knob has three serpent-like dragons with striated bodies and back-turned heads. The main frieze has a ground of tiny spirals and very fine granulations, a pattern of scrolls and arabesques, and stylized animals which are faintly recognizable as the heads of dragons and birds. Four zigzag, or lightning *motifs,* introduce a sharp contrast with the curves and countercurves of the decoration.

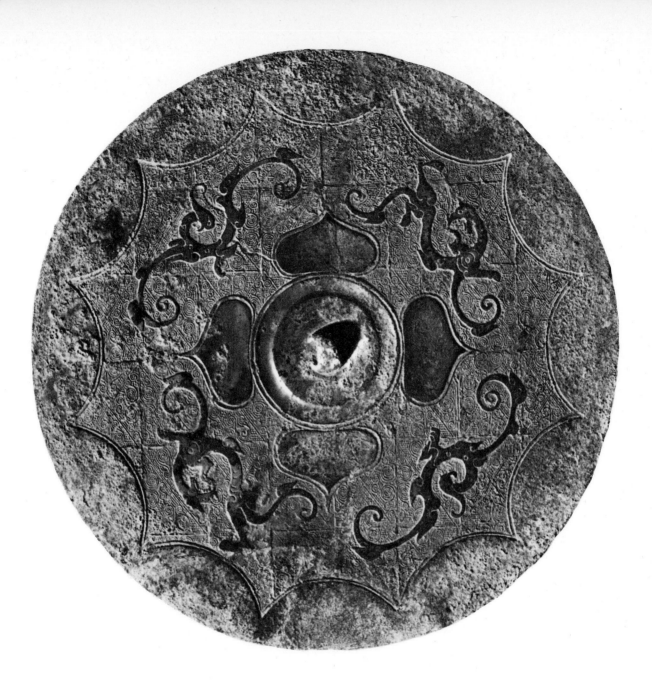

52. BRONZE MIRROR DECORATED WITH
DRAGONS AND BIRDS. END OF THE CHOU
DYNASTY. 4TH–3RD CENTURIES B.C.

D.18.2 cm. Private Collection

Another theme from the wealth of the Warring States period
is seen on the mirror here illustrated. The central knob for
hanging is placed in the middle of a circle, which is divided
by four heart-shaped petals. These are outlined by a double
incision. Around them are stylized animals – two dragons and
two birds, curved and swirling. Their long serpentine tails are
counterbalanced by purely decorative spirals.

This design stands out from a background of very delicately
traced geometrical *motifs*. Rectangles, diagonally divided, are
covered with an ordered spiral design on a ground of close
and regular granulations. It is interesting to remember that
these rectangles, carefully juxtaposed, had first to be impressed
into the clay mold with a very finely incised matrix.

The mirror is framed by a border of festoons.

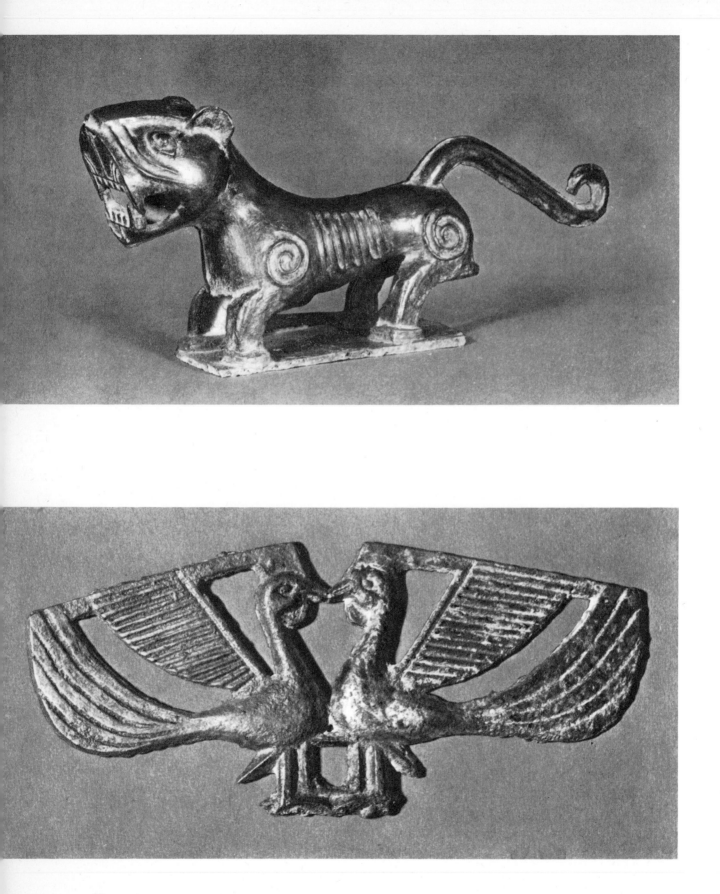

53. THE HANDLE OF A BELL OR DRUM
HAN DYNASTY (206 B.C.–220 A.D.)

L. 36 cm. Formerly Collection Mme J. Ramet, Paris

The three-dimensional tiger on this bell or drum handle is a good example of the simplified style which the Han artists introduced into bronze work, and especially into their handling of animals.

It is interesting to compare this piece with the tigers facing one another on the bell in Plate 40. The curving and flexible style is a perfect example of the artistic essays and almost fretful rhythms which are typical of the Warring States. The Han vision is more direct, more natural in its manner of expressing the essential character of a piece.

The object shown here is crudely cast, but manifests great force and realism within the limits of a restrained, linear vision. The head of the tiger, though much simplified, is still full of power. The influence of barbarian art can be seen here, and particularly of art from the region of the Ordos desert, where a definite animal style, at once stylized and realistic, had evolved.

Exhibition: Bronzes Chinois, *Orangerie Museum, Paris, 1934, No. 338.*

54. APPLIED ORNAMENT. HAN DYNASTY
(206 B.C.–220 A.D.)

L. 25 cm. H. 11 cm. Guimet Museum, Paris

These two stylized symmetrical birds, with outstretched wings and tails, recall the art of Western Asia. Han China had extended her sphere of influence as far as the Persian frontiers, and much art of the period shows the influence of Iranian and Mediterranean peoples.

The rigid treatment of this design – perhaps the crowning piece of a larger and, to us, an unknown work – is far removed from the free and animated modeling usually associated with Han bronze founders.

This bronze has a green patina with traces of gilding.

Exhibition: Arte Cinese, *Venice, 1954, No. 154.*

55. INCENSE-BURNER. HAN DYNASTY
(206 B.C.–220 A.D.)

H. 17 cm. Collection Frau Mary Mantel, Zurich

The spherical shape of this small bronze is reminiscent of the *tou* which was made at the end of the Chou dynasty.

The lower hemispherical part stands on a tall stem, and has no decoration. The cover, forming the upper half of the sphere, has pierced *motifs* of stylized dragons, and is surmounted by a sculptured bird. This bird is in the Han style, familiar on the pottery tomb figures – purely naturalistic reproduction without decoration except for the tail, which is stylized in the form of a flower.

A very light green patina is shaded with patches of azurite.

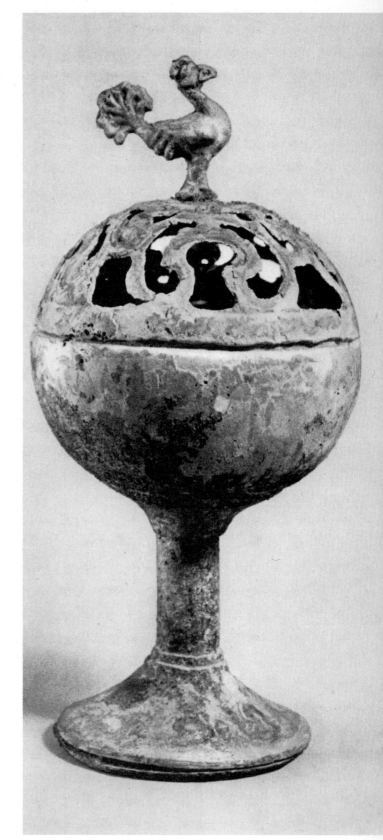

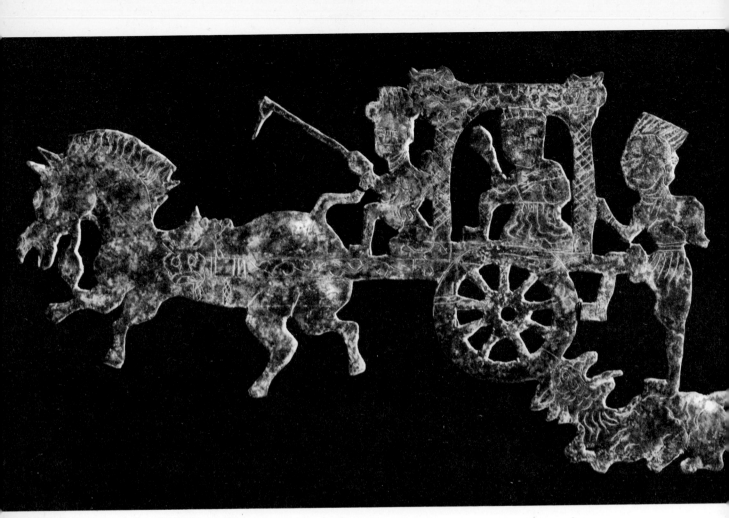

56. BRASS PLAQUE OF FRETTED DESIGN
HAN DYNASTY (206 B.C.–220 A.D.)

L.23 cm. H.12.5 cm. Collection Frau Mary Mantel, Zurich

If, in so far as they reflect the more dignified contemporary
painting, Han carved stone blocks can be called "popular," then
it is also true of this decorative plaque. Its purpose is unknown. Here, as on the tombstones, the outline is the most
important part, and it is enhanced by engraving which high-
lights the detail.

The scene is vividly realistic and, at the same time, naïve. Faces
and costumes are only lightly indicated. Fabulous elements
intervene, and heads of monsters decorate the chariot and its
poles. A threatening beast, crouching behind, supports a standing man. This is typical, and part of the charm of the Han
period, in which real and imaginary worlds are depicted side
by side.

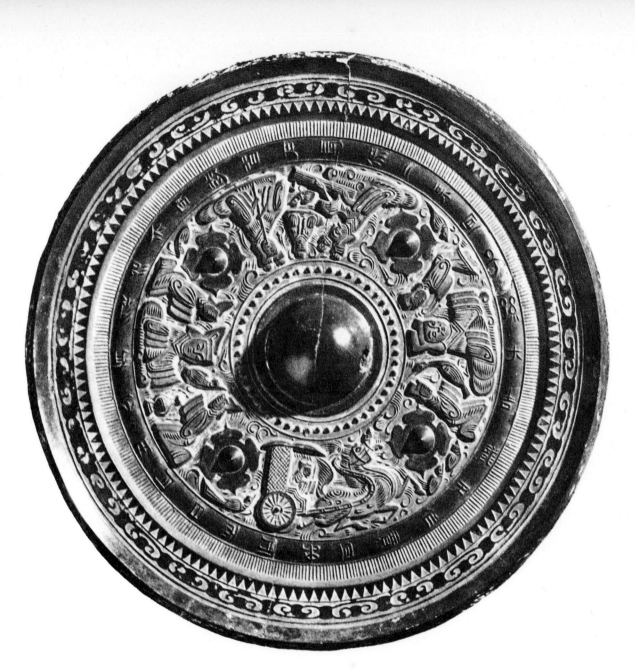

57. MIRROR WITH A DECORATION OF FIGURES
PERIOD OF THE THREE KINGDOMS (220–265)

D.18.5 cm. Private Collection

This type of mirror, of which there are many examples, is typical of the style of the period of the Three Kingdoms, although some specimens can be dated from the end of the Han, and some to the early 4th century. They nearly all come from Shao-hsing (the Yüeh Chou of T'ang times) in North Chekiang Province, and they are often known as the "mirrors of Yüeh" for this reason.

They are made of thick bronze with a large central suspension knob. Many of them have four "buttons" in high relief on the decorated part, and bear inscriptions referring to public or private events, or even sometimes to vows. They have decorations of human figures, gods, spirits, and symbolic animals in rather overloaded compositions, which are handled in a very realistic style.

All these characteristics are to be seen on the mirror shown here. Some ancient *motifs* still survive, such as the petals surrounding the prominent knobs (cf. Plate 52), and also the bands of parallel striations and denticulations, all of which were quite usual on Han mirrors. The design seems to depict scenes in the life of a high dignitary. A chariot drawn at the gallop can be discerned, and two scenes of homage, in which musicians surround a Winged Being.

Birds appear below the knobs, and in each little scene. Their presence, and that of the Winged Spirit, are probably symbolic of the "God-Bird," which Florance Waterbury saw as an Escort of Spirits, or perhaps even the symbol of the Spirit of Ancestors.

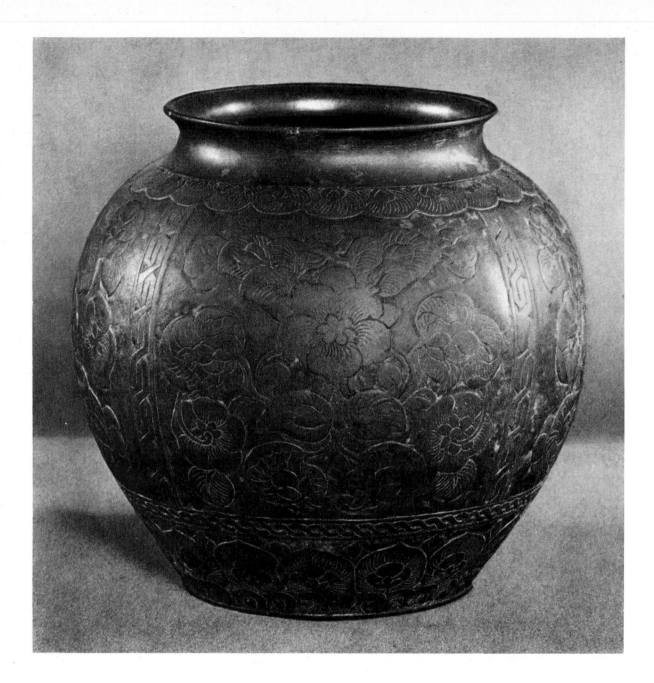

58. VASE WITH INCISED DECORATION
T'ANG DYNASTY (618–906)

*H.15.5 cm. Collection His Excellency M. Hugues Le Gallais,
Venice*

The bronze founders of the T'ang period preferred to copy
contemporary ceramic shapes rather than the ancient ritual
bronzes. The vase illustrated here is typical of their style (cf.
Plate 135).

The swelling shape surmounted by the small flaring neck has
an incised decoration of flowers and leaves which is quartered
by four vertical bands decorated with meanders. The upper
border has petals and leaves. A rope-like *motif* encircles the
lower half of the vase above a broad frieze of leaves and lotus
flowers.

The style of decoration, clear and delicate, relates this bronze
to the silverwork of the T'ang dynasty which has the same
elegance and skill.

A green and red patina very lightly coats the surface of the
metal.

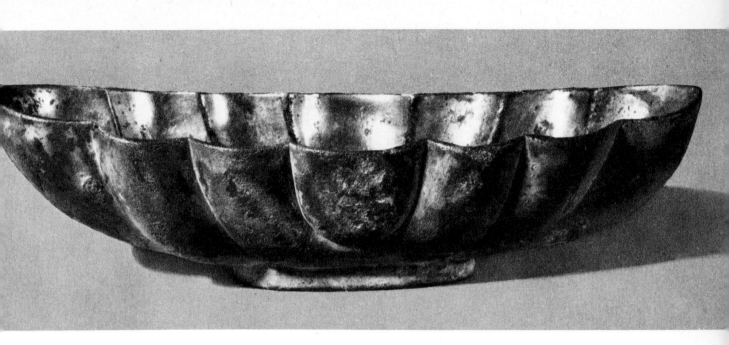

59. SMALL OVAL DISH WITH TWELVE LOBES GOLDEN BRONZE. T'ANG DYNASTY (618–906)

*L.16.3 cm. W.7.1 cm. (Enlarged). Formerly Collection
Mr. & Mrs. Desmond Gure, London*

This dish on its slightly raised foot is a remarkable illustration of the influence of Sassanian Persia on the art of the T'ang dynasty. There are, indeed, Persian silver dishes which are entirely identical in form. A similar T'ang dish, but with eight lobes, has been in the Shōsōin Pavilion at Nara, in Japan, since the middle of the 8th century. Incrustations of malachite can be seen on the surface as a result of many years of burial. Formerly in the Schoenlicht Collection.

60. CELESTIAL SPHERE IN GILDED BRONZE. CH'ING DYNASTY. REIGN OF K'ANG HSI (1662–1722)

D.37 cm. Collection Xavier Givaudan, Geneva

Astronomy, in the European sense of the word, was a comparatively late development in China – about the 5th century B.C. it seems. There is an immense time-lag between the birth of astronomy in Chaldea (before 3000 B.C.), followed by Greece and India, and its appearance in China.

In the beginning, Chinese cosmography used the sun, the moon, and the Great Bear (Ursa Major) as its landmarks. Their movements were imagined as a journey through the sky. Serious mistakes in their calendar forced the Chinese to invent new instruments, by means of which their theories were modified. About 124 A.D. the astronomer Chêng Hsien worked out the first armillary sphere. Foreign influences from India in the 7th century, and Persia in the 13th, combined with the introduction of mathematics into China, all contributed to the transformation of knowledge, both theoretical and technical.

The celestial sphere shown here is worked like a clock, by weights and counterweights, an escapement regulating the movement of the balance. The names and positions of the different constellations, with their cyclical dates, are marked on the sphere. This consists of two dovetailed hemispheres made of a rather fine, thin bronze, some parts of which are gilded. A very fine engraved design can be seen on the partitions which divide it.

It is possible that the rectangular parallelepiped in the interior is meant to represent the earth (which the Chinese believed to be square) and is similar to the small globes fitted into European armillary spheres.

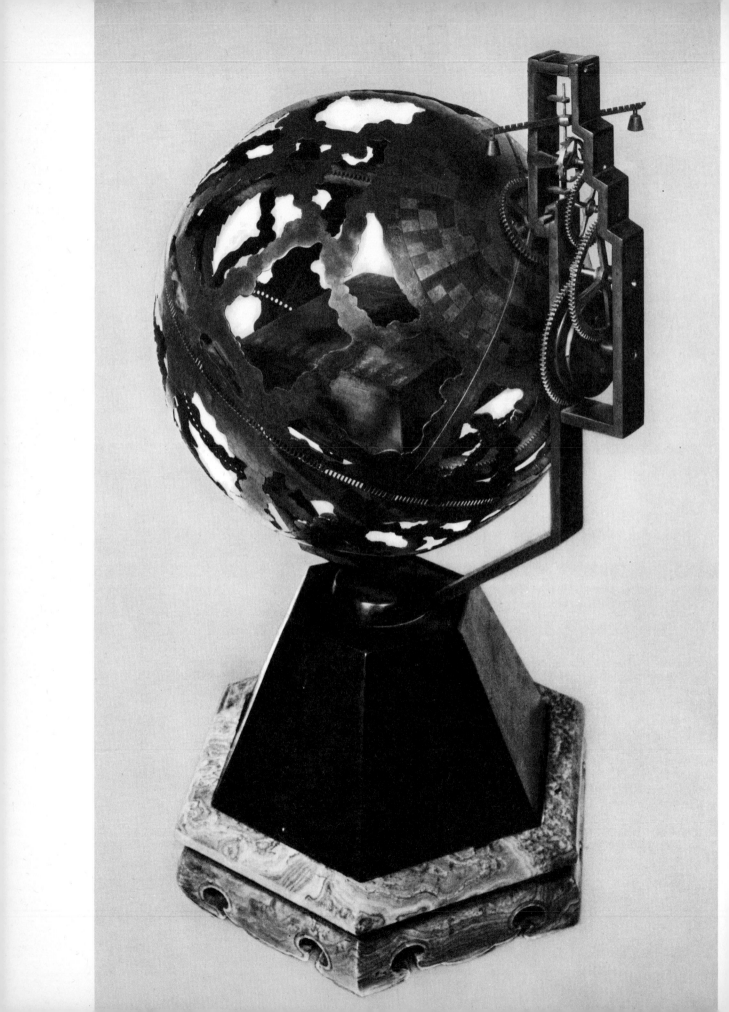

JADE

EVEN A BRIEF STUDY of jade presents great and varied difficulties in the light of our present knowledge.

To start with, we have so few definite archaeological facts around which to build a chronology. This is equally true of the two thousand years of our era as it is of the distant and early period before Christ. Most of the objects in museums and private collections have not been found as the result of properly conducted research, but have often either been stolen from burial grounds or dug up in a haphazard way. There is, for this reason, no background information which would help to date them or to determine their significance. The symbolic or ritual meaning of the archaic pieces is scarcely understood at all. Very little serious work has been done on the history and style of jade, even on the more recent period since the Han dynasty. Another obstacle is the fact that the jades, as opposed to the bronzes, have no inscriptions. Finally, apart from the fact that some pieces have slightly decomposed through burial, jade preserves its original appearance, so it is impossible to attribute it or to date it accurately using the effects of time as a guide.

Jade has always been held in the highest esteem by the Chinese. It ranked above gold or precious stones. But here we stumble against an ambiguity. The word *yü* – jade – did not always mean jade as we understand it, but was also applied to other materials of the same kind which were hard and took a high polish – agate, quartz, serpentine, marble, and others.

Also, the greater number of the old texts only add to the confusion, and must be used with extreme caution.

Again, the word "jade" in the West means two different minerals: the first, nephrite which is calcium and magnesium silicate of a fibrous structure with a hardness of 6.5 on Mohs' scale; and the second, jadeite, which is sodium and aluminium silicate of crystalline structure, more translucent, and with a hardness of 7. The difference between these two is not always easy to see, and the only certain way of telling is by analysis. Many of the colors are alike – more or less pure white, gray, a bluish shade, fawn, yellow, brown, and russet tones, as well as all the shades of green. The green tones become more or less intense as the proportion of iron in the stone varies*.

"True jade" (*chen yü*), that is nephrite, is the material of which all the archaic Chinese jades were carved. Its purity, durability, the ease with which it takes an edge, its beautiful colors, and finally, its sonority, made it a miraculous stone in the eyes of the Chinese. They attributed to it a supernatural

---

* Mohs' scale is a method of differentiating between minerals, utilizing the fact that a stone will always scratch another which is softer, or will be scratched by one which is harder. Steatite has a hardness of 1 on this scale, and a diamond of 10. The other minerals are located between these two points. Glass has a hardness of 5.5 and will be scratched both by nephrite and jadeite. A normal steel knife blade has a hardness of 6 on this scale, and will scratch neither type of jade. (Translator's note).

origin, and associated it with the mystic principle of the *yang*, the male element in the Cosmos. So jade itself became the symbol of vitality, hence its sacred character and wide powers, its important role in religious and funerary rites, and its significance as an emblem of rank and authority. It was not only held to be the most noble material, but was also very rare and expensive.

Whatever the old Chinese texts may say on the subject, it is doubtful whether it was ever found in China. It came either from the distant regions of Khotan and Yarkand in Chinese Turkestan, or from Lake Baikal in Siberia, and the nephrite from these places was of a dark green with small black spots caused by the presence of graphite in the stone. Wherever its origin, nephrite is supposed to be harder than steel. This is only true if the stone is in perfect condition, but sometimes in the course of years underground, perhaps in contact with the products of decomposition in the tombs, the jades have become discolored and changed, as it were decomposed or "perished," by different chemical reactions. Originally, many of the pieces were coated with red ochre (cinnabar), a substance which was supposed to have magic life-and health-giving properties. Many archaic jades still bear traces of it.

Jadeite comes from Burma, and was probably only first brought to China at the end of the 18th century. It has very vivid tones, and is more translucent. It will take a much more brilliant polish than nephrite. The emerald green jade used for modern jewelry is a form of jadeite.

The earliest Chinese jades were found on Neolithic sites. These are rounded axes, chisels, and fragments of rings, all undecorated. Other Neolithic peoples have also used jade, and these are all Pacific civilizations – Northwest American Indians, Aztecs, Mayas, and Maoris in New Zealand. In Central Asia the jade carved by the Turkestan Chinese seems to belong to the Neolithic culture of the Gobi desert, earlier than that of China.

At the Neolithic stage, jade must have been a luxury which seems to disappear everywhere at the beginning of the Bronze Age, except in China, where its use was continued but transformed. During the Shang dynasty jade was used for ritual objects, emblems of power, insignia of rank, and for ornaments reserved solely for the Emperor and the aristocracy. Although the finds at An-Yang have been published, there has been no information on the subject of jade, though it seems certain that many pieces must have been found there, in company with the bronze, pottery, ivory, and carved marble. It is, however, possible to date them and identify them by analogy with these other techniques. Using the chronology of Bernhard Karlgren, we shall group the jades of China's first historical period with those dating from the early Chou dynasty.

Up till now, no site from Karlgren's Middle Chou period (10th–6th centuries B.C.) has revealed any jade. On the other hand, several finds at Hsin-chêng and Chin Ts'un in Honan Province have produced objects of varying form having an advanced technique and a remarkable unity of style. These can be dated between the 5th and 3rd centuries, that is, to the period of the Warring States. Finally, some pieces – veritable landmarks – have been found near Ch'ang-sha in Hunan Province, confirming the important part played by the Chou kingdom in the development and elaboration of the contemporary style.

There are scarcely any Han pieces with a known provenance. At Lo-lang in Korea, however, some researches have been conducted by Japanese archaeologists with the greatest care, and they have unearthed a very significant set of funerary objects. Some pieces were also found at Noin-ula, in Northern Mongolia, a site worked on by the Russian expedition of Kozlov in 1924–25.

These are the only really scientific facts known at the moment about the archaic jades. Without permitting the establishment of a rigid succession of form and *motif*, they do, however, allow a general definition of style. Thus, by comparison with better-known techniques (bronze, and especially sculpture), one can make an attempt at classification, assuming that the other arts followed a parallel course of development. But one must not lose sight of the fact that jade in the early period was, above all, a ritual art, and thus remained faithful to unalterable tradition. Certain shapes – the *pi* disks, for instance – remain the same for centuries, and the only means of discrimination – and that only tentative – is a study of the technique.

METHODS OF JADE CARVING

The working of a stone as hard as jade must always present many problems. It cannot be cut without using abrasives harder than itself, but if the abrasive is efficient, the tool is less important. Observation of the Maori, who remained at a Neolithic stage for so long, has proved interesting. They cut jade with fine knives of sandstone or slate, using them like a saw in conjunction with an abrasive made from powdered quartz mixed with water which formed the cutting edge of the knife. It was a very long process. It has been calculated that it took a month of unceasing work to cut a slab of jade less than 4 cm. thick and the size of an octavo book into a roughly triangular slab. The Maori used the same method for engraving and drilling, employing pointed drills which they rotated.

Probably the methods of the Neolithic Chinese people were much the same, but their skill was immeasurably greater. The "saw" was probably a special kind of stone knife, examples of which have been found on prehistoric sites. Holes were made by drilling, and traces of this sometimes remain, especially where the two ends have been drilled simultaneously and the point where they meet is uneven. The hole is conical when drilled from one end only. The drills were often tubular in shape, and may have been made of bone, though more likely of bamboo shoots, which were quite efficient, and at the same time, provided a ready-made scale of dimensions.

The possibilities for the engraver were much increased after the beginning of the Bronze Age. A kind of grease, which was much more adherent, had taken the place of water as a medium for carrying the abrasives, and a further step forward was made with the introduction of the lathe. This invention, apparently, dates from the 6th century B.C., and the renaissance in jade decoration to be seen in the Period of the Warring States was certainly caused by it. From now on, there were stone disks for sawing and cutting, drills and chisels, and tools of wood or leather for sharpening and burnishing. The most common abrasive, apart from quartz sand, was powdered granite. In this way the patience to work for months on the decoration of a single piece enabled the skilled Chinese craftsman to create masterpieces in a unique art with only these simple tools.

The immense difficulty of working jade, and the skill needed to carve it, combined with the beauty and rarity of the material itself, explain the admiration felt for it by the Chinese. This developed into a kind of cult; a worship of the venerable qualities which jade possessed in Chinese eyes.

SHAPES AND THEIR INTERPRETATION

Our knowledge of the part played by jade in the life of China is based on the *Chou li*, or the Ritual of the Chou, a work which dates from the 4th or 3rd centuries B.C., and which purports to describe the rites and customs in use at the beginning of the dynasty. In fact, at the time when it was written, the traditions had been forgotten, and all the ideas of the ancient ritual completely lost in the course of the upheavals which had taken place in China. The only possible things which could have survived the centuries of political and social disintegration were vague memories of the significance of certain shapes. These would be renewed by the natural desire to strengthen traditional ties felt by the peoples of the Warring States period. The version of the *Chou li* which has come down to us was, in any case, edited in the Han period, and obscured by the moralizing tendencies of Confucian commentators. It is, therefore, not possible to put any scientific value on these texts, though they have served most modern authors as a starting point.

It is more than likely that many of the ancient jades were at the outset really copies of tools and weapons made of bronze or stone, and were probably intended for tomb furnishings. The prototypes are axes, knives, chisels, and halberds, which perhaps had a particular religious significance, but which certainly had no definite symbolic meaning originally. Among these is the *ko* or dagger-axe, found all over ancient China and especially at An-Yang, where different models in bronze and jade have been found alongside the remains of the Shang civilization. The *ko* has a triangular blade, with one or sometimes several ribs, fined and slightly asymmetric edges, and a "tongue" or tenon, often decorated lengthwise with striations. Like most objects imitating weapons, the *ko* has a hole which must have been used to attach it to the belt. Long flat objects with a rounded end must be derived from a primitive type of ax: tradition confers on them the symbol of virtue. Rectangular plaques, called *kuei*, which at present go under the name of sceptres and are faintly reminiscent of a primitive knife, seem to have been the insignia of high dignity, and to have been connected with certain sacrifices dedicated to the regions of the East. These and other objects of similar origin were symbols of rank and power. They were also used in sacrificial rites and the complicated hieratic ceremonial minutely described in the *Chou li* texts.

Of the most important emblems, six are mentioned as having been made in honor of the cosmic deities and the "Four Directions of Space." They had to be buried with the dead in definite ritual positions, but we do not know the date of the origin of this custom. Nor is much information available about the emblems themselves. The *kuei* scepter, as we saw, was used for Eastern sacrifices. The *hu*, in the guise of a white jade tiger, was intended for sacrifices to the West, while the South was honored by the *chang*, half a pointed *kuei*, and the North with a half *pi* (*huang*). The latter was a kind of crescent perforated at each end, sometimes in the form of a dragon or a fish.

The *pi* and the *ts'ung* are the best known of these pieces. A disk of variable size, the *pi* had a hole in the center (Plate 75) and is thought to have been a symbol of heaven, though this interpretation is not later than the 2nd century B.C. It is more likely that it represented originally the Supreme Power, in the cosmic meaning of the term, and was used in certain sacrifices, or given as an offering from subjects to their overlord. It is given different names according to the varying proportions between the hole and the disk – *pi*, when the diameter of the perforation is the same or less than half the diameter of the whole, *huan* when these two measurements are equal, *yüan* when the disk is reduced to a still narrower ring. The *pi* is generally undecorated, especially in the early period, but it has relief decoration by about the end of the Chou dynasty (Plate 62 b).

The "weapons," and the *pi* – like nearly all primitive jades – consist of thin flat plaques, varying in thickness between 2 mm. and 1 cm. The *ts'ung* is exceptional; a cylinder encased in a rectangular block of variable height (some are as tall as 50 cm.), or flattened to resemble a massive ring. It has angled edges and regular horizontal notches delineating flat bands with cellular patterns, often with a small incised circle near them (Plate 65). If Karlgren's hypothesis is correct, the prototype of the *ts'ung* was a kind of box protecting a tube in which were kept the Imperial or princely scrolls. This was made of four sections held together with cords, and the notches represent the grooves made to hold these cords in place. The *ts'ung*, traditionally an earth symbol as opposed to the *pi*, was also the emblem of the Empress. It is also possible that it was an astronomical instrument, perhaps used in conjunction with the jagged disk called the *hsüan-chi*. This object, which was undoubtedly used for observing the stars, always has three oblique indentations rotating, as it were, in the same direction (Plates 61 and 62). Henri Michel has advanced an ingenious theory (Plate 61) as a possible use for the *hsüan-chi*. The *ts'ung*, like the *pi*, was a funerary object. It was placed on the chest, and the *pi* under the back of the corpse.

A completely different group of jades consists of objects found in tombs which were probably part of the dead person's possessions whilst still on earth. They are mostly small; little ornaments which could be sewn on to the clothes – pendants, hairpins, bows, and so on – or sometimes seals and tiny sculpted figures with no immediately obvious purpose. There are many small animal plaques among them – the tiger (Plate 70 a), *k'uei* dragons (Plate 73), the hare (a moon symbol), and the antelope and the deer (Plate 70 c). There is also the buffalo, and, among the birds, the cormorant – a fish-eating bird which was undoubtedly associated with some unknown rite (Plate 71 b). Added to these are the goose and the owl, and, finally, bears, fishes (Plate 71 a), and tortoises. The animal plaques are cut in silhouette, and the outlines are vivid and well-designed. They are often engraved with lines which accentuate the limbs and sense of movement. Sculpted pieces (Plate 72) are extremely rare in the early periods, as are human figures.

Later on, ornamental objects increased, and at the beginning of the Period of the Warring States there were innumerable belt-hooks, pendants, belt buckles, and sword ornaments.

Our last category comprises the amulets which were made solely for burial with the dead. Because it did not deteriorate and by reason of the magic properties with which it was endowed, jade was thought to preserve bodies from decomposition. Many small objects were used to this end, and were carved to plug the orifices of the corpse according to a complex ritual which was not, however, clearly fixed till the beginning of the Han period. The amulet that was most widespread, and often mentioned in the old texts, is the cicada – a symbol of rebirth (Plate 63). It was placed on the tongues of the dead to represent the new life of the soul after the spirit had left the body. Sometimes the cicada amulet is treated in a geometric way, but it is more often realistically carved in relief. Imitations of larvae, though fairly rare, are amazingly real. The eyes of the dead were covered with oval closures; small octagonal tubes and tampons were intended for the ears, nostrils, and other orifices.

Finally, weights have been found in Han tombs which were intended to keep the folds of the clothes in place. Little pigs, sometimes very realistic, were used for this purpose, though no one knows why this should have been so.

These are the main types of very early Chinese jades. It goes without saying that the scope of jade carving increased as the technique advanced, and the artistic horizon retreated further and further beyond the limited ritual demands of former times.

Sculpted figures – chimerae, dragons (Plates 80, 66 and 79), vessels, bowls, boxes, and mirrors were made after the Han period. Copies of bronze and other ancient vessels, made in Sung times when archaizing work was fashionable, appeared in their turn among the enormous artistic repertory of jade (Plates 84 and 85).

CHRONOLOGY

As we have already said, the only possible means of dating jade is by a study of the methods of carving, and by analogy with objects which have been more scientifically dated. Reference to the styles, which have been clearly defined in the study of bronze, is the best guide in any attempt to outline the development of the archaic jades. During the dynasties which followed the Han period, comparison of the methods of decoration in the other arts, or a general study of the esthetic climate in any given period, may be used as a means of attribution.

The style of the Shang dynasty

During the Shang period the method of making weapons is not especially remarkable. The carving is already skilled and the objects are well polished. Perforations are clean, whilst the ribs and striations of the *ko* show technical mastery.

Animal plaques sometimes have unbroken contour lines, and at other times these are interrupted with hooks and indentations recalling the jutting ribs of certain bronzes, and the teeth of the astronomical disks (Plates 61 and 62). The outlines are often beveled. Some of these creatures have a kind of beveled appendage, sometimes pointed and sometimes spatulate (Plate 71 c) which can be found on the tail, on the head, or under the animal's feet. It has been suggested that this is a vestigial trace of a weapon, taken over finally by this animal substitute. These beasts, whether natural or imaginary, have generally a modest form of decoration, often obtained by different methods. The *motifs* may form a fine fillet in relief on a flat ground (Plate 73), or a double line may be used to produce a similar effect, but without the relief. Or the design may be a simple incised line. The decoration itself consists generally of rather rigid spirals, or single or double chevrons with striations and lozenges. A relationship with the bronzes can be well seen in all these *motifs*, but they are not handled with the same freedom owing to the difficulty presented by the material.

The styles of the Chou dynasty

In the early Chou period the jade styles are still very like those of the preceding dynasty, and we have no means of recognizing and establishing a historical sequence as we have with the bronzes.

It is probably about the middle of this dynasty (Karlgren's Middle Chou period) that the cosmic symbols, *pi* and *ts'ung*, make their appearance. The *pi*, however, or some kind of ring at least, was already in existence in the Shang period, though it had probably not yet acquired its symbolic meaning. It must have been more difficult to transpose the Chou bronze decoration into jade than the engraved linear ornament of the Shang. Nevertheless, it is possible to date from this period the disk emblem on Plate 76, with its broadly carved dragons and birds, and gentle curves recalling themes on certain contemporary bronzes. The period from the 10th to the 6th centuries is a time when jade with very little relief ornament is to be seen.

The following period on the other hand sees this art at its finest. The craftsmen were extraordinarily skilled, the material and the tools were to hand, and their imagination soared, enabling them to produce an abundance of forms and a large range of fantastic decoration. The result was an era of master pieces.

Pi are covered with a "grain" pattern, often in the form of spirals starting in relief and ending in incised lines (Plate 62 b). Some famous pieces of this kind are decorated with feline creatures, and pierced dragons coiling round the edges. Other forms of the *pi* have a chequered design imitating basket-work. On most of the jades, relief spirals give the effect of rich embroidery enclosed within the curved incisions which follow the outlines (Plate 78).

The animal decoration is inspired more by fantasy than by real creatures; dragons, tigers, and crested birds, often sharing the same features (wings, paws, crests, etc.), stretch along the curving bands. These spirited compositions have their own peculiar rhythms and balance, and are characterized by opposing *motifs* and backward-looking heads. Imbricated scales, crosses, triangles, scrolls, cord and plait *motifs*, and parallel striations cover the surface of the jades with many contrasts. Subtlety and richness, balance and flexibility, seem to be the outstanding characteristics of this compelling and brilliant art. Jade became an ornament, either alone on belt-hooks, buckles or belt plaques, pendants, and jewelry of all kinds, or combined with bronze in hooks (Plate 48), rings, or on precious boxes such as those in the Winthrop Collection in the Fogg Museum at Cambridge, Mass. Immense skill was needed to hollow out a cup, or to cut two disks held together by movable cylindrical catches, from a single piece of jade.

The style of the Han dynasty

The fabulous kingdom of the Warring States gives place under the Han dynasty to a more realistic repertory, in which sculpture plays a greater part. Although it is rather difficult to draw a clean line between the two periods, in general the geometric *motifs* can be said to be simpler and less elaborate than in the preceding period. The forms, on the other hand, become freer, and have more dash and vigor. The steady progress of new tools enabled the jade-cutter to throw off the limitations which reduced his field to plaques and low reliefs. The figures in Plate 80, and the wonderful dragon and *djinn* in the Desmond Gure collection (Plate 66) bear comparison with the finest sculpture, which reached its apogee during the Han dynasty.

The later dynasties

After the Han period it is only possible to date jades to certain periods by comparing them with contemporary sculpture (Plate 81). The exuberant naturalism of the T'ang period is sometimes moderated by that innate gift of the Chinese sculptor which enables him, by simplification, to draw out the essential meaning of a shape (Plates 67 and 68). Sometimes he is guided by the urge to express powerful movement (Plate 82). The jade artist also uses nuances in the color of the stone, as well as extraneous marks, to vary his effect (Plates 67 and 68) and to enhance the shape of the model.

The Sung period is characterized by a leaning towards the archaic which expressed itself in a genuine feeling for the ancient art of China. But although digging was done by order of the Emperor Hui Tsung at An-Yang itself, and despite the fact that the enormous number of examples and of copies shows that there was a knowledge of the archaic bronzes, still the information given about jade is improbable and fantastic. In this field, apparently, only Han objects were copied. Pendants ending in dragons face to face (Plate 83), and the *hu* skillfully and abundantly decorated (Plate 84), confirm this impression. The treatment of spirals in graduated relief, and the outlining of contours are characteristic of the style which, it is at present agreed, can be attributed to the Sung dynasty. This attribution, however, can only be tentative in face of the very limited information available.

Very little more is known about the Ming jades, but it does seem possible to attribute some large pieces to this period, namely mountainous landscapes in high relief, as well as a variety of small fantastic objects, and a number of horses, buffalo, and other animals carved in the round (Plates 88 and 89) These are sometimes quite large. Naturalistically treated, they are lively and attractive.

The jades of the Ch'ing dynasty are almost the only ones which have inscriptions and dates. It is difficult to understand the absence of inscriptions on the early pieces since they are so frequent on the bronzes. In the reign of K'ang Hsi, and even more under Ch'ien Lung, there was great activity in the jade-carving workshops. As in other fields, the scope widened enormously. The Court needed jewels, ornaments, ritual and ceremonial objects, vases, cups, and trinkets. The precious material was used by the Buddhists for votive figures and altar-pieces (Plate 90). The skill of the artists was prodigious, and all problems were solved. Jadeite and nephrite were used interchangeably at this time. Undecorated cups are generally attributed to the reign of K'ang Hsi. They are certainly masterpieces of poise and simplicity (Plate 69), but the attribution is not absolutely proven. During the reign of Ch'ien Lung there was such perfection of techniques, such a large increase of fine contrasts and of purity in the stone used (Plate 90), and such a large number of important inscribed pieces, that it is possible to attribute precisely where so many guiding factors are present.

The long tradition continues, and the modern artists, at least in so far as care, patience, and skill are concerned, are worthy successors to past centuries.   *D. L.-G.*

Note: A number of jade objects proved to be too small for effective reproduction in their natural size. They have, therefore, been considerably enlarged.

61. *Hsüan chi.* ASTRONOMICAL INSTRUMENTS
END OF THE SHANG OR BEGINNING OF THE
CHOU DYNASTY C. 1100–1000 B.C.

D. 33 cm. Formerly Collection D. David-Weill, Neuilly-sur-Seine

At the end of the 19th century Wu Ta-Ch'êng identified this
type of object for the first time with the *hsüan chi* mentioned
in the pre-Han texts. These were supposed to be astronomical
instruments for "regulating the Seven Governors," which
probably meant observing the seven stars of the Great Bear
(Ursa Major or the Big Dipper) as well as other constellations.
Henri Michel advances an interesting hypothesis in a recent
article which would explain not only three oblique points which
rotate, as it were, in the same direction, but also the three
series of notches on the edge (which are not, however, always
the same number or shape) and the two incised lines, one
single and the other double, which cross the disk. He associates
the *hsüan chi* with the *ts'ung* (Plate 64), suggesting that if the
neck of the *ts'ung* is inserted in the disk, its hollow body then
acts as a theodolite. In this way it would be possible, by
arranging the points and notches in a certain way in relation
to the Big and the Little Dipper (Ursa Major and Minor) to
determine the position of the Pole Star. The single incised line
was used to calculate the points of the solstice on the ecliptic
when the instrument was in the proper position. These calcu-
lations were necessary for the making of a calendar, which
must have been essential to an agricultural people.

The disk illustrated from the David-Weill collection is undoubtedly one of the earliest examples of this type of instrument. They are thought to date from 1100–1000 B.C. This one
is of exceptional size, and is made of a beautiful nephrite,
touched here and there with bluish gray.

Exhibition: Arts de la Chine Ancienne, *Orangerie Museum, Paris
1937, No. 89.*

62a). *Hsüan chi.* ASTRONOMICAL INSTRUMENT
EARLY CHOU DYNASTY
10TH–8TH CENTURIES B.C.

D. 10.8 cm. Collection Frau Georg Hasler, Winterthur

This disk is of the same kind as the preceding one, but it has
a very large central hole, reminiscent of the *yüan* rings (Plate
133). The notches are in regular groups of four, and the jade,
much spotted, is of fine quality.

62b). *Pi.* END OF THE CHOU DYNASTY
PERIOD OF THE WARRING STATES
5TH–3RD CENTURIES B.C.

D. 8.5 cm. Collection Frau Georg Hasler, Winterthur

The *pi* was the symbol of Heaven in ancient China, and
possibly also of the sun. In the early period it was undecorated
(cf. Plate 75), but during the period of the Warring States it has

small incised, and often (as here) counteracting spirals. The
edges are outlined with circles.
The jade, rather a bluish green, is partially decomposed.

63/64. A JADE AMULET AND ORNAMENTS

a) Cicada amulet. End of the Chou dynasty. 6th–3rd centuries B.C.

L. 5.8 cm. Collection Frau Georg Hasler, Winterthur

The cicada, symbol of rebirth, was placed on the tongues of the
dead, and was part of a whole collection of ritual funerary
objects (cf. Plate 134). The piece shown here is carved and incised with great realism and keen observation. It certainly
dates from the late Chou dynasty.

*b) K'uei (dragon). End of the Chou dynasty. Period of the Warring
States. 5th–3rd centuries B.C.*

L. 6.2 cm. Collection Frau Georg Hasler, Winterthur

The *k'uei,* or single footed dragon, here takes on the aspect of
a tiger. Its jaws are carved in the traditional way with jagged
edges and two fangs (cf. Plate 70). The large paw with its curving claws is joined to the lower jaw, and a notched crest indicates the back. The tail ends in a dragon's head with a round
hole in it, and the serpent-like shape of the dragon is to be
inferred from incised lines and scales. The whole piece is
covered with an incised decoration of hooks and sharp points.

*c) Plaque in the form of a t'ao t'ieh mask. Period of the Warring
States. 5th–3rd centuries B.C.*

L. 5.2 cm. Collection Frau Georg Hasler, Winterthur

The mask on this small plaque of translucent jade is a far cry
from the archaic *t'ao t'ieh.* The composition has interlaced
dragons and serpents, with a single head which forms the nose
of the mask. The sinuous movement, accentuated by the
incisions, is typical of the period of the Warring States. Engraved lines form parallel striations or scales. The piece has
three holes for attachment.

*d) Pendant. End of the Period of the Warring States. 4th–3rd centuries
B.C. or Han dynasty (206 B.C.–220 A.D.)*

H. 4.7 cm. Collection Frau Georg Hasler, Winterthur

This little object, pierced and finely engraved with striations
and interwoven lines, is a kind of stylized ornament, perhaps
inspired by a plant.
The greenish-gray jade is slightly decomposed.

e) Ornament. Period of the Warring States. 4th–3rd centuries B.C.

H. 6.2 cm. Collection Frau Georg Hasler, Winterthur

Joined, counterpoised hooks form a deeply incised swarming
motif, recalling intertwined dragons. Here and there very tiny
engraved circles perhaps represent eyes.
The jade is a dark green of fine quality, with splashes of
vermilion.

65. RITUAL SYMBOL. *Ts'ung.* BEGINNING OR MIDDLE OF THE CHOU DYNASTY 11TH–7TH CENTURIES B.C.

H.22.5 cm. Östasiatiska Museet, Stockholm (Formerly Collection H.M. the King Gustave VI Adolphe)

The *ts'ung* was a symbol of the earth, which, at that time, was believed by the Chinese to be square. This object takes the form of a rectangular block of square section, drilled through the center to form a circular tube. At each end is a short collar. Each side is divided into eight sections by deep horizontal incisions cut at the angles, and these are divided into two by a polished vertical band lying flat on the surface. Three striated horizontal bands decorate each section, the top one being shorter than the others. Two small circles are engraved on both sides of the ribs, placed at the end of the shortest of these bands. These may, perhaps, be the eyes of a primitive mask, with the central band as its axis.

The craftsmen must have encountered great difficulty in drilling this type of object, which was pierced from both ends. The interior of this one decreases towards the center, and the two openings are far from being equal in size.

The material is speckled, almost translucent nephrite. It is brownish-green, with a slight yellow tinge, and has some dark brown and reddish spots.

The dating of these objects is controversial. M. Palmgren, who has prepared the catalogue of the collections of H.M. The King of Sweden, puts this *ts'ung* in the Shang or early Chou period, whereas Salmony places it in the middle of the Chou dynasty.

Exhibition: Arte Cinese, *Venice, 1954, No.187.*

66. CHIMAERA RIDDEN BY AN ANTHROPOMORPHIC FIGURE HAN DYNASTY. 2ND–3RD CENTURY A.D.

L.14.6 cm, H.8.6 cm. Formerly Collection Mr. & Mrs Desmond Gure, London

This winged feline creature of a type generally called chimaera is a masterpiece of the art of jade. The tension of the arched pose gives it a majestic air which recalls the huge stone lions erected near burial grounds during the period of the Six Dynasties in South China. The carving of this creature is a fine example of the advanced technique achieved by the Han. The body is arched on powerful striding feet armed with claws, and this movement is accentuated by the weight thrown on the back left leg. Three groups of wings on the shoulder, flank and thigh, a long lashing tail, and a beard curving on to its breast, all add to the fabulous appearance of this beast. Intermittent striations indicate the fur. The kneeling figure, with its simian aspect, is undoubtedly one of the demons from the complex Han mythology. His long arms cling to the beast's mane.

This is the earliest known example of a jade chimaera.

67. SEATED GREYHOUND. BEGINNING OF THE T'ANG DYNASTY (618–906)

L.8.8 cm. H.4.3 cm. (Enlarged). Formerly Collection Mr. & Mrs. Desmond Gure, London

This greyhound, though very small, has all the powerfully realistic and vigorous appearance of T'ang animal sculpture. The somber formality and exact perceptive treatment have tempted some authorities to put it to an earlier date – under the Wei or Sui. The attribution given here, however, rests on evidence brought to light by new excavations in China, and accords with the opinion of the owner of this beautiful piece, himself a fine scholar and a connoisseur of jade. Similar figures of recumbent greyhounds can be fairly often found among the T'ang tomb figures.

The artist who carved this piece was a master of his craft, whose use of the color variations to enhance the modelling is particularly brilliant.

68. RECUMBENT RAM. T'ANG DYNASTY (618–906)

L.5.6 cm. (Enlarged). Guimet Museum, Paris (Paul Cosson Bequest)

The vigor and power seen in the previous example are repeated in this sculptural piece, but on a much smaller scale. The ram was a favorite theme with the T'ang, especially for bronze lamps which have the same sober realism. Here again the lapidary has used the colors of the jade most skillfully to achieve his effects.

69. MOTTLED JADE BOWL. CH'ING DYNASTY REIGN OF K'ANG HSI (1662–1722)

D.17 cm. Calouste Gulbenkian Foundation, Lisbon

A bowl such as this, delicate and regular and carved from a single piece of nephrite, must have taken many hours of arduous work.

The stone, translucent and extremely beautiful, has a cloudy and mottled appearance. Its shape, with lightly flaring lip, is reminiscent of porcelain bowls of the same period.

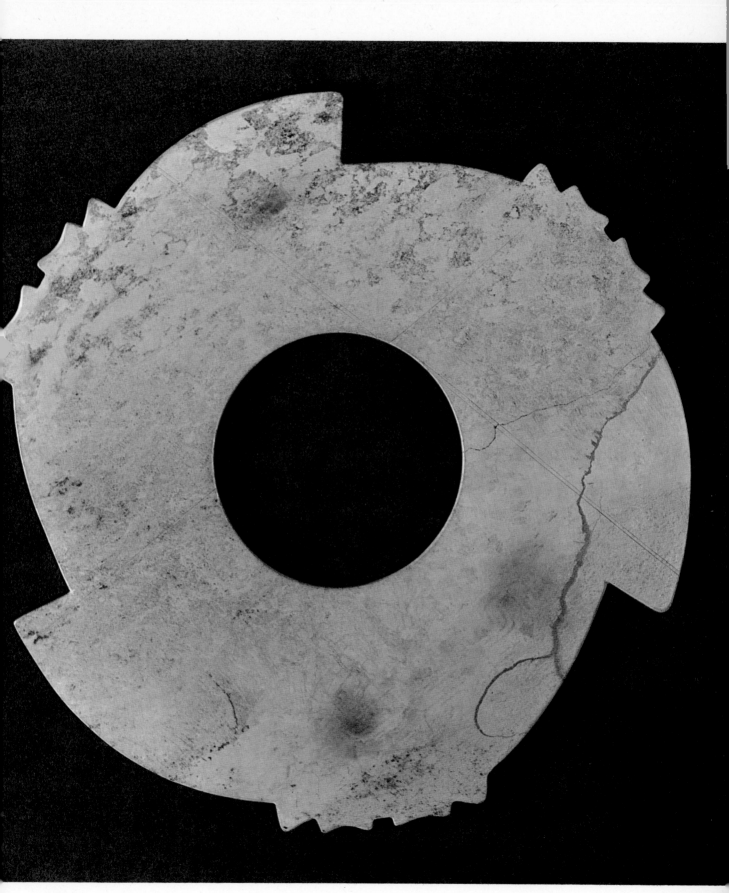

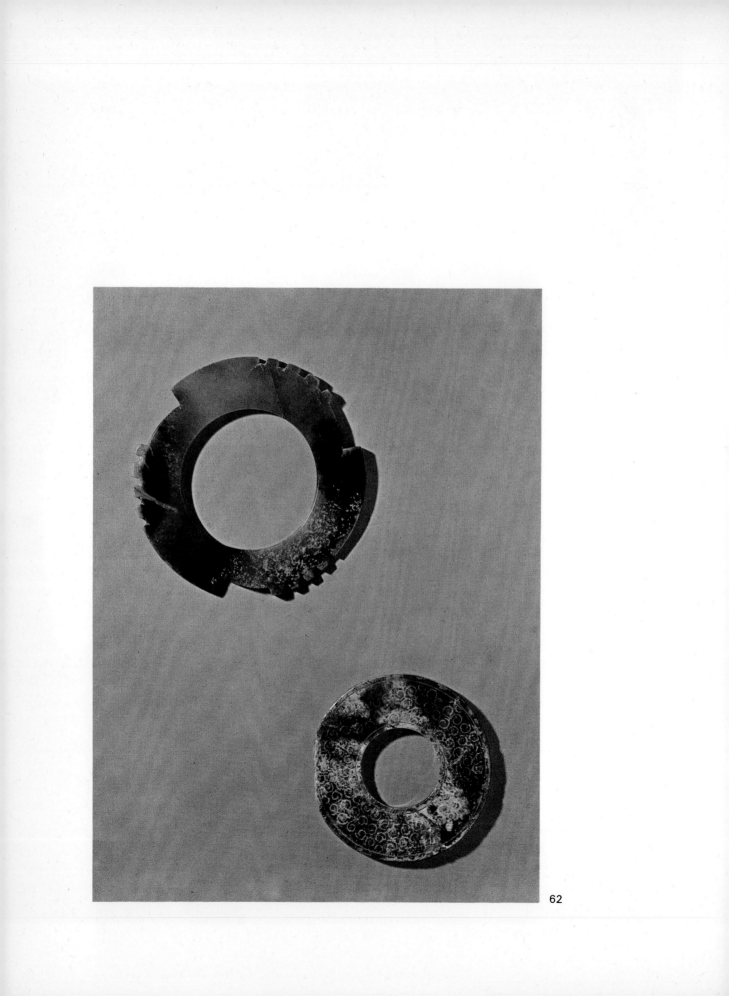

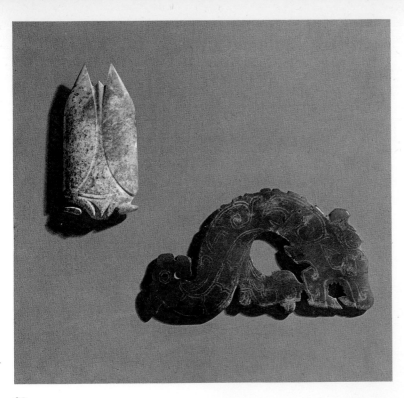

63

64

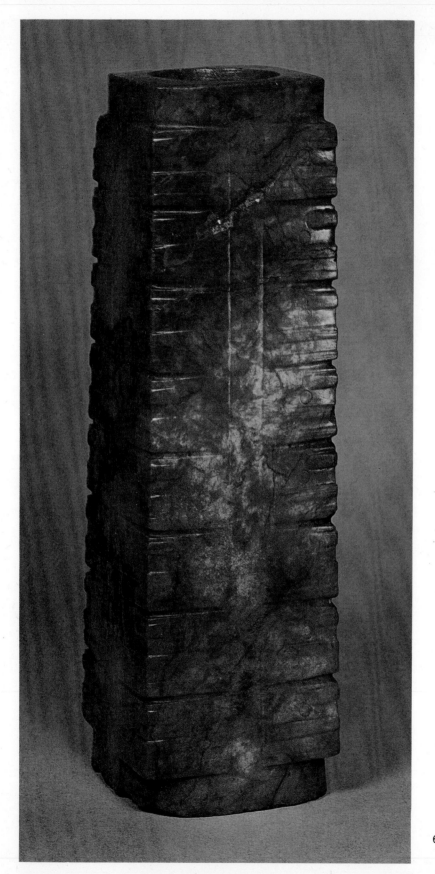

65

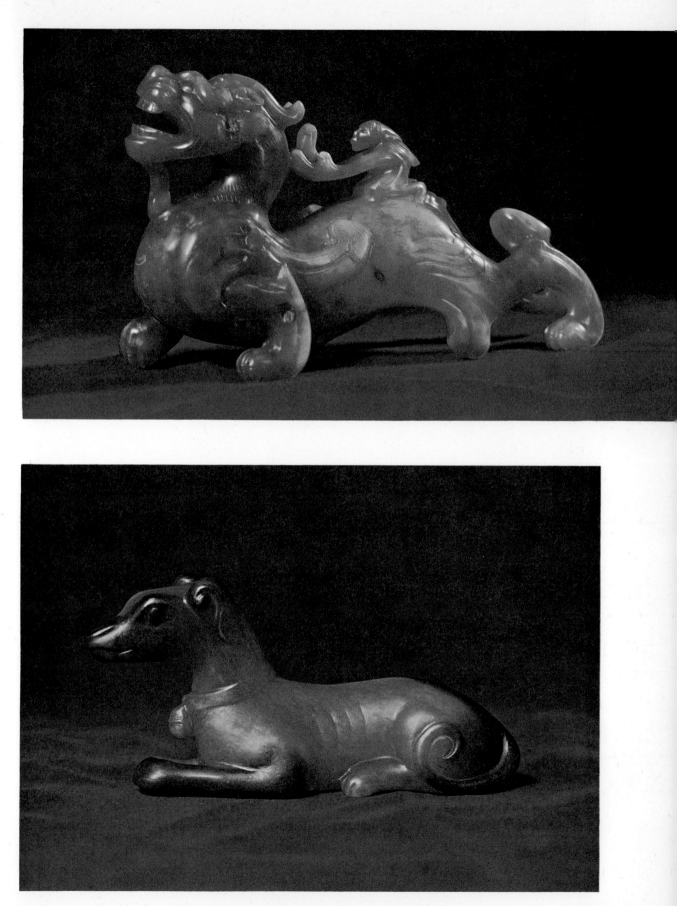

66

67

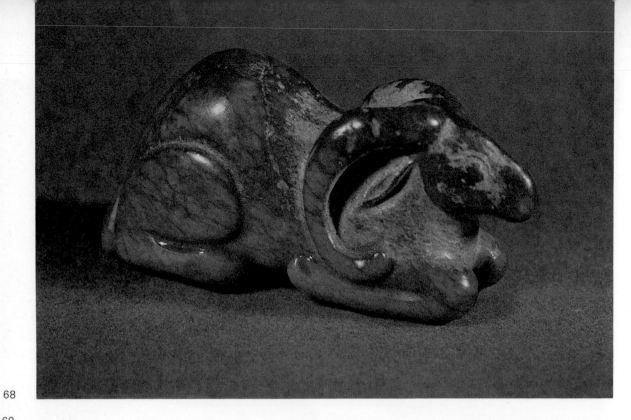

68

69

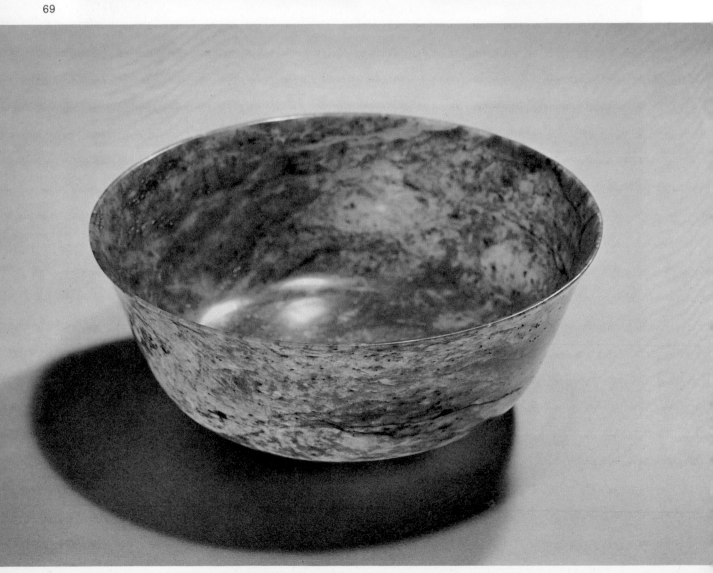

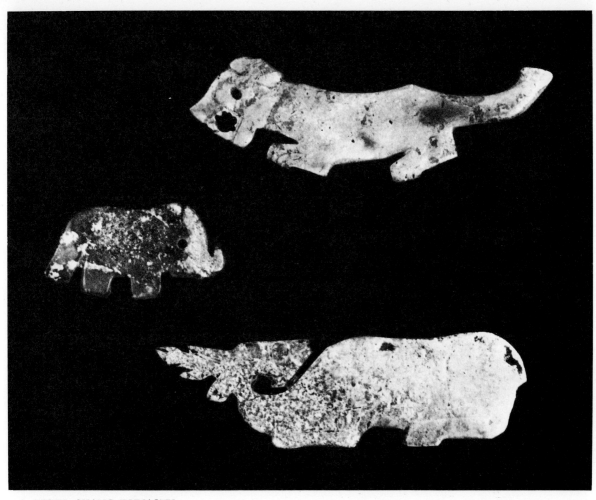

70a). TIGER. SHANG DYNASTY
14TH–11TH CENTURIES B.C.

*L.7.9 cm. Thickness 0.2 cm. (Enlarged). Musée Guimet, Paris
(Michel Calmann Bequest)*

Carved from a thin flat piece of jade with beveled outlines, this
cat is typical of the animal *motifs* of the Shang period. It was
found at An-Yang. Its large C-shaped ears are in relief. The
eye is indicated by a round hole, and the jaw is jagged, with
two carved and beveled fangs. The feet have incised claws.
The ivory-colored jade, which has patches of green, is partially decomposed.

70b). ELEPHANT. SHANG DYNASTY

*L.4 cm. Thickness 0.1 cm. (Enlarged). Musée Guimet, Paris
(Michel Calmann Bequest)*

This little plaque, carved in green jade which is slightly decayed
and touched with a cream color, is in a very simplified style
which perfectly depicts the characteristics of the animal. Its
eye is a pierced hole, the ear traced by a line. The elephant
appears fairly often in Shang bronze decoration, almost always
treated in a very naturalistic way (cf. Plate 22).

70c). RECUMBENT DEER. SHANG DYNASTY

*L.8 cm. Thickness 0.5 cm to 0.1 cm. (Enlarged). Musée Guimet,
Paris (Michel Calmann Bequest)*

For a long time it was thought that the *motif* of the deer
appeared for the first time about the 6th century B.C., the
result of Scythian influence, and, indeed, this piece was
first attributed to the Warring States period. However, the
deer does not appear on carved bone and bronze of the Shang
period. Possibly it was a symbol of light and fire, connected
with the concept of rebirth by the annual casting of its antlers
and their subsequent renewal.
The position of the animal is suggested here purely in profile,
carved with great verisimilitude. The two antlers are indicated
separately. The eye is shown by a circle outlined with an engraved line. The mouth is turned towards the haunches, and
the hooves are shown by light incisions.
The jade is cream and green in color, rather decomposed, and
bearing traces of vermilion. The plaque grows gradually thinner
from head to tail.

Exhibition: Chinese Art, *London, 1935/6, No. 291.*

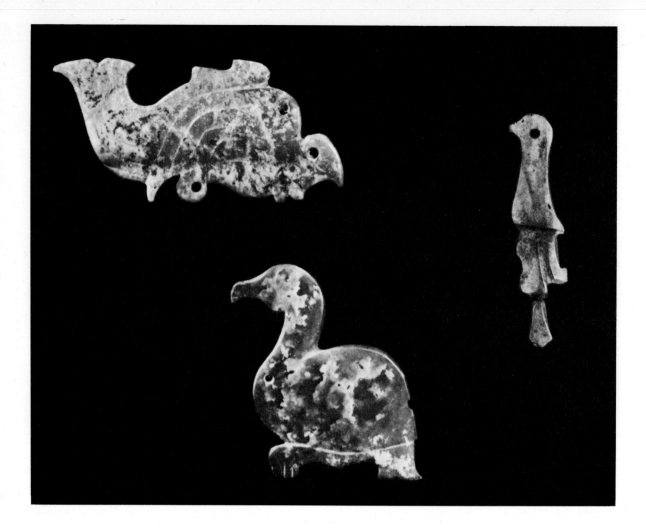

71a). FISH. END OF THE CHOU DYNASTY
6TH–3RD CENTURIES B.C.

L.6.5 cm. (Enlarged). Collection Bataille, Paris

This fish is rather like a dolphin, though its head is lengthened into the beak of a bird. There was often a connection in the art of ancient China between the themes of the bird and the fish. The jade is carved with considerable freedom. The parallel incisions draw attention to the tail and fins, whilst the mouth is in light relief. There are three attachment holes in the object, one of which serves as an eye.
The jade is greenish yellow, with traces of vermilion.

71b). CORMORANT. HAN DYNASTY
(206 B.C.–220 A.D.)

H.5.5 cm. (Enlarged). Collection Bataille, Paris

A very popular bird in China, the cormorant is here treated with the vigor and realism common in Han art. The piece has a hole for attachment. The engraving is of the simplest. Two circles indicate the eye and the pupil, and a wavy line separates the body from the feet which are only lightly etched in. The jade is green with patches of yellow, and has some vermilion markings.

71c). SMALL BIRD SITTING UPRIGHT. SHANG
DYNASTY. 14TH–11TH CENTURIES B.C.

H.4.3 cm. (Enlarged). Musée Guimet, Paris (Michel Calmann Bequest)

Of yellow-green jade, this little object is smooth on the upper part, and carved on different planes near the tail and feet. A hole marks the eye. The spatulate tail juts below the feet in a manner characteristic of many jades of the Shang period.

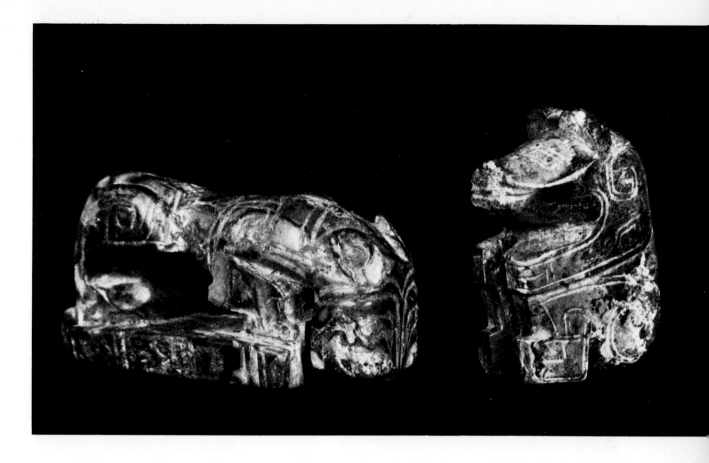

72b). SMALL SEATED BEAR. JADE. SHANG
DYNASTY. 12TH–11TH CENTURIES B.C.

H. 4.4 cm. Musée Guimet, Paris (Michel Calmann Bequest)

The bear, while playing an important part in ancient Chinese
mythology, only makes a very rare appearance in art before
the Han dynasty. Here we see the animal crouching, its front
feet forward and its head sunk between the shoulders. The
shape much resembles the original block of jade. The two sides
are flat, giving the appearance of two distinct but connected
silhouettes. The shape of the body is suggested by spiral engraving which outlines the limbs, whereas the head is treated
sculpturally, its smooth planes being very skillfully carved.
Like the marble tiger there is a naturalistic feeling here which
belies the stylistic surface decoration. The eye is lozenge-
shaped, and the rounded back decorated with incised chevrons.
The ornament is consistently executed with double line incisions. The piece is jade of a discolored green. A hole between the ears for some kind of pendant joins another at the
back of the neck.

Exhibition: Chinese Art, *London, 1935/6, No. 283.*

72a). TIGER IN MARBLE. SHANG DYNASTY
14TH CENTURY B.C.

L. 8.5 cm. Musée Guimet, Paris (Michel Calmann Bequest)

This tiger with flexed feet and its head bent down is mounted
on a rectangular base. The simplified handling and the broad
treatment of the material admirably reproduces the suppleness
and power of the animal. The body is lightly incised with two
t'ao t'ieh masks, and perhaps the marks on the head represent
the striped hide of the tiger. Although this precious piece of
marble, found at An-Yang, really belongs to the art of sculpture
(cf. Plate 93), it is interesting to see it here contrasted with one
of the rare jade sculptural pieces. In this way, the difference
between the two materials is made very plain – the first, easy
to carve and shape, and the second, jade, of a hardness which
enormously increased the difficulties of the lapidary.

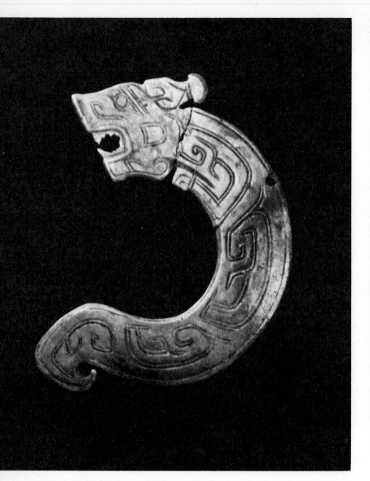

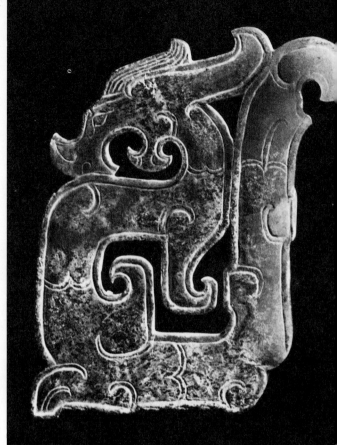

73. JADE PENDANT IN THE FORM OF A
DRAGON. SHANG OR EARLY CHOU DYNASTY
11TH–10TH CENTURIES B.C.

*D.9.2 cm. Östasiatiska Museet, Stockholm (Formerly Collection
H.M. the King Gustave VI Adolphe)*

The solidity and simplicity of this small semi-circular plaque
brilliantly expresses the power of the symbolic beast. The
typical *k'uei* paw, folded back and engraved, fits well into the
outline. A glance at the dragon opposite makes one realize at
once the differences in interpretation of the same subject from
one period to another.

The dragon's mouth is pierced and fretted (cf. Plate 70a) and
the horn is in the form of a club. The decoration, which covers
the whole surface, is a slender relief line standing out from the
grooves in a typically Shang technique. The hooks and meanders are very like those on the marble buffalo of Plate 93. An
engraved line outlines the shape, and a hole for attachment is
drilled in the animal's back.

The material is a brownish gray nephrite with traces of vermilion.

Exhibition: Chinese Art, *London, 1935/6, No. 316.*

74. PLAQUE IN THE FORM OF A DRAGON
END OF THE CHOU DYNASTY. PERIOD OF THE
WARRING STATES. 5TH–3RD CENTURIES B.C.

*H.6.4 cm. (Enlarged). Art Council of Great Britain (Formerly
Collection Mrs. C.G.Seligman), London*

The dragon is shown here with its head turned back, a position
characteristic of the period of the Warring States. The plaque
is almost rectangular in shape, whilst the contours of the
fabulous creature are drawn by means of complicated perforations. Incisions mark the oval eye and the crest, and link the
limbs and the tail. A continuous incised line accentuates the
border.

The jade is green with touches of white.

Exhibitions: Chinese Jades, *Oriental Ceramic Society, London, 1948,
No. 56.* – Arte Cinese, *Venice, 1954, No. 205.*

110

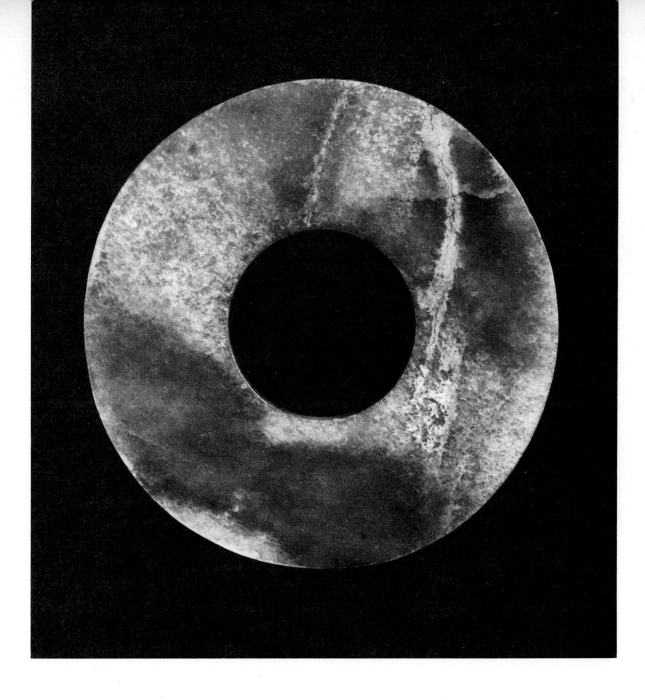

75. RITUAL DISK. *Pi*. EARLY CHOU DYNASTY 11TH–9TH CENTURIES B.C.

D. 15 cm. Thickness 0.5 cm. Collection His Excellency
M. Hugues le Gallais, Venice

The *pi* – ritual symbol *par excellence* – is one of the most venerable of all jade forms. It dates from the Neolithic period, and is traditionally interpreted as a symbol of Heaven, in contrast to the *ts'ung* which is the symbol of Earth. However, this interpretation can only be dated back to the 2nd century A.D., when it is found in a commentary of the *Chou li* (Chou ritual). Since then, it has been completely accepted in China. The *pi* seems to have been an emblem offered to their Emperor by the Princes, or which they received from him in certain circumstances, perhaps as an insignia of rank. It was undoubtedly a symbol of the divine power.

It was also used in the funerary ritual, and some archaeological research leads one to think that it may have been laid as a charm on the backs of the dead, who were buried face downwards.

The large hole in this *pi* relates to the form known as *huan* (cf. p. 93). The disk is cut and perforated from a beautiful olivegreen and brown nephrite, with large flecks. The marks of the cutting tool can be seen on both sides.

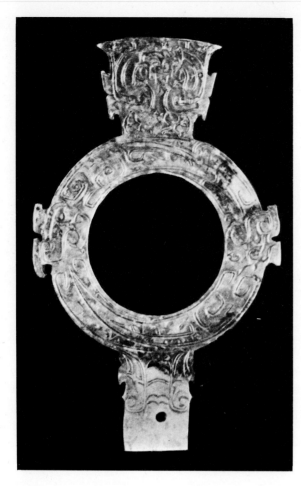

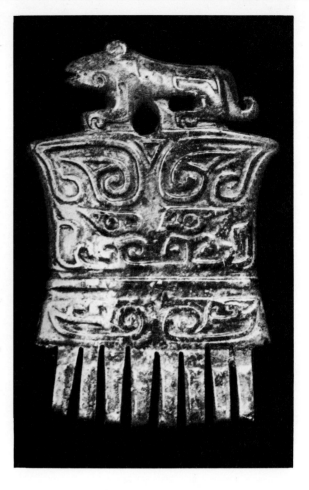

76. PERHAPS AN EMBLEM. CHOU DYNASTY 9TH–7TH CENTURIES B.C.

H.16 cm. B. 10 cm. Thickness 0.6 cm. Guimet Museum, Paris (Collection Gieseler)

The purpose of this object is not known, but it is a very fine example of the style known as Middle Chou. The large central ring is decorated with two dragons extended into a triangle. A double spiral forms the open jaw and the muzzle. The escutcheon crowning the piece bears two birds face to face, their long tails erect. The heads are raised, joining the hooked beaks, and each has a crest curving forwards and not backwards as is usually the case. The feet, too, are exceptional, being composed of two symmetrical claws. The decoration on the lower part is difficult to decipher. It may be a degenerate form of mask, or perhaps the wings of a bird. The discoloration of the jade, and the presence of a hole at this point, seems to show that the piece fitted into a slot, or formed the crest or finial of an unknown object.

The whole decoration is most precisely incised in double oblique lines, giving the illusion of relief. Professor Salmony, who thought very highly of this piece, saw in it a simple copy of the "thread pattern" of the Shang period. The jade is green, with reddish lights, and is faintly touched with white.

77. COMB. SHANG OR EARLY CHOU DYNASTY 11TH–10TH CENTURIES B.C.

H.7.7 cm. B. 4.7 cm. (Enlarged). Thickness 0.4 cm.
Musée Guimet Paris (Michel Calmann Bequest)

The two facets of this short-toothed comb have a decoration of broad bands in relief on a flat ground – a characteristic Shang technique. The *t'ao t'ieh* masks are separate and very stylized, suggesting that the attribution might be fixed slightly later. A triangle has replaced the traditional lozenge between the horns of the masks.

The comb is surmounted by a bear, its feet armed with long sharp claws. It is carved in the round, and has an incised decoration.

The jade is light brown and faded green, with traces of vermilion.

Exhibition: La découverte de l'Asie, *Cernuschi Museum, Paris, 1954, No. 453.*

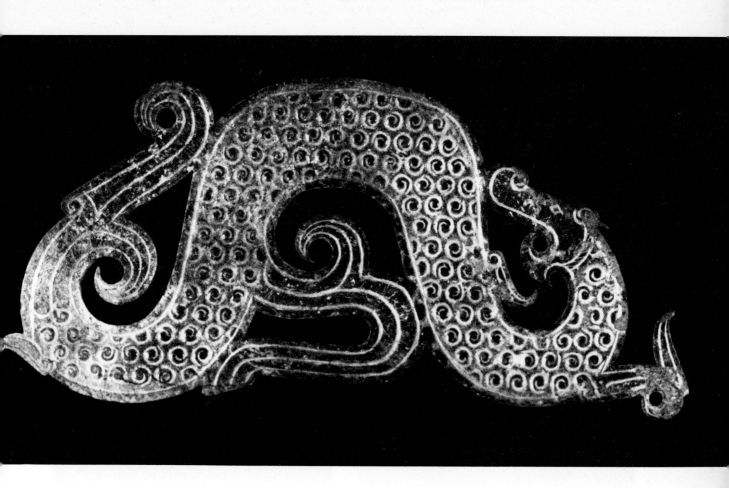

78. PLAQUE IN THE FORM OF A DRAGON
END OF THE CHOU DYNASTY. PERIOD OF THE
WARRING STATES. 6TH–3RD CENTURIES B.C.

*L.18.5 cm. Thickness 0.4 cm. Guimet Museum, Paris
(Collection Gieseler)*

Carved from a very slim flat piece of jade, this dragon is typical of the style of the period of the Warring States; both the sinuous design and the decoration are characteristic. The elongated body coils in the form of an *S,* and the head is turned backwards. Outlined with an engraved line, the muzzle and jaw form a scroll. The decoration, which covers the whole body, is composed of small spirals in relief. Curves and countercurves hold the balance, and a long spiral from the tail serves to balance the head.

The piece has three holes for attachment. The jade, which is dark green, has some traces of deposit due to burial.

Exhibition: Arts de la Chine Ancienne, *Musée de l'Orangerie, Paris, 1937, No. 127.*

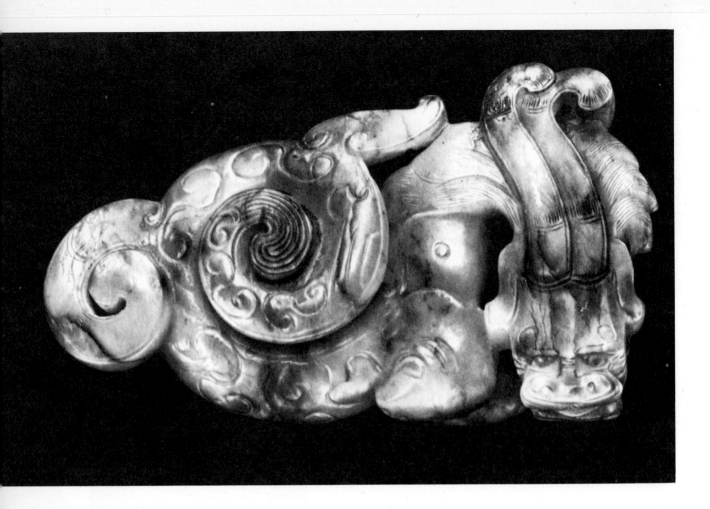

79. DRAGON. GREENISH-WHITE JADE, WITH
TOUCHES OF BROWN AND BLACK
BEGINNING OF THE HAN DYNASTY
3RD–2ND CENTURIES B.C.

L.10.2 cm. B.5.7 cm. (Enlarged).
Formerly Collection Mr. & Mrs. Desmond Gure, London

This fabulous creature belongs to the vivid composite world of
Han mythology. *Djinn,* demons, dragons, serpents, and
monsters, as well as half-men and half-birds, filled the imagination of the time.

This beast has folded feet, a crest formed by two parallel curving bands, a large muzzle between horns curving forward, and
a square open mouth revealing fangs and rows of teeth. A
large and finely striated mane falls from either side of the
crest, and a long beard, also striated, sweeps from the lower
jaw along the underside of the head. The beast's body extends
into two powerful spirals, twisting and turning on themselves.
An extraordinary impression of power emanates from this
piece. The rhythmic backward movement of the spirals is
especially vigorous and powerfully supple. The whole surface
is decorated with incisions – hooks and curves on the front,
and double striations on the back.

There are some parallels with this type of crested dragon in
Han art, particularly a jade ornament in the same collection
which was intended for attachment to a bronze belt hook.

114

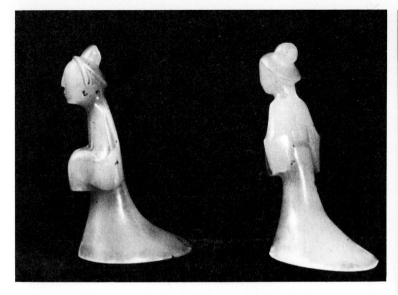

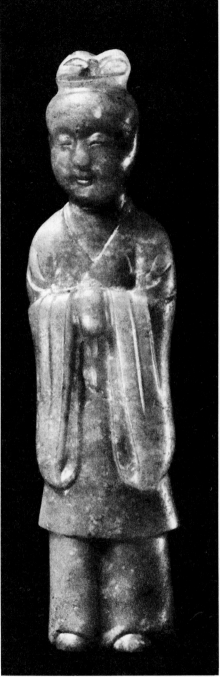

80. A PAIR OF FEMALE FIGURES IN WHITE JADE HAN DYNASTY (206 B.C.–220 A.D.)

H.6.3 cm. (Enlarged). Formerly Collection Mrs. Walter Sedgwick, London

The skillful simplicity and restrained style of these two charming small figures endows them with a certain grandeur. They have the typical appearance of Han statuary. The hands are joined and covered by the sleeves. The flowing robe hides the feet, and ends in a train which lightly follows the walker's swaying steps. Subtle in form, and completely unadorned, they evoke all the grace and elegance of a high-ranking lady.

Exhibitions: Chinese Art, *London, 1935/6, No. 559.* – Chinese Jades, *Oriental Ceramic Society, London, 1918, No. 1.*

81. STANDING FIGURE. GREEN JADE, SHOWING SIGNS OF LONG BURIAL. SUI DYNASTY

H.9.6 cm. (Enlarged). Formerly Collection Mr. & Mrs. Desmond Gure, London

The sensitive carving of this figure illustrates perfectly the sculptural vision of the Sui, as much in the proportions of the body as in the vigorous, integrated treatment of the whole piece, which is somber and smooth.

Figures of this quality which can definitely be attributed to the short-lived dynasty of the Sui (561–618) are very rare indeed.

A large vertical perforation extends from head to foot at the back of this piece.

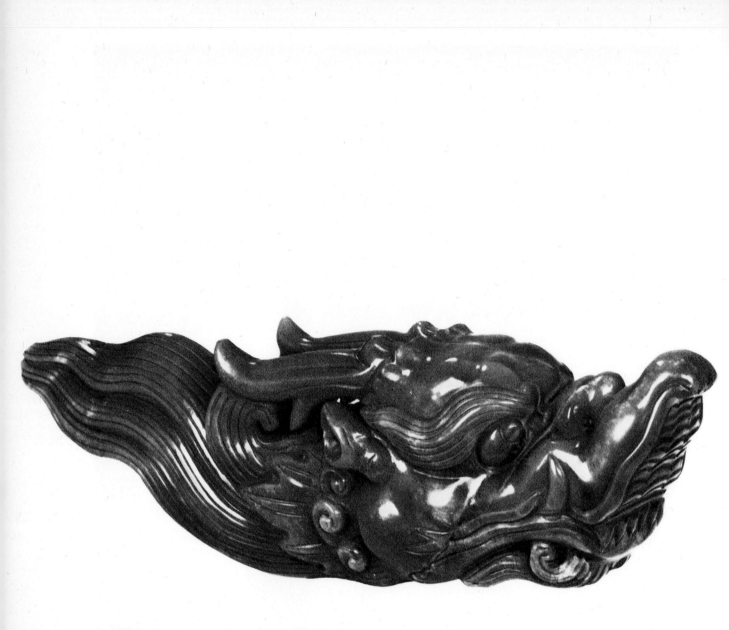

82. HEAD OF A DRAGON. GRAYISH-GREEN JADE WITH FAWN PATCHES. END OF THE T'ANG DYNASTY OR PERIOD OF THE FIVE DYNASTIES 9TH–10TH CENTURIES

L.24.7 cm. H.6.9 cm. Formerly Collection Mr. & Mrs. Desmond Gure, London

Professor Salmony considered this object to be a masterpiece of jade sculpture. The powerful treatment, and the sense of movement, are typical of the end of the T'ang dynasty. Several other dragons of the 9th and 10th centuries in various materials are known. All have the same characteristics – prominent eyes, ears stylized in the form of a flower, and an upper lip curling over jutting fangs.

Exhibition: The Arts of the Sung Dynasty, *Oriental Ceramic Society, London, 1960, No. 280.*

83. PENDANT. SUNG DYNASTY (960–1276)

H.17.2 cm. B.11.3 cm. Guimet Museum, Paris (Collection Gieseler)

Two symmetrical dragons hang face to face from a chain which closes with a kind of yoke. The decoration consists of relief spirals, and the rather smooth type of design is generally attributed to the Sung style, though in the present state of our knowledge it is impossible to be definite about it. The jade is an ivory white, with grayish-black veining.

Exhibitions: Chinese Art, *London, 1935/6, No. 694.* – Arte Cinese, *Venice, 1954, No. 226.*

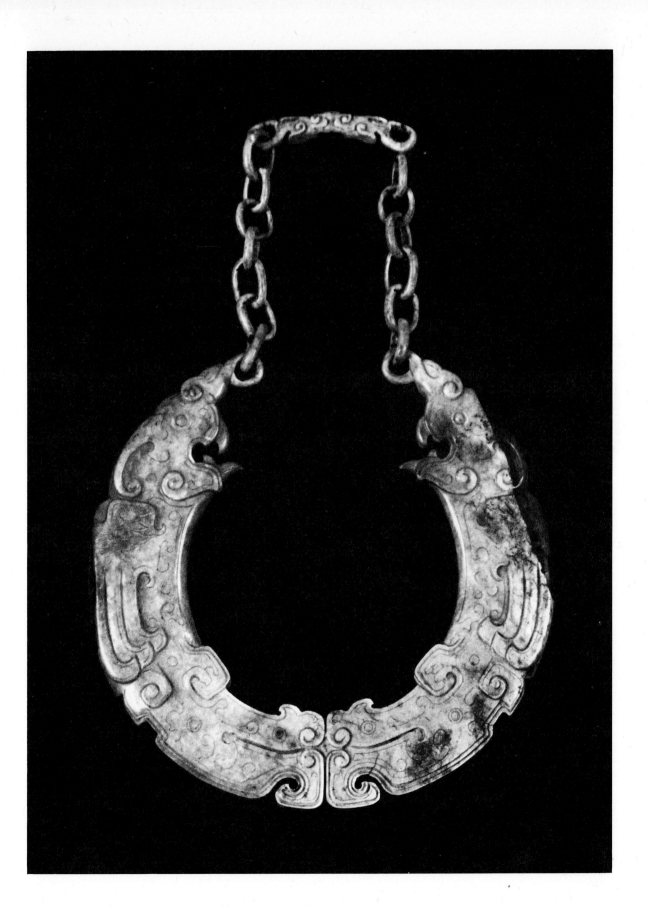

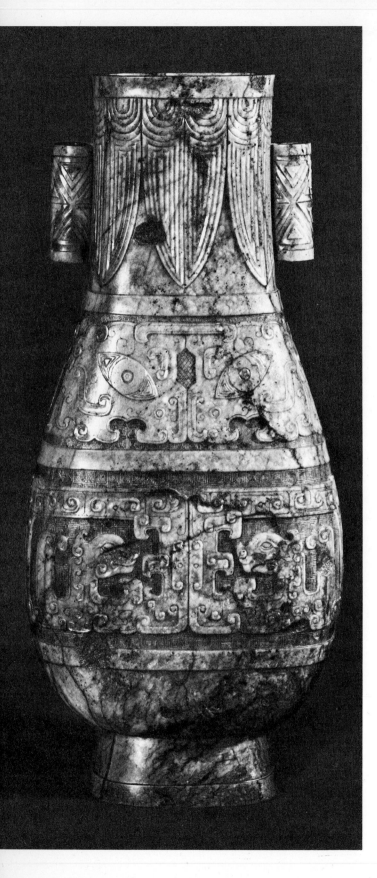

84. VESSEL. *Hu.* END OF THE SUNG OR EARLY YÜAN DYNASTY. PROBABLY 14TH CENTURY

H. 58 cm. Private Collection, Paris

During the Sung dynasty much research was done on the sites of the ancient capitals, especially at An-Yang, where ritual bronzes were found which became the pride of the Imperial collections and of the high Court officials. Catalogues of these were published. From then onwards the decoration on the archaic vessels was copied in bronze, porcelain, and jade in a style which was intended to be a faithful imitation, but which, on analysis, turns out to be a little fantastic. This large jade vase, green with black and gray veining, is a copy of a *hu*. It is splendidly incised, with both skill and accuracy. The archaic style, with the scrolls carved in light relief on a ground of regular square spirals, seems to accord with this kind of work done under the Sung. However, certain details have persuaded Mr. Desmond Gure, the eminent authority, that it ought to be placed a little later. The decoration is divided into three parts, separated by smooth bands. The central part is reminiscent of an old *t'ao t'ieh* mask, but only the eyes are clearly indicated, and these are handled in a very peculiar way. On the lower part, two dragons face one another, but their bodies are lost in a mass of bands and scrolls. Tubular handles, typical of the *hu,* are incised with closely fitted triangles.

118

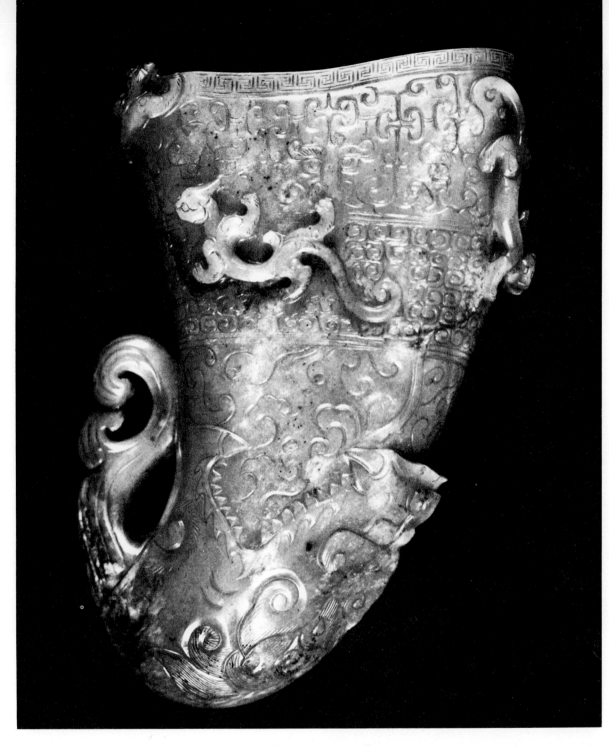

85. RHYTON IN WHITE JADE STREAKED WITH RUSSET. SUNG DYNASTY (960–1276)

H.18 cm. Guimet Museum, Paris (Collection Gieseler)

The earliest known rhytons date from the T'ang period (cf. Plate 173). They were used as libation cups, and are fairly common in jade after the Sung dynasty.

In the shape of a horn, this piece from the Guimet Museum is made in the form of a deep bowl, apparently engulfed by the open jaws of a powerfully fanged dragon. The handle is a double arc or scroll, perhaps representing the creature's tail. The cup itself is decorated with three different engraved *motifs*. On the lower part broadly drawn spirals and waving lines; in the center, relief spirals set closely in opposition (a *motif* which had become traditional since the period of the Warring States – cf. Plate 78), while above a freely handled *t'ao t'ieh* mask stands out from a geometric decoration of straight lines and hooks in the form of a *C*. Dragons carved in high relief encircle the two upper friezes.

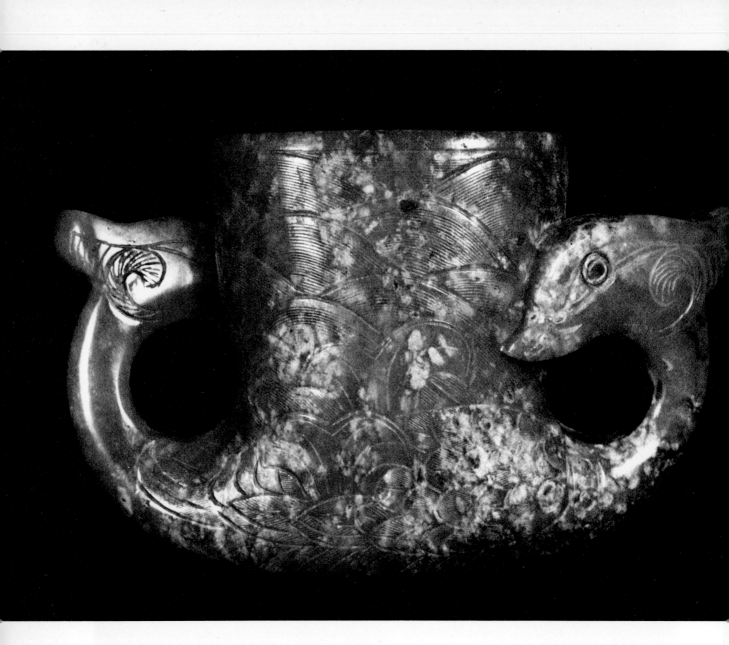

86. JADE CUP. END OF THE SUNG DYNASTY
(960–1276)

B.14 cm. (Enlarged). Art Council of Great Britain (Formerly Collection Mrs. C.G.Seligman), London

This rare piece in the form of a tall cup is composed of two mandarin ducks joined together, the heads and curving necks forming the handles. The beautiful pale green jade, translucent and touched with brown, has a lightly incised decoration depicting the birds' plumage and the waves. This cup, which was always formerly attributed to the Ming dynasty, is now thought by specialists to be slightly earlier.

Exhibition: The Arts of the Ming Dynasty, *Oriental Ceramic Society, London, 1957, No. 345.*

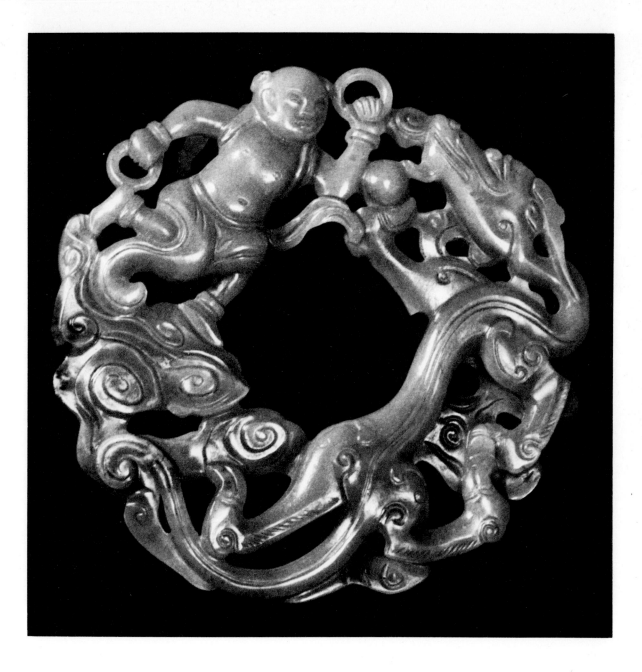

87. PIERCED RING. GREEN JADE WITH TOUCHES
OF BROWN. MING DYNASTY

*B.11.3 cm. (Enlarged). Formerly Collection Mr. & Mrs. Desmond
Gure, London*

The circular composition of this ornamental object is extremely adroit. A small boy, a ring in either hand, faces a dragon
with spreading feet and a long, coiling tail. They are riding on
stylized clouds. Placed between them is the pearl which traditionally accompanies dragons in later periods of Chinese art.

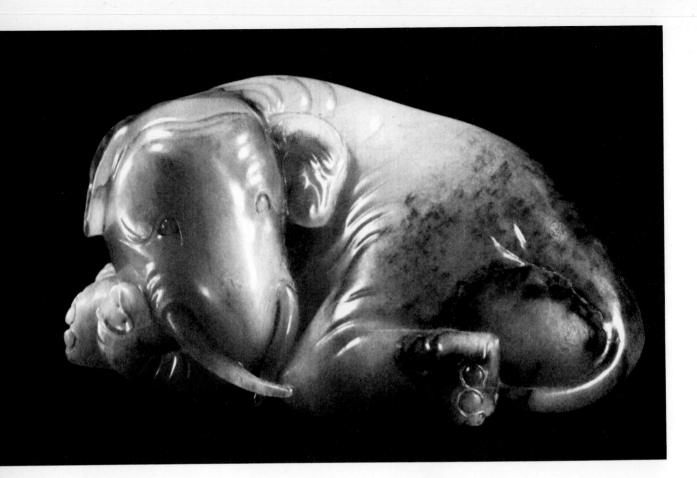

88. RECUMBENT ELEPHANT. JADE
GREENISH-WHITE WITH YELLOW AND
BROWN SPOTS. MING DYNASTY

*L.12.1 cm. H.5.2 cm. (Enlarged). Formerly
Collection Mr. & Mrs. Desmond Gure, London*

Jades of the Ming dynasty exhibit great virtuosity in form.
Among the very wide choice of subjects – religious figures,
heavily decorated goblets, landscapes in relief, and the like –
the most popular subject seems to have been small statues of
animals. They are carved with acute perception, particularly
evident in the figure shown here, where a sense of the great
weight of the beast portrayed emanates from this small object.
Accurate dating of Ming jades is almost impossible within the
present limits of our knowledge. In general, attributions have
to be based on analogies with styles and *motifs* to be seen in
other branches of art which are less obscure, for instance
porcelain or painting.

Exhibitions: Arte Cinese, *Venice, 1954, No.233.* – The Arts of the
Ming Dynasty, *Oriental Ceramic Society, London, 1957, No.352.*

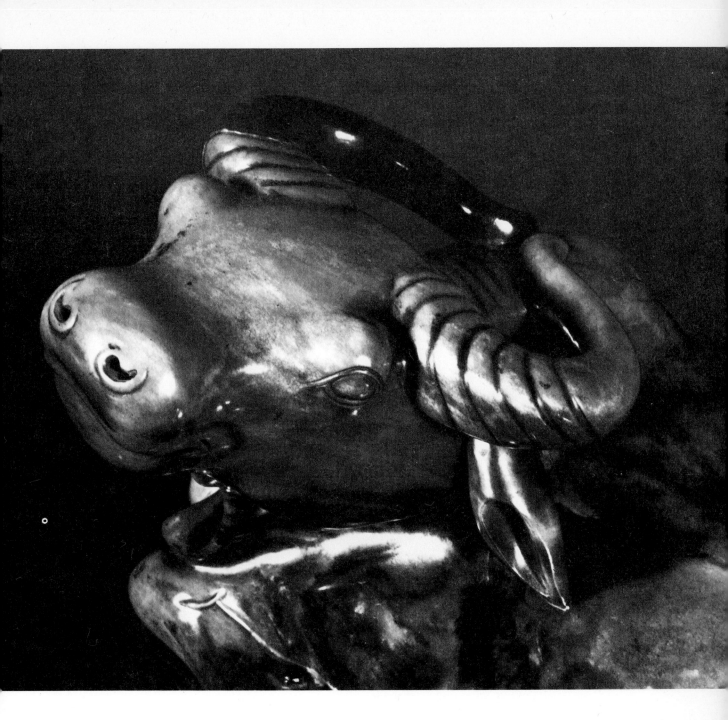

89. LARGE RECUMBENT BUFFALO (DETAIL)
MING DYNASTY (1368–1644)

L.38 cm. Collection Eskenazi, London

The buffalo *motif,* associated with symbols of the earth, is a recurring theme in Chinese art, both in archaic bronzes (cf. Plates 93 and 39), sculpture and painting, and the ceramic art where the animal often acts as a mount for Shou Lao, the god of Longevity.

The naturalistic Ming style is well seen here in this fine recumbent buffalo. Its large placid head is lifted, and turned in a movement which has been well caught by the observant jade carver. The beast is most skillfully handled, and the artist has expressed a poetic conception with great subtlety.

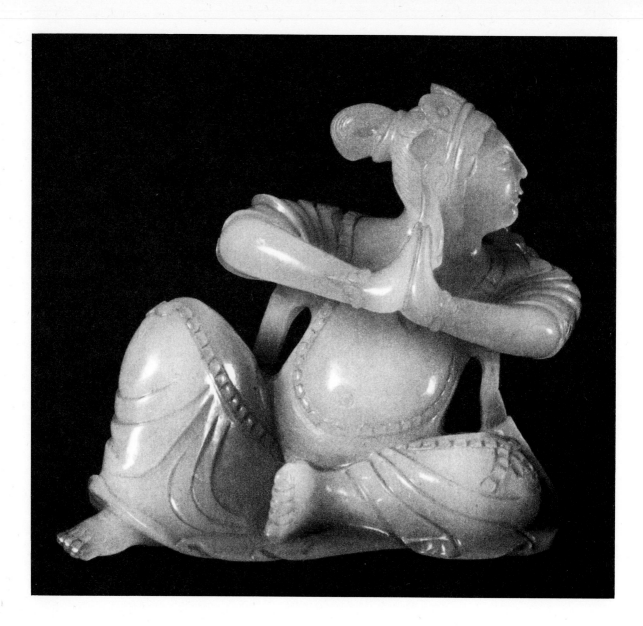

90. SEATED BODHISATTVA WITH HANDS
CROSSED IN ADORATION. WHITE JADE
CH'ING DYNASTY, REIGN OF CH'IEN LUNG

*H.7.5 cm. (Enlarged). Formerly Collection Mr. & Mrs. Desmond
Gure, London*

This beautiful Imperial piece has the reign-mark of Ch'ien Lung
engraved as a seal on the base. It is an excellent example of the
interest taken by the 18th century court of China in antiquity,
inspired, as it was, by T'ang Buddhist sculpture, which itself is
derived from the art of India. The jade is an exceptionally pure
white. The carving is of high quality, although a certain stiff-
ness can be seen in the handling of folds and ornament, foreshadowing the decadence which befell the art of China in the
19th century.

SCULPTURE

BEFORE ANY ATTEMPT can be made to examine the historical development of Chinese sculpture it is necessary to underline the great differences which distinguish it from the plastic arts of the Western world. We expect a concrete subject to be handled spatially in three dimensions, and that sculpture, contrasting reality with artistic expression, will reproduce life and movement. Classical Greek sculpture and the traditions of art since then – even, to a certain extent, the art of the Middle Ages – have all led us to accept, and expect, this point of view.

The Chinese approach is completely different. In the first place, the human figure does not play the preponderant role assigned to it in our civilization, and in others, such as that of ancient Egypt. In China, man is only one of the diverse manifestations of life. He is only rarely an individual, and always on the same plane as other beings – divinities, *djinn*, and animals especially. These occupy, as it were, the foreground of the picture. Man does not impose his image on the gods, nor dominate the world in which he lives. In the archaic periods supernatural forces are expressed by abstract designs, by multiple unreal shapes in which he has no part. Even when man does assume an important role in Chinese art – introduced through Buddhism which is an alien tradition of thought – the sculptor makes no attempt at all to glorify the beauty of either the body or its movement. He draws not a portrait, but a vision of the soul – an intellectual or philosophic concept. The body, or more often the face alone, is only the medium through which thought is expressed.

It is not that the Chinese were unobservant; there are many examples to prove the contrary. Vivacity, animation, and humor fill the Han bas-reliefs, and enliven the informal world of funeral personages. But, even here, the essential point is the crystallization of an idea or an emotion, whether it be strength, reverence, struggle, mercy, or contemplation. This is achieved by means of an attitude, a gesture, the expression in a face – a whole range of formulae expressing a universal language. In this way, Buddhist iconography, which was to be the subject of infinite variations on a richly spiritual theme, was always dominated by strict tradition. Even in the very early days, on a quite different plane of ideas, rigid conventions bound the art of the Shang and Chou peoples in all its aspects.

It may be argued that this is a characteristic common to all primitive civilizations, and in this respect one could say that China, in spite of her amazing virtuosity, remained at this stage for a long time. However, some of the technical limitations of sculpture must have been self-imposed. True sculpture, in its three-dimensional sense, only appears very late. The plastic interpretation of form remains for a long time static and frontal. In Buddhist art the human figure is placed with its back supported, a rather flattened conception almost without a profile. A graphic and linear view dominates the form, and was to continue to do so until the relatively late T'ang period. It must be added, however, that like all generalizations, these brief remarks are by no means absolute. The ancient animal bronzes are an exception, and also the vivid little world of the *ming ch'i* or tomb figures which give a lively portrayal of all aspects of daily life. But it was precisely at this point where they diverged from tradition, and this unusual interest in verisimilitude must have provoked the severest censure from the Confucian moralists.

Chinese sculpture covers a wide field, although it cannot claim the continuity of other art forms, such as bronze, pottery, and porcelain, nor the outstanding pre-eminence enjoyed by painting and calligraphy.

In the Chinese scale of values sculpture does not rank as a major art. Sculptors were scarcely even thought of as artists. Craftsmen serving a funerary tradition, a religious ideal, or a ritual commemoration, they remain anonymous. Whereas the names of painters are venerated, and their lives described in the smallest detail, sculptors, apart from a few exceptions during the Ming period, have left no names to posterity. Yet they have enriched the artistic heritage of mankind with some of its greatest masterpieces.

Since it is within the scope of this book only to illustrate works from private and public collections, it would be very difficult to follow the history of sculpture in China through all its phases. For instance, the great groups from the Buddhist temples can only be suggested by isolated figures which come from them. We would, therefore, suggest that the reader refers, wherever possible, to two or three important works, such as that of Professor Siren, or the publications of the Chavannes and Segalen archaeological missions. Here, in chronological order, we shall follow the successive developments of the many varying sculptural concepts. On the one hand these follow the traditional Chinese course created by the Shang peoples which continues by way of animal and funerary sculpture almost to our own day; on the other, a completely different trend is evident – the influence of Buddhism from India. Although this was an alien art, it was rapidly absorbed. It brought a new conception of life and the world, introducing a fertile iconographical repertory, and breathing fresh life into the sculpture of China which soared to great heights on this new-found faith.

SCULPTURE OF THE SHANG AND CHOU PERIODS

For a long time it was thought that there was no sculpture in the very early periods of Chinese history, but this has now been disproved. Scientific research at An-Yang, carried out by the Academia Sinica of Peking between 1928 and 1936, brought to light a series of sculptured figures which were a revelation to scholars. In size they are often small, varying between 8 and 50 cm., but they are handled boldly, and have a monumental quality. The themes are single animals, which were, of course, already known in the zoomorphic bronzes of the *tsun* group – the owl, the elephant and the ram, the buffalo and the tiger (Plates 93 and 72 a). The material is white marble, or a close-grained limestone akin to alabaster. The beasts seem to huddle in on themselves, hardly standing out from the stone block, although the essential structure is well-defined. Even though the form is only suggested, it always has an aura of the beast and reveals its salient character. Some human figures belong to this group. One of these, a man crouching with head and shoulders turned and resting on outstretched arms, is unusual and remarkable for the realism of its attitude.

In contrast to this rather summary frontal immobile realism, many pieces are also decorated with incised lines. Here, once more, we find the *t'ao t'ieh* and the single footed dragon, *k'uei*, in company with the spirals and hooks of the bronze and jade decorative "grammar" – a surprising stylistic unity seen in every branch of Shang art.

Several of these little figures have a groove at the base, which seems to show that they were part of an architectural or decorative group which has now disappeared. They were all found in tombs and must have been symbols of protection or good fortune.

Small jades representing crouching bears (Plate 72 b), human, or animal heads, confirm the existence in the Shang period of a coherent tradition in the plastic arts which was already bound by definite conventions. The character which was to dominate the whole of Chinese sculpture was already apparent – the broad viewpoint which saw not the detail, but the essence and the potential within a block of stone.

The same may be said of the animal heads on some bronze vessels (Plate 27). On the other hand, some of the bas-relief masks are intensely alive, in spite of the unreal elements in their composition. It is interesting to learn that imprints have been found in the tombs at An-Yang of vessels in carved wood, which could well have been the prototypes of some of these bronzes. Noteworthy is the *li* on Plate 20, which has masks "apparently cut from some carved material" to quote the Abbé Breuil, which points to the possibility of such a relationship.

The sculptural character of the archaic bronzes is even more striking in the zoomorphic vessels. The famous tigers in the Freer Gallery at Washington, the elephant in the same collection and in the former Camondo Collection now in the Guimet Museum, and all the rhinoceroses, buffalos, and birds powerfully affirm the characteristics of their origin.

Their solid power successfully overcomes the conventional, swarming design with which they are often decorated. This remains true through the early centuries of the Chou dynasty (Plate 39). Even in hybrid forms, such as the *kuang*, the spirit of the animal loses none of its power (Plate 22). The human figure appears more rarely, but it is realistically treated, and is almost always free from traditional ornament. The Freer Gallery has a *huo* with a lid in the form of a finely modeled head of a man crouched between the paws of an embracing monster. As in the piece illustrated on Plate 30, the realism of the man, simple and unclothed, contrasts sharply with the brooding fabulous beasts enfolding him.

It is not until the end of the Chou dynasty, during the period of the Warring States, that the human figure takes on any importance. A group of bronze figures was found in the tombs of Chin Ts'un in Honan Province, on the site of ancient Lo-Yang, which was the Chou capital for several centuries. These are kneeling figures, arms outstretched and holding in their hands cylindrical cups which must have been intended to hold torches or candles (Plate 94). Although the carving is superficial, the turn of the face and the attitude of the body are well caught. They all have rather complicated *coiffures*, and some, for example the figures in the Minneapolis Museum in the U.S.A., wear clothes with a frieze relief on the borders. There are some bronze figures of acrobats which are rare examples of funerary art. This took its models from the most unexpected aspects of daily life.

Even earlier than the pottery *ming ch'i* of the Han and T'ang periods is an astonishing bear-leader in the Freer Gallery. The sense of balance governing the naturalistic attitudes of man and beast reveals one of the earliest expressions of movement in sculpture at the time. In spite of their controversial nature, we must mention the very small human models in black stoneware which appeared about fifteen years ago, and are said to come from Hui Hsien in Honan Province. They do, in some sense, approach these bronze figures, although they are cruder. The sense of depth and the supple movements of both dancers and musicians are very skillfully produced, although the arms, ending in a point, as well as the flattened faces, are scarcely more than rudimentary. The authenticity of these pieces is much in question today, but it is possible that they were the first of the early *ming ch'i*, made as a substitute household to accompany the dead man on his journey to the next world.

The painted wood figures from the tombs at Ch'ang-sha (Hunan Province) also date from the period of the Warring States. These figures, about 50–60 cm. in height, are much elongated, and their faces almost caricatures. They are very expressive, despite a rather uniform approach. The gestures are varied, and the clothes soberly but exactly defined. This is a provincial art, only recently discovered, which must have developed apart from the main – the more classic – trends. Animal art also has a very original character, combining extreme stylization with an acute power of observation. This can be seen most clearly in the three large lacquer wading birds perched on coiled snakes in the Museum at Cleveland, Ohio.

The realistic tendency to be observed under the Shang only in a few rare models of deer in bronze found at An-Yang, strengthens and develops about the 5th century B.C. with the small sculptured pieces found on the covers of *ting*. Ducks, rams, and reclining buffalo, are mounted on the bronzes discovered at Li-yü (Northern Shansi) and most of these are in the Guimet Museum. The detail of the carvings is astonishing. Even the fabulous beasts at this time were imbued with a life which is somehow in harmony with an imaginary animal kingdom. The tiger on Plate 43, and, even more, the wonderful winged dragon in the Stoclet Collection (Plates 44 and 45) tense their muscles and quiver with powerful effort. It is necessary, if we are to understand the transformation in style which these creatures represent, to remember that during the period of the Warring States China was at war with her northern neighbors – barbarians whose methods she copied the better to resist. In this way many new influences were absorbed, among them the animal traditions of the steppes. These contacts brought new forms, new decorations. Gradually the animalistic art broke away from the age-old formulae inherited from the Shang. Strong rhythms now govern the bodies of the animals, now interwoven, now opposing (cf. the handle of the bell, Plate 40), and movement succeeds the traditional rigidity. This is the source of the vitality and animation in the work of the later centuries of the Chou dynasty, and herein lies its fascination.

The Han dynasty sees the beginning of the great monumental sculpture. It is also a period during which funerary art, both in relief and in the round, developed vigorously.

Animal sculpture in stone is first seen in a classical monument which was thought for a long time to be the starting point of all Chinese sculpture. This is the "Horse attacking a barbarian" which was erected in Shansi at the foot of the burial mound of General Huo Ch'in-Ping who died in 117 B.C. At that moment China, still waging her centuries old struggle against the barbarians, was making incessant cavalry expeditions as far as the borders of the Parthian Empire. The Emperor Wu Ti (140–87 B.C.) erected this monument in honor of one of his most distinguished officers, a man famous for his victories over Hun tribes. The animal is huge, immobile; the defeated man lies on his back between its legs, embedded, as it were, in the granite block. The dominant power of the beast is commanding, although the carving is crude and worn by time. To quote Victor Segalen – "Here is a splendid fragment of tragic sculpture." Originally, there must have been other figures in this group, but we are ignorant of their placing. Some huge pieces still lie on the ground beneath.

Other tombs of the period, for instance the last resting place of the Wu family in Shantung, have stone lions. These are the first of a long series, which reappears later in the 5th and 6th centuries A.D. on the Royal tombs of the Southern dynasties. After the advent of the Han, they point to Western influence; the lion was, in fact, unknown in China. It must have been a relic of Assyria and Babylon, brought to China by way of her contacts with Persia after the expansion into Bactria and Central Asia. Some of these pieces have come to the West. One, in the Guimet Museum, although it has lost its paws, still embodies all the power and pride of the lion. Even the rather heraldic posture of the limbs is skillfully indicated.

Diverse traditions still continued in the realm of Han funerary art. The tombs had to be laid out according to plans which were subject to a strict convention. The grave, or tumulus, was erected in a funeral ground which was entered from the south along the "Road of Spirits" (*shên-tao*). Pillars ornamented with bas-reliefs flanked the entrance. In front of and behind these were monuments arranged in pairs – *stelae*, columns, or animal statues. The plans of these funeral ways remained the same for centuries, increasing in size till they achieved colossal proportions in the Ming tombs near Nanking and Peking. In the Provinces of Honan and Shantung a small funeral chamber, intended to protect offerings, was erected near the tomb itself. In the end, several rooms were added to this, often lined with molded or painted bricks. These funerary rooms were decorated with flagstones, carved, and evincing a surprising competence in the art of bas-relief. The world of the Han, a mixture of science and fable, passes before our eyes in huge compositions placed one above the other. Hsi Wang Mu, Sovereign of the Western Air, and other supernatural beings from the realms of Air and Water, fill the legendary scenes – the Seven Gods of the Great Bear (Ursa Major, or the Big Dipper), mythical Emperors, a whole army of *djinn* with wings and serpents' tail, sorcerers, demons, and fabulous animals exist among scrolled clouds, architecture, and magic trees (cf. Plate 95). Man is there too, earthbound, but vividly presented in animated scenes of worship, feasts, the hunt, battles, cavalcades, and funeral processions. The books of the Chavannes Mission which are responsible for our knowledge of this art reveal "a fantasy and inventiveness, and an astonishing impulse inspiring both themes and characters" (René Grousset). The most typical of these groups come from Shantung, Hsiao-t'ang Shan and Chou-wei, and date from the 1st century B.C.: also the Wu-liang Tsun (Wu family tombs) dating from 146–167 A.D. Sometimes a technique of outline engraving was used, at others a process of *champlevé* achieved by hollowing out the stone around the figures. This gave a series of flat surfaces which were then incised with decorative detail. The famous stone from the Rietberg Museum in Zurich well illustrates this complex and vivid art (Plate 95).

The dynamic linear work of the Han had been inherited from the Period of the Warring States, but was henceforth to be employed in a more logical and real way. Used with enormous skill and imagination, their graphic methods conferred life only by the indications of outline. If it is true, as it may well be, that these relief carvings are transformations into stone for the use of the dead of mural paintings which decorated palaces during their lifetime, then this point of view, in which the world is seen in silhouette, is easily explained. It would strengthen our impression that Chinese art is more at home with painting than with sculpture.

An echo of this art of carved stone can be seen in the terra cotta pillars and molded bricks from the tombs. Here the *motifs* were repeated by applying wet clay to a sculpted matrix. This, though, is a more popular art. The decoration has hooks which are akin to calligraphy, approaching painting or the engraving on contemporary bronzes. There is an attempt to portray depth and perspective in architecture and landscape, in which animals and people appear in profile behind the rocks and the mountains.

However, during the 1st and 2nd centuries A.D. a school of sculpture, in its real sense, grew up in Szechwan. The Segalen Archaeological Mission of 1914 found high-relief compositions on funeral pillars which are filled with movement – animal struggles, dragons creeping out of walls, riders on horseback; and, in bas-relief, skillfully modeled animals symbolic of the points of the compass. One of these is the famous Red Bird of the South on the Chen column, its wings outstretched, which is described by René Grousset as "elegantly imperious."

The Han tomb figures (*ming ch'i*) are of especial interest in their representation of people and animals, for the substitution of the inanimate for the animate was an entirely new approach. So the figures of servants, magicians, dancers, and fine ladies throw a wonderful light on family life of the time. Some of them are very lively, especially the broad sleeved sorcerers whose robes sweep the ground as they flex their knees and bodies in the dance. Others are more stately, the artist making the most of the new freedom of outline (Plate 98), or again, there are merchants and artisans going about their daily tasks. For the most part, however, the figures are motionless – standing men and women dressed in long robes fastened across the chest, and with enormous sleeves hiding their hands. These robes swing out to cover the feet (Plate 97). The body is also completely covered, but its shape is indicated by the massive folds and contours of the robe. This style was to continue beyond the Han period, and right through the 3rd century. It can also be seen in bronze or jade figures (Plate 80).

The pottery and bronze animals are also conceived on broad, simple lines, unencumbered with detail. The artist portrays each species with an acute eye for its characteristic pose, often adding good-natured touches which warmly reveal the Chinese sense of humor. Bears, horses, boars, dogs, and birds are all sketched with great vitality (Plate 101). There are many horses, often very large. The head and neck are both well-bred and nervous (Plate 100). They originally had legs of wood, but these have all disappeared, although researches in Korea have now revealed animals completed in poplar wood, which show what the beast was intended to look like originally. Bears, too, crouching or standing, are found everywhere. Sometimes they act as supports for tripod vessels, and the ones with the malicious expression, made in golden bronze, are among the most successful sculptural pieces of the Han.

FROM THE END OF THE HAN TO THE ACCESSION OF THE SUI (220–589)

The powerful Han Empire was replaced in 220 by three kingdoms which divided the territory. After a brief reunification by the Chin in 265, these kingdoms in turn took refuge in Nanking a few miles south of the Yang-tze-Kiang river, abandoning the whole of Northern China to the endless hordes of invading barbarians. But these nomads, in settling down, became themselves more and more Chinese. Ephemeral dynasties succeeded one another in both North and South, until unity was again achieved with the accession of the Sui in 589 when the ancient city of Ch'angan became once more the capital of the Empire. These long troubled years were the cause of deep spiritual unrest, and of a notable revival of Taoism in popular esteem. Han artistic traditions still survived, however, particularly in South China.

One outstanding example of this is seen in the wonderful animal sculpture beside the royal and princely tombs of Nanking. The Han lions here became grandiose chimaerae, with swelling chest and arching back, and they still stand proudly overlooking the Chinese landscape. These are masterpieces of sculpture in the round, no longer imprisoned in the stone, and they convey a powerful dynamic force unique in the history of Chinese art. This dynamism is revealed in the lordly pose of the turned head, the tension of the striding feet, the great jaws, gaping with lolling tongue as though uttering a prolonged roar. Although realistic in stance, and in their sense of life and movement, these lordly beasts are yet partly fantastic – wings start from their shoulders, and long stylized curls adorn the manes. They can be dated between the middle of the 5th century (the tomb of the Emperor Sung Wên-ti who died in 453), and the middle of the 6th with the tombs of the Liang Emperors (502–556) and the princes of the Imperial House. The winged lion of the Duke of Hsiao-hsiu (died 518) is the culminating point of this group – the vigorous carving has boldly chiseled features where the play of light accentuates the expression of dominant power.

The little terra cotta tomb figures, known everywhere as "Wei," may be recognized by their graceful restraint, and sharp, taut, treatment with excessive elongation of the human figure. Women, who played an important part in the artistic and literary Courts of the South, are frail and thin, perhaps a little stiff, but often endowed with a fleeting smile which gives a special character to their faces (Plate 99). The dresses are long and stiff, with very high waists and incised details. The commonest animals were the richly caparisoned horses with tiny heads, angular saddles, and saddle cloths reaching almost to the ground. Their riders are very often barbarians wearing heavy hooded cloaks. Camels now appear for the first time, with their whimsical hump realistically, and often wittily, depicted. Other, stranger, beasts fill the world of the tombs; tense nervous dragons and chimaerae freely and delicately modeled, and now in a style far removed from the rather weighty and massive treatment of the Han animal world.

Parallel to this traditional art, which was continuously transfused with new life, there runs a completely different development which arose from the introduction of the Buddhist religion into China. Buddhism was founded in the 5th century B.C. in the form of an atheistic moral code by Siddhārtha, a prince of the Sākya family. In retreat from the world, Sākyamuni (the monk of Sākya), or the Buddha, saw the Divine Light, and it was also revealed to him that it was possible to avoid the succession of rebirths, the source of pain, by the renunciation of all desire. This would lead to Nirvāna, a state of complete nothingness. Although the new doctrine was, at first, atheistic, succeeding centuries enriched it with legends and all kinds of divinities who gradually became more definite and individual. Two different forms of Buddhism grew up: the Hinayāna, or Small Vehicle, remaining rigidly faithful to the original precepts, and the Mahāyāna, or Large Vehicle, which was the source of immense development, being much more accessible to the people through the medium of merciful interceding gods. In fact, there were added to the historical Buddha, Buddhas of the past and of the future, or Bodhisattvas, who, having themselves achieved Nirvāna, renounced it for the sake of humanity. Of these, the most popular in China were to be Maitreya, the Buddha-to-come called the Consoler, and Avalokiteshvara (Kuan Yin in China) who was originally a male divinity, but was later to become goddess of pity and mercy.

The doctrine of Mahāyāna spread through the Punjab in Northwest India, and during the 1st century B.C. was adopted by the Kings of the Kushān Empire which covered also a part of Afghanistan and modern Pakistan. Slightly later, it began to gather an iconography, which now, for the first time, dared to represent the Buddha himself, who had formerly been worshipped only through symbols. This iconography developed in the 1st century A.D. in the schools of Mathurā and Amaravati in India, and Gandhāra in the region of Peshawar. These places still retained a sculptural tradition dating from the conquests of Alexander who brought elements of Greek civilization with him. Contacts with the Roman Empire kept this tradition alive, and now it became the foundation for a "Graeco-Buddhist" art. The sculpture of this area is full of classical allusions of a surprisingly hybrid character. Sākyamuni is an Apollonic figure with a Greek profile and curled hair, and the decoration has Corinthian capitals, with cupids and atlantes. Indian legend also established rigid iconographical formulae, and, among these, some signs by which the Buddha was to be recognized: *ushnîsha*, the protuberance of the skull which looks rather like a *chignon*; the *urnā*, a tuft of hair between the eyes, later changed by popular feeling into a jewel; the wheel of the law drawn on the palm of the hand; very elongated lobes to the ears, supposed to have originated from the weight of the earrings worn by Buddha when he was a prince. The Buddha was always clothed in the robe of a monk, although the Bodhisattvas were adorned with jewels and veils. The gestures (*mudrā*) and the attitudes (*asāna*) also became traditional and symbolic.

For a long time trade had been established with Gandhāra and the Punjab through Central Asia, and they were also connected by the "Silk Road" with China and Persia. It was on these trade routes during the 1st century A.D. that Buddhist missionaries undertook the conversion of the Indo-European peoples of Chinese Turkestan. It was not long before they arrived in China, and it is known that a Buddhist community was already established at Lo-Yang in the year 73. During the 3rd century the city was to become an active center of Buddhism, which gradually spread all over the empire.

In the 2nd century, the first Buddhist representations appeared in China on Taoist bronze mirrors, and, oddly, in conjunction with the ancient *motifs* of the dragon and the phoenix. These two religions were related for a long time, one supporting the other, so that they benefited from the confusion which kept them linked together, in spite of the interminable argument which continued unresolved even after the official victory of Buddhism in the 5th century. Primitive figures of haloed Buddhist divinities are to be seen also in Yüeh stoneware found at Chiu-yen in Chekiang Province which date from the 3rd century.

But it is only in the 4th century that a truly Chinese Buddhist sculptural art emerges. The small golden bronze Buddha of the Brundage Collection in Chicago, dated 338, is the earliest of a series destined to have a long history. It was doubtless inspired by an image of Central Asian origin. The Enlightened One is seated on a low plinth, with legs crossed and hands joined in the gesture of meditation (*dhyanāmudrā*). The thickset body, massive head, and slit eyes indicate a Chinese hand, as yet unfamiliar with a foreign model, but the Graeco-Buddhist influence is apparent in the parallel pleats of the monkish robe, and in the curled hair with its high *chignon*. A similar statue belonging to the Fogg Art Museum of Cambridge (Mass.) resembles even more the style of Gandhāra. The figure has a mustache in the manner of some Greek Buddhas, but the plinth is decorated with lions which are purely Chinese. Most other figures of the 4th century are in Japanese collections.

In the 5th century a whole series of dated figures shows the developing skill (Plate 108) and the new accuracy of observation. The faces become increasingly Chinese; flaming clouds serve as a background (Plate 109, 110); robes often have parallel pleats with clinging drapery as at Mathurā (Plate 110); or the figure is enveloped by soft elegant folds (Plate 108). There is often a sharp contrast between striations and flat surfaces. The high plinths look like hollowed cubes, and are surmounted by a circular pedestal in the form of a lotus or a throne. They are often decorated with inscriptions and figures in low relief, connected in some way with the main figure. There is enormous variety among these statues which arose in response to a demand for images for domestic worship. Early Buddhist art flourished with a freedom very remote from the restricting formulae of later years.

These small bronze statues throw light on the beginnings of the large stone sculpture of the Wei, which began to develop strongly about the end of the 5th century. It must be remarked that Buddhism spread most rapidly in Northern China, ruled at that time by a Turko-Mongol dynasty, the Toba or Wei, although they had been entirely absorbed by Chinese civilization. But even before the Wei, the petty barbarian kings ruling over Shansi and Shensi Provinces had protected the Buddhist monks.

In 444 the King Wei T'ai Wu Ti, during a period of fanatical proscription, ordered the destruction of the first rock sculptures at Yün-Kang, begun in 415, but the official conversion of his successor, Wên Ch'êng Ti in 454, gave a fresh impulse to sculpture, and the stone carvers again started work with renewed zeal.

Yün-Kang lies in the north of Shansi, several miles distant from the first Wei capital at P'ing Ch'êng, near the present day Ta-tung-fu. A whole kilometer of high rocky cliff was hollowed out into cave temples, the walls of which were covered with carvings. The idea of the rock temple came from India (Karli, Ajantā, Ellura) by stages from Bāmiyān in Afghanistan and the oasis of Tarim (Qyzyl and Turfan). In China it was first used at Tuen-huang, frontier post, market, and religious center in one, which was situated at the beginning of the Silk Road on the edge of the Gobi Desert. The first caves found there may be as early as 366. One can see the remote Indian origin in the architectural features of Yün-Kang – arches, pillars, and the outlines of openings and while some of the decorative *motifs* recall Hellenistic or Iranian themes, some of the secondary subjects, such as flying *apsaras*, doorkeepers (*dvarapālas*), or musicians, come straight from the iconography of India.

The walls of the caves are covered with figures arranged in richly decorated niches around, and at the feet of, the Buddha or the Bodhisattva. Their vast numbers constituted acts of piety, for the Mahāyāna taught that it was a virtue to make pious images and address worship to them. The burning faith of the Wei kings, who directed the construction of these temples, as well as that of the craftsmen working there, is revealed in these astonishing works, in which even painting had a part to play. All the complex iconography of the Large Vehicle is present: Buddhas surrounded by their disciples; the Boddhisattvas, or favorite disciples; the Buddhist saints (*arhat* or *lohan*); episodes in the earthly life of Sākyamuni or in his previous lives (*jātakas*); as well as *apsaras*, donors, and other figures. Generally, attribution is made according to the various features and gestures of the divinities, but there are still no definite rules, and the sculptors seem to have had comparative freedom in their composition.

In this first phase the caves at Yün-Kang can be dated between 453 and 494. The five colossal Buddhas of Caves XVI and XX belong to this period, and are reminiscent of the Indian style of Mathurā. The faces have a large forehead, narrow prominent nose, and a fixed smile. They are very impersonal. Massive in body, the figures are clothed in straight-pleated robes, sometimes revealing a naked shoulder. The headdress is not elaborate. After this first primitive phase, the style begins to evolve, and the figures grow more Chinese.

In Caves V and VI the faces are thinner, and the now elongated bodies disappear beneath a mass of tubular folds (Plate 104). An intense spiritual feeling emanates from some of these figures – Maitreya and Bodhisattva with their tender smiles, lowered eyes, and calm faces, reflecting an inner vision (Plates 103 and 104). An expression of fervor, of emotion even, which now appears for the first time, is the Chinese contribution to the cold, expressionless Graeco-Buddhist art.

At Yün-Kang we are faced with one of the great moments of religious art of all time, and it is not without good grounds that Yün-Kang has been compared with the carved groups in our Gothic cathedrals.

The caves of Mei-tsi shan which have only been very recently discovered in the Wei valley (Kansu Province) are contemporary with Yün-Kang. The style of the first carvings encountered here is remarkably fine, and very like that of Yün-Kang. Mei-tsi shan makes one realize the enormous radius covered by the art of Yün-Kang in Buddhist areas of the 5th century. It extended even as far as Manchuria, where there are more caves to prove the magnificent development of art under the Wei.

It was, however, at Lung-mên that the great religious work of the dynasty was to be carried out. In 494, with the idea of being in the very middle of the Kingdom, the Wei kings moved to Lo-yang, in Honan Province, the ancient capital of the Han and the most active Buddhist center in China. The new work was to continue that already completed at Yün-Kang. The chosen site, about 15 kms. from the town, was the rocky pass of Lung-mên, and work on the black limestone cliffs was begun in 495. It continued until the middle of the T'ang dynasty. The early Lung-mên sculptures were more coherent and more Chinese than those of Yün-Kang. The figures and decoration are more animated, as may be seen in the flying scarves of the *apsaras* (Plates 107 and 112), and in the clouds and plants. The bodies have slim waists and are thin and elongated (Plates 105 and 111). The faces are sharply carved, for the stone at Lung-mên is closer in texture and takes detail more easily than the softer limestone of Yün-Kang. An intense spirituality and fine sensitivity (Plate 105), sometimes overshadowed by a detached gravity (Plate 112), play around the smiling mouth and eyes. The symmetrical, geometrically arranged draperies flow in "architectural harmony" (Vadime Elisseef) with a schematic, linear rhythm. The pleats, arranged in a complex manner one over the other, cascade gently over the plinths, spreading outwards towards the base to give a "keyhole" effect (Plate 111). René Grousset describes them brilliantly: "They are no longer material beings beneath the huge pointed and flaming halo, but symbols of the cloak of Buddhism." Plate 106 is a fine example of this, despite its rather later date.

Of all the caves at Lung-mên it is those at Ku-Yang-tung and Lien-hua ssŭ which best embody the religious vision, despite the fact that they have, since the beginning of the 20th century, been subjected to commercial vandalism. The *stelae*, heads, and figures, brutally torn from the cliffs, are now in museums and private collections. The central cave of Pin-Yang, which can be dated between 499 and 535, has, as well as a large Buddha of supreme mystical power seated with his favorite disciples, Ānanda and Kāsyapa, two fine bas-reliefs representing the Emperor and Empress walking in their court (c. 535). Here in a secular, and, therefore, a freer subject – for religious art always, in every civilization, remains untouched by innovation, fearing diminution of the cult's efficacy – we find a distant echo of the great compositions of the Han. But now there is a scientific grouping and fluidity of the almost flat figures, an elegance and grace which raise these works to the highest level of the art of bas-relief. These secular frescos were also ravaged several years ago, and are now partly reconstructed in the Metropolitan Museum of New York and in the Kansas City Museum. Lung-mên was not the only center of important rock sculpture. About the end of the dynasty, work was started not very far away, at Kung Hsien. The statues of the cave of Chê-ku ssŭ, in a beautiful grayish-blue limestone, are worthy to rank among the best works of the Wei dynasty.

Here we must mention a series of monumental votive *stelae* in stone, of which two examples are in Boston (*anno* 529) and in Kansas City (c. 535–540). They are in the monumental commemorative style of the Han, and perpetuate a very ancient Chinese tradition, namely large protective dragons with their heads intertwined. Buddha and the Bodhisattva stand out from niches in high relief, surrounded by smaller figures – worshippers, *apsaras*, and donors, in very vivacious attitudes. In bas-relief round the *stele* is a concentrated decoration of scrolls, ornate canopies, trees and flowers, and even horsemen with caparisoned chargers, of which there is a multiplicity among the Wei tomb figures.

A golden-bronze statuary with the same pliant, nervous style of the Lung-mên caves has real grandeur. The *stele* on Plate 116, dated 517, is a good illustration of the clarity achieved in the metalwork. The face, crowned with an elaborate *coiffure* and lit by the "archaic smile," is the serene focal point of flamboyant surroundings. The same impression is gained from the famous little *stele* of the Guimet Museum (*anno* 518), where the Buddha and Prabhūtaratna converse together. They are almost unreal, for the faces and hands alone are visible beneath a swirl of folds which are broken and angular. In the altars of a slightly later date, now in the Metropolitan Museum, New York, this intense feeling concentrated on the head of Buddha is increased in some measure and accentuated by additions in which the flying draperies of the *apsaras* are like moving flames.

Art under the Wei seems to have pushed mystical expression to extremes. After the middle of the 6th century, new tendencies intervened with the Ch'i dynasty of the North (550–577). There was an amazing renaissance of plastic art; an attempt to make more realistic representations. The influence of Gupta art was probably at work here. There were carvings of chaste nudes, veiled in supple, transparent draperies. A second wave of Western influence was spreading, but it encountered the evolution taking place in the interior of China, which was reacting strongly against the linear art of the Wei.

The major work of this period is the sculpture in the first caves of T'ien Lung Shan, in the center of Shansi Province, which was started about 560 and continued under the Sui and the T'ang. The compositions are much more sober than those at Yün-Kang and Lung-mên, and there is not the same profusion of figures and decoration. The gods – trinities, in which the central figures are Sākyamuni, Maitreya, and Amitābha (Amita) – are carved in very high relief in the white sandstone cliffs. The robes still spread out symmetrically, like fins, beneath parallel pleated folds, but these are not so stiff, and the carving is deeper. The figures are not so angular but more softly rounded. The attitudes of the Bodhisattvas are more pliant, and no longer strictly frontal in relation to the Buddha. The air now seems to move between the folds of the scarves which surround them.

Indian influence is equally noticeable in a group of high relief carvings in white marble which come from Hopei Province (Plate 114). In these, the clothes cling closely to the figures, whilst narrow scarves twist round them, giving life to these massive statues. Rounded faces, supple hands and feet, make earthly mortals of these deities.

In the caves of Hsiang-t'ang Shan, on the borders of Honan and Hopei, there is another important group in which the handling of the human body is even freer. The poses are no longer stiff, and a kind of smiling strength pervades the figures. The walls are decorated with bas-reliefs, evocations of the Paradise of the Pure World, with the gardens of Eden which were part of the now popular cult of Amitābha. Two large reliefs from this same group are in the Freer Gallery in Washington. The decoration of flowers framing the gods is richly ornamental, a feature of many of the figures of the Bodhisattva which are adorned with numerous necklaces crossing and intertwining. The figure in gilded bronze on Plate 115, while still close to the later *stelae* of the Wei, is a good example of this dying traditional art. But the full face, rounded eyelids, soft hair, and human expression, clearly indicate the developments which have taken place (cf. Plate 116).

The statues of Bodhisattva in the University of Philadelphia have even more gorgeous jewelry. They are larger than life-size, with a majesty, dignity, and solemn serenity which are apparent only in masterpieces of religious art. A monk in the same Museum, an Amitābha in the Royal Ontario Museum of Toronto, and the Buddha of the Nezu Museum in Tōkyō, are all equally fine. The heavy drapery of their robes is intersected by fine relief fillets or light incisions, and these accentuate the falling folds of the Indian style. This beautifully balanced and moving art of the Northern Ch'i is a wonderful combination of sculptural inspiration and religious zeal. Far removed from the heavy languid styles and excesses which came later, it marks one of the finest moments of sculpture in China.

SCULPTURE UNDER THE SUI AND THE T'ANG DYNASTIES (589–906)

The short-lived Sui dynasty was represented by two men who devoted themselves to the re-unification of China, and to the restoration of her traditional cultural life, which had been completely disrupted by partitions and civil wars. They were very tolerant towards Buddhism, and undertook the completion of the work begun at Lung-mên and T'ien Lung Shan. They were also responsible for many of the rock sculptures of Shantung and Hopei. It is written in Chinese texts that a fabulous number of Buddhas was constructed at that period. The first Emperor, Wên Ti, alone, is said to have caused to be made more than 106,000 statues in varying materials.

Sui statuary is very different from that of the Wei, and there was now a clear reaction against the free, smooth Ch'i sculpture, and against the Indian influence it reflected. A rather cold rigidity characterizes the work of this period, but far too many pieces (in bronze, wood, and lacquer) have disappeared to allow absolute statements. The bodies tended to be huge blocks, often ovoid, and in no way reminiscent of the sweeping garments of the preceding period. The heads are also egg-shaped, and the faces square, with heavy chins. The immense Amitābha in the British Museum, in white marble from Hopei, appears like a kind of column. The dress is finely carved in pleats with prominent fillets, and enfolds the body without acknowledging its shape. The head, carried high on a stiff cylindrical neck, is almost a perfect oval, and the face is smooth and formal. The same may be said of the painted marble statues of Ānanda and Kāsyapa in the Guimet Museum. Their frozen simplicity and almost tubular shape contrast sharply with the tense art of the Wei, and with the mobile power which was to be the prerogative of the T'ang.

One model which is more expressive, while still retaining its simplicity, is the white marble Bodhisattva, 3 m. in height, in the National Museum at Tōkyō, naked but for the scarves and jewelry. Some of these calm, smooth faces express a serenity and sense of meditation which are accentuated by the seeming simplicity of the carving (Plate 118). Much more time has been devoted to some of the others, particularly those in the Polignac and Stoclet collections (Plate 118). Here, a special characteristic of the period can be seen in the double lines of the eyelids and the mouth. These two pieces also have carved tiaras which are said by Mizuno, the Japanese archaeologist, to represent the luxury of the immoral and dissolute Court of Yang Ti (605–618).

Parallel with this rather severe art there runs a developing taste for profuse ornament, for decoration which fills the niches and covers the balustrades and *stelae*, as well as the haloes and robes of the Bodhisattva. There is an abundance of roses and lotuses, acanthus leaves, garlands, and jewels. These *motifs* are even found on the gilded bronze figures, which were descendants of a very ancient line. The deities are loaded with heavy crowns and long interlaced necklaces adorned with flowers. The Buddhist altars (the most typical of these is in the Museum of Fine Arts, Boston, and dated 593) have an animated composition, in which the head of the Buddha stands out from a round halo, and the branches of the Sacred Tree form a kind of canopy. Some exceptional pieces, though, have kept the simple dignity and charm of the Ch'i statuary. One of them in the Guimet Museum, and the one illustrated on Plate 117 for example, have all the dignity of monumental sculpture, and are subtly radiant. They are the final expression of an art which has learned to use the dimensions whilst remaining loyal to the demands of the faith which was their inspiration.

T'ang sculpture is, in some ways, an outpouring of the developments which had been gathering and crystallizing since the end of the 6th century. Now the artists were to go far beyond the Ch'i and the Sui in their grasp of space and form, and in their attempts to depict the human form in movement, as well as in the customary immobile attitude.

After the reconquest of the territory by the genial Li Shih-min, the future Emperor T'ai Tsung "the Great," China embarked upon an epoch of proud grandeur in which research advanced on all sides. The renaissance was to last almost 150 years, and it was to be seen in every field of art. Prodigious military successes carried the empire into close contact with Western Asia; economic prosperity was the direct result of contacts with the foreigner; and religious fervor multiplied the Buddhist sects and instituted study and research on the sacred texts. It is also the Golden Age of poetry, philosophy, and painting.

Ch'angan was the Imperial capital. A cosmopolitan city of growing influence in the world, it plays the role, in the Far East, of ancient Rome in the Mediterranean. Ambassadors, traders, students, and missionaries poured into China from all parts of Asia. Here, all races converged; differing religions were accepted with rare and unusual tolerance. Luxury increased and the life of the Court in the 8th century was magnificent in the extreme. In the world of art vigor, child of a conquering era, was allied with curiosity in seeking new forms and exotic fashions. This will clearly be seen in the manner of the development of the ceramic art.

In the realm of sculpture renewed influence from India is apparent, inspired by the fresh contacts with Central Asia, and by returning Buddhist pilgrims who had piously made the long journey. Of these, the most famous was Hsüan-tsang, who stayed away for sixteen years, to return triumphant in 645. He brought back sacred books, and seven statues of Buddha in gold, silver, and sandalwood. They were venerable icons, obviously Gupta or post-Gupta, and were solemnly deposited in a specially constructed temple. These undoubtedly had an enormous influence on the development of Chinese figures.

Sculptural activity intensified after 650. These often dated works were intended for pagodas and monasteries which were constantly being erected, or were carved into the walls of rock temples. The work at Lung-mên, and in Shantung, was resumed early in the 7th century. At this time the figures were still the rigidly heavy and over-decorated statues inherited from the Wei. However, between 672 and 676 at Lung-mên, near to the cave of Fêng-hsien ssŭ, a more significant group, filled with new vision, was to be erected on the command of Wu-tsou tien, the all-powerful concubine of the Emperor, Kao Tsung. On a terrace, with its back to the rocks, the "Great Buddha" was raised – a giant figure 12 m. in height, undoubtedly representing Vāirōtchana, the primordial Buddha and manifestation of the Universal Essence. He is depicted in a sitting posture with legs folded. Behind his head is a delicately carved halo, chiseled in the rock, and, with him, two Bodhisattvas, two disciples, two Guardian Kings (*lokopāla*), and two Temple Guardians (*dvārapāla*). This is one of the most famous of all Chinese sculptured figures. "Superhuman, impassive... it transcends space and time, and, far above the world, looks beyond the level of human infirmity" (René Grousset). The face is full and softly modeled, and the perfectly proportioned body seems to breathe under the light garment covering it.

In the early part of the 8th century, both at Lung-mên and elsewhere, many figures and bas-reliefs bear witness to the progress made. There is a great variety of pose and freedom of movement, many nudes, and a more human, sometimes almost individual, character in the faces (Plate 121). Now, in most cases, the purely frontal approach has disappeared. The sculptors had mastered their art. This is clearly to be seen in the figures of the Temple of Pao Ch'ing at Ch'angan, now in American and Japanese museums, and even more in two headless white marble figures of Ling–yen Ssŭ (Shantung). A fine balance is achieved in these works (Boston Museum, Rockefeller Collection) between vigor and flexibility, the nude figure and the drapery, and they have an elegance and purity reminiscent of classic Greek art. A slightly flexed position of the leg accentuates the hip movement of the figure, inspired by the triple flexion of the rules of Indian iconography (*tribhanga*). One could mention many other statues of the same kind, all inspired by Indian esthetic theories, with naked breast scarcely covered by a floating veil (nudity is contrary to Chinese tradition), and the clothes draped on the hips to mold the legs in a symmetrical way, typical of an Indian *dhoti.*

Indian influence is even more remarkable in two groups of rock sculpture, the one quite recently discovered at P'ing-ling Ssŭ (1951) on a fine site on the upper reaches of the Yellow River in Kansu Province, and the other at T'ien Lung Shan in Honan, where the Wei had previously done some work (cf. p. 208). The carvings of the first of these groups are not dated, but a date between 650 and the early part of the 8th century seems tenable. The whole ensemble is intact, untouched, whereas the statues at T'ien Lung Shan, dated between 684 and 755, are, for the most part, lost. The style at P'ing Ling Ssŭ is massive and powerful. The figures stand out in very high relief from the rough face of the stone, and they are grouped in shallow undecorated niches, level with the rocks. The bodies are strongly carved, the faces broad and heavy. Indian-style draperies cling to the firm flesh. Some of the figures are in a frontal attitude, but the Bodhisattvas inclined in the *tribhanga* pose have an S-shape which is more accentuated here than in any other Chinese sculpture known today (vide William Willetts). The effect at T'ien Lung Shan is very different, for here the rock is a dense limestone, almost white in color. The Buddha and the Boddhisattva are graceful, gentle; sometimes standing, leaning, or seated in attitudes which are no longer ritual. The artist has worked with extreme sensitivity, and the figures are slim, a little effeminate, and only lightly veiled by the transparent material clinging to their limbs. But the culminating point of balance has now been passed, delicacy leans already towards softness, and opens the way for wilting decadence.

This, however, is only one aspect of T'ang sculpture, and although undoubtedly one of the most fascinating, it still remains an exception. The influence of India was an episode. The essential Chinese character lies in the attempt to portray a living being seen in attitudes which are no longer strictly frontal, but moving in three-dimensional space. More than the art of any other period, that of the 7th and 8th centuries imposed its Chinese character on assimilated foreign influences. No T'ang figure could possibly be confused with one from India, Central Asia, or even Japan where Chinese art did, indeed, have a strong influence. Solidity and power, a kind of complacent aloofness, can be seen in the faces and attitudes; there is an exuberance in the carving which was soon to degenerate into bombast and excess. These characteristics gave new life to the strong ancient traditions, in spite of the marked leanings towards greater reality.

It is, however, less in Buddhist art than in the tomb-figures and animals that tradition continues. The finest point is reached in the tomb of Tai Tsung, who died in 649, at Chao-ling in Shensi Province. Six huge bas-reliefs decorated the tomb, which was ordered by the Emperor in 637. Two of these are now in the University Museum at Philadelphia. Each one is a portrait of a favorite charger belonging to this famous horseman. They are true likenesses, attributed by tradition to the hand of the great painter, Yen-li Pên. Even the names of the horses are known, since they took part in the triumphal epic of their master. Some of them have been wounded by enemy arrows, and their attitude is full of pain and suffering. These powerful beasts, depicted in all their paces, are masterpieces of animal art, and are handled with close attention to anatomy. The carving has great breadth, and is vigorously realistic in the manner of the period, but this does not exclude precise and careful detail. Also in Shensi Province is the tomb of Chao-tsung, who died in 684. It is reached by a traditional funeral road flanked by carved animals. A particularly majestic figure is a winged horse, a descendant of the chimaerae of the Liang dynasty. The wings are wonderful curved scrolls, a linear conception derived from archaic decoration. Next to this are resting horses, and a huge bas-relief ostrich much less vital in comparison. In the figures beside the tomb of the Empress Wu Tsu T'ien (c. 700) this art is already becoming stiff and conventional, the lions are heavy and thickset, and the attendants dressed in rigidly pleated garments.

We must look elsewhere for life and movement; to the small figures in gilded bronze which seem to be the Buddhist cave sculpture come to life; or again, to the seated lions in stone or marble, of which there are two outstanding examples in the Guimet Museum. One of these, ravening its prey, bristles with impatience and ferocity.

It is, however, in the tomb figures, lineal descendants of the Han and the Wei, that this taste for vital expression is above all revealed. Aspects of daily life, and of life at the Court, are depicted, with all the freedom permitted by the material – fine ladies of the Imperial Court (Plate 133), musicians (Plate 134), and dancers; graceful little figures which show the T'ang ideal of beauty. Sometimes they are frail and slim, and sometimes of a noticeable plumpness which seems to have been fashionable in the time of Hsüan Tsung, perhaps because the favorite, Yang Kuei-fei, was herself a lady of no mean proportions. These courtesans are clothed in an astonishing variety of well-cut clothes, with a range of designs for collars, necklines, and sleeves, which can only be the reflection of refined and rapidly changing fashions. Even the hair styles are complicated, and heavily swathed. Also mirrored in this small world are all the foreigners who came to Town – Indians, Iranians, Tartars, Syrians, Jews, and Turks, each one pictured after his nationality and costume. But the favorite subject was undoubtedly animals, and, above all, the horse. Scarcely a museum or a collection is without one (Plates 130 and 131). Robust, muscular, and vital, they are portrayed in every pose – resting, rearing "*en piaffe*," or extended in the gallop. They often have riders, and these equestrian figures recall the military raids of a period of conquest, or even the games of the women riders, polo, for instance, which is said to have been the favorite pastime of Yang Kuei-fei.

Besides the horse, which is also to be seen in other materials, (Plate 125) we find the camel, a beast of immense importance to the Chinese on their long journeys; also the buffalo (Plate 172), and, more rarely, hounds, geese, and ducks. The figures are nearly always heightened with painting for a more realistic effect, and some have a shining glaze which adds to the splendor of the costume.

The finest period of T'ang sculpture, and, indeed, of all Chinese sculpture, ends in the middle of the 8th century. At that time threatening forces were gathering round the Empire. After the fall of Hsüan Tsung in 755, China lost her foreign possessions, which were gradually wrested from her by the Turks and Tibetans. Internal revolts followed one after another, bringing in their train an increasingly violent reaction against foreign religions. Systematic persecution of the Buddhists started in 845. The monasteries were closed, and 260,000 monks forced into secular life. Temples were partially destroyed and bronze figures sent to be melted down. Sculpture, already declining, was now deprived of its main source of inspiration, and it never recovered, even when the artistic climate became more favorable. The later T'ang works are almost without artistic interest; pale repetitions of themes which had lost their driving force, they too often sink into extravagance, affectation, and insignificance.

SCULPTURE UNDER THE SUNG AND THE LATER DYNASTIES

A very important monument follows immediately on the heels of T'ang art. This is the tomb of Wang Ch'ien, discovered in 1943 at Ch'êng-tu in Szechwan. He was one of the ephemeral Emperors who emerged during the political troubles at the end of the 9th century. The Emperor is depicted within a vast funeral chamber, seated in European fashion on a high stool. His face is very expressive, and recognizably bears the characteristics by which he is described in contemporary texts – deep-set eyes, long straight nose, and thin lips. His sarcophagus rests on a rectangular pedestal of carved stone, 7.45 m. in length. Decorative panels in bas-relief, ornate with peonies, garlands, and representations of the phoenix, demonstrate the use, on a large scale, of *motifs* used by the T'ang jewelers and metalworkers. They are pictorial rather than sculptural (cf. Plate 58). Alternating with these panels are smiling, roundfaced dancers and musicians in high relief. They move freely in supple garments recalling the terra cotta tomb figures. Twelve warriors besides, helmeted and in armor, are oddly represented half-buried in the ground and supporting the stone platform, their arms and hands tensed with effort. These are wonderful figures in the round, reminiscent of the Buddhist Lokopāla. Their faces are very individual, their stance varied, and they are filled with athletic vigor – a survival of the vitality and power of the finest periods of T'ang sculpture.

Comparable with this work are the guardian emperors of T'ai-yüan fu, in Shansi Province, made of cast iron and dated 1097. Also remarkable for the charm of the female figures, and for the floral decoration, is the platform supporting a huge Kuan Yin at Ch'êng-ting (Hopei Province), which was erected in 971, but is now very much mutilated. The figure itself is of ungainly proportions, and is in a mannered style – a return to the sculptural styles of the Wei and the Sui. This archaizing tendency is, moreover, one of the characteristics of early Sung figures.

The nomad tribes of Khitan or Liao (936–1122), and finally, the Chin Tartars (until 1234) whose rulers rapidly became completely Chinese, dominated Northern China, where Buddhist influence survived, and where the larger number of temples and figures were made. New work was started by the Liao at Yün-Kang, and restoration of the old was undertaken. The great Buddha and his companions in the 3rd cave, handled in the manner of the Sui, were accepted as genuinely of this period for many years. The same thing happens in the North, where the Hopei marbles are faithful to a tradition which was already very old, but which, in this case, showed some tendency towards a more exuberant decoration than formerly.

More and more, sculpture followed a path which led nearer to painting, and from there it was a short step to the almost complete abandonment of stone in favor of less recalcitrant materials – wood, clay, lacquer, and iron. This type of statuary is represented mainly by large wooden figures of Kuan Yin in a characteristic style which continues till the 14th century. The Bodhisattva Avalokiteshvara, and indeed the whole of the Buddhist pantheon, were, in principle, sexless, supposedly transcending such human differences; but in China the characteristics become more and more feminine, to turn finally into the goddess of Mercy, Kuan Yin, the compassionate – popular since Sung times.

In the 12th and 13th centuries she appears as a beautiful and mature woman, plump and passive. The walls of the temple were painted to encourage the illusion that these goddesses, with eyes of glass, were accessible living beings. Their bodies were half-nude, and adorned with knotted veils, which were pleated sharply with mannered folds, so as to suggest movement by the play of light among shadows. In their sinuous lines and flowing hair, there is a fluid, almost calligraphic effect, which is in direct opposition to the early Buddhist statuary. Almost, one could say, it is painting transposed into three dimensions.

Statues of this kind are very numerous. Examples can be seen in London, Amsterdam, and in the Guimet Museum, and a more important series in Toronto and Kansas City. Sometimes Kuan Yin is depicted standing, sometimes seated in a new ritual pose called "The Pose of Royal Relaxation" – the left leg hangs down, or rests upon a rock, the right is folded under, with the right hand resting on the knee (Plate 126). It is a position which offers opportunities for affectation and mannerism, but it is not without sculptural value in the balance created between the vertical figure and the opposing movement of the limbs.

The art of the Liao and the Chin can be seen in a famous series of *Lohan*, the disciples of Buddha, and of monks, in lacquer and glazed pottery. The seated figures of *Lohan* in the British Museum and various American Museums, are really striking portraits, with zealous faces, the modeling exhibiting a remarkable knowledge of the anatomy of the face and head. At the same time as the many moving dieces of sculpture, there are, too, the ceramic masterpieces in which there is a renaissance of the glistening colored glazes evolved by the T'ang.

After the 14th century Chinese sculpture degenerates into lifelessness, with an obvious falling off in technique. Faces grow flat, and draperies harden into parallel pleats. This is the type of the Ming dignitary, of Confucian origin, made in cast iron. They are stereotyped figures, sometimes almost caricatures, used to flank the funeral alleys of the Imperial tombs.

The Ming and Ch'ing dynasties are remarkable for the restoration of Buddhist temples and innumerable figures. Statuary grows more and more lifeless, probably following the decadence in the Buddhist cult, which, from the end of the 13th century, was contaminated by Lamaism from Tibet. With this came a rigid, complex iconography drawn from Nepalese sculpture which finally suffocated all Chinese inspiration. From now onwards there was to be no more sculpture on a grand, a national scale. The plastic arts took refuge in the decoration of the Imperial Palaces, or in minor works in jade (Plate 90), wood, or ivory, and here the work of the sensitive artist could still be seen in surviving traditional themes.   *D.L.–G.*

91. POTTERY FIGURE OF A MAN
PERIOD OF THE THREE KINGDOMS (220–265)

H. 58 cm. Collection H.E. & Mme H. Hoppenot, Paris

Very strong realism has been allied with simplicity to produce this fine figure. The face, much more expressive than is usual with tomb figures, is sad and reflective. He seems to be a servant carrying a ritual vessel, or some emblem, in his hands. He is perhaps dressed in mourning – a tunic of coarse dyed cloth, hempen belt, a headband of the same material, and shoes of straw. If this is so, then the slight flexing of the knees to be seen under the tunic could be explained by his leaning on a funeral staff clasped between his hands. The piece, which should be envisaged among many similar figures, suggests participation in the mourning ritual as it is described in the *Li chi,* the "Record of Rites," which explains the ceremonies in detail.

This example of social life, classified according to Confucian principles, tempts one to suggest the existence of a "Confucian" art, though really it cannot be said to have existed as such.

The gray pottery still bears traces of painting.

92. CAPARISONED AND SADDLED HORSE
WEI DYNASTY. EARLY 6TH CENTURY B.C.

H. 22.7 cm. Musée Guimet, Paris (Michel Calmann Bequest)

This painted gray pottery tomb figure is a very fine piece. The horse is saddled and almost completely covered with armor (or a saddle-cloth?) which is decorated with swan-like *motifs*. A rigid mask ornamented with relief flowers covers the head and neck. Painted tassels hang from the trappings. The stocky aspect of the horse and harness give it a stiff and solemn air which contrasts sharply with the free handling of the horses of the T'ang period.

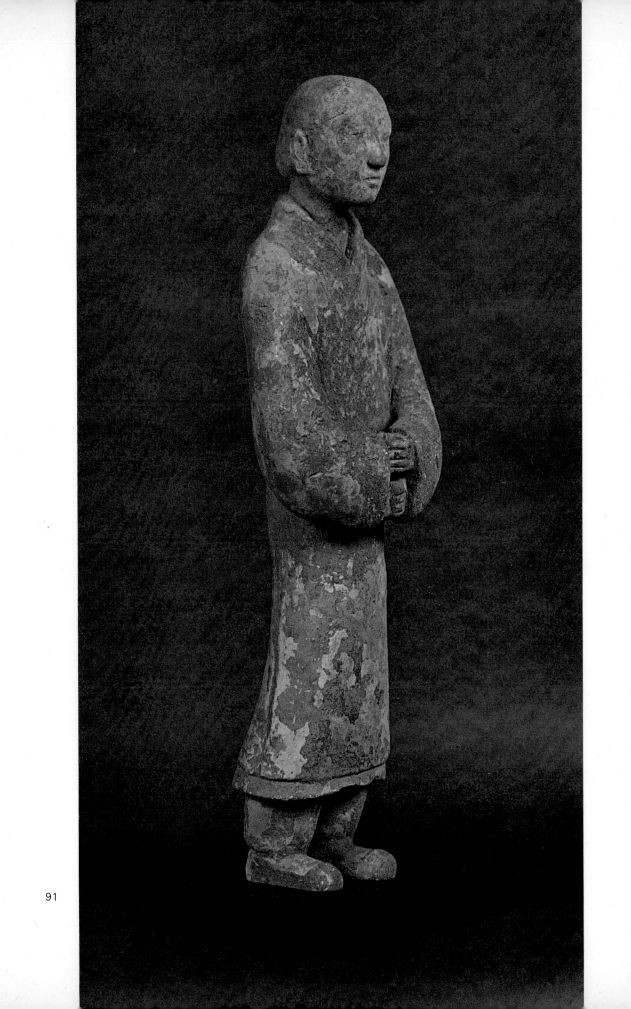

91

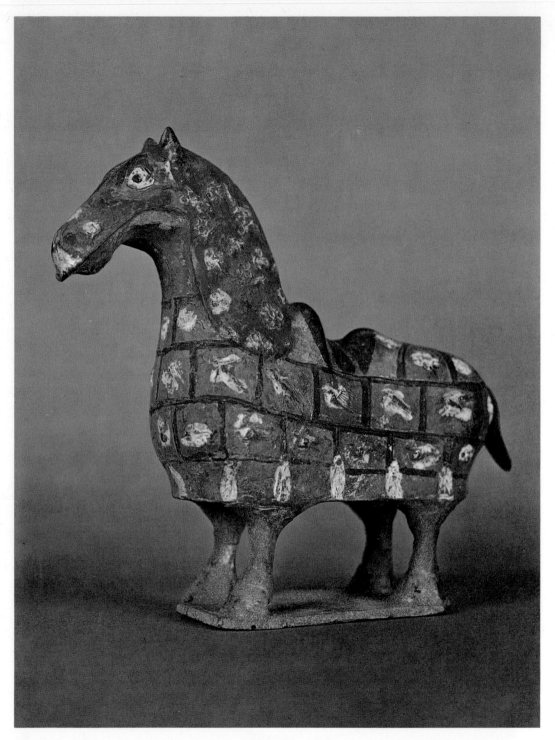

92

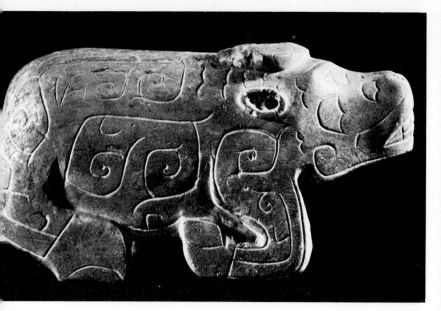

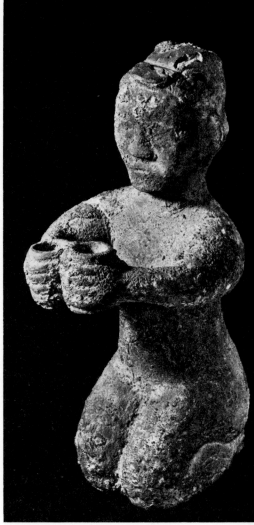

93. WHITE MARBLE BUFFALO. SHANG DYNASTY
AN-YANG PERIOD (1300–1028 B.C.)

L. 21 cm. Formerly Collection Mrs. Walter Sedgwick, London

This small marble piece carved in the round was found about
1930 with other carved pieces, ritual vessels, and richly decorated weapons, in the royal tombs at An-Yang. They brought
to light the existence of a hitherto undreamt of primitive plastic
art, which is closely related to other forms of Shang art.

Although the shape of the beast is only suggested in the
stone, the sculptor has successfully transmitted, an impression of its weight and strength. The position and general proportions of the buffalo, its placid expression, the ears and horns
carved in relief, all exemplify the artist's power of observation.
The surface is covered with engraved *motifs* recalling those on
contemporary bronzes (*k'uei* dragons, spiral hooks, and shields),
and these are skillfully contrived to underline the details – the
muzzle, the turn of the foot and shoulder.

Exhibition: Chinese Art, *London, 1935/6, No. 268 A.*

94. KNEELING BRONZE FIGURE. END OF THE
CHOU DYNASTY. PERIOD OF THE WARRING
STATES (5TH–3RD CENTURIES B.C.)

H. 21 cm. Formerly Collection Pincket, Brussels

We only know a few examples of this type of bronze figure
which was found in the tombs of Chin Ts'un in Honan Province. They are probably the first of the funerary figures, which
were to throng the tombs of the Han and later dynasties.
Originally it was probably a question of providing substitutes
for the humans sacrificed in the royal tombs, of which traces
have been found in the Shang tombs at An-Yang.

This interesting little figure of a kneeling man holds in his
hands two sockets, perhaps for flagstaffs or some other kind of
insignia, or, more likely, torches. The face, broad with high
cheek bones, has a short flat nose, and, as in other figures in
this group, is crowned with an elaborate headdress.

The bronze is very corroded, and has a fine green patina.
Similar pieces are in the Minneapolis Museum (U.S.A.) and in
the Royal Ontario Museum of Toronto (Canada).

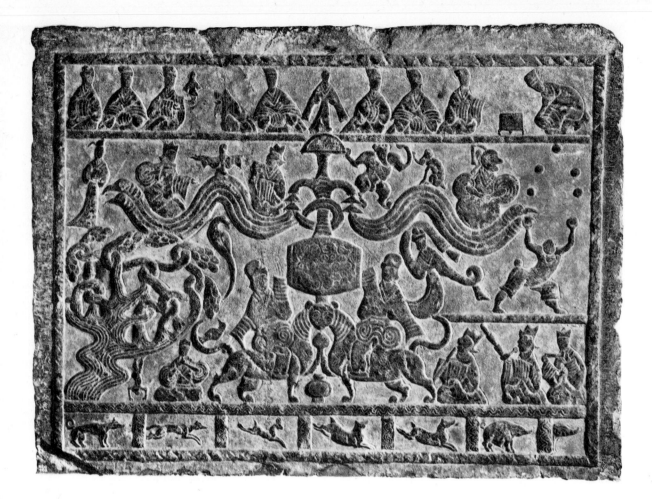

95. TOMBSTONE. PERIOD OF THE EASTERN HAN (A.D. 26–220)

L.118 cm. H.88 cm. Collection von der Heydt, Rietberg Museum, Zurich

This wonderful carved stone is one of the finest known, and it is a good example of the art of bas-relief which is so typical of the Han. Its date corresponds to 114 A.D. and below it is carved in a brownish marble-like limestone. The decoration is in light relief, accentuated by engraving. It is full of the lively fantasy and animation encountered everywhere in Han art.

The large central theme has two narrow borders. The upper frieze has several seated figures, a standing man between them, and, on the extreme right, a man kneeling before a tripod. The third person from the left is showing a child to a crouching chimaera.

The upper part of the central frieze has a large ax, sinuous serpents with birds' heads carrying men and animals on their backs, and on the left side a man standing at the serpents' heads. The serpents' tails seem to swirl round the ax, which is suspended above the two men beating a drum. These men are mounted on two griffon-like beasts with a single head. On the right there is a juggler, a dancer, and musicians: on the left, the magic tree has intertwining and twisted branches reminiscent of dragons. A bird sits on a branch, and another on the griffon on the left. They stress the presence of this beast which was sacred to funeral rites (cf. Plate 57). A small acrobat and a musician under the tree complete the composition.

The lower part has an animal frieze (wolf, hare, boar, and the like) framed, and handled in the clear dashing style of the Han.

150

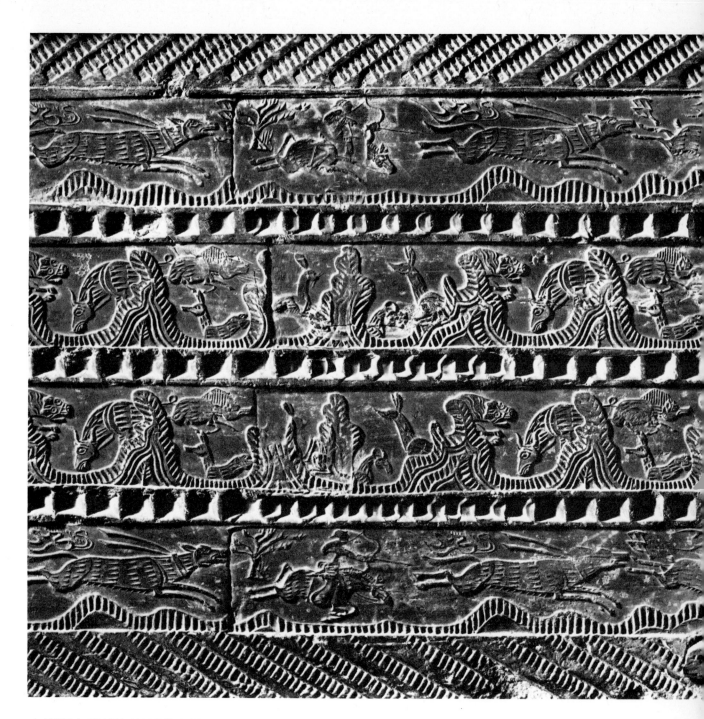

96. TERRA COTTA TOMBSTONE
HAN DYNASTY. (206 B.C.–220 A.D.)

L. 34 cm. H. 30 cm. Formerly Collection Pincket, Brussels

Engraved bricks, such as this one, lined the funeral chambers of the Han tombs, notably in Szechwan. They are related to the carved tombstones of Shantung, and have the same type of decoration. Repetition of *motifs* shows that the pattern was imprinted in plastic clay by means of molds before firing.

On two of the friezes a hunting scene is depicted in which an archer, riding a galloping horse, is about to shoot his arrow. He is close on the heels of his hound, which is hunting a wildly coursing deer. On the other friezes animals wander freely; a tiger surprises a drinking buffalo, a deer is on the watch, and there are hares and a running bear.

The life and movement in these scenes, the vivid realism achieved by a rapid stripcartoon technique, are characteristic of Han art which was always executed with prodigious *élan*. For the first time appear tentative impressions of landscape: rocks and trees which put the animals into perspective.

151

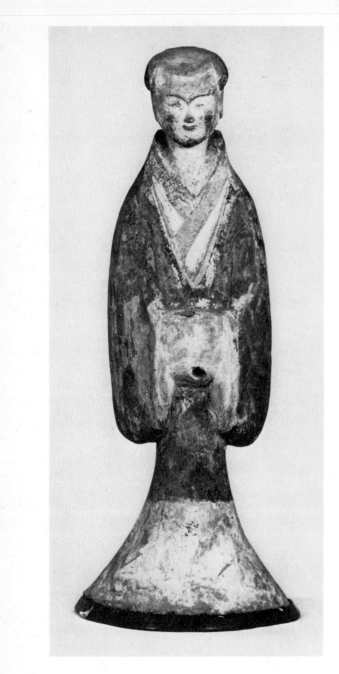

97. POTTERY FIGURE OF A SERVANT
CHIN DYNASTY. C. 300 A.D.

H. 74 cm. Musée Guimet, Paris (Michel Calmann Bequest)

This unusually large statue is still very close in style to some of the Han tomb figures. It has the same stylized dress with symmetrical sleeves, which hides the body and flares out at the foot into a kind of pedestal. It is only the fine modeling of the face, framed by smooth hair, which indicates an attribution to a later date. The body leans slightly forward. The attitude, entirely frontal, is well-balanced and elegant. The joined hands are only just seen protruding from the sleeves, and they seem to be holding an object – perhaps an insignia, which was fastened into holes above and below.
The gray body is painted in a brick red and white.

Exhibition: Arts de la Chine Ancienne, *Musée de l'Orangerie, Paris, 1937, No. 298.*

98. FIGURE OF A WOMAN. PERIOD OF THE
THREE KINGDOMS (220–265 A.D.) OR
EARLY CHIN DYNASTY 265–420 (A.D.)

H. 46 cm. Private Collection

This attractive terra cotta figure is full of character. In contrast to the foregoing plate she is depicted in graceful movement, and may perhaps be a dancer. Her outstretched arms swing out the deep voluminous sleeves. She wears a scarf in the neck of her dress, which broadens at the foot into a sweeping line so as just to uncover the tips of her toes.

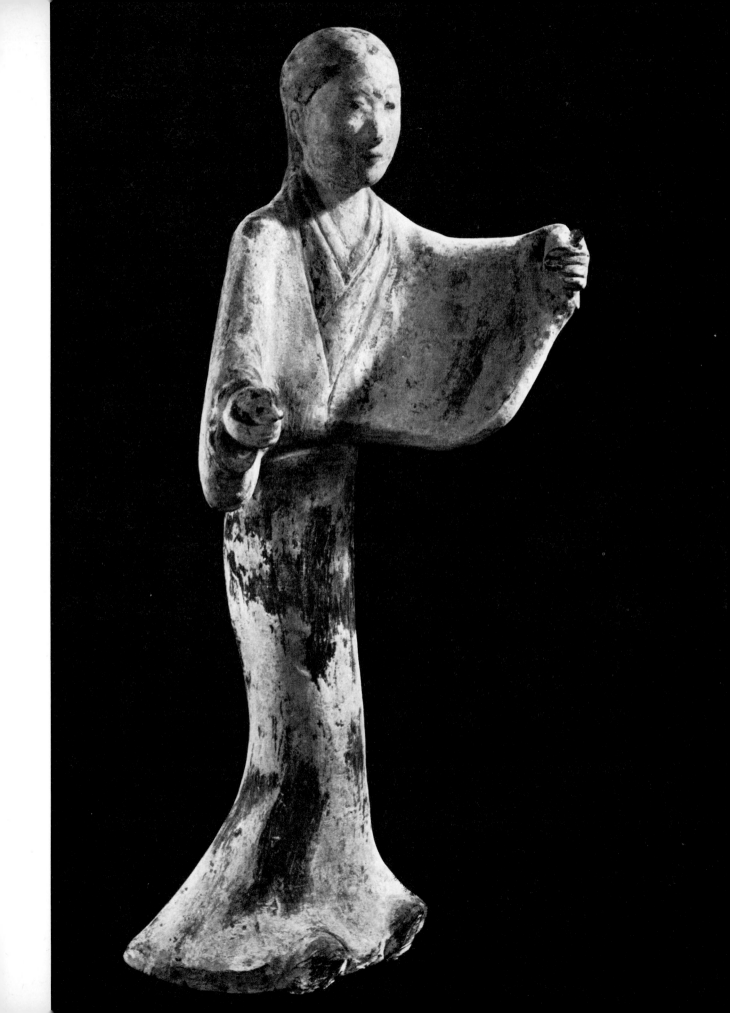

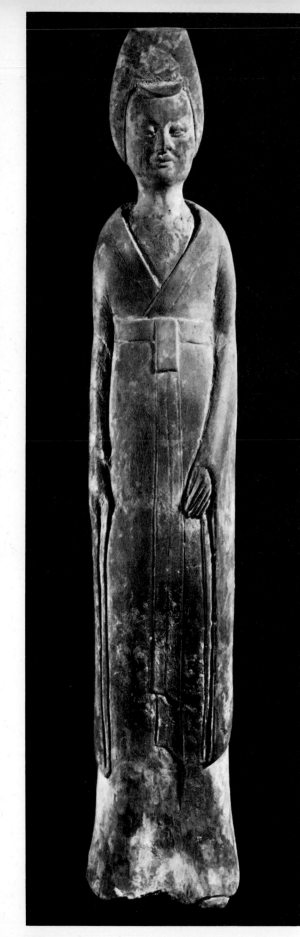

99. TERRA–COTTA TOMB FIGURE
NORTHERN WEI DYNASTY (398–534)

H.63 cm. Private Collection

This very elongated figure, dressed in a stiff straight-pleated gown, has a fine perceptive face and simple pose, which enable us to attribute it to the tomb figures of the Wei period. This traditional attribution is based on the analogy with similar pieces in stone and bronze of the same period.

Both men and women wore this type of gown with a high belt, so it is difficult to determine which this may be. The tall, plain *coiffure* agrees with that of some of the Court dignitaries, but one also sees it on figures which are clearly feminine. The fine features, however, seem to indicate that this figure is of a woman. It is certainly very attractive.

The hard dark gray body was originally decorated with colored pigment.

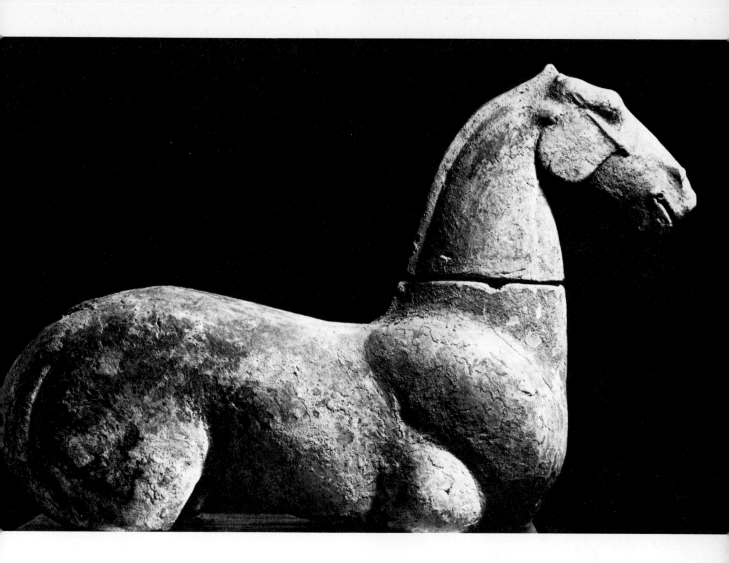

100. POTTERY HORSE. EASTERN HAN DYNASTY, OR PERIOD OF THE THREE KINGDOMS

L. 47 cm. Collection Dr. Schotte, Ghent

Terra cotta horses of this kind were mounted on legs of wood which have disappeared entirely (except for some found in Korea), and the body was in two parts held together by a tenon.

This horse has a finely nervous head. The artist has stressed the prominent features – the jaw, the eye, and the trembling nostrils. The mane is indicated by a simple ridge. The modeling of the animal's body skillfully portrays its powerful chest and supple spine. The artist has taken great pains to express the nobility of his subject.

This one is obviously a Bactrian pony, descended from the Perso-Arab horses brought to China in large numbers from Eastern Turkestan to serve as mounts for the cavalry.

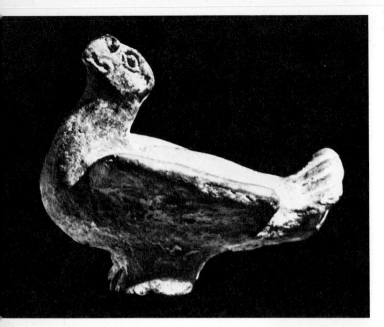

101. POTTERY EAGLE. EASTERN HAN DYNASTY
OR PERIOD OF THE THREE KINGDOMS (26–265)

L.11 cm. H.8.5 cm. (Enlarged). Private Collection, Paris

The artist who modeled this fine eagle sought to bring out only
the essentials: those qualities which would best illustrate its
strength and pride – the lifted, half-turned head, the staring
eye, and the wings, lifted and ready for flight. It is an acute
piece of observation.

The grayish-black body was covered with a green lead glaze.
Some slight iridescence, due to long burial, can be seen on the
body of the bird.

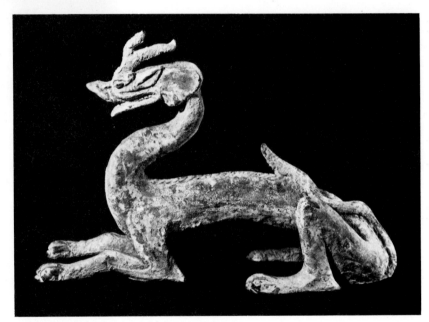

102. POTTERY DRAGON. DYNASTY OF THE
NORTHERN WEI (398–534)

L.25.4 cm. Collection Mrs. Walter Sedgwick, London

This piece, a descendant of the ancient dragons of the period
of the Warring States, is sculpturally very fine. The powerful
yet supple curves illustrate the skill of the Wei sculptors, whose
work is more defined and vibrant than that of the Han. In
company with other contemporary tomb figures, the details of
the decoration are outlined by engraving.

The body is of a brownish-gray, and traces of pigment remain.

Exhibition: Chinese Art, London, 1935/6, No. 2431.

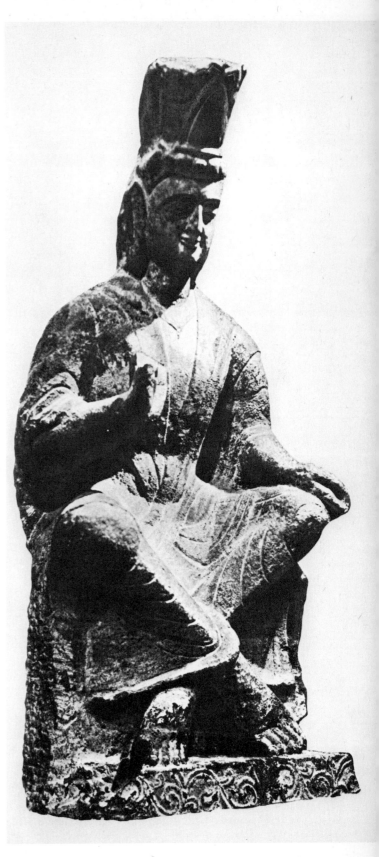

103. BODHISATTVA. PERIOD OF THE NORTHERN WEI. SECOND HALF OF THE 5TH CENTURY

H.130 cm. Cernuschi Museum, Paris (Donor Wannieck)

This fine statue comes from the wall of a cave at Yün-kang, and is carved in the gray sandstone of the cliffs where the Wei built their first great rock temple. The flat folds of the robe are in the Graeco-Buddhist tradition, molding the pliant curves of the body. Here is a very definite development compared with the five huge Buddhas of the first phase of Yün-kang sculpture. The scrolled leaves on the base are reminiscent of Hellenistic design.

The pose of the figure, seated "in the European manner" with crossed ankles, is by tradition that of Maitreya the Consoler, who will return to earth as the savior of mankind. This position illustrates the influence of Sassanian Persia. The right hand (which is much broken) is raised in the gesture of calm re-assurance, of fearlessness *(abhaya mudrā)*. The face, sensitive and serene, slightly smiling and with lowered eyes, is radiant with the gentle spirit which characterizes the most moving sculpture of Yün-kang.

A similar statue is in the Metropolitan Museum of Art, New York.

Exhibition: East-West, *Cernuschi Museum, Paris, 1958/9, No. 185.*

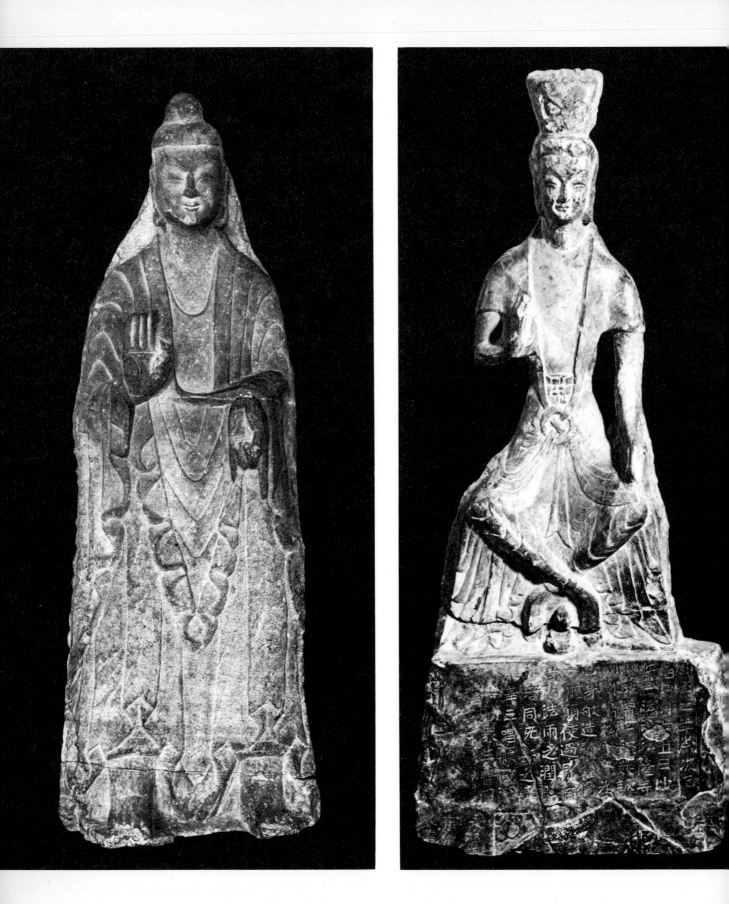

104. BUDDHA. PERIOD OF THE NORTHERN WEI SECOND HALF OF THE 5TH CENTURY

H.192 cm. Guimet Museum, Paris (Donor D. David-Weill)

The rounded style of the Wei, which predominates in the Buddhas of Yün-kang, can be seen in this gentle, almost dreaming figure. It is one of the finest pieces in the collections of the Guimet Museum, and probably comes from the sixteenth cave of Yün-kang.

The face is small and oval, the eyes half-closed – an expression characteristic of the mystic passivity of sculpture of the late 5th century. Rounded pleats terminate in scepter shapes, and the dress has conventional trimmings. It completely covers the figure. Only the hands can be seen – the right in the gesture of reassurance *(abhaya mudrā)*, the left in that of bestowal *(varada mudrā)*.

The clothes are traditionally monastic, without ornament of any kind. The protuberance on the head *(ushnisha)* is much accentuated, as are the long ears. This figure is not carved in the round, but in very high relief. A piece of the wall to which it was attached can be seen behind the shoulders.

Exhibition: Arts de la Chine Ancienne, *Orangerie Museum, Paris, 1937, No. 11.*

105. FIGURE OF A SEATED BODHISATTVA DYNASTY OF THE NORTHERN WEI (398–534)

H.66 cm. Private Collection

The beautiful figure on this plate comes from Lung-mên, most probably from the cave of Kuyang Tung which is one of the earliest, having been started sometime after 508. Both the grayish-black limestone, and the tense style of the artist, are very characteristic.

This Maitreya is in the traditional attitude, seated in the European manner with ankles crossed. The body is slightly elongated and the waist very small, while the face, lit by a secret smile, has a detached spiritual expression. A high tiara accentuates the length of the figure. The draperies are handled in a way characteristic of the late 5th and early 6th centuries. A veil covers the shoulders like a shawl, and falls in ribbons, crosswise, through a ring below the waist. The sharp pleats of the robe mold the legs in a rather arbitrary fashion, ending in points and *ruches*. It spreads out and completely covers the throne. The work has a special fascination. The hieratic angular style, and a certain mannerism, are very typical of the art of Lung-mên in its early stages.

106. BUDDHA WITH NIMBUS IN LIMESTONE C.550

H.164 cm. Museum für Kunsthandwerk, Frankfort on the Main

This beautiful blackish-gray limestone *stele* is of exceptional quality, and is also an admirable illustration of the transition between the style of the Wei and that of the Northern Ch'i.

The Buddha, Sākyamuni, is depicted standing. The mutilated hands must have been in the gestures of *abhaya mudrā* and *varada mudrā* (cf. Plate 104). His monastic robe is in regular pleats which fall in symmetrical ruching in the manner of the Wei, but they are handled more broadly and flexibly than the angular style of the early 6th century. The foreshortening of the figure, round face, and the impression of solid grandeur made by the whole piece, are very near to the art of the Northern Ch'i.

The nimbus is completely covered with decorative incised work featuring the two Bodhisattvas, Sākyamuni's assistants, standing on a lotus. Around them flying *apsaras* and musicians converge on a Buddha seated on a throne. He is representative of the *Dhyani-Buddha*, the metaphysical Buddha of the past. The round halo is decorated with scrolls of lotus leaves, and at the top is the head of a dragon with gaping jaws.

107. FLYING *Apsaras*. DETAIL OF THE NIMBUS ON A BUDDHIST STONE STELE. DYNASTY OF THE NORTHERN WEI. EARLY 6TH CENTURY

Stele: H.205 cm. Detail: H.23 cm. (Enlarged). Rietberg Museum, Zurich

This is an interesting detail from one of the fine stone Buddhist *stelae* now in the Rietberg Museum at Zurich. This section belongs to a nimbus which supports a standing Buddha assisted by two Bodhisattvas. All three are in high relief. The decoration is incised, and has eight compositions of the same type – persons seated in adoration, with flames and Buddhist symbols. Their animated style contrasts sharply with the hieratic principal figures.

This progeny of the *apsaras* of Indian iconography, seems to have halted in full flight to kneel, with joined hands, turned towards the Buddha in an attitude of respect and devotion.

The engraving has been done with an admirably sure hand. The pliant living body moves in perfect harmony with the flying veils and the folds of the robe. The blackish-gray limestone is related to the dark-colored rock of Lung-mên.

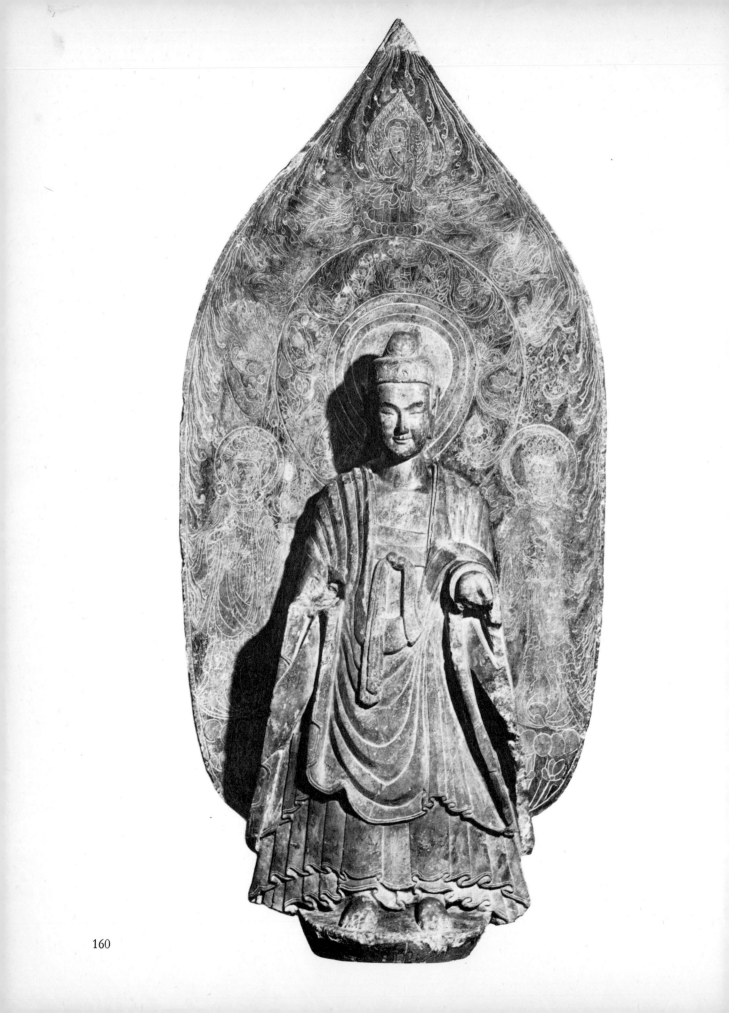

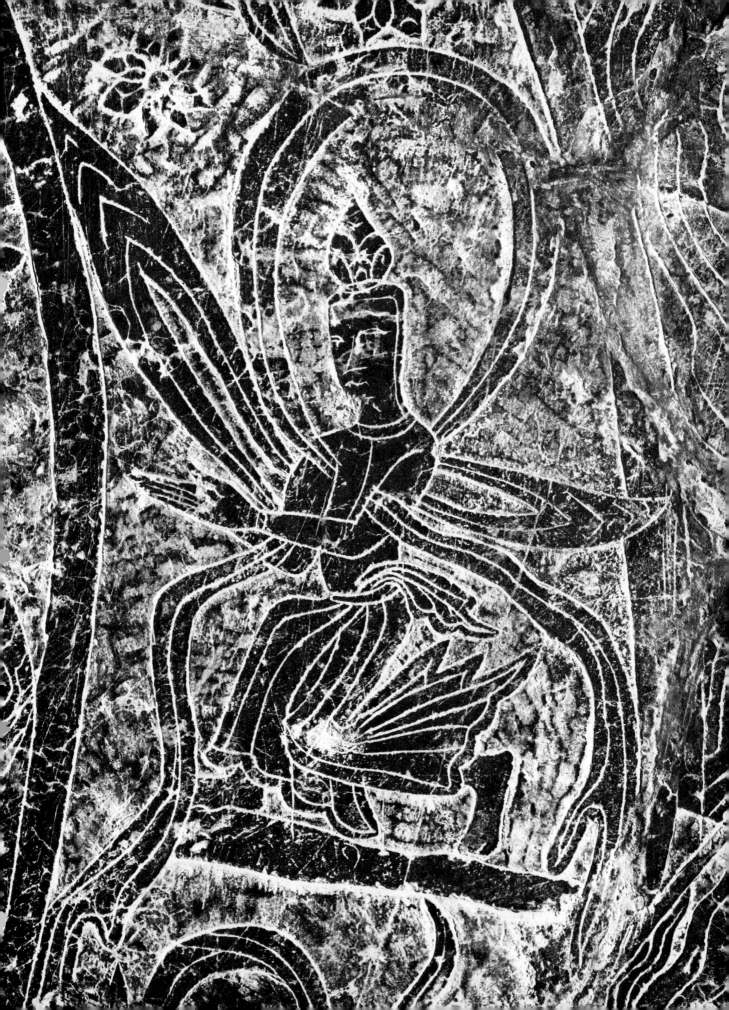

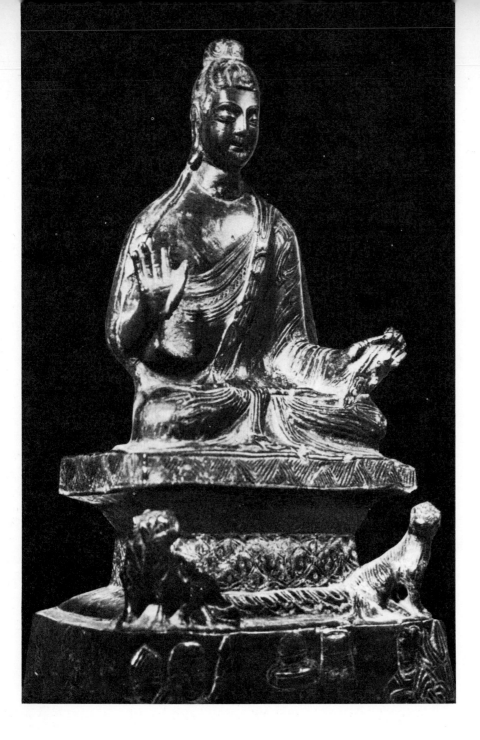

108. SEATED BUDDHA IN BRONZE
DYNASTY OF THE NORTHERN WEI (398–534)

Collection H.E.M.Giacinto Auriti, Rome

The bronze votive figures are the earliest dated Buddhist pieces known in China. This fine specimen clearly belongs to a group which is placed among the 5th century figures. It bears the date equivalent to 478.

The Buddha sits in the Indian position, the feet flat against the knees, and makes the gesture of the first predication. Originally the figure must have been supported by a huge pointed nimbus. The relationship with Graeco-Indian art is clearly to be seen in the face, which is still close to the Buddhas of Gandhāra. So, too, is the deeply waved hair. A most elegantly draped garment covers the body in facile pleats; the right hand and part of the torso are uncovered. It resembles some of the *stucco* Buddhas found in the caves of the Tarim valley in Chinese Turkestan, and especially those in Qyzyl. The same style and arrangement of pleats, in points on the left arm, is also to be seen on the huge Buddha in the twenty-second cave at Yün-kang.

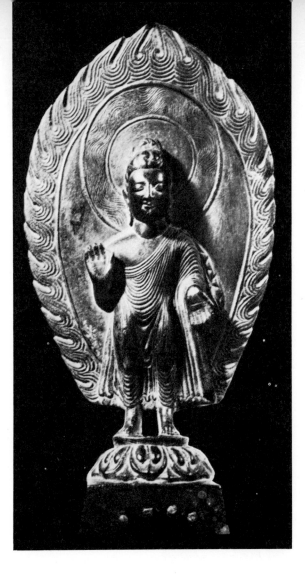

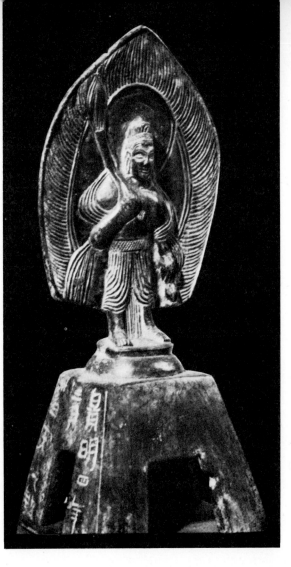

109. MAITREYA, THE BUDDHA-TO-COME
DYNASTY OF THE NORTHERN WEI (398–534)

H. 29 cm. Collection H. E. M. Giacinto Auriti, Rome

This small dark-colored bronze figure, which bears the date
444, is one of the earliest known dated pieces of the 5th century.
Maitreya, the Buddha-to-come, stands on a lotus flower, his
right hand raised in the gesture *abhaya mudrā* (which banishes
fear), and the left in the gesture of giving *(varada mudrā)*. He is
supported by a flaming nimbus, in the center of which is a
round halo incised with waving lines.

The face has obvious traces of Graeco-Buddhist art, whilst the
clothes, molding the limbs in parallel pleats in relief, are faintly
reminiscent of the Indian prototypes. However, the fore-
shortened figure, and the smiling face, betray a Chinese interpretation of a foreign model.

110. STANDING BODHISATTVA
DYNASTY OF THE NORTHERN WEI (398–534)

Collection H. E. M. Giacinto Auriti, Rome

The date on the base of this figure is 503, which prolongs a
whole group of bronze figures from the end of the 5th century
to the beginning of the 6th. The Bodhisattva carries what seems
to be either a thunderbolt or a fly-swat in the right hand and a
ritual vase in the left. The figure wears a kind of loincloth, one
end of which falls between the legs and is bound by a jeweled
belt. A long scarf is wound about his shoulders and arms.

The rather heavy style is a good example of the simple vigor
and slightly naive effect which is noted in some of the 5th
century work of Northern China by the Japanese archaeologist,
Seiichi Mizuno. The piece has certain analogies with Taoist
sculpture of the same period. The pointed nimbus has a halo
surrounding the head which is incised with parallel lines re-
placing the conventional flame *motif*. These accord well with
the treatment of the clothes, the hair, and the accessories.

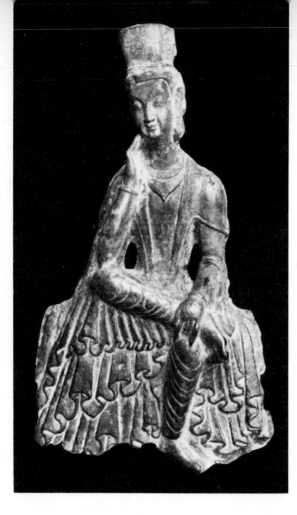

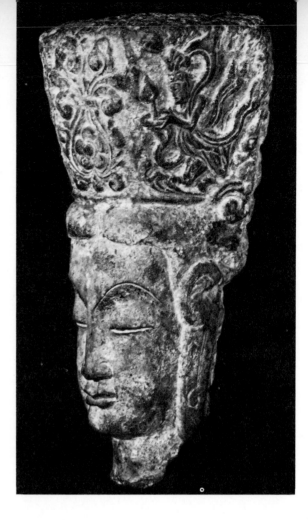

III. SEATED BODHISATTVA
DYNASTY OF THE NORTHERN WEI
EARLY 6TH CENTURY

H. 41 cm. Musée Guimet, Paris (Michel Calmann Bequest)

The Buddha, Avalokiteshvara, is seated in a position known as
the "Royal Relaxation" which is very characteristic of Kuan
Yin in the later periods (cf. Plate 126). Like the figure on Plate
105, this piece, carved in blackish-gray limestone, comes from
Lung-mên where it was situated in the cave of Lao-ch'un. By
analogy with dated carvings in the same style, it can be placed
to about 520.

The graceful charm of this figure is beyond mere words. The
remarkable skill of the sculptor confers a sense of harmony on
it by the almost geometrical equilibrium to be seen in the
position of the arms and legs. The contrast between the rich
folds of the skirt, and the simple upper part of the robe, is also
interesting. The ends of the pleats are ruched together to form
a "keyhole" or "ace of spades" design in the mannered style of
the early 6th century.

Exhibitions: Chinese Art, *London, 1935/6, No. 481.* – Arts de
la Chine Ancienne, *Orangerie Museum, Paris, 1937, No. 37.*

112. HEAD OF BODHISATTVA. DYNASTY OF THE
NORTHERN WEI. 6TH CENTURY

H. 30.5 cm. Musée Guimet, Paris (Mme J. Ramet Bequest)

This beautiful head of a Bodhisattva came from Lung-mên, but
the cave from which it was taken is not known.
The long face is noble and austere. The arched eyelids, and
half-closed eyes, the cleft chin, rolled *coiffure*, and tiara, are all
details which can be found on many of the Lung-mên sculptures (cf. Plates 105 and 111). The very restrained handling
well depicts the detachment of a supernatural being, in which
there is only spirituality. The definite modeling of the mouth
alone gives a human, a sensual and earthbound character to the
face.
The tiara is typical of those worn by figures at Lung-mên, but
this one is also decorated with bas-relief ornament finely incised. One can distinguish flying *apsaras* which carry incense
burners, and, in other parts, a floral *motif* perhaps representing
the lotus. The richness of this decoration, and the contrast thus
formed with the serene and calm face, makes a fine sculptural
effect.

Exhibition: Arts de la Chine Ancienne, *Orangerie Museum, Paris,
1937, No. 40.*

164

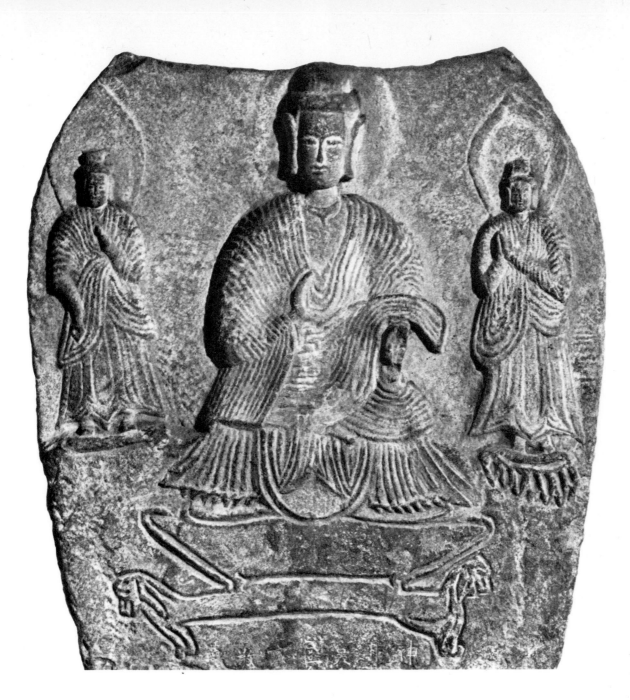

113. BUDDHIST TRINITY
DYNASTY OF THE NORTHERN WEI (398–534)

H.92 cm. Museum für Kunsthandwerk, Frankfort on the Main

This large *stele* bears an inscription which dates it to the period of Shên Kuei (518–526). The style is characteristic of other examples which are also of the early 6th century.

Carved in the soft gray limestone of Shansi Province, the style is rather crude. Although the subject represents the Buddha and two holy men, it is very close to similar Taoist *stelae,* which also represent a trinity. An example of a very similar *stele* is in the Museum of Far Eastern Art in Cologne. Probably the very slow spread of Buddhism in districts far from the religious centers was the cause of some confusion in the minds of the artists. Taoist imagery borrowed freely from Buddhist iconography at this period. We have indicated the connections between the two religions elsewhere; it is natural that they would make some impression on each other in the realm of art.

The group to which this *stele* belongs is notable for the rough background, and for the ingenuous character and summary handling of the composition. The relief is not very pronounced, and the regular parallel pleats give a crude corded effect. The engraving of the Buddha's throne, and the guardian lions, is touching in its spontaneous naïveté.

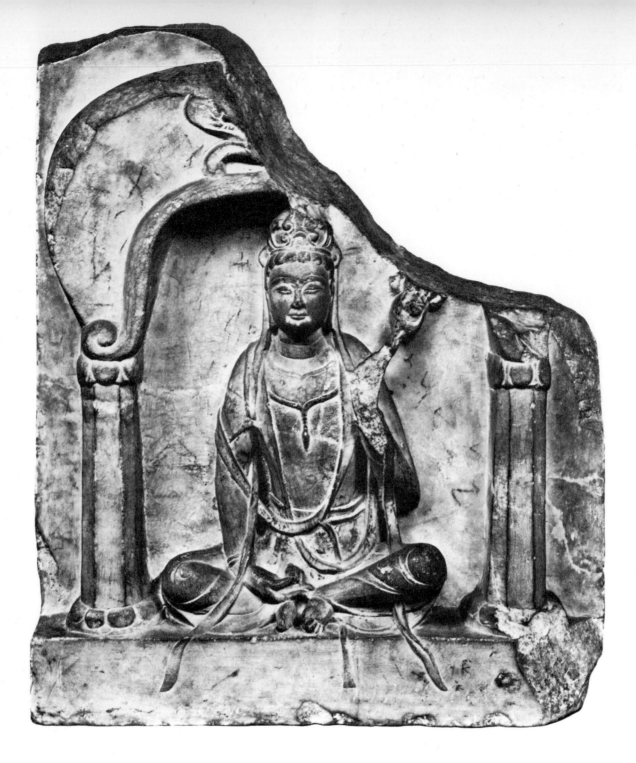

114. BUDDHIST STELE
DYNASTY OF THE NORTHERN WEI (550–577)

H. 53 cm. B. 46 cm. Private Collection, Paris

This piece can be recognized as one of a series in high relief
from Hopei by the beautiful micaceous marble in which it is
carved.

The Bodhisattva wears a tiara and is seated in a niche, framed
by a curving lintel supported on hexagonal columns. The bases
and capitals of these are decorated with lotus flowers.

The carving is facile and rounded, making a noble work of art.
A slight mutilation of the nose has changed the gentle expression of the face. The robes cling to the body in fluid lines,
and narrow loose scarves break the frontal impression. Both
hands and feet are handled in a lively, sensitive manner.

Indian influence is to be seen in the architecture of the niche,
and in the flow of the draperies. The work, however, is certainly Chinese; as much may be seen from the grave serenity
of the face and the roundness of the limbs.

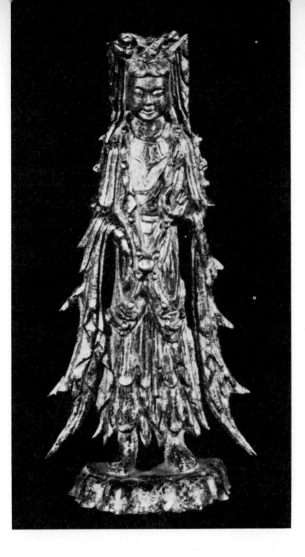

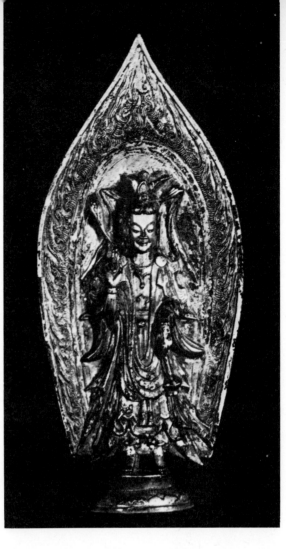

116. BUDDHIST STELE IN GILDED BRONZE
DYNASTY OF THE NORTHERN WEI
EARLY 6TH CENTURY

H.25.5 cm. Formerly Adolphe Stoclet Collection, Brussels

This precious little *stele*, bearing a date corresponding to 516 or 517 on the base, is a fine and very characteristic example of Buddhist art in the early 6th century.

The elongated face with high forehead has the famous "archaic" smile of the Wei. Attention is drawn to it by the flamboyant draperies which accentuate the serene expression. The piled hair is surmounted by a crown in the form of a lotus. The robes, the veil on the head, and double draped scarf, seem to move in the wind, spreading out in angular pleats which completely cover the body. The pointed nimbus makes a harmonius background to the figure. It has a very delicate decoration of incised flames.

The Bodhisattva, Avalokiteshvara, stands on a round base holding the ritual symbols, the lotus stem in the right hand, and the vessel containing the "Elixir of Life" *(amrita)* in the left.

Exhibitions: Chineesche Kunst, *Amsterdam, 1925, No. 87. –* Chinese Art, *London, 1935/6, No. 797.*

115. STANDING BODHISATTVA IN
GILDED BRONZE
DYNASTY OF THE NORTHERN CH'I (550–577)

H.22 cm. Formerly Collection Mme J.Ramet, Paris

Since both the halo and the base of this beautiful little figure have been lost, it is difficult to give an accurate date, but it probably belongs to the period of the Northern Ch'i, that is to say, about the middle of the 6th century. The face is broadly handled and has an expression full of charm, especially in the sensitive carving of the eyelids and the very human smile.

The body, elongated but with fine carriage, shows beneath the tightly folded and pointed pleats of the cloak. The Bodhisattva wears a long necklace which crosses beneath a heavy jewel. The feet are a little apart, with a slight flexing of the left leg. The figure is surrounded with pointed flying drapery formed by the falling veil from the head, and the long scarf passed over the forearm, though in a less exaggerated way than in the accompanying *stele*.

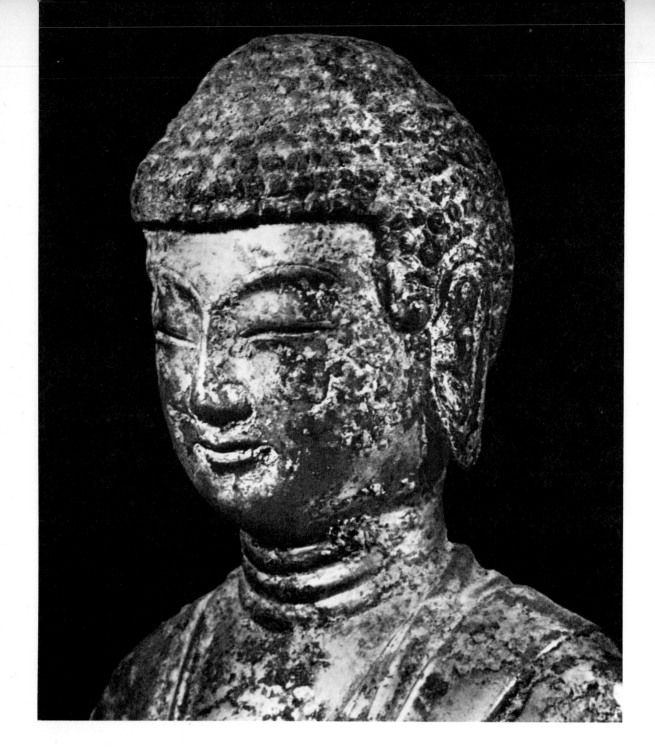

117. DETAIL OF A FIGURE OF BUDDHA IN
GILDED BRONZE. SUI DYNASTY (589–618)

Figure: 22 cm. Head 7 cm. (Enlarged).
Formerly Collection Jean Daridan, Paris

We have chosen to illustrate only the head of this little Buddha
the better to apprehend its exceptional beauty and perfection
of casting.

The work represents a standing Buddha, the right hand raised
in the gesture *abhaya mudrā,* and the left in *varada mudrā,* and it
may be said to be one of the finest pieces of all Chinese sculpture. In spite of its small size, the figure possesses a monumental grandeur.

The face is modeled with great feeling. It has an expression of
profound spirituality and gentleness, which is rare in the usually
rather rigid statuary of the Sui. It more nearly approaches the
charming dignified style which is typical of the Northern Ch'i
(c. 570–585). The tracing of the eyelid, and the triple roll on
the neck, are innovations of the Sui period.

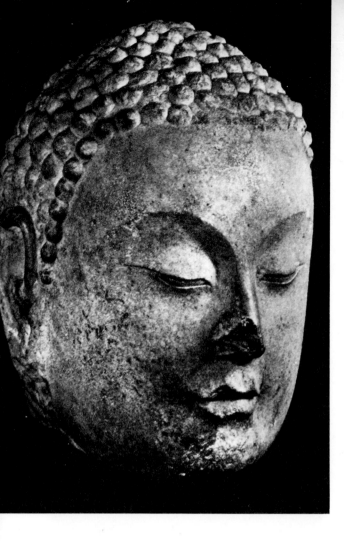

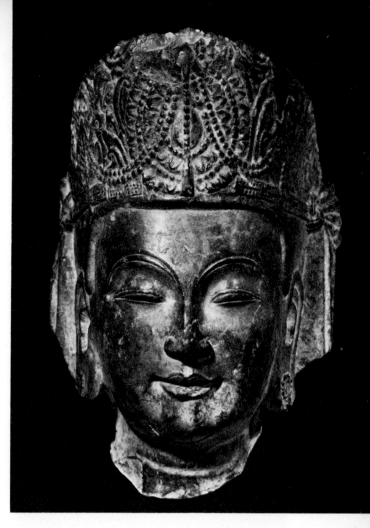

119. HEAD OF A BODHISATTVA. SUI DYNASTY
(589–618)

H. 36 cm. Collection Féron-Stoclet, Brussels

"A face full of distinction and dignity" were the words used
by René Grousset to describe this fine head. He also noted the
persistence, even until the 7th century, of the Greek profile,
which had been introduced into China with the Graeco-Buddhist
figures from Gandhāra. The serene spiritual expression of this
face is purely Chinese, however.

The carving is both firm and delicate, with subtle details, such
as the double line of the eyelids, eyebrows, and lips. The
features are already less rigid than in characteristic Sui sculpture, for we are now on the threshold of the T'ang period, at
the end of the reign of Yang Ti (605–618). The Japanese
archaeologist, Seiichi Mizuno, thinks that the richness of the
tiara, decorated with precious stones and strings of pearls, is a
reflection of the untold luxury enjoyed at the Court of this
Emperor. Precious stones can be seen on the long lobes of the
ears, which are now broken. The whole statue would certainly
have been thus adorned in the manner of the Bodhisattvas of
the period.

The stone is a fine dark brown limestone.

*Exhibitions: La découverte de l'Asie, Cernuschi Museum, Paris, 1954,
No. 98.*

118. HEAD OF BUDDHA IN WHITE MARBLE
DYNASTY OF THE NORTHERN CH'I OR SUI
(550–618)

H. 26 cm. Collection H. E. & Mme H. Hoppenot, Paris

The smooth carving of the face of this Buddha, facilitated by
the close-grained micaceous marble of Hopei, gives it a grave
dignity and serene detachment. The regular curls and Apollonic
features show a return to the Graeco-Buddhist style, but the
curving outline and radiant face are outstanding Chinese
characteristics.

Buddhist sculpture of the Northern Ch'i stands at one of the
finest moments of Chinese plastic art, and it often achieved the
technical mastery and harmony to be seen here.

However, some details, for instance the sinuous curve under
the eyelids, suggest that this work could be dated to the Sui
dynasty.

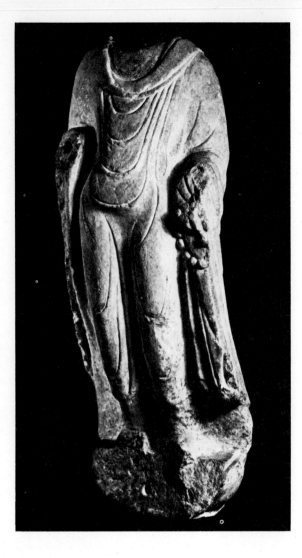

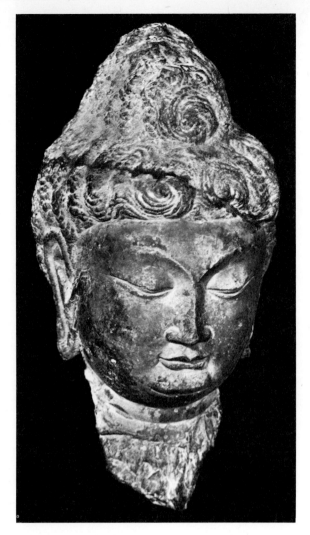

120. BUDDHIST FIGURE IN MARBLE
T'ANG DYNASTY (618–906)

H.42 cm. Collection M. Michel Beurdeley, Paris

Although this small figure is seriously damaged, it still retains its characteristically T'ang grace and dignity. It depicts a holy man holding a rosary in the left hand. Indian influence, which made a deep impression on T'ang art of the 7th and 8th centuries, is here very noticeable, especially in the curve of the hips. This gives an impression of flexible movement to the body. The robe hangs from the draped neckline, covering and accentuating the entire body. The falling pleats are indicated by concentric incisions – a traditional Chinese mannerism.

The figure, carved in fine white marble probably from Hopei, belongs to the Northern school of sculpture which had been responsible for many fine works in preceding periods.

121. HEAD OF BUDDHA
T'ANG DYNASTY. 7TH CENTURY

H.30 cm. Collection M. & Mme Léon Velluz, Paris

This fine head of Buddha comes from the caves at Lung-mên, and is a good illustration of early T'ang art in the 7th century. It wears an expression of devout meditation, and one is reminded that there was in the reign of Kao Tsung (650–683), and of the Empress Wu Tse Tien after him, a revival of religion and piety which stimulated Buddhist art enormously. Chinese statuary is here at its finest "classical" period, which was, however, to prove ephemeral.

The carving is firm yet free. The broad face is typical of the T'ang ideal of beauty, with curving outline and cleft chin. It is handled with clarity, and an individual, human approach which was to disappear in the following centuries and give place to an impersonal, almost degenerate heaviness.

122. *Dvārapāla* STANDING ON A ROCK
T'ANG DYNASTY. 7TH–8TH CENTURY

H. 190 cm. Guimet Museum, Paris (Donor D. David-Weill)

This threatening spirit, a Temple Guardian, comes from the
Cave of the Lion at Lung-mên, and is a fine example of one of
the most typical of T'ang subjects. Eyes starting from his head,
distorted, shouting mouth, and swinging hips which bulge with
tensed muscles all add to the ferocious concept of the *dvārapāla,*
ready to fight and destroy evil spirits.

T'ang realism is here seen at its height, but a leaning towards
the baroque is apparent in the dramatic force and twisted
rhythms. It points to the coming decadence in Chinese sculpture.

The figure is carved in fine gray-black limestone with yellow
streaks, and this has taken on a polish like marble.

Exhibition: Arts de la Chine Ancienne, *Orangerie Museum, Paris,
1937, No. 30.*

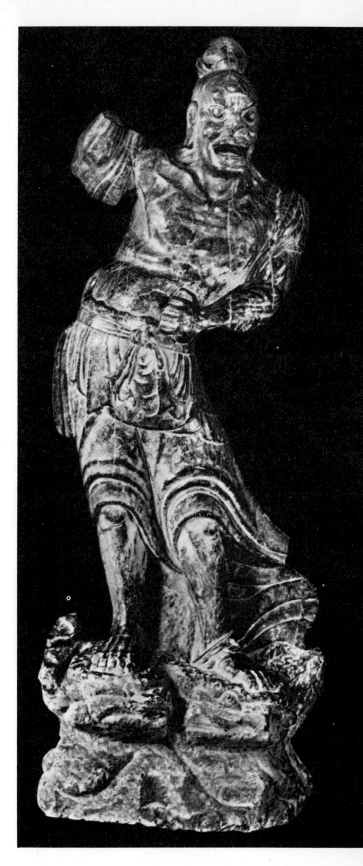

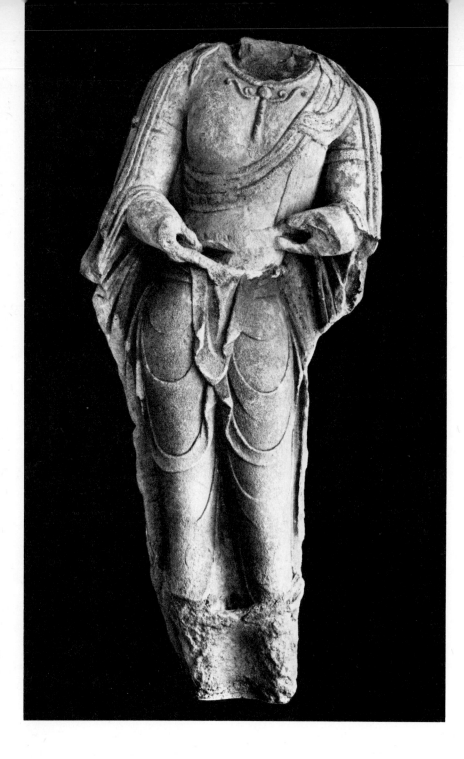

123. BODHISATTVA FROM T'IEN LUNG SHAN
T'ANG DYNASTY. EARLY 8TH CENTURY

H.95 cm. Museum of Far Eastern Art, Amsterdam

This figure is typical of the art of T'ien Lung Shan, and comes from Cave XIV, which is one of the most important of this famous site in Shansi Province. Two figures from the same group belong to the von der Heydt Collection, and a third is in the National Museum of Tōkyō.

Although much broken, this work is still a fine illustration of sensitive carving which sets out to express the graceful movement of the body. The naked torso, covered only by a knotted scarf, the robes clinging like a second skin, the light symmetrical pleats, and, most of all, the inclined position of the breast, are all clearly influenced by Gupta art, which was dominant in early T'ang sculpture.

The light colored sandstone still bears traces of red paint.

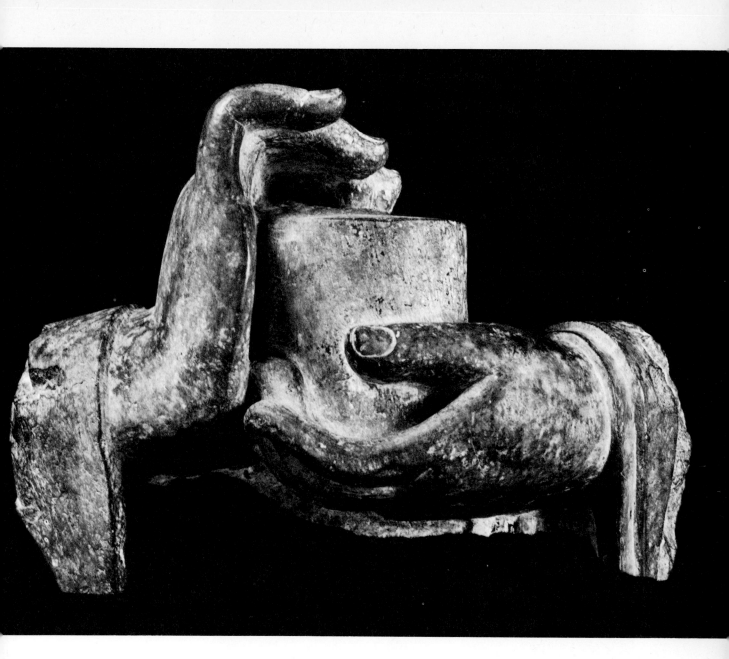

124. HANDS OF A BODHISATTVA
T'ANG DYNASTY. 7TH CENTURY

H.36 cm. B.50 cm. Formerly Collection K.L.Essayan

The size of this beautiful fragment, carved in grayish-black limestone, shows that the Bodhisattva was much more than life-size. The hands are carved with great strength and sensitivity. The gesture expresses meditation and religious awe. The hands hold the *sintāmani,* the Sacred Jewel "which fulfills all desires."

This is a fine piece of Chinese sculpture. Its beauty serves to stress what we have lost.

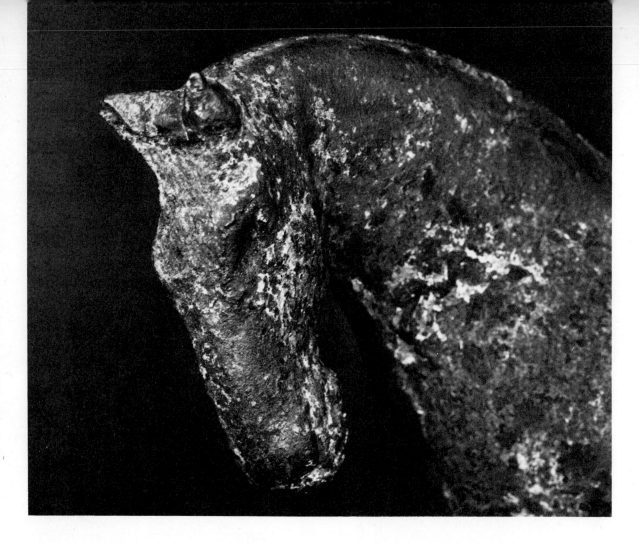

126. KUAN YIN IN GILDED BRONZE
SUNG DYNASTY (960–1276)

*H. 18.5 cm. (Enlarged). Museum of Eastern Art, Oxford
(Formerly in Sir Herbert Ingram's Collection)*

During the Sung period Avalokiteshvara, took on the female form of Kuan Yin, Goddess of Mercy and Compassion. Buddhist sculpture often depicts her in this pose – the "Royal Relaxation" *(mahārājalila)*. Usually she is seated on a rock which supports her left arm and leg, while the other arm rests on her right knee.

This beautiful figure is a replica of the large figures in wood which formed the greater part of the production of Northern China between the 11th and 12th centuries. Buddhist traditions were keenly upheld under the powerful barbarian Emperors of the Liao and the Chin, who had become completely Chinese.

The pose is free, but not lacking in dignity. The swirl of the scarves and belt, and the flowing hair, add life and movement to the figure. Characteristic mannerisms of the period can be seen in the conventional twist given to the ends of the scarves, and in the "pictorial" effect of the ornament.

Exhibitions: L'Art de la Chine des Song, *Cernuschi Museum, Paris, 1956, No. 8.* – The Arts of the Sung Dynasty, *Oriental Ceramic Society, London, 1960, No. 236.*

125. DETAIL FROM THE FIGURE OF A HORSE IN CAST IRON. T'ANG DYNASTY (618–906)

*L. 58 cm. H. 58 cm. H. of the head 20.5 cm.
Collection M. & Mme H. Halban, Paris*

The use of cast iron became fairly frequent at the end of the T'ang dynasty, and even more so under the Sung. Although iron does not lend itself to the same refinements as bronze, one has only to see this sensitive, powerful head to feel its quality as a sculptural medium. It recalls the proud stance of the terra cotta horses of the same period, and it is even probable that one of the pottery horses, so popular in the T'ang era, served as a model.

The rust, which has eaten into the material, only increases the impression of vigor in the piece. Traces of polychrome painting can be seen on the surface.

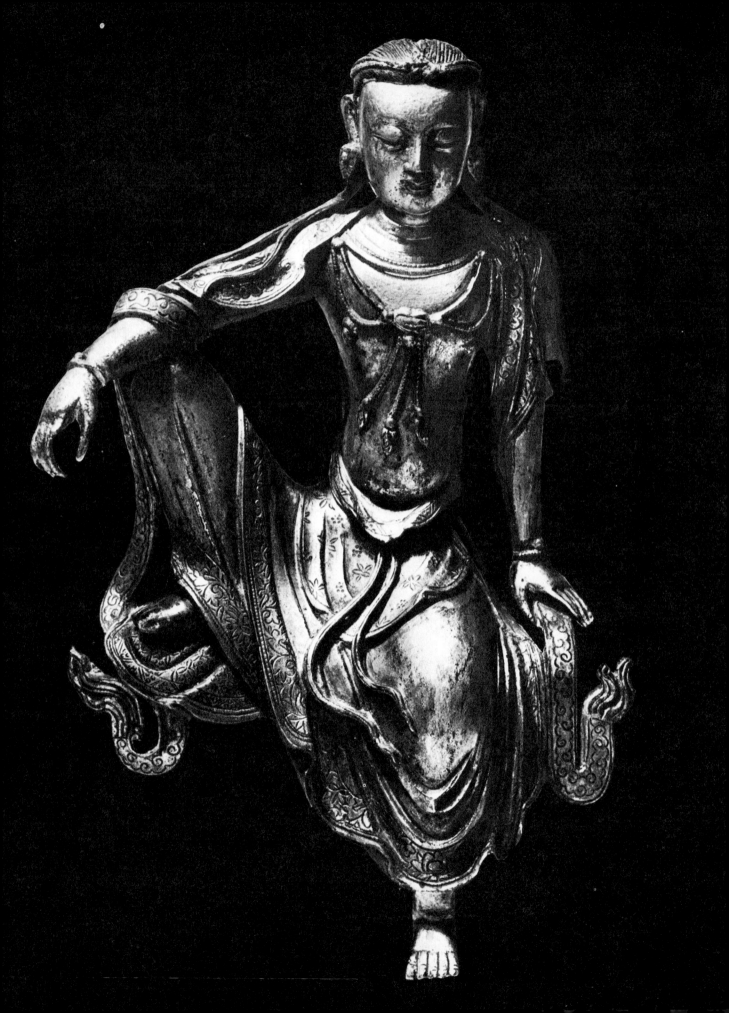

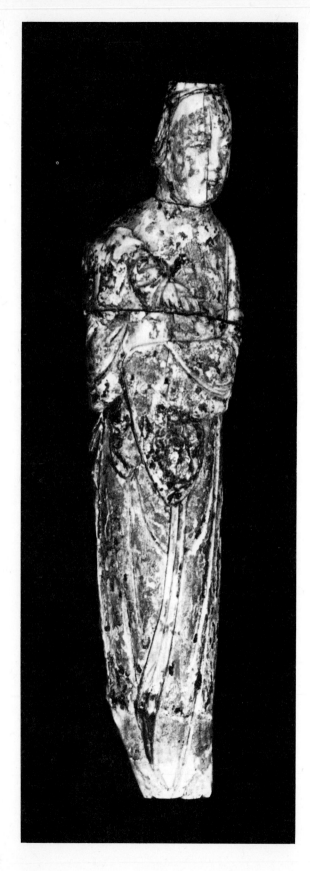

127. KUAN YIN IN IVORY
MING DYNASTY (1368–1644)

H.19 cm. Private Collection

Kuan Yin in this beautiful ivory figure is depicted in female form, carrying an infant in her arms. The Bodhisattva has now become a Protector of the Hearth, and Goddess of Childbirth. This belief was still valid not very long ago. People wanting children offered their prayers to Kuan Yin, and burned incense on her altar.

At a time when sculpture in bronze and stone had lost its vigor and creative force, it reappeared in works on a small scale, and often in precious materials. The best specimens are to be seen in ivory. The piece illustrated is sensitively and simply carved. Buddhist art has here abandoned its hieratic dignity, to take on this familiar (and now truly Chinese) aspect. The sculptor has known how to envisage an elegant shape in the form of his raw material.

The carving bears considerable traces of the original red and blue painting, which can be seen on the surface of the ivory.

CERAMICS

POTTERY AND porcelain in China show an incomparably greater diversity than any other branch of Chinese art. Even ignoring Neolithic pottery (2nd millenium, B.C.), and so putting aside an unbroken tradition of 3,000 years, we are still confronted with a prodigious variety of themes of form, of color, and of decoration. However, the unity of Chinese art is as evident in this field as elsewhere. It remains constant through successive metamorphoses, and this in spite of frequent borrowings from abroad, each of which, being quickly assimilated, soon became Chinese. This unity was born of a respect for tradition, of faith in an image, which, through years of groping experiment, remains loyal to certain fundamental concepts in an unbroken continuity to be seen in no other civilization. A leaning towards logic and simplicity, and towards quiet severity, gives a "classical" character to all Chinese ceramics, in contrast to the sometimes anarchic caprices and crude experiments to be found elsewhere. These exacting demands concern equally the form of a vase, the balance of a decoration, the harmony of color, and the transparency of a glaze, and, whatever the particular aspects and potentialities of a certain period may have been, they alone distinguish a Chinese piece, and enable it to be recognized as such at first sight. The whole civilized world marvels at such virtuosity: Chinese pottery and porcelain has been acclaimed by all ages since it first became known beyond the frontiers of China. Its fascination took hold of Japan, southeast Asia, the Near and the Middle East, from a very early date, and enthralled Europe from the 15th and 16th centuries onwards, when the urge to imitate was born and spread westward.

NEOLITHIC POTTERY

The early history dates from the 2nd millenium B.C., in the Neolithic Age, and reveals an agricultural people who already kept herds of domestic animals. The site at Yang-shao (Honan) where the Swedish scholar, J.G. Andersson, first discovered pottery painted with geometric *motifs*, has given its name to this primitive culture. Many funeral vases of vigorous form and more complex decoration have also been recovered from different burial grounds much farther east, in the Province of Kansu, at that time beyond the frontiers of China. At Pan-Shan the refined clay was baked to a high temperature: the decoration on the upper part is broadly painted in black and dark red on a light orange ground (Plate 166). The designs consist of interwoven spirals, triangles, undulating or indented lines, sometimes with trelliswork, with representations of cowrie shells, or even human figures, though these are very stylized. At Ma-Chang the technique is not so good. The clay is coarser, and the decoration, which has horizontal parallel lines, concentric circles, and meanders, is not so fine. It shows affinities with some of the geometric *motifs* which decorate the bronzes at the end of the Shang period, and also with the white pottery related to them. Later, at Hsien-tien, earthenware vessels of a different character with a very wide mouth are decorated with widely spaced hooks, scrolls, and zigzags.

The chronology of Neolithic pottery is controversial. A date of between 1900–1300 for Pan-Shan, and from 1300–1000 for Ma-Chang seems tenable. Its distant origins may, perhaps, be attributed to Western Asia, whence, starting from the high Iranian Plateaux, it may have spread towards Southern Russia and the basin of the Danube on the one hand, and towards the Far East on the other. Undoubtedly there is a real affinity between all the Neolithic products of the immense region of Euro-Asia. It was, however, in China that this pottery, majestic in form and balanced decoration, achieved perfection.

THE FIRST DYNASTIES

Painted pottery has an episodic quality, and seems unrelated to the real development of ceramic art in China. It continues alongside local and sometimes more skilled techniques. A varied and elaborate form of black pottery from a culture known as the "Lungshan" (Shantung Province), finely potted, with polished surface and incised decoration, has been found from Honan to Shantung.

A white earthenware was discovered at An-Yang, the capital of the last Shang Emperors, mat and engraved with meanders in the style of contemporary bronzes. Its use is a still unanswered riddle.

There did exist, however, everywhere in China a kind of domestic pottery dating from before the Neolithic period right up to the Christian era. It was of gray earthenware and fairly crude, decorated only with the so-called "mat markings," or with parallel lines traced with a "comb." It has no real artistic value, but it is historically interesting as a proof of the continuity of a primitive folk industry. Its main interest lies in the purely Chinese shapes, namely, the *ting* and *li* tripods, which are the forerunners of these shapes in bronze (cf. p. 16).

About the 5th and 6th centuries B.C., towards the end of the Chou dynasty, an important change took place. Progress had gradually been made with methods of firing, and, with the achievement of high temperatures, the first stoneware appeared. The body, fused and vitrified, was of a hardness hitherto unknown. The feldspathic glaze was fired at the same time as the body in the high-temperature kiln and is an integral part of it. It was a glaze originally produced, doubtless accidentally, by contact with burning wood ashes. So, whereas pottery, an essentially primitive industry, is common to the human race everywhere, stoneware, impervious as well as strong, is a purely Chinese invention. The first attempts appeared in widely scattered areas. They were the forerunners of the protoporcelain of the Han period, and heralded long years of evolution which culminated in the discovery of porcelain.

During the Han dynasty (206 B.C. to 220 A.D.) the two types of pottery developed side by side. The wares are sometimes gray, close-grained and hard; sometimes, however, a reddish-buff, which was enriched by a new technique – a lead glaze. This reduced the porosity of the body, and gave it a warm green or yellowish tone at the same time. The glaze is a thin skin on the surface of the objects, but it endows them, as the result of long years of burial, with a delicate gold or silver iridescence (Plate 167).

Han pottery was essentially funerary, and made up the complex trappings destined to accompany the dead into the hereafter. Vases of noble form, massive imitations of bronze vessels with relief masks holding imaginary handles, and often with a molded frieze depicting hunting scenes, have been found in tombs, with urns, cups, lamps, and candleholders. Among the furnishings one is confronted with realistic models of buildings and household objects, and figures of people representing the deceased's staff – maid – and manservants (Plate 97), acrobats, dancers, magicians – as well as domestic animals (Plate 172). These were called *ming ch'i*-objects made for burial with the dead. Flagstones, pillars, and bricks, all decorated with geometric designs, or animated shapes sometimes set in sketches of landscape (Plate 96), form the structure and background to the funeral chamber.

Stoneware was already a great step forward. The most characteristic examples are urns without a neck, and protoporcelain vases which already contained, in part, the *kaolin* which was to be an essential part of the porcelain to come. They are bold pieces, with a clear and vigorous outline. The upper part is decorated with fine incised hooks, stylized birds, or "combed" *motifs* in parallel borders. Over this a thin covering of olive colored glaze flows unevenly to end in heavy vitrified drops (Plate 169).

The first Yüeh stoneware also dates to the Han period, and many of the kiln sites have been uncovered in different places in the eastern Province of Chekiang. They are very varied in form, and often enormously complicated – bowls, huge waterpots with the head of a chicken for a lip, ewers in the shape of crouching lions, boxes, and lamps. The glaze is an improvement on that of protoporcelain. It is thick and regular, translucent, crackled, and colored pale green or olive, or a grayish hue, which foreshadows the celadons of the Sung dynasty.

The manufacture of Yüeh continued all through the long and confused era of the Six Dynasties which followed the downfall of the Han Emperors. Apart from Buddhism, the four hundred years of continuous anarchy which preceded the unification of China under, first, the Sui dynasty (581–618) and then the T'ang (618–906) may, by introducing new ideas, have played an important role in the history of sculpture, (cf. p. 203) but they brought no new discoveries in the realm of ceramics. The tradition of Han pottery continues with monochrome, often iridescent, glazes. Shapes, however, did evolve, and show greater variety. On the other hand, the tomb figures are quite different. Their body is hard, and of a somber gray, with very little glazing, while the characteristic style shows elongated silhouettes, thin faces, and linear treatment of the draperies, giving them a weird charm reminiscent of the stone sculpture and the bronzes of the Wei dynasty (Plate 99).

THE T'ANG DYNASTY

At the beginning of the T'ang dynasty (p. 210) there was an almost immediate renaissance, which is reflected in the thriving ceramic industry. A period impatient for progress, for luxury and the exotic, it manifests a vigor and vitality of form, a remarkable taste for polychrome, and the important achievement of technical perfection.

Pottery begins to be more widely used. Freed from the influence of bronze, the shapes become very varied – covered vases and vessels of pronounced ovoid form; long-necked bottles with cup-shaped mouths; ewers with cylindrical spouts; bowls, cosmetic boxes, and pilgrim bottles. There are many examples of Western inspiration: *amphorae* with long, arched, handles showing the influence of the Hellenistic world, ewers with birds' heads, lobed cups, and plates, copied from the silver of Sassanian Persia. They have broken and angular outlines, and the beveled base is flat and unglazed, revealing a pinkish-white body. The rebirth of the ceramic art is even more noticeable in the use of colors. The monochrome glazes of previous centuries give way to a range of fresh and brilliant colors, often mingled- or used side by side – transparent straw, amber, orange red, bright green, and deep blue, on a white slip ground, which enhances their brilliance. The liquid glazes are allowed to flow in uneven streams which blend in the kiln. Some plates give an impression of mosaic, where the colors are separated by incisions (Plate 128) – a new technique which led to the "three color" pottery of the Ming period. Ornament borrowed from the Mediterranean is often added to the colored decoration – palm leaves, roses, medallions, strings of pearls, and so forth, molded and applied in relief to the belly of the vase or ewer (Plate 173). Finally, there are some especially subtle developments, among them the "marbled" pottery, obtained by mixing black and white clay and then covering this with a transparent, or sometimes a colored, glaze (Plate 132).

Of all T'ang pottery, perhaps the tomb figures are the most charming. The outcome of a secular tradition, they show a characteristic freedom, a depth and sense of realism, which gives us a glimpse of Chinese life of the period (cf. Plate 130 and 133). They are modeled in clay painted with delicate unfired pigments, sometimes enlivened with gold (although, for the most part, only traces of this remain), or covered with the colored glazes found on useful wares.

T'ang pottery had a wide influence. Imitations appeared in Japan and Persia from the 8th and 9th centuries. On the other hand, the barbaric emperors of the Liao were ruling over the northern regions, on the borders of China and Manchuria, from 907 to 1126. Despite this, the T'ang techniques survived, though in pieces of rather specialized form, but still having the same glazes, particularly the green and yellow on a ground of white slip as in the earlier examples (Plate 136).

In the realm of stoneware decisive progress led to the discovery of porcelain. Stoneware, as we have seen, was produced by firing clay at such a high temperature as to cause fusion and vitrification throughout the body. Impervious, strong, and resonant, stoneware has a glistening appearance at the point of fracture. Some clays become white and translucent when they are fired at 1,380 degrees Centigrade. The paste is then like glass, and the surface is so hard that a steel file makes no impression on it. This is the traditional definition of porcelain. It is composed of a mixture of a feldspathic clay called *kaolin* with a fusible feldspathic rock, *petuntse*. These, melting in the kiln, fuse together, binding the particles of *kaolin* like cement. Both porcelain and stoneware are covered with a glaze which also has a feldspathic base and is fired at the same time as the body in the high temperature kiln.

The use of these basic materials in China was the result of years of groping experiment using the primitive stoneware as a jumping off point. The technique of kiln management, and of fuel combustion, was improving all the time, and by the end of the 8th or the beginning of the 9th century the craftsman's skill had evolved a material which was to have a brilliant future. It was not until the 18th century, however, that Europe, in spite of keen and unremitting efforts, at last discovered the secret of Chinese porcelain.

To be exact, the Chinese do not apply the term "porcelain" (*tz'u*) only to the white and translucent wares. They make a distinction between pottery (*t'ao*) on the one hand, and the hard vitrified bodies which give a clear ringing sound when struck on the other. There is a famous text of the 9th century which boasts of the bowls "white as snow" of Hsing Chou (Hopei Province). So far no one has discovered the site of the kilns where they were made. The Middle Eastern merchants who traded with China at the time were amazed at this near-miraculous substance, and sent cups and vases to the Middle and Near East which have come once more to light under the spade of the 20th century archaeologists.

Examples of white T'ang porcelain are generally not large; mostly wide mouthed bowls (Plate 175), lobed cups, and very small ewers, all showing great variation in the whiteness and perfection of the paste, as well as in the purity of their glazes. The Chinese of the period prized most highly the Yüeh wares of the 9th century, which they compared with jade – the highest praise. Yüeh, at the close of the T'ang dynasty, is incised under a grayish-green or greenish-olive glaze with decorations of lotus flowers or leaves, birds, or overlapping petals, which are both vigorous and elegant – sensitive harbingers of Sung (Plate 137). Some of the stoneware, splashed with lavender blue or with a black glaze, is, perhaps, a forerunner of *temmoku* and some of the black wares of Honan.

THE SUNG DYNASTY

The Sung dynasty is the "classical" period in the history of Chinese ceramics and some of the finest work of all time dates from this era. Pottery has, so to speak, disappeared and given place to stoneware and porcelain, and to all the intermediate stages in the development of the more or less porcellaneous wares resulting from the widely differing experiments which were carried out in scattered workshops over the whole of China. There is great variety and the classification is by no means uniform. Old Chinese texts refer to many groups, some reserved for the Court and others for more general use. It is impossible to identify them all, and the origin of many is guesswork – one can say definitely that certain pieces were made at great distances from others. In spite of uncertainties, however, it is still possible to classify a good many of the distinctive products, while admitting that many pieces are still problematical.

The history of the Sung dynasty is divided in 1127 by the invasion of the Chin barbarians, who drove the Imperial Court away from K'ai-fêng, the Northern capital, to take refuge at Hangchow, in Chekiang Province. From that date China was isolated within her borders and cut off from outside influences. The new capital was prosperous and, in this favorable climate, a new intellectual class emerged, whose life was dominated by philosophic and esthetic speculation. Poetry, painting, and the lesser arts, flourished in this cultured and subtle society, where restraint was considered the greatest felicity. Porcelain became a mirror of its time. The vigorous T'ang forms give way to refinements of simplification and subtlety, to a more gentle line. The monochrome glazes take on a deeper, less vivid tone, but their throbbing brilliance and unctuous quality have never been equalled. The material is of such quality that the decoration is almost superfluous, but, restrained and austere, it is always in close relation to the form – graceful incised or relief patterns underglaze, crackle in several colors, and patches of color, all subtly contrasted.

Ju ware, with its pure form and fine thick, cloudy glaze, is among the rarest of Imperial pieces. The colors range from a bluish-gray to a soft lavender-blue (Plate 141). While early 12th century Ju ware is the product of a workshop within the precincts of the Palace at K'ai-fêng, Kuan represents the essential Imperial productions of the Southern Sung, centered on Hangchow. The body of the pieces is gray or somber brown, and can be seen through the polished gray-green or bluish glaze, strongly crackled, with richly varied tones and combinations of colors (Plate 142 and 183).

From Northern China comes Ting ware, originally from Ting-Chou (Hopei Province) – a true white porcelain, heritage from the T'ang era. After 1127, however, some potters who had followed the exodus to the South opened workshops at Chi Chou in Kiangsi Province. Ting ware has a very close-grained and translucent body covered with a creamy white glaze of variable shade, flowing like wax on the reverse of the pieces. The best known forms are wide-mouthed cups, and plates, bowls, vases, and ewers, almost always decorated with a finely incised design in calligraphic style, or sometimes with delicately molded relief *motifs* (Plate 177 and 178). Bowls are often protected by a copper bord at the rim. Very close to Ting in form and decoration is *ying ch'ing* (shadowy blue), also known as *ch'ing pai* (bluish white). This important class, of which some kiln-sites have been discovered in Kiangsi Province, is not mentioned in Chinese texts and seems to have had its greatest admirers abroad, numerous fragments having been found in Korea, Japan, and even Egypt. It is a very fine white porcelain of fragile nature, less close-grained than Ting, and with a very hard and brilliant glaze, deepening to light blue where it gathers and lies thickly (Plate 182). This type of porcelain was produced before the advent of the Sung Emperors, and continued with some changes into the 14th century.

The group called Chün is well-known in the West. These pieces are of heavy stoneware with a lavender-blue glaze sometimes splashed with purple. Kilns established near Chün Chou (Honan Province) supplied the Court with jardinieres, bulb bowls, and garden pots. These forms are complicated, with thick glazes resembling those known as *flambé*. A more delicate type, mostly cups and bowls, is a wonderful shade of pale blue with opalescent violet splashes (Plate 143). Very exceptional pieces have soft gray, impure white, and sometimes deep yet tender green glazes.

The last Yüeh wares of the T'ang epoch have not entirely vanished, and their manufacture continues until towards the middle of the 11th century. They were, though, soon to give way to the true celadons, which are the most famous of all the Sung innovations. The kilns at Lung Ch'üan (Chekiang Province), the origin of the best pieces, were prosperous for hundreds of years. These pieces, with their close-textured, clouded glaze, subtle green tone, and polished unctuous surface reminiscent of jade, are perhaps the most perfect of the Sung monochromos. The bluish pieces are the most sought after (Plate 144). The later examples are sea- or olive-green. The celadon group has a body very near to porcelain, but which is red when fired. This property has sometimes been used to make a contrasting decoration of red fish or dragons in relief. Most pieces are decorated with incised or relief patterns under the glaze: lotus or poppy flowers, petals, fish in curving waves (Plate 181). Some celadons, however, have decorative iron-brown splashes (*tobi seiji*). Already, during the Sung period, and much more in the Yüan and Ming dynasties, celadon was exported in immense quantities to Japan, the Philippines, the Malay States, and to Western Asia. The Museum of the Old Seraglio at Istanbul, and also the Teheran Museum, have large collections amassed by the Sultans and Caliphs from the 12th century onwards.

The Northern celadons, coming from different sites in Honan, are much less varied. Among them we find vases and bottles, but principally conical bowls with a tapered foot (Plate 138). These celadons may be recognized by their fine brownish-gray paste, elegant form, and glassy, hard glaze, which is dark olive-green, almost brown. The ornament is incised deeply and more lavishly than on the other celadons, with "combed" *motifs* and stipples, reminiscent of Yüeh.

In addition to the clear monochromes there are black pieces in considerable variety, and the best known of these are the Chien teabowls made in Fukien, and much appreciated in Japan where they are known as *temmoku*. These conical bowls of blackish stoneware are heavy and rugged and their blue-black glaze forms an irregular vitrified roll above the unglazed foot. Small ewers and cylindrical cups belong to the same group. The glaze is brightened by a metallic sheen caused by many little streaks ("hare's fur") or by round iridescent splashes ("oil-spots") (Plate 179).

Pieces rather like these come from Chi-an fu in Kiangsi Province. They are of light colored stoneware, the glaze splashed with brown or decorated with floral designs. Honan Province was the birthplace of fine vases, cups, and jars in a deep and brilliant black with sometimes a lustrous brown decoration (Plate 176 and 180).

The pottery of Tz'ŭ Chou (Hopei Province), and of the nearby districts, is distinguished from other groups by its completely different decorative approach. There appears here for the first time in China a real painted decoration – vigorous floral *motifs*, swirling poppies, fabulous animals in black on a white slip ground, covered with transparent colorless or green glazes (Plate 140 and 185). The broad treatment and bold composition give Tz'ŭ Chou wares of the Sung period a serene beauty which was gradually to be lost in the more stylized decoration of the later Tz'ŭ Chou, for the workshops have never stopped working. A different kind of Tz'ŭ Chou ware is the "carved" decoration, where the thick glaze is cut and incised to form contrasts of texture, color, and relief with the ground (Plate 184). Finally it is here, at Tz'ŭ Chou, that enameled ornament first appears, limited, it is true, to red and green, but still a discovery of the first magnitude, for this ability to put low-temperature enamels over the high-temperature glaze was to be the foundation for all the later polychrome developments of the Ming and Ch'ing dynasties.

THE YÜAN DYNASTY

During the Yüan period potters clung to some of the Sung traditions, notably the celadons, which now become monumental, with accentuated relief ornament (Plate 188). In the realm of white porcelain there are certain rare and precious small pieces called *shu-fu* (after an official mark: "Central Palace," which can be found on certain of these pieces, in relief, concealed in the decoration) which approach *ying ch'ing*. Their opaque glaze, however, distinguishes them from these; but otherwise they are related to the first blue-and-white, marking an important milestone in the history of Chinese porcelain.

The most important discovery of this period, probably at the beginning of the 14th century, was the use of blue underglaze, destined for a brilliant future. Painted decoration in cobalt blue was a technique imported from Persia, and its journey to the Far East had been favored by the Mongol conquest of Asia. The decoration is painted on the unfired body, and covered with a glaze which becomes translucent and brilliant during the single firing. This process continues down the centuries, in the course of which blue-and-white is remarkable for its evolution of form and decoration and variation in color. The decorative range was already rich at the end of the 14th century. The style is naturalistic and vital (Plate 189), but gives way to a more conventional treatment after the beginning of the 15th century. The porcelain is pure white, and the designs extraordinarily spontaneous and free.

THE MING DYNASTY

After the Mongol domination of the Yüan there appeared a native dynasty which gave new impetus to China. New trends appear in the realm of ceramics which were to direct and integrate the work in certain definite directions. This influence came for the most part from a centralized production at Ching-tê-Chên, in the favored Province of Kiangsi, which had already been responsible for many earlier types. The Imperial products of ever-increasing importance, and the products of small private kilns nearby, were to turn this city into a metropolis of porcelain. From now on both pottery and porcelain made in provincial workshops fall into the background.

The main feature of porcelain from the Ming period was the painted decoration, which was either underglaze in blue or red, or in enamel colors. Imperial pieces from the outset were made only of material which was technically perfect. The slightly wavy glaze gives them a vibrant quality, whereas the smooth icy surfaces of the later Ch'ing porcelain makes it seem cold by comparison. Pieces made for commerce and export were cruder: often with faulty glaze, ill-concealed joints, or a badly finished base. Some provincial wares, for instance, the so-called "Swatow" plates which were exported primarily to southeast Asia, have spontaneous or schematic decoration of considerable charm. They are the antithesis of the chaste and refined work of Ching-tê-Chên.

Ming shapes are characteristic: *mei-ping* vases with high shoulders and a narrow neck (Plate 146), wide mouthed jars, bulb-shaped and baluster vases, gourds and double gourds, ewers inspired by models from the Near East (Plate 197). The cups are often on a stem. Besides these, the essentials for a scribe: brushholders, waterpots, small table screens, and also figures of gods or legendary heroes. Later, there was a fashion for decorative small animal models (Plates 156, 157 and 164).

After the beginning of the 15th century the range of decoration became fixed. The great classic *motifs* were inspired by designs on embroidered silks – lotus leaves, fabulous animals, clouds, arabesques and so on. Others copy contemporary pictures, illustrate stories and legends, or depict symbols borrowed mainly from Taoism and the search for longevity.

The use of marks became general at the same time. Nearly always under glaze in blue, they are painted on the base, though sometimes on the edge of the piece (Plate 152). They show the "reign mark" (*nien hao*) chosen by the Emperor at his accession, and the mark of the dynasty. These marks are often in the form of seals during the 18th century (cf. p. 297). One must be careful in making attributions, for it was usual to mark pieces with that of an earlier reign, not with any intention to defraud, but as a mark of respect for the quality of its products. Also, there are cyclical marks, giving a date; studio, symbolic, and emblematic marks (especially under the Emperor, K'ang Hsi); and also votive marks.

Blue-and-white reigned supreme from the 14th to the 17th century. Big plates with stylized floral *motifs* characterize the beginning of the 15th century (Plate 190). The reign of Hsüan-tê (1426–1435) is the golden age of this technique with its vigorous decoration applied in broad sweeps of the brush and dotted with blackish spots, due to oxidation in the kiln. In the reign of Ch'êng Hua (1465–1487) vigor gives way to a delicate refinement of design and color, which becomes a soft, almost silvery blue (Plate 193). A heavy body with a slightly greenish glaze is typical of the reign of Chêng Tê (1505–1521). It often has Arabic or Persian calligraphy, framed with conventional Islamic *motifs*, and pieces so decorated were made for the educated Mohammedan, of whom there were many in China at that time (Plate 194). Quite different is the blue-and-white of Chia Ching (1522–1566), where Taoist inspired decoration (for the Emperor was a fervent disciple) is applied in a vivid purplish blue (Plate 195). Most of the products in the reign of Wan Li (1573–1620) were made for export and deteriorate accordingly. Decoration grows heavy and complicated. This was the period which produced the thin porcelain with its grayish blues, which flooded the European market, and had such decisive influence on the faience of Delft and Germany. The period called Transitional, that is, from the end of the Ming dynasty to the beginning of the Ch'ing (about 1630–1680), is represented by a very fine quality porcelain in new shapes and with a warm, deep blue decoration (Plate 196). This class of porcelain also had an enormous influence on European faience (Delft, Nevers, Rouen, and so forth). Underglaze red decoration goes through the same process as blue-and-white, but, being very difficult to control, never got really under way (Plate 145).

The first polychrome masterpieces were made in the reign of Ch'êng Hua (Plate 148). Enamel colors were used for a long time with underglaze blue to give the "five-color" technique (*wu ts'ai*), of which the reign of Wan Li (Plate 152) and the Transitional period were the classic epochs, or the style called *tou ts'ai* (contrasting colors) where the outlines are traced in pale blue, contrasting softly with the clear toned enamels. Mention must also be made of the red and green, often enlivened with turquoise and yellow, precursors of the *famille verte*, and of the two-color decoration of the period of Chia Ching, which marries violet and yellow, red and green, and red and yellow, sometimes on a blue ground (Plate 151).

The quality of white Ming porcelain was such that it could be used alone, or with only such decoration as enhanced its perfection – the "secret" decoration, a fine linear, almost invisible, underglaze design or with relief and pierced decoration. The first *blanc de Chine* was made at Tê Hua, in Fukien Province, at the beginning of the 17th century. Figures, cups, teapots, and the like, may be recognized by their thick unctuous glaze, which is of a warm, almost ivory white (Plate 153).

The colored monochromes are not so popular, though the Hsüan-tê period is famous for its red, and Chia Ching for its blue. Some of these monochromes have decoration in gold, others have applied white ornament in relief. Some Sung types still survived, notably the celadons. Made mostly for export, they are immense, heavy pieces of a dark or yellowish green.

A very well-known group from the 15th and 16th centuries is the "three-color" (*san ts'ai*). This comes from provincial factories making architectural pottery. They made vases of vigorous outline, religious figures, and garden seats. The stoneware body is covered with glazes similar to those of the T'ang, but with areas of color divided either by pierced decoration or by clay threads. The colors are for the most part, dark blue, turquoise, aubergine, and white (Plate 146). This bold association of colors clearly illustrates the characteristically Ming taste for a rather gaudy polychrome palette, and contrasts sharply with the austere subtleties looked for by the potters of the Sung dynasty.

THE CH'ING DYNASTY

Even before the fall of the Ming Emperors, and until about 1680, times were troubled in China, and in no way favorable to the development of ceramics. The town of Ching-tê-Chên was largely destroyed during the continual civil wars, but the Imperial kilns, reconstructed in 1683, were soon to enter a long era of prosperity. Under the continued direction of three great men, the work was closely organized, and the original, creative artist flourished. The town itself became an industrial city. At the beginning of the 18th century the population was already a million. Three thousand kilns were working, and the extent of the production shows an incomparable mastery of the technique, as much in the preparation of the body as in control of the kiln.

The reign of K'ang Hsi (1662–1722) shows characteristically vigorous shapes, designs, and colors. It is enough to indicate the blue-and-white of the period – beautiful sapphire tones, brilliantly graded, and depicting romantic scenes, landscapes, or flowers, mostly borrowed from contemporary painting. Polychrome subjects are not very different.

Famille verte takes the place of the "five-color" decoration and of the "red and green" family, with a more varied palette in which different greens, a very intense black, and sometimes gold, are used with an enamel blue, which now replaces the traditional underglaze cobalt blue (Plate 161). *Biscuit* is decorated with the same enamels. They are applied to the fired but unglazed body. Their tones are, therefore, subdued, and stand out from the colored grounds, black, yellow, and green, which serve to mask the mat surface of the body (Plate 154). The K'ang Hsi monochromes are justly famous; white from Fukien, still in the Ming tradition; brilliant blacks enhanced with gold; apple green; intense reds universally known as *sang de bœuf* (Plate 160); and a mottled rose-red called "peach bloom".

Important, too, are the powder-blues, which produce mottled effects and serve as a ground for gilded decoration, or for reserves painted in blue and white, or enameled in *famille verte* colors. Underglaze blue in conjunction with gold and iron-red is known as Chinese Imari; copied from Japanese porcelain, it was made only for export.

In the reign of Yung Chêng (1723–1735) *famille verte* disappears, and its place is taken by *famille rose*. The new enamels are softer, and, among them is a new color, a mauvish rose of European origin. Vigor gives way to delicacy in the soft colors, fine eggshell pastes, and graceful patterns of flowers and birds (Plates 162 and 163). A very heavily decorated type was the result of the demands of European taste, with its enthusiasm for anything bizarre. The best known examples of this are the ruby-backed plates, which have many closely detailed borders framing cockerels, peacocks, and groups of women and children. Here is the beginning of a decline which increases under Ch'ien Lung. On the other hand, the cultivated taste of the period is reflected in an archaic bent which produced copies of the old Sung models, and a renaissance of the Ming *tou ts'ai*, though with rather insipid colors.

Increasing virtuosity marks the long reign of Ch'ien Lung (1736–1796). Technical *tours de force* and flights of imagination in questionable taste defy the ceramic laws. Pierced work, double walls, superimposed enamels, shaded colors, pitted surfaces, heavy gilding, *mésalliances* of color, imitations of bronze, jade, and lacquer, combined with increasing complication of design, are only some of the technical skills which were to lead Chinese porcelain into a decadence from which it has not recovered. The only important work of the reign is the theme called the "*mille fleurs*" (the thousand flowers). Some pieces, though, are faithful to the true Chinese tradition, and some of the *famille rose* of this period is equal to that of Yung Chêng.

Otherwise, during the whole of the 18th century, export porcelain – for the East India Companies, that is – took up most of the potter's time. Armorial services, which were rare in previous centuries, now had an enormous success in Europe. The borders surrounding the Arms faithfully reflect the successive styles of Western decoration, so it is possible to follow their evolution, and to date them with accuracy (Plate 198). After the K'ang Hsi period there appear also copies of European decoration inspired by prints and drawings sent specially from the West. There is a wide range of subjects – religious scenes, *fêtes champêtres* and *galantes*, portraits, fantastic personages (Plate 165), pictures of boats, towns, and so forth. The Chinese interpretation of these foreign subjects, which were often imperfectly understood, is full of zest and charm.

The 19th century, in spite of immense productivity, manufactured only copies and repetitions, which were often very skillful but without real artistic value. The soaring impulse towards original creation is no longer seen after the reign of Ch'ien Lung, which closes the history of ceramics as an art in China. *D. L.-G.*

MING dynasty (1368–1644)

德年製　大明宣

HSÜAN TÊ (1426–1435)

化年製　大明成

CH'ÊNG HUA (1465–1487)

治年製　大明弘

HUNG CHIH (1488–1505)

德年製　大明正

CHÊNG TÊ (1506–1521)

靖年製　大明嘉

CHIA CHING (1522–1566)

曆年製　大明萬

WAN LI (1573–1619)

CH'ING dynasty (1644–1912)

熙年製　大清康

K'ANG HSI (1662–1722)

正年製　大清雍

YUNG CHÊNG (1723–1735)

隆年製　大清乾

CH'IEN LUNG (1736–1795)

189

128. PLATE DECORATED WITH COLORED GLAZES. T'ANG DYNASTY

D.31.5 cm. Musée Guimet, Paris (Michel Calmann Bequest)

Colored glaze pottery which, in both form and decoration, was inspired by Western models is exemplified by this magnificent dish, itself clearly akin to the silver wares of Sassanian Persia. The plate is supported by three feet, a characteristic more suited to metal work than to the ceramic art.

The radiating design shows a crane flying in clouds surrounded by an octagonal *motif* of stylized lotus flowers. In this design the glazes are divided by incised lines to keep the colors separate, whereas the blue of the reverse is allowed to flow freely over a cream ground. The feet are covered with orange and green glazes. The intense, fresh palette is characteristic of the T'ang era.

The traces of three stilt marks are to be seen on the reverse.

Exhibition: Arts de la Chine Ancienne, *Orangerie Museum, Paris, 1937, No. 314.*

129. POTTERY VASE DECORATED WITH COLORED GLAZES. T'ANG DYNASTY

H.27 cm. Musée Guimet, Paris (Michel Calmann Bequest)

This vase, with its cylindrical neck, is typical of the T'ang dynasty, particularly in the way in which the different formal elements are accentuated by horizontal lines incised in the clay. However, the gentle line of the belly, and the rolled border at foot and neck, forecast the subtle curves of the following period, and suggest that this piece may belong to the end of the dynasty.

A clear buff in tone, the paste is close-grained and highly polished. The vigorously colored, free-flowing glazes are remarkably decorative in their effect.

Exhibition: Arts de la Chine Ancienne, *Orangerie Museum, Paris, 1937, No. 359.*

130. HORSE AND RIDER. POTTERY FIGURE IN COLORED GLAZES. T'ANG DYNASTY

H.46 cm. Musée Guimet, Paris (Michel Calmann Bequest)

This beautiful little model is vigorously sculpted. The rider, characteristically Tartar, illustrates the interest which T'ang artists took in observing and depicting foreigners. The proud and sturdy mount is a fine example of the famous T'ang horses, which are so much sought by modern collectors. It came originally from the Northern Province of Shensi. A similar figure is in the Museum of Fine Arts, Boston, Mass.

131. HORSE AND GROOM
T'ANG DYNASTY (618–906)

Horse: L.87 cm. H.77 cm. Groom: H.60 cm.
Collection Comte & Comtesse de Bismarck, Paris

After the beginning of the T'ang dynasty China extended her rule to include Bactria (the Afghanistan province of Balkh), and new contacts affected every branch of art. Sculpture, ceramics, and jewelry all reflect the Western influence thus introduced. Many new things appear, and especially in the pottery tomb-figures.

The horse shown here, powerfully muscular, tall, and with a broad thick neck, is quite different from the earlier examples, and certainly belongs to a breed imported from the West. The groom wears a costume with a large *revers* which is in no way Chinese, but rather that of the nomads of Central Asia.

This kind of horse, very common in the T'ang era (cf. Plate 130) was buried beside the dead, apparently waiting for its rider.

The pinkish-buff pottery of these two admirable pieces is covered with a fine manganese glaze relieved with lighter tones, in which an orange-yellow is dominant. The harness is decorated with leaf *motifs*. At this period these usually took the place of buckles and rings.

132. THREE SMALL POTTERY BOWLS WITH MARBLED DECORATION. T'ANG DYNASTY (618–906)

D. (from left to right) 8.9 cm. 8.5 cm. 6 cm. Musée Guimet, Paris (Michel Calmann Bequest)

The technique of marbled decoration is one of the most delicate of the T'ang skills. It consisted in mixing light and dark clays so that the more or less regular veined decoration is in the body itself. The pieces were then covered, either with colorless, yellow, or green glazes. These rare bowls show the different effects attained by the use of each of these three methods.

133. FIGURE OF A STANDING WOMAN
POTTERY DECORATED WITH COLORED GLAZES
T'ANG DYNASTY

H.39 cm. Musée Guimet, Paris (Michel Calmann Bequest)

The extreme elegance of a T'ang court lady is well illustrated by this model. A long scarf hides her hands, the bell-shaped dress reveals shoes with upturned toes, and her *coiffure* is elaborately tall. It seems, from figures which survive, that feminine fashion of the period was amazingly varied and elegant, both in the cut of the clothes and in the startling fantasy of the hair styles.

The paste is close-grained and polished. It appears, a pale buff-white, on the hair, face, and neck, which have long since lost all trace of their original cold pigments.

Exhibition: Arts de la Chine Ancienne, *Orangerie Museum, Paris, 1937, No. 342.*

134. PLAYER OF CYMBALS
T'ANG DYNASTY (618–906)

H. 36 cm. Private Collection

Figures of musicians, seated or crouching, are among the most attractive of the T'ang tombfigures. They are often arranged in groups, and it is rare to find one as large as the charming woman shown here.

Her dress is elegant and daring, an example of the pomp of the T'ang Court under Hsüan Tsung (713–755), during the ascendancy of the favorite ballet and music mistress, Yang kuei-fei. A magnificent deep blue glaze, splashed with yellow, only partly covers the figure, allowing the pinkish white of the paste to show here and there. The smiling face, half-closed eyes, and the very elaborate *coiffure* were originally painted also.

135. POTTERY VASE WITH MONOCHROME GLAZE. T'ANG DYNASTY

H. 20.3 cm. Collection of His Excellency Sir George Labouchère, London

This massive vase is typically T'ang. Its accentuated globular shape and high shoulders, the cylindrical neck with its jutting horizontal rim, and the flat base, are quite characteristic. The composition gives an impression of primitive vigor.

The lively tone of this monochrome glaze is due to the use of copper oxide, and it well illustrates the developments and achievements since the days of the somber green glazes of the Han dynasty.

136. VASE. THREE-COLOR GLAZES. LIAO DYNASTY (MANCHURIA) (907–1125)

H. 35.5 cm. Musée Guimet, Paris (Michel Calmann Bequest)

This brilliantly colored vase well illustrates the art of the barbarian dynasty, Liao, who reigned over Manchuria during the 10th and 11th centuries. The use of *san ts'ai* glazes over a white slip is a surviving T'ang technique.

The piece, however, shows development in form, and in the freedom of the floral design, which is characteristic of contemporary Sung art.

Exhibition: The Arts of the Sung Dynasty, *Oriental Ceramic Society, London, 1960, No. 128.*

137. BOWL. NORTHERN CELADON
SUNG DYNASTY (960–1276)

D. 11 cm. H. 7.5 cm. Private Collection

The group known as Northern Celadons has not, so far, been identified with any of the categories mentioned in the Chinese texts. Sir Percival David classes them with the *Tung* group, of which very little is known. The Japanese, on the other hand, have suggested that they were made by the potters of Ju-Chou before their transfer to Kai-fêng, the capital of the Northern

Sung. Indeed, the very abundance of the production poses many problems. They are undoubtedly related to the Yüeh of Chekiang (see below), though their decoration is heavy and more complex, whilst the glaze is much glassier and rather brown in color.

The bowl reproduced here, with its upright sides and raised foot, has an incised design of stylized peonies and trailing foliage. The glaze, thin and free-flowing, gathers in the hollows, giving a shaded effect of relief, which is characteristic of this group of celadons.

The body is a reddish-beige stoneware, and the treatment is both extremely delicate and acute.

138. YÜEH STONEWARE BOWL. END OF THE T'ANG OR BEGINNING OF THE SUNG DYNASTY

D. 14 cm. Art Council of Great Britain (Formerly Collection Mrs. C. G. Seligman), London

The Yüeh stonewares derive their name from Yüeh Chou, near Shao Hsing, in Chekiang Province. Here, as well as at Chiu Yen nearby, were found the earliest olive-glazed pieces which were the forerunners of the celadons to come. The first Yüeh wares were made from the beginning of our era until the sixth century, but there seems to have been a revival in the ninth century in the same area, not far from the lake of Shang-lin-hu. These Yüeh wares differ from the early ones (cf. Plate 170) in their decoration – very sensitive incised designs with some likeness to the Northern celadons of the Sung dynasty. They were greatly treasured by the Chinese of the period, who compared them with jade. It is indeed possible that the potters were trying to imitate the green tones of that precious and revered material.

The bowl shown here is of an exceptional quality. The decoration is at once vigorous and restrained in the composition of folded lotus leaves, and delicate in the treatment of the finely drawn veins. Lotus petals decorate the reverse.

Exhibition: The Arts of the T'ang Dynasty, *Oriental Ceramic Society, London, 1955, No. 263.*

139. KUAN BOTTLE. SUNG DYNASTY (960–1276)

H. 21.5 cm. Private Collection

The modeling of this beautiful octagonal vase is exceptionally fine, and it is accentuated by eight lightly indicated ribs with horizontal lines in relief. The round body is flattened at the top, and the slim neck has a broad flat rim. The sides are thin, and the body, appearing here and there on the lower edge, is of a somber color and delicate quality. The opaque and polished glaze, unctuous to the touch, is lightly crackled, and of a soft bluish gray. It covers the whole piece, including the base.

These characteristics lead us to classify this vase among the ceramic masterpieces made at the kilns of Ch'iao-tan (the Altar of Heaven) near Hangchow, which started production after the Southern Sung capital had been established in the 12th century. In 1952 at an Oriental Ceramic Society Exhibition in London this bottle (at that time in another collection) was shown side by side with another almost identical piece from Lung Ch'üan. The two were the same, except for the quality of the paste and the difference in the color of the glaze, the Lung Ch'üan specimen being sea-green. This juxtaposition revealed the problems inherent in the study of the enormous category grouped together as "celadons," their shapes and superficial appearance often leading to confusion.

This beautiful celadon may be compared with the pieces illustrated on Plates 142, 144, and 183.

Exhibition: Ju and Kuan Wares, *Oriental Ceramic Society, London, 1952, No. 33.*

140. TZ'Ŭ CHOU VASE. SUNG DYNASTY (960–1276)

H. 35 cm. Private Collection

During the Sung dynasty the kilns at Tz'ŭ Chou, in the southwest of Hopei Province (formerly Chihli), were the most important center of the ceramic industry in the north of China. Their influence spread widely, especially in Honan, and notably in the village of Chü-lu-hsien, which was destroyed by the flooding of the Yellow River valley in 1108.

The varied techniques of the Tz'ŭ Chou potters brought innovations to Sung ceramics. Now, for the first time, we see painted and *champlevé* (carved) decoration which had previously been unknown in China. These new techniques employing incised designs and sometimes enameling, exhibit an original taste for contrasts in material and color which places the work of Tz'ŭ Chou in a different category from all other contemporary products.

The rare vase illustrated here is of exceptional quality, and is certainly one of the finest specimens from these kilns known in Europe. The decoration makes use of painting and carving at the same time, so that the main design stands out clearly from the ground. The painting in black is of a peony encircled by leaves, and a transparent green glaze covers the vase. The details are incised into the body. The foot is painted black under the glaze, and the striations incised into it represent opening petals.

Exhibition: Arts de la Chine Ancienne, *Orangerie Museum, Paris, 1937, No. 730.*

141. JU BOTTLE. SUNG DYNASTY

H. 20.3 cm. Formerly Collection Mrs. Alfred Clark, Fulmer, Bucks.

The Ju wares are among the rarest and most precious of all the Imperial Sung products. They seem to have been made between 1107–1127 during the building of the palace of K'ai-Fêng, the first capital of the Sung dynasty. The workshop was destroyed by invading Mongol nomads, who seized the city and looted the Imperial collections.

This wonderful vase from Mrs. Clark's collection is one of the most perfect examples of Ju ware known today. It combines all the qualities for which these pieces are renowned – simplicity and elegance of form, the pure outline of the typical Sung piece, and a thick unctuous, clouded, and slightly mat glaze, delicate in tone and finely crackled. The base, which is also glazed, has traces of oval "stilt" or "spur" marks within the footring.

Exhibitions: Arts de la Chine Ancienne, *Orangerie Museum, Paris, 1937, No. 517.* – Ju and Kuan Wares, *Oriental Ceramic Society, London, 1952, No. 3.* – The Arts of the Sung Dynasty, *Oriental Ceramic Society, London, 1960, No. 63.*

142. KUAN VASE. SUNG DYNASTY (12th CENTURY)

H. 18 cm. Percival David Foundation of Chinese Art, London

The vase shown here is a most graceful example of the Imperial official *(kuan)* workshops of Hangchow, the Southern Sung capital after 1127.

Shaped like a pear, its long cylindrical neck has a wide flaring mouth. The somber tone of the body can be discerned through the lustrous, rich glaze, exquisite in tone, which covers it completely. A copper rim embellishes the foot and mouth, and an irregular crackle, spiraling up the neck, covers the whole surface.

From the Imperial Collection, Peking.

Exhibitions: Chinese Art, *London, 1935/6, No. 875.* – Arts de la Chine Ancienne, *Orangerie Museum, Paris, 1937, No. 498.* – The Arts of the Sung Dynasty, *Oriental Ceramic Society, London, 1960, No. 160.*
Catalogue of the Percival David Foundation, by S. Yorke-Hardy, 1953. – Section 1, No. 4.

143. DISH. CHÜN WARE SUNG DYNASTY (960–1276)

D. 18.5 cm. Percival David Foundation of Chinese Art, London

This small dish is of a gray porcellaneous stoneware. The body, to be seen on the unglazed footring, has assumed a reddish tinge from contact with the fire. The wonderful opalescent glaze is suffused with splashes of purple fairly evenly dispersed over the surface. On the reverse it is olive green. Chün ware of this quality was produced during the second half of the 10th century in Honan Province, not only at the site of Chün Chou as formerly thought, but also at different places in the same province.

Exhibitions: Chinese Art, *London, 1935/6, No. 1068.* – Arte Cinese, *Venice, 1954, No. 472.*
Catalogue of the Percival David Foundation, by S. Yorke-Hardy, 1953. – Section 1, No. 72.

144. SMALL CYLINDRICAL CELADON VASE
SUNG DYNASTY. (960–1276)

H. 15.7 cm. Musée Guimet, Paris (Michel Calmann Bequest)

Although the workshops of Lung Ch'üan are famous for the fine celadons made there, they were not the only source of production. After the Sung transferred their capital to Hang-chow in 1127 there was an immediate ceramic renaissance in the neighborhood, as well as in the Imperial Palace itself. These two famous centers of art produced the Kuan wares (cf. Plate 142), some of which have a bluish glaze which is very near to the finest celadons of Lung Ch'üan. Indeed, it is often difficult to distinguish between them.

This small vase is of a very rare shape, and has a fine tawny colored crackle. It belongs to the class of celadons known as Hangchow. The subtle bluish tone and cloudy unctuous glaze add to its exceptional quality. The body is a sandy-colored porcellaneous ware.

Exhibition: L'Art de la Chine des Song, *Cernuschi Museum, Paris, 1956, No. 89.*

145. BOTTLE DECORATED IN UNDERGLAZE
COPPER RED. MING DYNASTY. C. 1400

H. 14.5 cm. Collection Garner

The development of the technique of underglaze decoration produced enormous quantities of blue-and-white from the 14th century onwards. Probably underglaze copper red would have had the same success had it not been so difficult to control this color. It tended to volatilize in the kiln, and to emerge as a greenish black. Successful pieces, such as this one, are remarkably rare. The technique of underglaze copper red was to disappear for a time after the reign of Hsüan-tê (1426–1435), and the only red to be seen was an iron-red enamel which was much easier to handle.

This little bottle, with its rounded body and slender spout, and the cylindrical enlarged neck, is a copy of the Indian *"Kendi"* or drinking bottle. The design of peonies among the trailing leaves is handled in the powerful, naturalistic style of the 14th century. Borders of petals form a frame for the design. The neck and spout are decorated with scrolls and stylized leaves.

Exhibition: The Arts of the Ming Dynasty, *Oriental Ceramic Society, London, 1957, No. 153.*

146. *Mei p'ing* VASE. *San ts'ai* (THREE-COLOR)
PORCELAIN. MING DYNASTY. C. 1500

H. 42.3 cm. Formerly Collection Mrs. Alfred Clark, Fulmer, Bucks.

The *san ts'ai* (or three-color) technique is very well seen in this vase, one of the finest known. The *mei p'ing,* known since the Sung dynasty, was designed to hold a single branch of prunus blossom. Here it is seen in the form characteristic of the 15th century; tall shoulders accord perfectly with the small flared mouth and the gently spreading foot. The decoration, of the

type referred to as *cloisonné (fa hua),* consists in fine threads in relief which were used to prevent the intermingling of the colored glazes. Detailed decoration is delicately incised. The *motif* of decoration is frequently encountered in work of the period. Three sections are filled with a sensitively free pattern of lotus flowers growing in water and surrounded by aquatic plants. A stylized border of waves and acorns strung together with pearls surrounds the main *motif.*

Exhibition: The Arts of the Ming Dynasty, *Oriental Ceramic Society, London, 1957, No. 160*

147. PORCELAIN STEM-CUP. MING DYNASTY
SECOND HALF OF THE 15TH CENTURY

H. 10.5 cm. Formerly Collection Mrs. Walter Sedgwick, London

Stem-cups, such as this one, were used for ritual purposes, and were probably kept on the altars to hold flower offerings or water. It is probable that they are derived from metalwork of the Near East. The beautiful shape of the cup illustrated here is typical of the 15th century. The decoration is a combination of red and blue, but no longer underglaze colors only – the cobalt blue and copper red of the beginning of the century – but underglaze blue in conjunction with iron red enamel. Two firings were necessary, therefore; the first at 1350 degrees Centigrade for the body and for the blue pigment, and the second in the so-called "muffle" kiln at 800 degrees Centigrade for the red enamel color.

The design represents mythical creatures, dragons, horses and winged elephants, galloping over foaming waves. In the middle of the interior, a blue dragon coils amid red waves.

Exhibition: The Arts of the Ming Dynasty, *Oriental Ceramic Society, London, 1957, No. 189.*

148. SMALL CUP WITH ENAMEL DECORATION OF
THE KIND KNOWN AS *tou ts'ai.* MING DYNASTY
REIGN OF CH'ÊNG HUA (1465–87)

D. 9.5 cm. Formerly Collection Mrs. Walter Sedgwick, London

The first *tou ts'ai* enameled porcelain was made during the reign of Ch'êng Hua. Imperial pieces of this period are very rare, and Chinese connoisseurs have always counted them among the most precious examples of fine porcelain. These small "chicken" cups represent a kind of porcelain which is unsurpassed for subtlety and *finesse.* The soft harmonious colors which characterize the *tou ts'ai* enamels were achieved by painting the outlines of *motifs* in underglaze blue before applying the enamels. The Chinese call this the technique of "contrasting colors," perhaps because the decoration is produced by opposing methods – underglaze blue drawing followed by the application of the colored enamels over the glaze.

This type of decoration was repeated during the reign of Wan-li (1579–1620) and again in the reign of Yung Chêng (1725–35), when copies exact in every detail were made, a proof of the reverence in which they were held. There is no need to stress the delicate beauty of the charming cup shown here. The cockerel with the hen and her chicks is one of the classic themes of the period. It is repeated on the far side of the piece and the two *motifs* are divided by rocks and blossoming branches.

The piece has the reign-mark of Ch'êng Hua, six characters in a square in underglaze blue on the base.

Exhibitions: La découverte de l'Asie, *Cernuschi Museum, Paris, 1954, No. 532.* – The Arts of the Ming Dynasty, *Oriental Ceramic Society, London, 1957, No. 174.*

149. PORCELAIN BOWL DECORATED WITH UNDERGLAZE BLUE. MING DYNASTY REIGN OF CHIA CHING (1522–1566)

D. 16 cm. Collection Junta do Baixo Alentejo, Beja, Portugal

The chief point of interest in this fine bowl is the inscription written in Portuguese on the periphery of the inside border which shows that it was made for Pero de Faria in 1541. This man, well known to Portuguese historians, held important positions in the Far East, one of which was the Governorship of Malacca from 1537 to 1543. A bowl with "ears," of identical shape but different decoration, can be seen in the Museo Duca di Martino at Naples. Both examples have the mark of the Hsüan-te on the base (1426–1435) in underglaze blue surrounded by a double circle. The marks of former reigns were quite commonly used in China after the end of the 15th century. These two pieces, and a ewer decorated with the Arms of the King, Don Manuel I, exhibited in the Museu Nacional de Arte Antiga of Lisbon, and which can be dated to about 1520, are the oldest known blue-and-white pieces which were definitely made to fill European orders.

150. LARGE JAR IN BLUE-AND-WHITE PORCELAIN. MING DYNASTY REIGN OF CHIA CHING (1522–1566)

H. 50 cm. Private Collection, Paris

The period of Chia Ching produced a large quantity of blue-and-white porcelain which is characterized by vigorous design and an intense blue with warm violet tones. Influenced by the Emperor himself, Taoist themes play an important part in the decoration, but traditional *motifs* like the dragon continue alongside this trend.

The firing of large jars such as the one reproduced here had to be done in special kilns, and was not without difficulties which are mentioned in contemporary Chinese texts.

This piece is a good example of the art of the middle 16th century. It has a strong decoration of dragons chasing each other among clouds. These are divided by two characters – *fu,* the symbol of happiness. The lower part of the vase has a frieze of *ju-i,* or scepter heads. Originally, a short neck (which has since been ground down) must have surmounted the shoulder which is decorated with scrolls of flowers painted in the style of the 16th century.

On the base is the mark of Chia Ching – six characters within a double circle.

151. SQUARE BOX WITH ENAMEL DECORATION MING DYNASTY. REIGN OF CHIA CHING (1522–1566)

L. (one side) 16 cm. Collection A. de Medeiros e Almeida, Lisbon

This beautiful box, with its lobed corners and slightly arched cover, belongs to the rare and precious class known by the name of two-color ware. The vigorous designs and harmonious clear colors are typical of the reign of Chia Ching, whose six-character mark is painted in underglaze blue on the base.

The *motifs* in yellow enamel – dragons, clouds, the *ling chih,* or longevity fungus, and stylized leaves – are outlined and accentuated with iron red. The brilliant contrasting background in underglaze blue was painted and fired at the same time as the body in the high-temperature kiln, the enamels being added afterwards.

152. SQUARE VASE WITH THE ENAMELED DECORATION KNOWN AS *Wu ts'ai* ("FIVE COLOR"). MING DYNASTY REIGN OF WAN-LI (1579–1620)

H. 34.5 cm. Collection A. de Medeiros e Almeida, Lisbon

This beautiful vase decorated with enamels in polychrome on white is typical of the reign of Wan-li. It is inspired by the square variant of the archaic bronze *tsun.*

A wonderful example of the "five color" technique, the decoration uses underglaze blue in combination with colored enamels. The reign of Wan-li is the classic period for this type of decoration – sinuous dragons chasing the sacred pearl twine among the flower *motifs.* The foot of each panel is decorated with stylized waves.

The reign mark in six characters is painted on the upper rim of the vase. The mark in this position, though generally less usual than on the base, is often encountered in the reigns of Chia Ching and Wan-li.

153. FIGURE OF KUAN YIN. WHITE PORCELAIN. FUKIEN PROVINCE. 17TH CENTURY

H. 31.3 cm. Guimet Museum, Paris (Collection Grandidier)

The factories at Ching-tê Chên became the focal point of Chinese ceramics early in the Ming dynasty. From then onwards they absorbed almost all active potters, and eclipsed most of the earlier provincial studios. However, at Tê Hua, which lies in the southern part of the Province of Fukien, a local clay was discovered which made fine quality porcelain of a rose or ivory tone. The glaze blends into the body, and is rich and unctuous to the touch.

These are the renowned *blancs de Chine.* First produced in the 17th century, production went on almost unaltered, even beyond the 18th century, faithful to a strong technical and iconographical tradition. For this reason it is very difficult to date these pieces exactly, though it does seem that exceptional examples, such as the one shown here, were probably made in the 17th century. They may be distinguished by their pure white, the delicacy of the modelling, fine detail, and sharply edged draperies.

Best known are the religious figures representing the Buddhist and Taoist gods and disciples, but the potters of Tê Hua also made libation cups, vases, brush holders, teapots, and even figures of Europeans.

Kuan Yin, goddess of Mercy and Pity, is derived from the Indian Bodhisattva, Avalokiteshvara, and is, in some ways, his feminine counterpart. She is seated in the attitude of meditation, with lowered eyes and her hands hidden in the thick folds of her cloak. The image of the Buddha, Amida, can be seen in her crown.

This figure, as is often the case, has a potter's signature on the back.

154. LARGE BALUSTER VASE. ENAMEL ON BISCUIT. CH'ING DYNASTY. REIGN OF K'ANG HSI (1662–1722) END OF THE 17TH CENTURY

H.67 cm. Calouste Gulbenkian Foundation, Lisbon

This immense vase is a fine example of the famous "enamel on *biscuit*" made in the early part of the reign of K'ang Hsi. The majestic form, the harmony of color, and the brilliant elegance of the design speak for themselves.

Enamel on biscuit reached its finest point in the reign of K'ang Hsi. It continued the tradition of the Ming three-color wares, of which the last, made at the beginning of the 17th century, was its precursor. Enamel on *biscuit* diverges from the usual Chinese method of decoration. The body was first fired unglazed, and this accounts for the heavier tone of the enamels, which were applied to a mat surface which had none of the brilliance of a glazed ground. Of course, it was necessary to cover the whole of the surface. Black was sometimes used for this purpose, accentuating the brilliance of the enamels, and less often, green or yellow, which produced a softer effect.

On this kind of vase the decoration is always homogenous, painted from top to bottom without reserves or borders. The main *motifs* are placed at the point of greatest expanse; in this case, a pair of birds perched on a gnarled prunus branch (a symbol of Spring), the flowering branches reaching to the top of the vase. Rocks painted in broad flat washes, and bamboo shoots, complete this fine decoration. The vase has no mark.

155. JUNK. ENAMEL ON BISCUIT. CH'ING DYNASTY. REIGN OF THE EMPEROR, K'ANG HSI (1662–1722)

L.33 cm. H.33 cm. Collection Paul Duboscq, Paris

By using the *biscuit* technique in which the paste was fired before the application of glaze or enamels, the potter could achieve a finely detailed effect. This rare junk is a perfect example.

The use of enamels of three colors was a reintroduction of a palette dating from the T'ang period, and which the Emperor Wan-li had already brought back into fashion at the end of the 16th century, when it is known as *san ts'ai* (three-color) ware. The colored decoration is so applied as to allow the mat white porcelain to show through here and there on the junk.

Exhibition: Chinesische Kunst, Berlin, 1929, No. 978.

156. HARES CARRYING THE FUNGUS OF LONGEVITY. CH'ING DYNASTY REIGN OF K'ANG HSI (1662–1722)

L.13.5 cm. H.12.5 cm. Collection Xavier Givaudan, Geneva

The nocturnal frolics of the hare at the time of the full moon impressed the Chinese very early in their history, and the animal became a lunar symbol which is commonly encountered in Chinese ceramic art. It is also related to the study of longevity undertaken by the Taoists, and it is the hare which prepares the drug of immortality on the moon. It is here depicted carrying the *ling-chih* fungus, an essential part of this elixir of life, and a classic symbol of longevity. It is noteworthy that the heads of the *ju-i* scepter (which grants all desires) that are everywhere encountered in the various decorative schemes, seem to derive from this fungus (cf. Plate 150).

The turquoise blue glaze appears for the first time in China on certain wares from Tz'ŭ Chou made during the 14th century. It was to become very popular during the Ming dynasty. At the end of the 17th century a more intense blue tone was perfected by Ts'ang Ying-hsüan, and this was much used in the 18th century.

In the reign of K'ang Hsi this blue is especially luminous and light in tone, well seen on the pieces in the illustration.

157. PAIR OF TOADS ENAMELED ON BISCUIT CH'ING DYNASTY. REIGN OF K'ANG HSI (1662–1722)

L.12 cm. H.18 cm. Collection Xavier Givaudan, Geneva

The toad, which often appears in Chinese porcelain, is connected with many legends about lunar eclipses. These were supposed to occur when the toad swallowed the moon. Certainly he always seems to be gazing upwards.

Biscuit figures are especially numerous during the K'ang Hsi period, and the subjects are often taken from ancient legends. The technique was particularly suitable for pieces with complicated shapes which needed sharp modeling, where realism and humor were both sought after.

The monochrome glaze of these little beasts contrasts well with the "three-color" base, which recalls the T'ang figures decorated in the same softly blended tones.

158. COVERED JAR AND DISH, GLAZED ON BISCUIT. CH'ING DYNASTY
REIGN OF K'ANG HSI. (1662–1722)

Jar H.44 cm. Dish D.47 cm. Collection M. & Mme Léon Velluz, Paris

In the reign of K'ang Hsi there was a fashion for monochrome glazes which appeared in great variety. Yellow, which was a semi-high temperature color used on *biscuit,* seems to have been the prerogative of the Emperor since the Sui period (589–618), perhaps by analogy with the color of loess, the most fertile of all Chinese soils.

The invention of many new colors has been attributed to Ts'ang Ying-hsüan, who directed the Imperial factory after its re-opening in 1682–3 until about 1710. Among these new colors were several yellows – eel yellow, trout yellow, and the like.

The two pieces in this illustration are finely matched. The translucent luminous yellow, and the classic restraint typical of the products of this reign, contribute to their exceptional quality.

159. SMALL BOTTLE. 18TH CENTURY

H.16.2 cm. Collection Garner

Like the so-called *sang de bœuf* red glazes (right), green enameled porcelain was produced by the use of copper oxide. They are among the rarest of the monochromes of the reigns of K'ang Hsi and Yung Chêng. The tones are variants on an apple green, camellia, leaf, and cucumber green.

The piece illustrated here belongs to the last of these categories. The green enamel, which stops short a little above the foot, is superimposed over a fine colorless glaze, which is finely crackled. The smooth curving shape is typical of the 18th century.

Exhibition: Monochrome Porcelain, *Oriental Ceramic Society, London, 1948, No. 154.*

160. VASE WITH A MONOCHROME GLAZE
Sang de bœuf (Lang-yao). CH'ING DYNASTY
REIGN OF K'ANG HSI. (1662–1722)

H.16.1 cm. Guimet Museum, Paris (Collection Grandidier)

One of the great triumphs of the reign of K'ang Hsi, the red monochrome glazes, illustrate the revival of certain old techniques – a renaissance of ancient skills which had been developed during the reign of Hsüan-tê (1426–35). This was, in Chinese eyes, the Golden Age of porcelain. The 15th century was renowned for its skill in handling copper red, a high temperature underglaze color. The secret of this was then lost, and only recovered two hundred years later.

The squat bottle shown here belongs to the group of deep red glazes known as *sang de bœuf* (oxblood) – the famous *Lang-yao* of the Chinese. It may, perhaps, date from a little before the reign of K'ang Hsi. The glaze is very brilliant, bluish near the mouth

and on the four handle *motifs,* which were reserved during the first application of the color.

161. DISH IN *Famille verte* ENAMELS. CH'ING DYNASTY. REIGN OF K'ANG HSI (1662–1722)

D.57 cm. Formerly Collection K.L.Essayan

Enamels of the *famille verte* were the triumphant result of a long ceramic journey. With the discovery of a blue enamel, which came much later than that of the other enamel colors, the potters were freed from the limits imposed by the underglaze blue, and had the whole range of porcelain colors at their disposal (cf. Plate 152). The variety in decoration is now infinite, as can be seen on this fine plate which uses most of the techniques and available *motifs.* The central theme is characteristic of one of the most vigorous styles of the period. A gnarled prunus tree, a bamboo, flowers, and birds perching on a branch fill the circle. Eight fan-shaped reserved panels have landscapes, decorative objects, and flowers with birds and butterflies. The small medaillons on the border are filled with animals. Scroll *motifs,* borrowed from contemporary silk embroidery, cover the ground. The whole composition radiates strictly from the middle. The colors are in perfect accord, brilliant and vigorous, and especially remarkable for the use of aubergine for the border panels. The design is very delicately handled, the *motifs* detailed and sensitive, while the colors of the enamels show up brilliantly against the white ground.

The dish is decorated on the reverse with lotus flowers and arabesques. It has the mark of a studio potter in a double circle underglaze.

162. SMALL SAUCER DISH. *Famille rose* PALETTE CH'ING DYNASTY. REIGN OF YUNG CHÊNG

D.19.7 cm. Formerly Collection Mrs. Alfred Clark, Fulmer, Bucks.

This beautiful small saucer-dish is a very fine example of *famille rose* decoration, the finest pieces of which date from the reign of Yung Chêng and the first years of Ch'ien Lung. The reverse is completely covered with a rose-pink enamel of the intense shade known as ruby. The decoration of the obverse is beautifully composed, and painted with immense skill and detail. A large part of the dish is left unpainted, showing the pure white of the porcelain. The cockerels are a favorite *motif* of the period. Here, they are pictured pecking about on a mound, and perched on the stem of a flowering peony. The flowers are most delicately shaded. A very simple trellis border encircles the dish.

The porcelain, which is very translucent and of fine quality, is of the kind known as "eggshell."

Exhibition: Enamelled Polychrome Porcelain, *Oriental Ceramic Society, London, 1951, No. 237.*

163. BOWL PAINTED IN *Famille rose* ENAMELS CH'ING DYNASTY. REIGN OF YUNG CHÊNG (1723–1733)

D.14 cm. Formerly Collection K.L.Essayan

The pictorial and free handling of this fine bowl is much more consistent with true Chinese taste than the overloaded compositions often seen on porcelain of the 18th century. The peonies are painted in a naturalistic way, and with the spontaneity and freedom which makes a very attractive design. The contrast between the delicate *famille rose* enamels and the brilliance of the white porcelain is effective and beautiful.

This bowl is one of a pair. Both pieces have the mark of Yung Chêng in six characters on the base.

164. PHEASANT PERCHED ON A ROCK. CH'ING DYNASTY. REIGN OF THE EMPEROR, K'ANG HSI (1662–1722)

H.43 cm. Collection Harari, Paris

In ancient China the pheasant was the symbol of thunder, and was always a venerable bird. One could quote many examples. There was, for instance, a "Dance of the Pheasants" – perhaps a fertility rite – which took place in Spring each year. Also, the Phoenix *(fêng huang),* emblem of the Empress and sacred bird of the South, was a combination of characteristics borrowed from the pheasant and the peacock, among others.

This bird must have been a constant challenge to the ceramic artist, and many models made in the 18th century have the same attention to detail as may be seen in the one reproduced here. The well-balanced vigorous pose of the bird is enlivened by the brilliant application of the colors.

165. PORCELAIN DISH, MADE TO A EUROPEAN DESIGN (C.1750–1770)

D.39.5 cm. Collection Pechère-Wouters, Brussels

The decoration of this fine dish, called "aux sonneurs de trompe," or the Indian Trumpeters, shows a rather exceptional example of a European theme ordered in China for export. By their costume the people seem to be Indian. It is possible that services of this kind were made for British Governors, or other officers living in India, who wanted a souvenir of life in the East. The black enamel ground covering the porcelain makes a fine contrast with the delicately shaded enamels of the central subject, and with the gold border surrounding it. The lanceolate *motif* of the border is typical of the style of the middle of the 18th century.

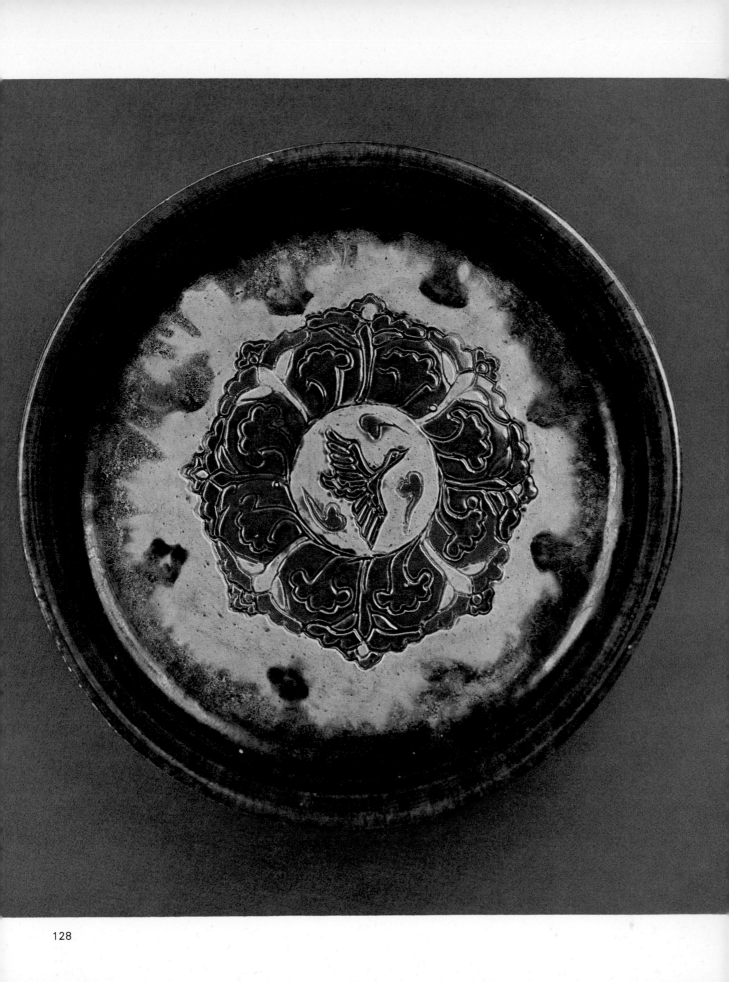

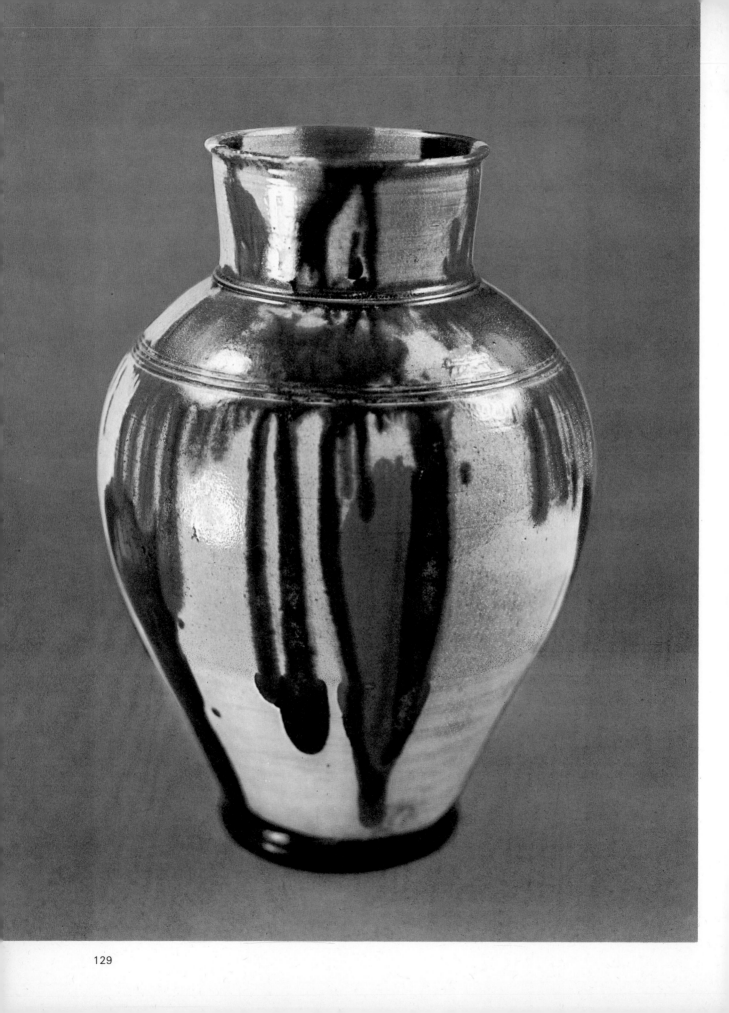

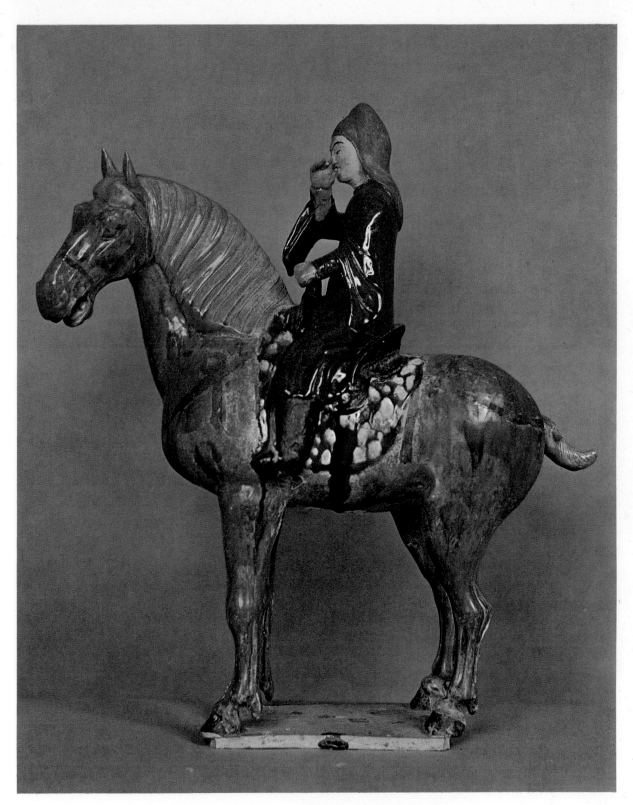

130

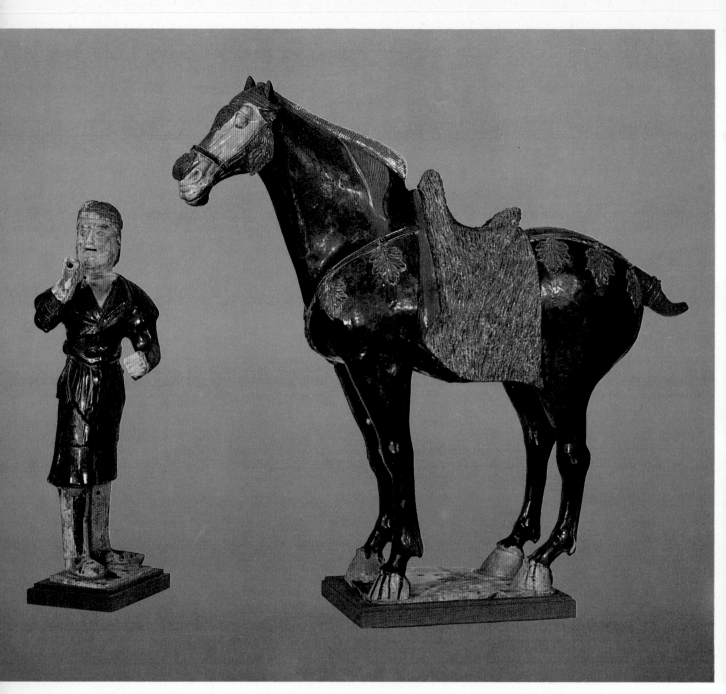

131

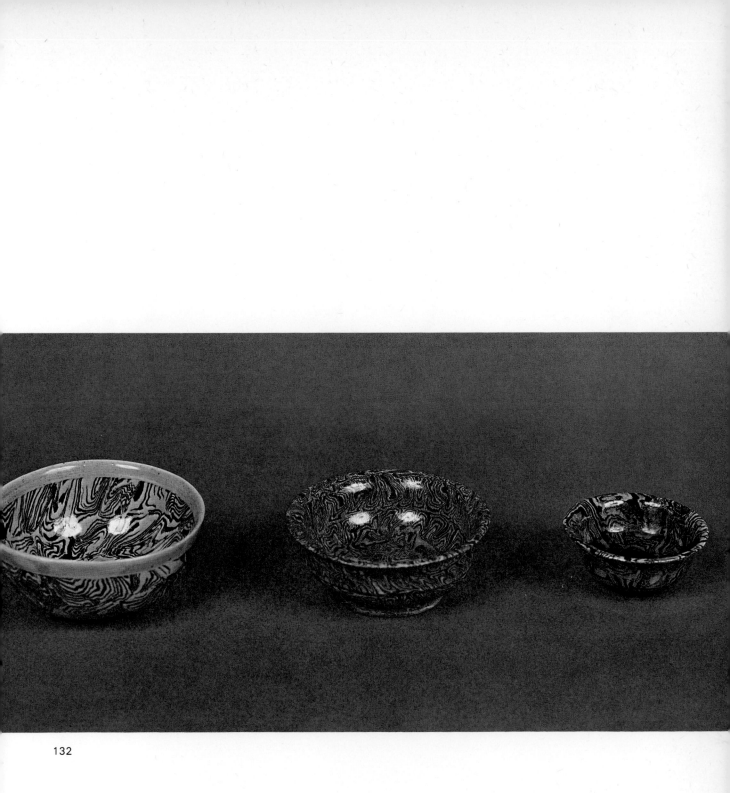

132

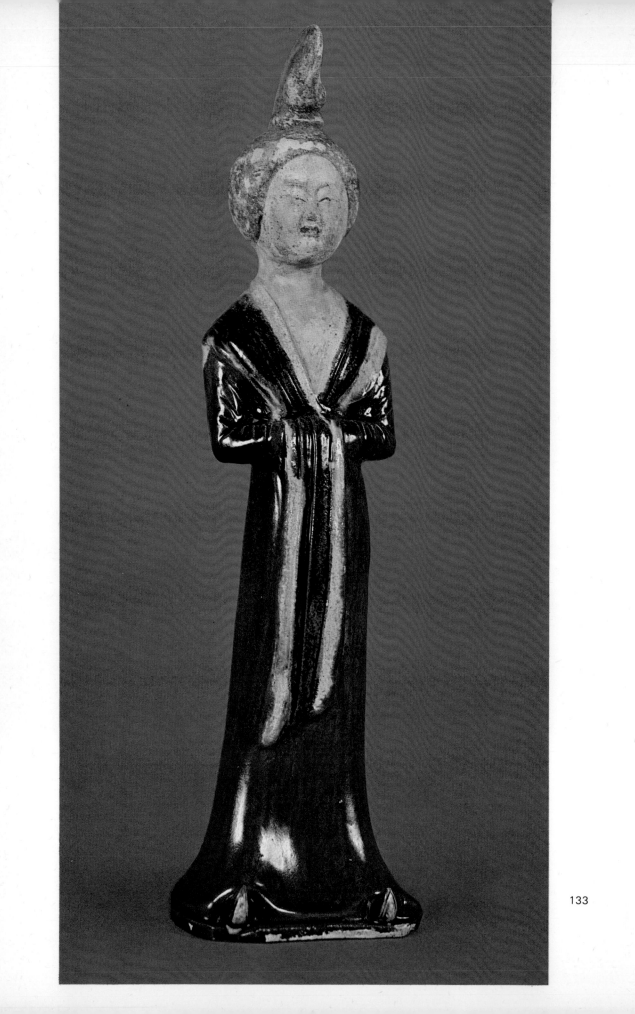

133

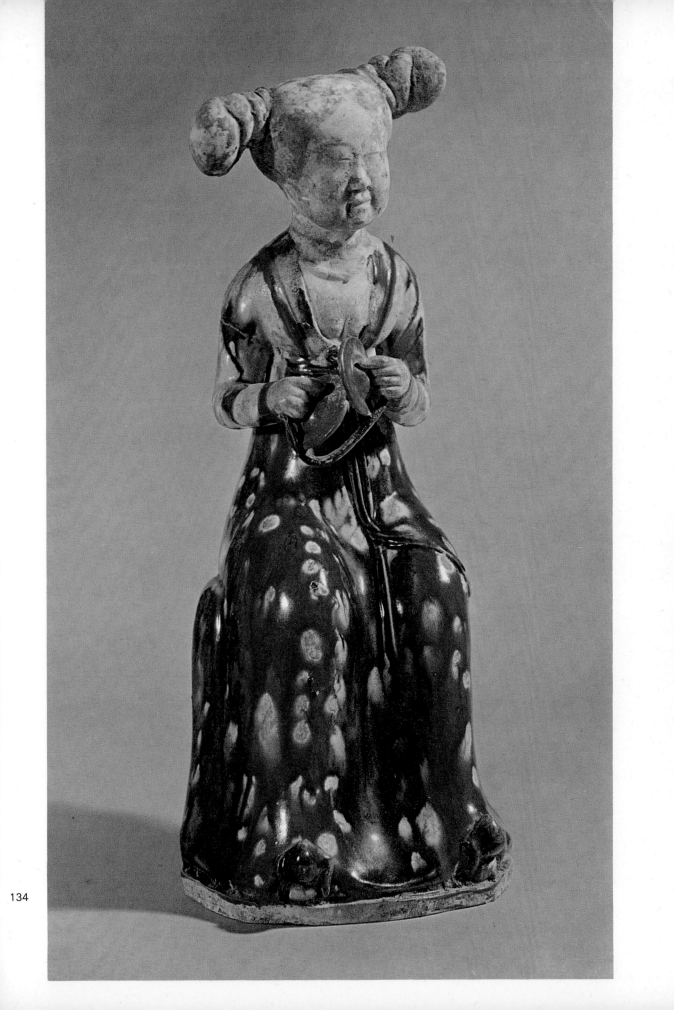

134

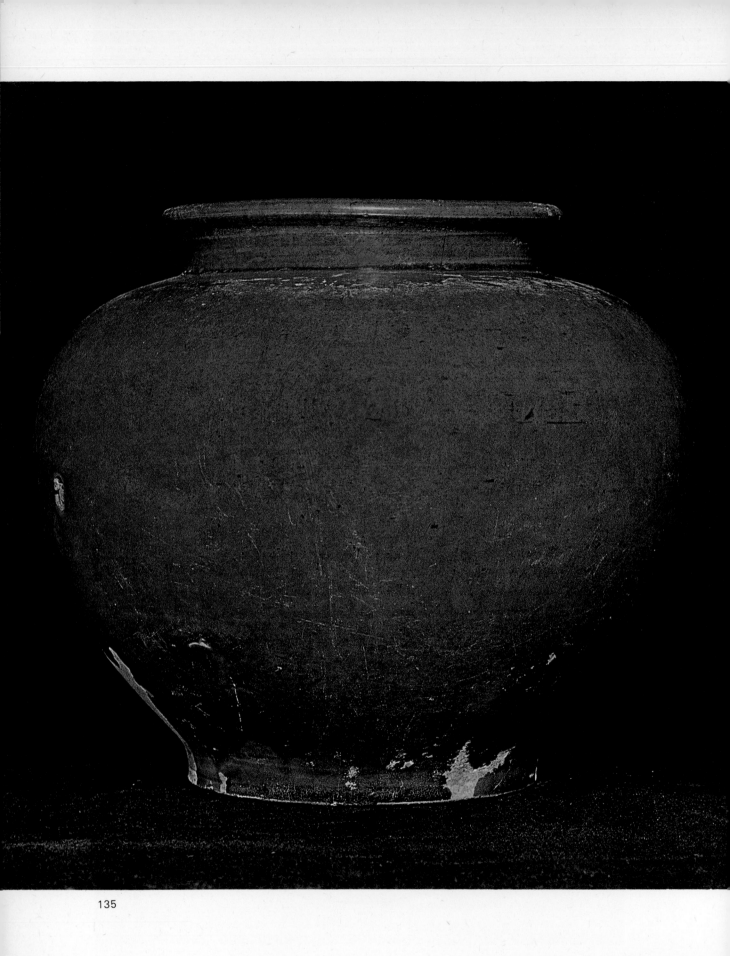

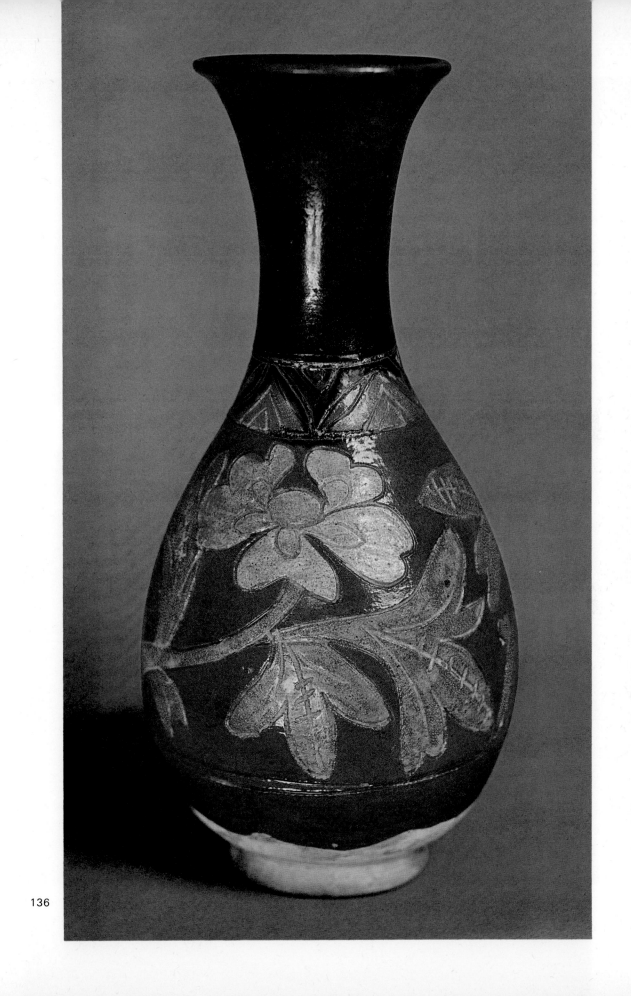

136

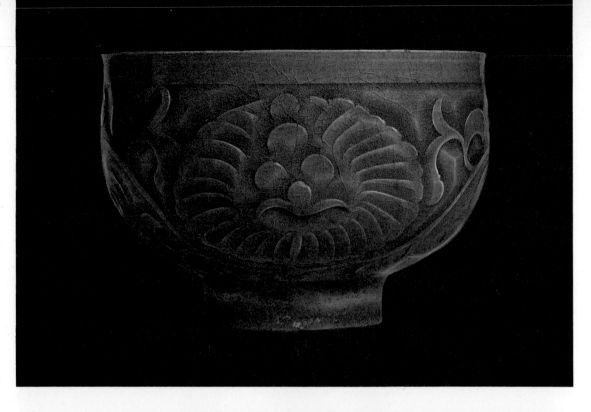

137

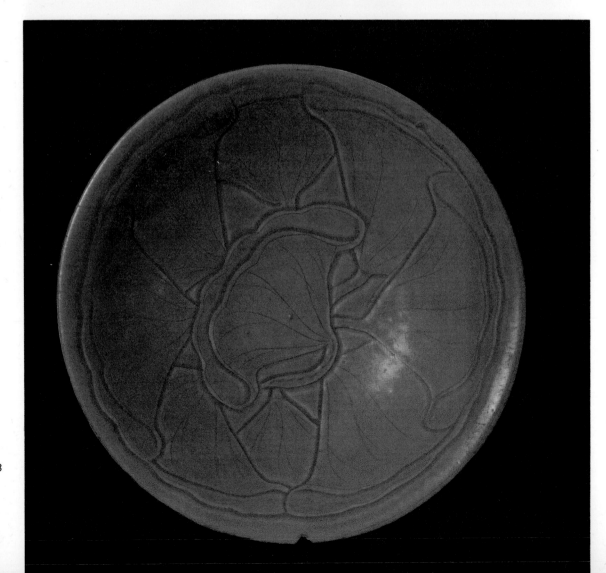

138

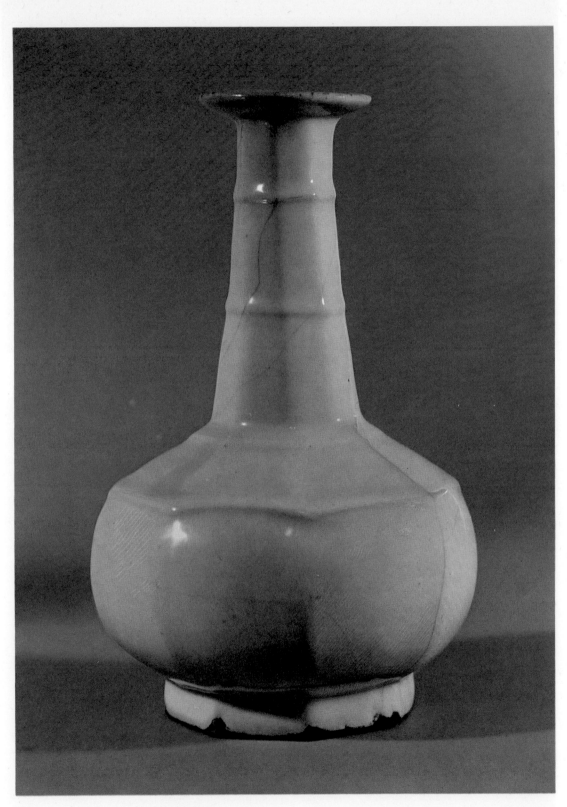

139

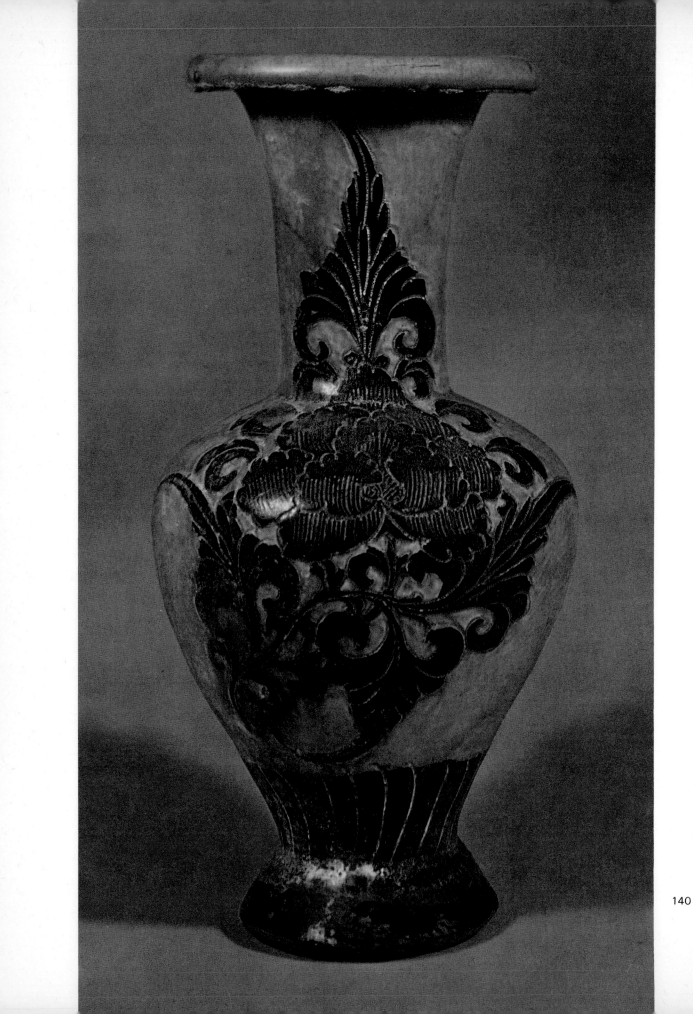

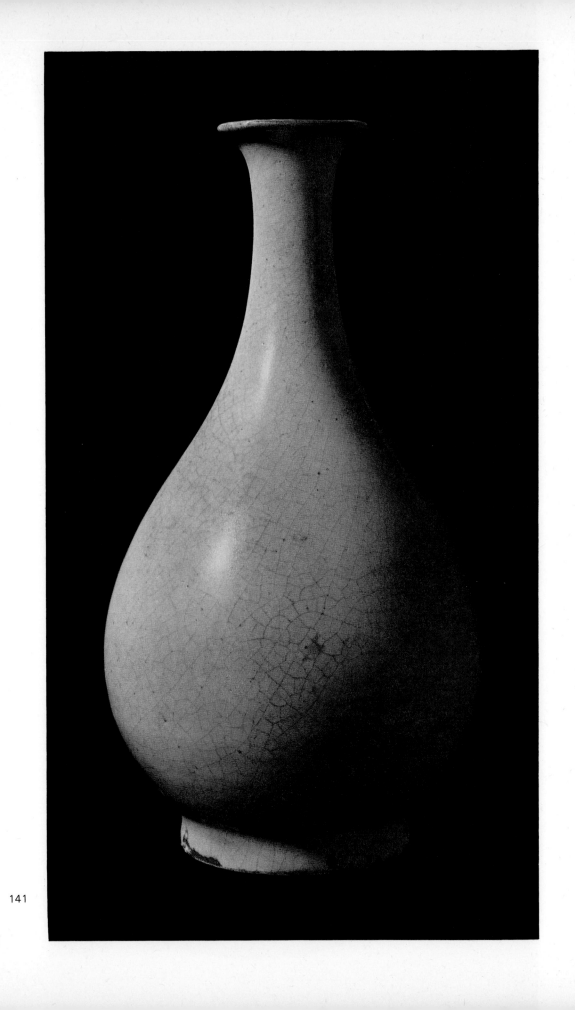

141

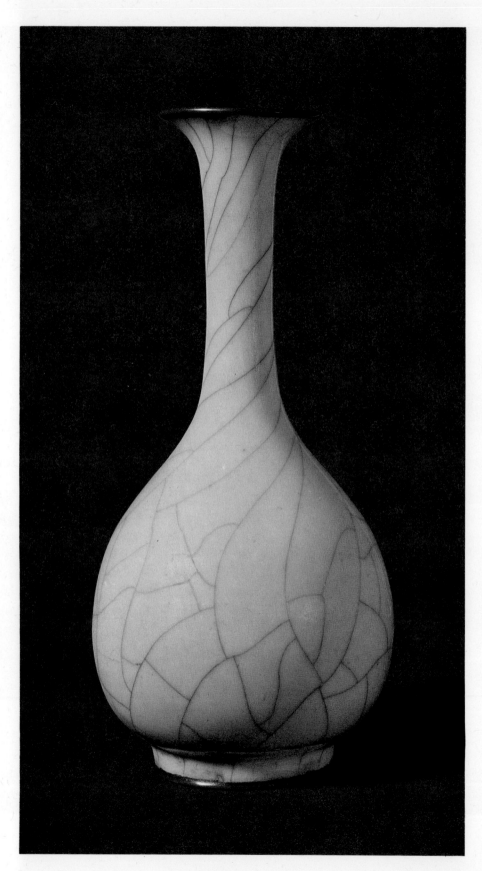

142

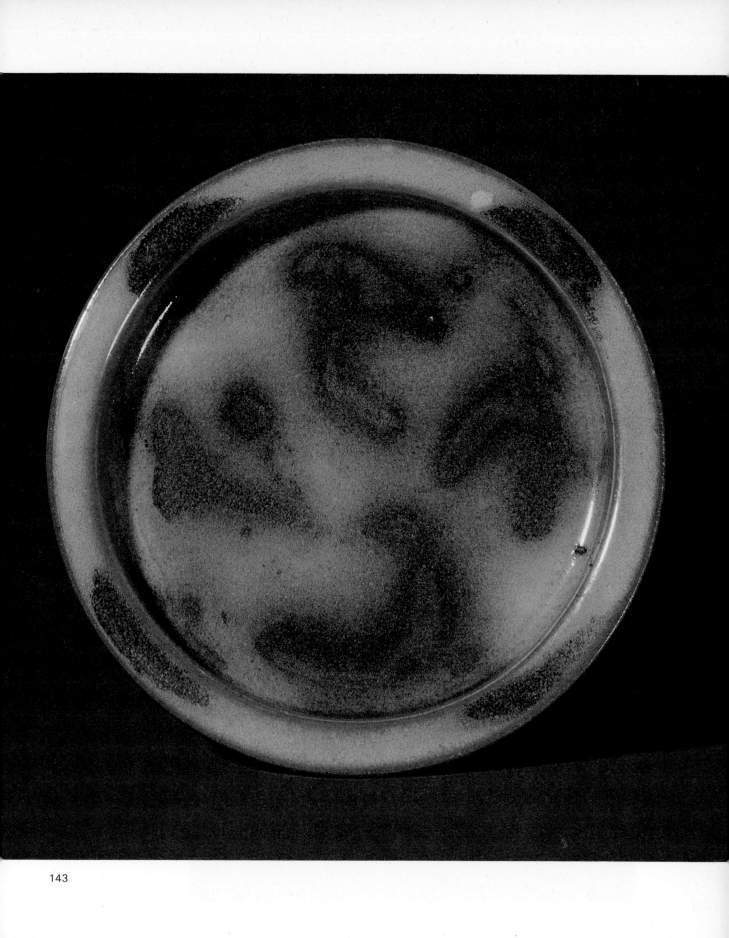

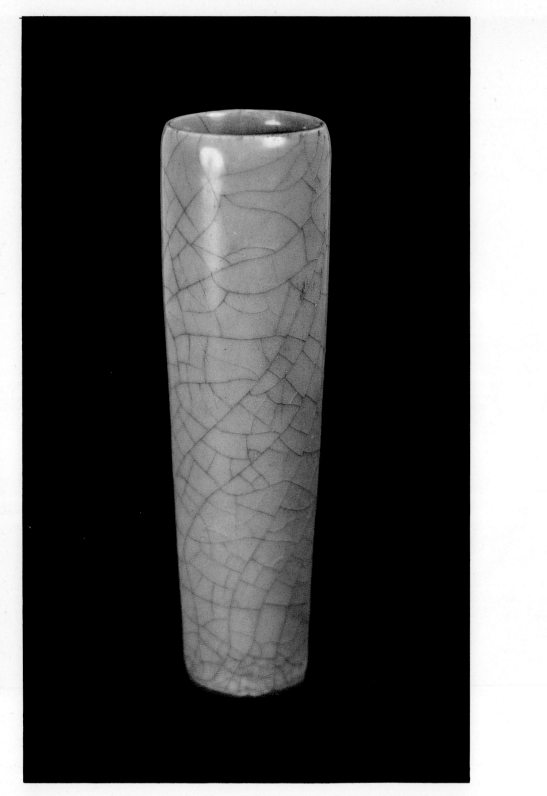

144

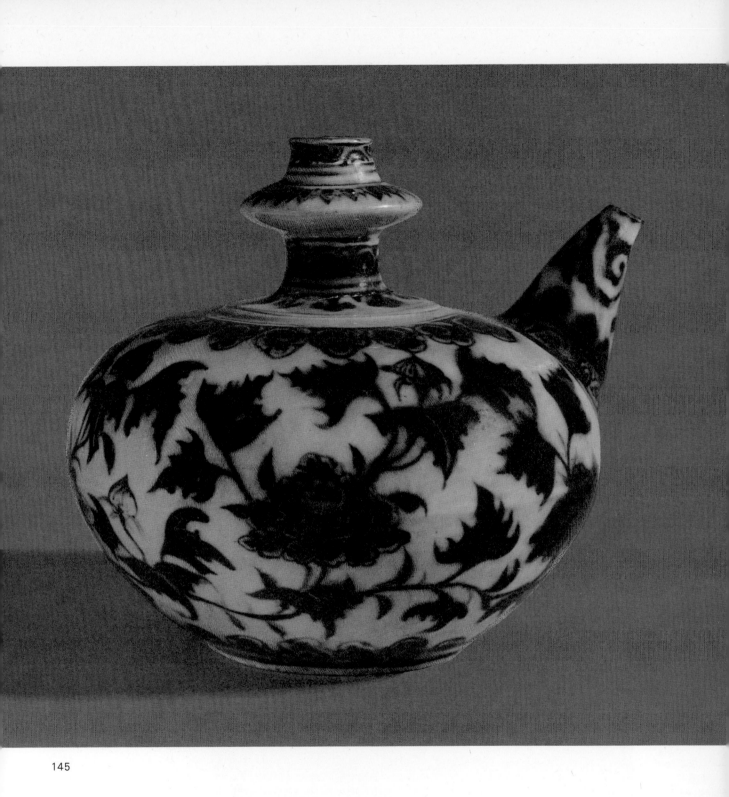

145

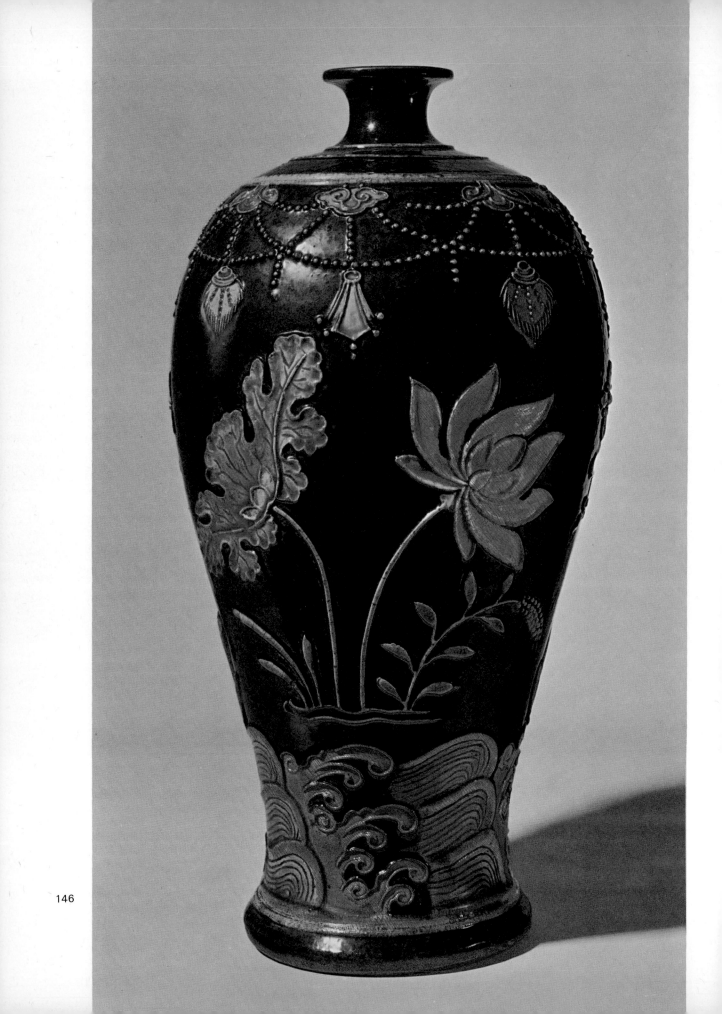

146

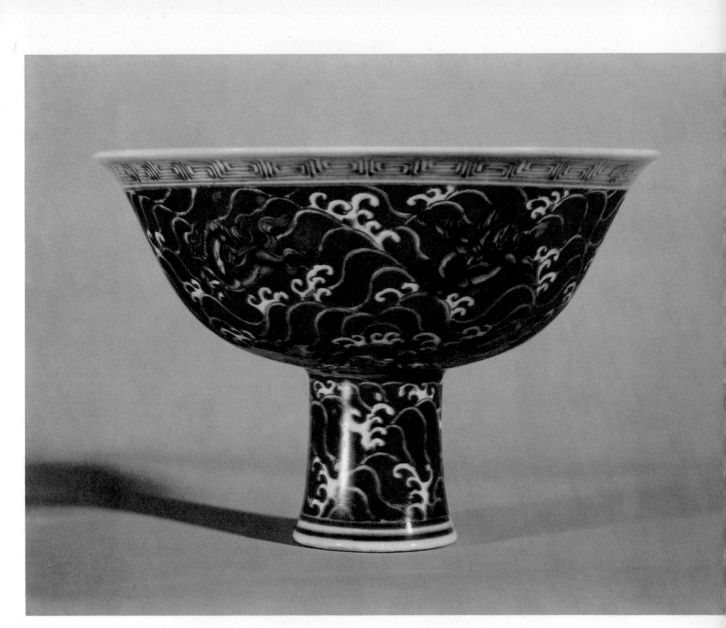

147

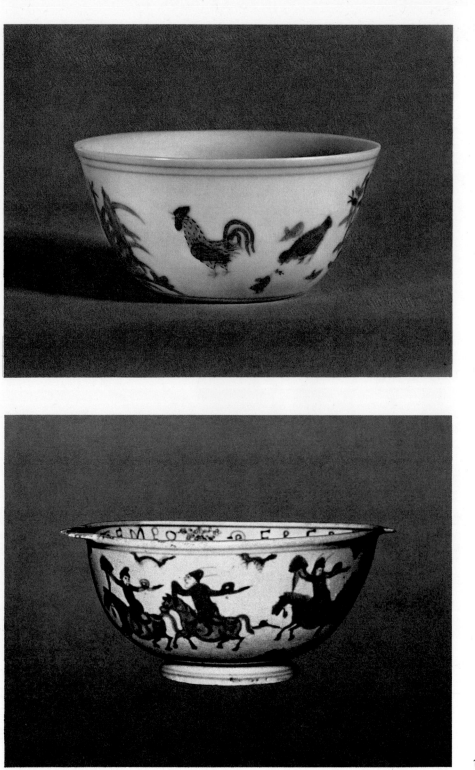

148

149

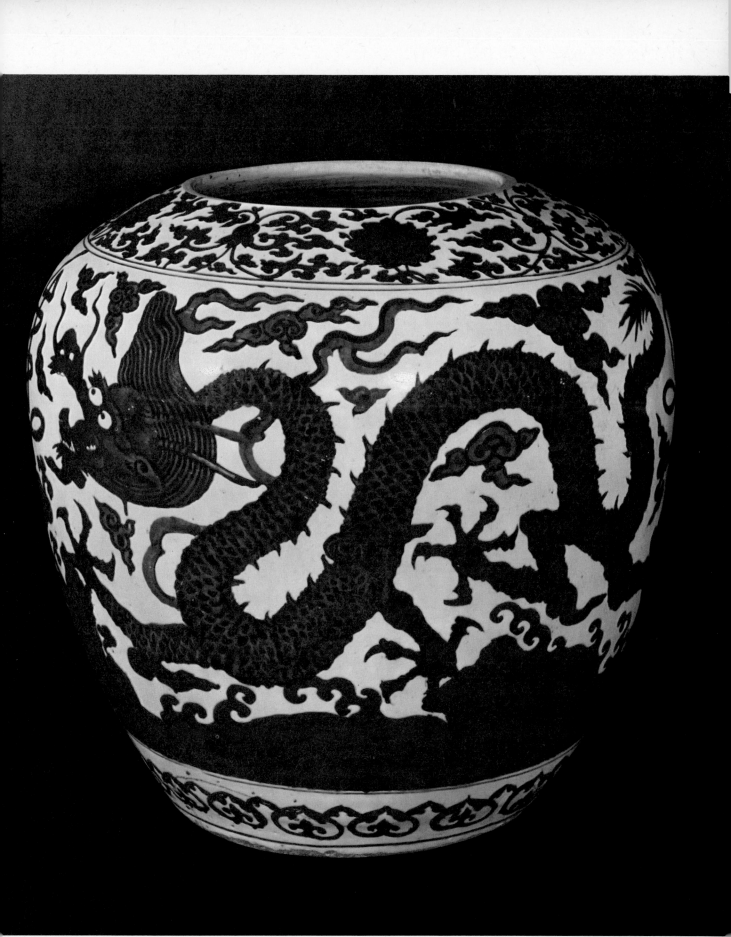

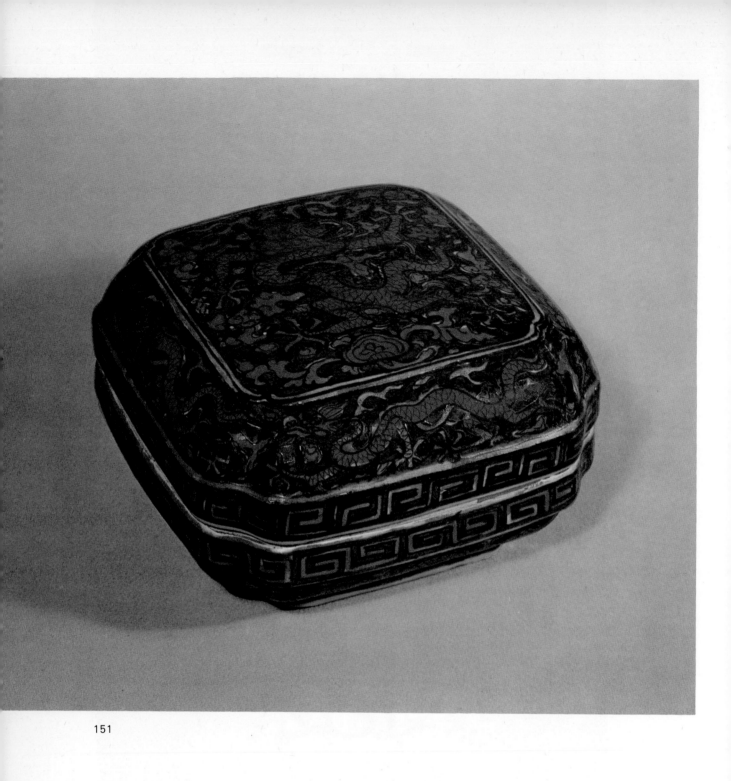

151

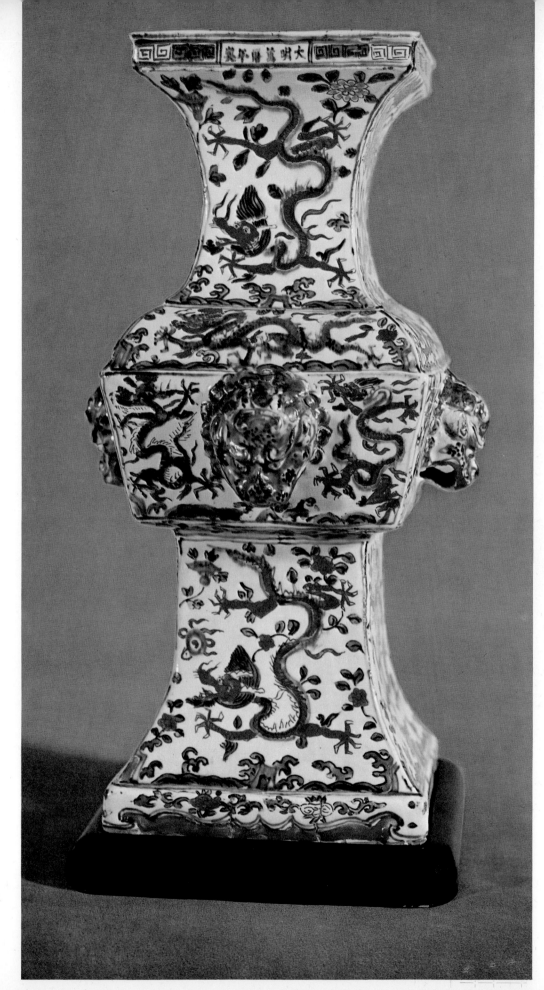

152

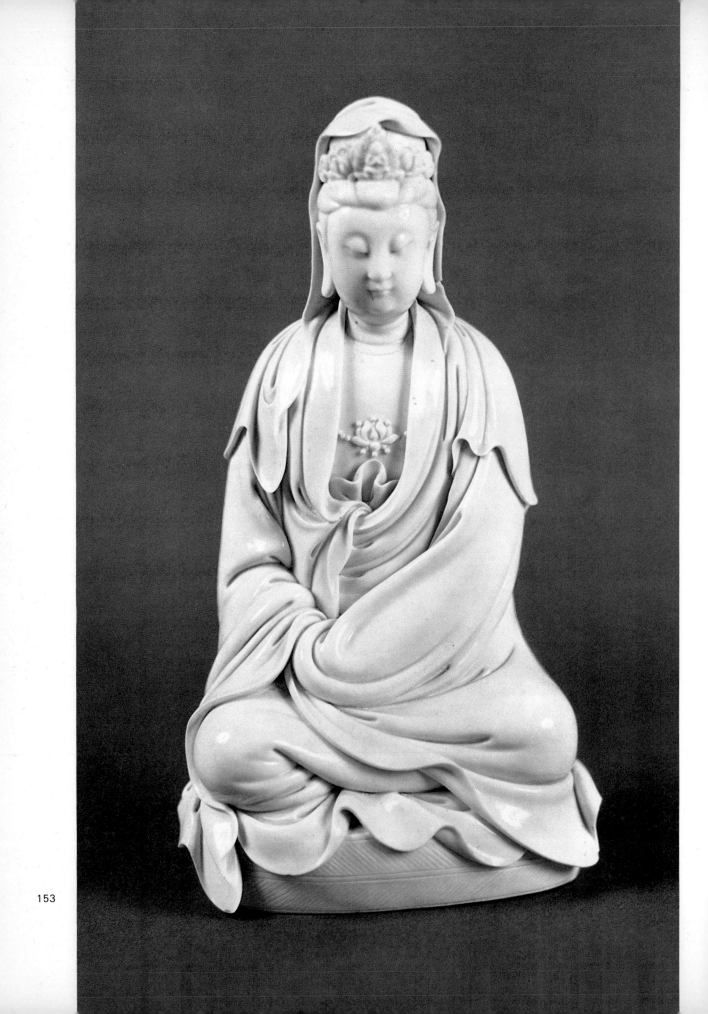

153

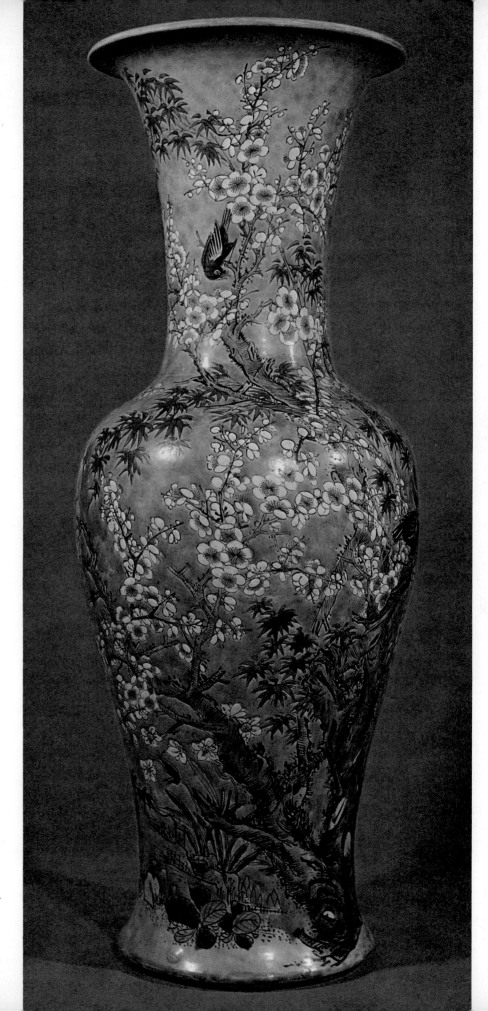

154

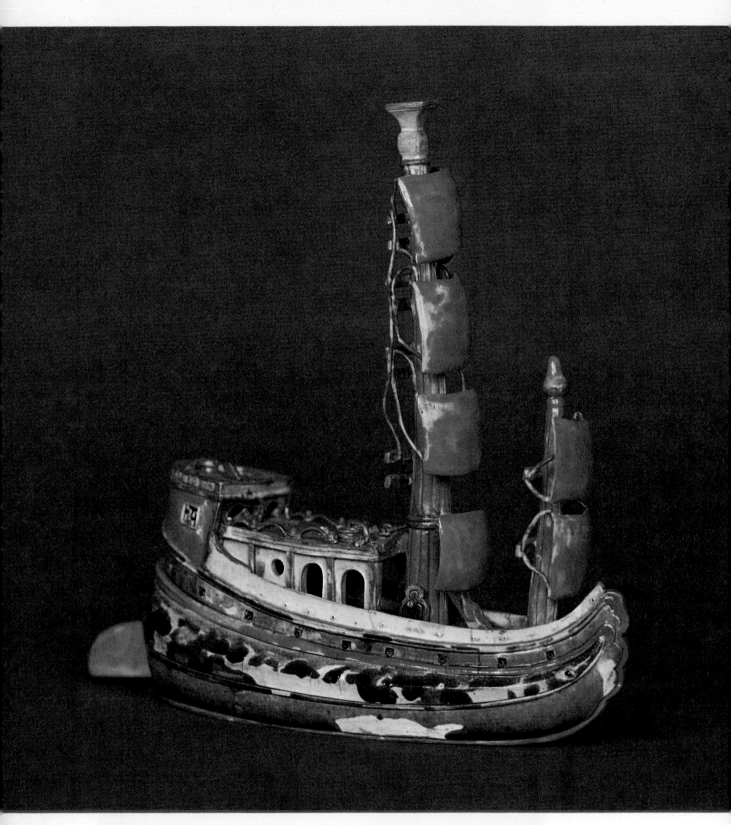

155

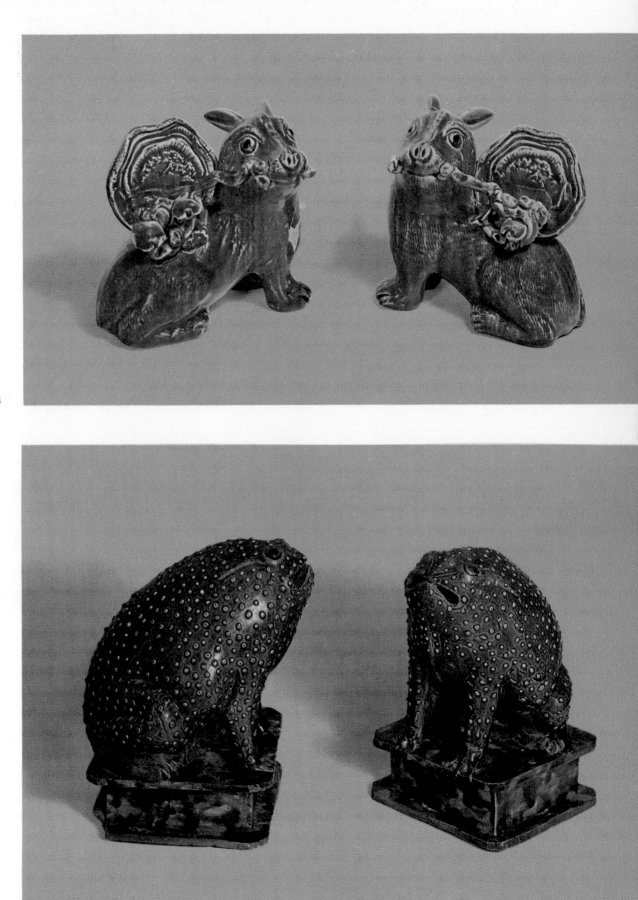

156

157

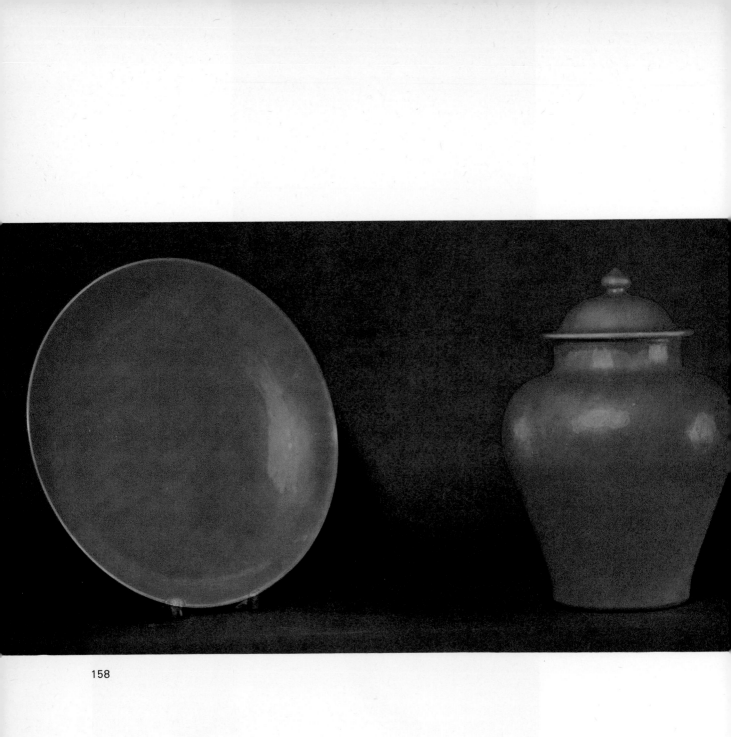

158

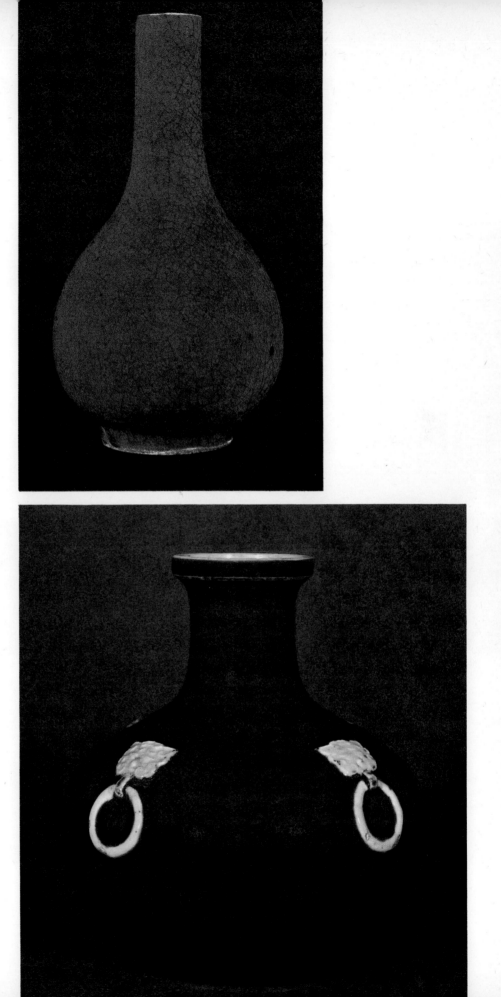

159

160

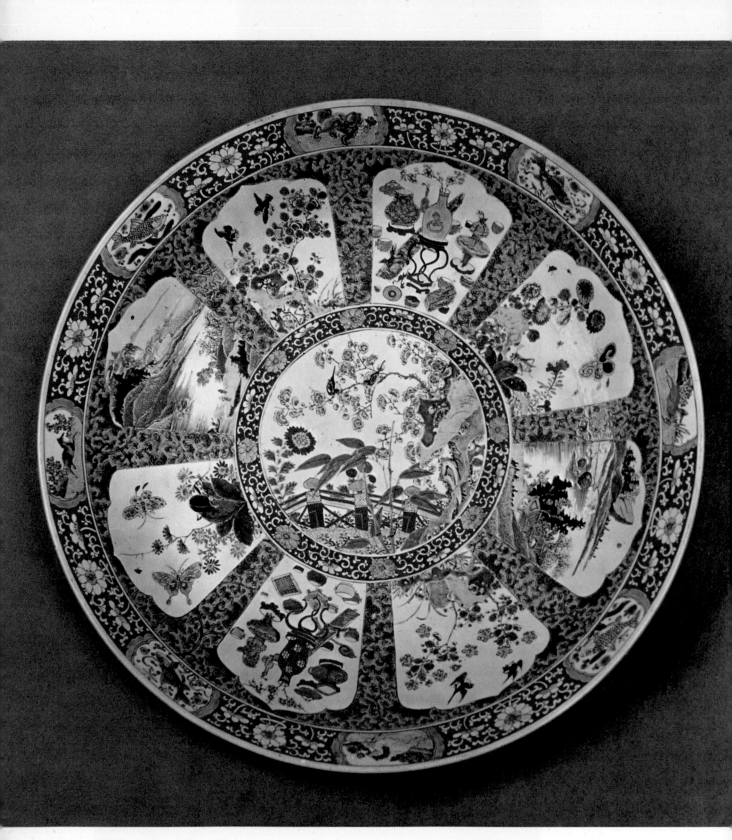

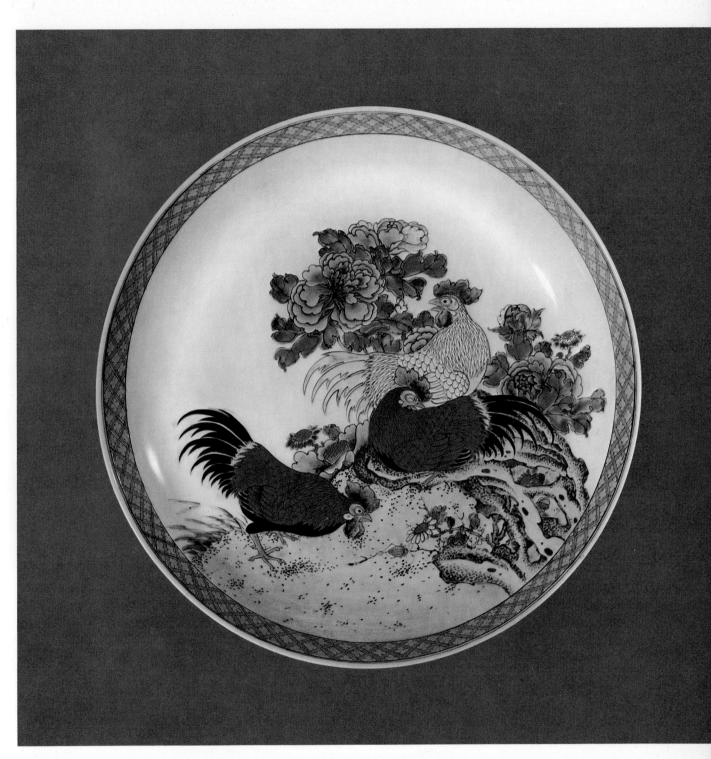

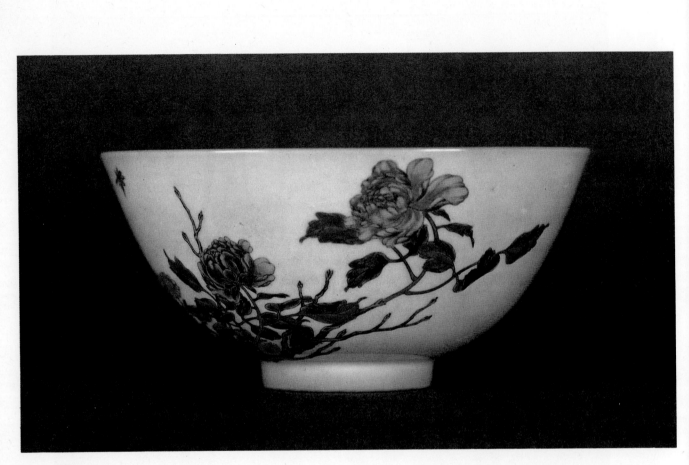

163

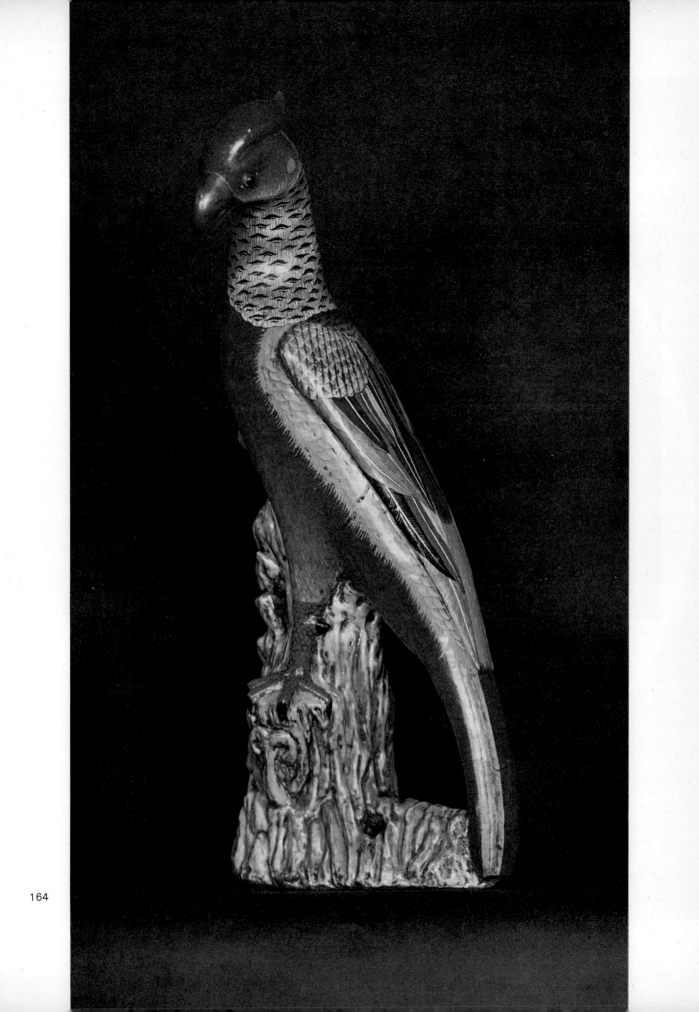

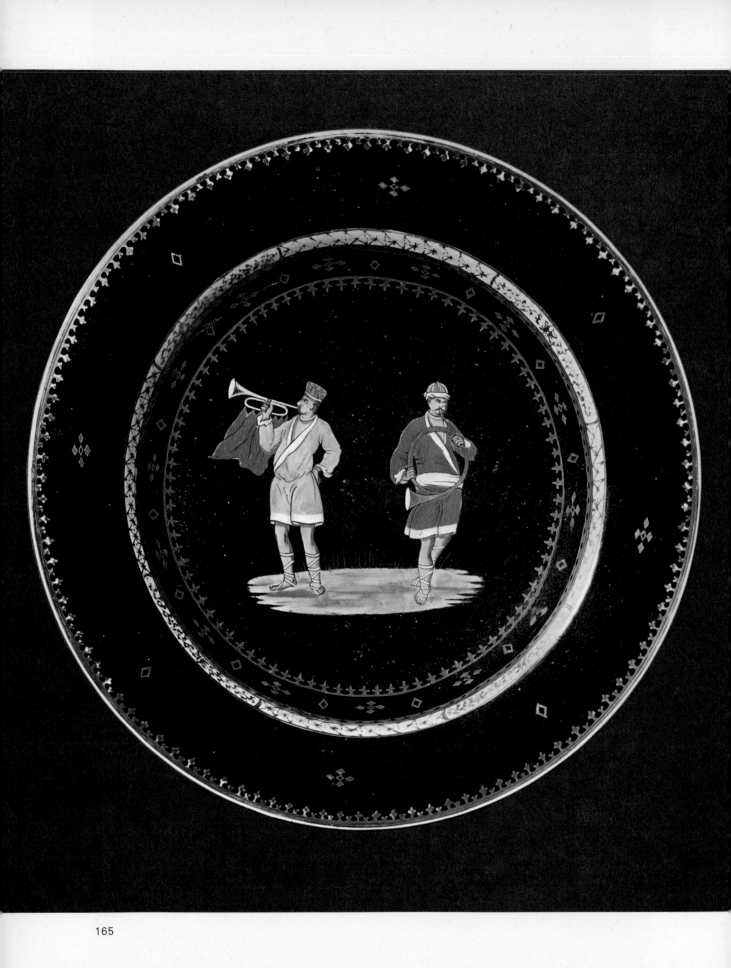

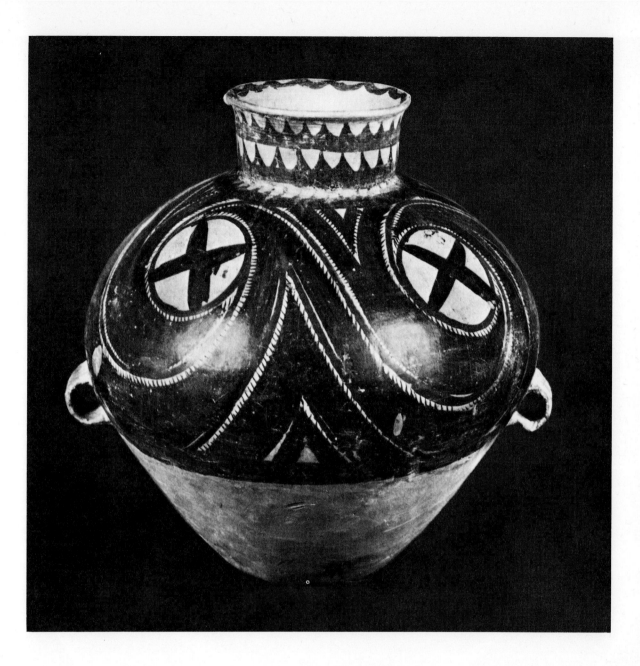

166. POTTERY VASE WITH PAINTED DECORATION
NEOLITHIC PERIOD

H. 36 cm. Formerly Collection of His Excellency M. Jacques Coiffard, Paris

Both in form and decoration this beautiful piece is typical of the pottery found at Pan-Shan in the western Province of Kansu. Unearthed from burial grounds, these are always funerary vases, and were intended to hold offerings of food for the dead. The fine clay was formed by hand and fired at a high temperature. The coiling spirals of the decoration, painted dark red and brown over light orange, have a noble breadth and balance. The neck is decorated with a denticulated pattern called the "Motif of Death."

The renowned Swedish scholar, J. G. Andersson who first discovered this painted pottery in 1920 held that the Pan-Shan pottery should be dated about 1900 B.C. Today, it is generally thought to be a little later, and to have continued, in any case, until the early days of the Shang dynasty, namely about 1300 B.C.

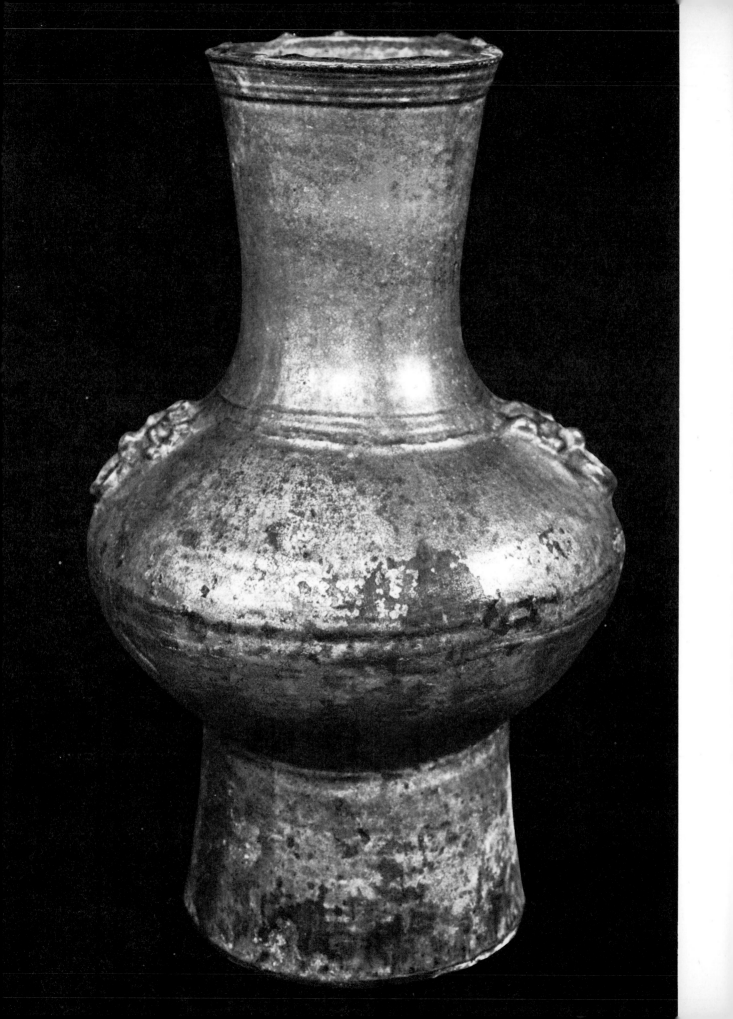

167. HU. POTTERY VASE. HAN DYNASTY

H. 37.5 cm. Collection A. de Medeiros e Almeida, Lisbon

During the Han dynasty many vases were made in the form of
the *hu;* inspired by the late Chou bronzes they were sweeping
and massive. The very simple decoration of the example shown
here is characteristic – fillets in relief and two jutting masks
reminiscent of bronze handles. The piece has a monochrome
lead glaze, perhaps originally green, but this color has gradually
disappeared with the passage of centuries of burial in the earth,
leaving in its place a golden iridescence – a source of added
beauty.

168. INCENSE-BURNER IN POTTERY
HAN DYNASTY (206 B.C.–220 A.D.)

H. 36 cm. Collection M. Jean Mahé, Paris

This type of incense-burner was part of the funeral trappings
generally buried with the dead in the Han period. It is very
close to some bronze models, although the base – which is
decorated with people and animals in relief – is reminiscent of
the friezes depicting hunting scenes to be found on pottery *hu*.
The cover has pierced holes, and these relate the piece to the
group called "hill censers" and "hill jars" – round vessels and
incense-burners with a cover in the form of a mountain, recalling the Taoist Isles of the Blest surrounded by the waves of the
sea.
Originally there was a green glaze, but this has given way to a
silvery iridescence.

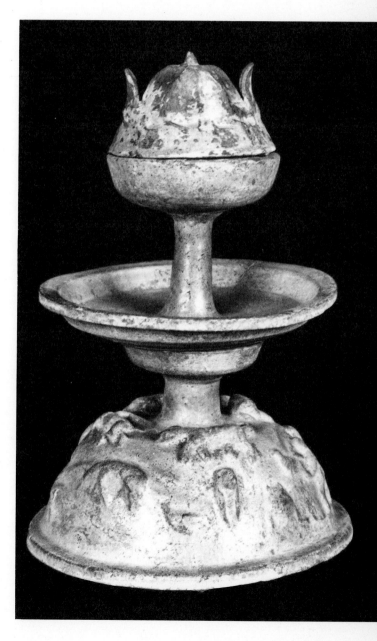

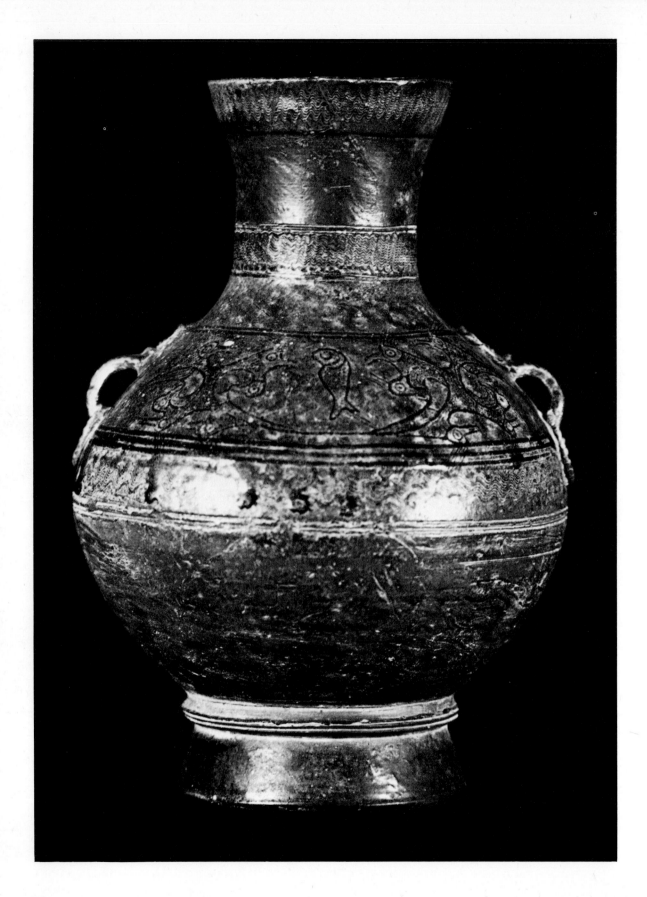

236

169. HU. VASE IN PROTO-PORCELAIN
HAN DYNASTY

H.28 cm. Guimet Museum, Paris

This vase is an exceptionally fine specimen of a type of stoneware which was identified for the first time by Berthold Laufer after discoveries had been made in Shensi Province in 1915. He called it proto-porcelain because he found a certain amount of impure *kaolin* in the body of this group. But even without this, the hardness of the body alone would certainly have established the relationship with the later porcellaneous wares.

The proto-porcelain wares are of heavy, close-textured, stoneware, covered with reddish slip. The upper part has a speckled olive green glaze which gathers in irregular drops towards the base. The form of this vase is very close to the contemporary bronze *hu*. It has the same vigor and clean lines. Friezes in relief divide it into horizontal bands, three of which are decorated with wavy lines drawn with a comb. The largest of these friezes, on the shoulder, has engraved scrolls, curves and counter-curves, ending in birds' heads, and among these a fish can be seen. There are two handles mounted with masks to carry the imagined chain ring.

170. NORTHERN CHINESE STONEWARE VASE
6TH CENTURY

H.30.5 cm. Musée Guimet, Paris (Michel Calmann Bequest)

The light olive-green glaze in this biscuit-colored stoneware vase has a fine crackle. Stopping about 7 cm above the foot, it flows down in long rivulets. The decoration on the neck, and the cup-shaped mouth, are almost peculiar to the T'ang period, but the outline of the vase and the four double handles on the shoulder justify a slightly earlier attribution.

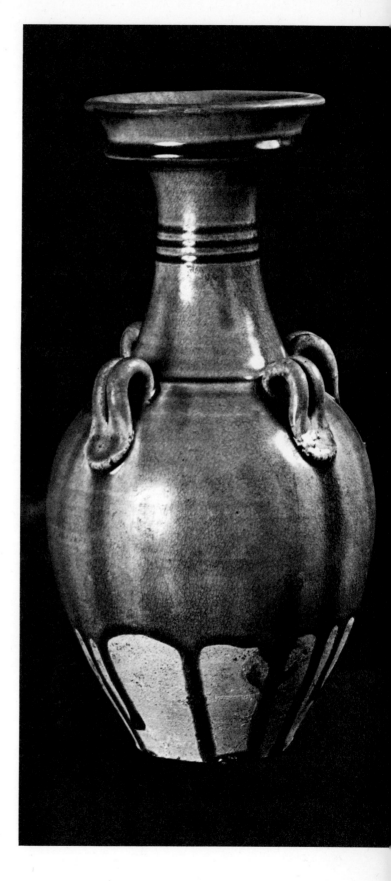

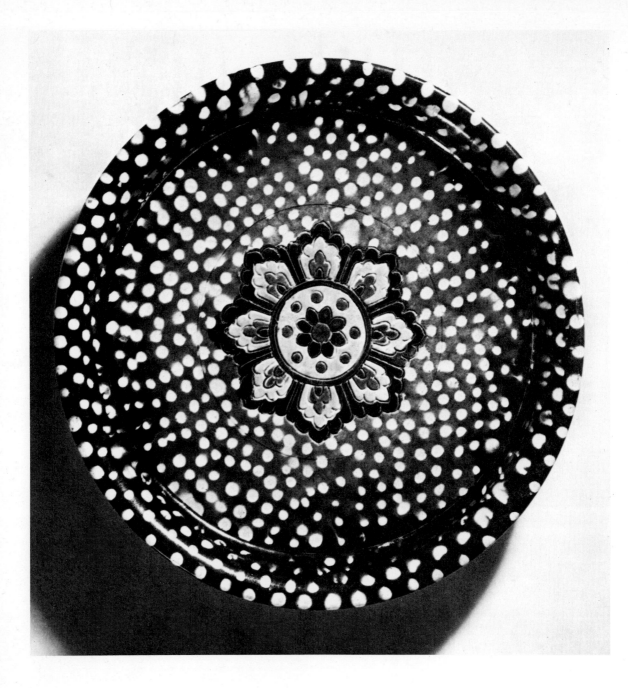

171. DISH DECORATED IN THREE-COLOR GLAZES
T'ANG DYNASTY (618–906)

D. 31 cm. Formerly Collection Mrs. Alfred Clark, Fulmer, Bucks.

This is one of the most beautiful of all known glazed T'ang dishes. It may be compared with the one shown on Plate 128. The central medallion is entirely floral, and decorated with blue and yellow glazes which are separated by incised lines. The ground is an amber yellow with irregular white spots. The reverse is covered by a blue glaze. Like all other pieces of this group, it is supported by three feet. An almost identical dish can be seen in Professor Koyama's book, *Céramique Ancienne de l'Asie* (Plate 21).

Exhibition: The Arts of the T'ang Dynasty, *Oriental Ceramic Society, London, 1955, No. 78.*

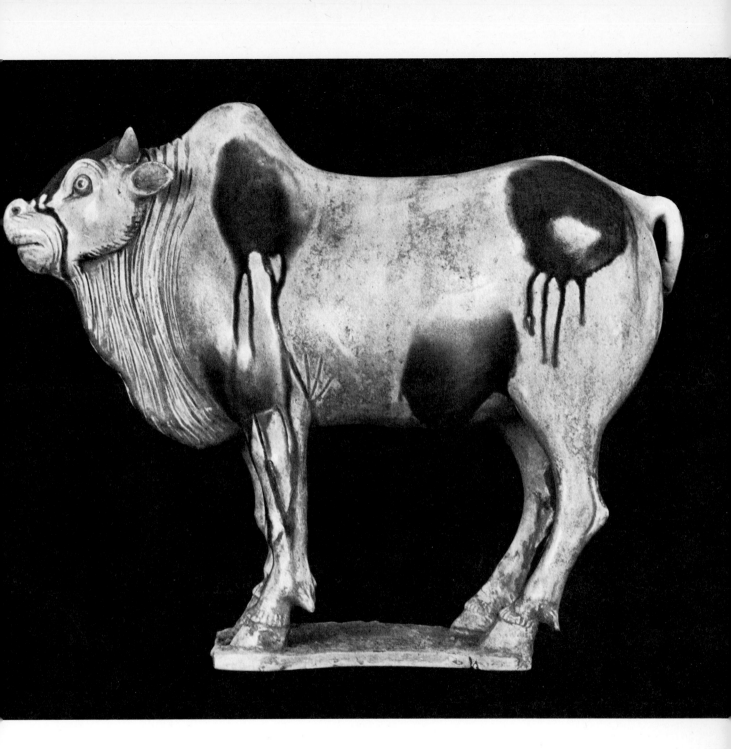

172. SMALL FIGURE OF A BUFFALO
T'ANG DYNASTY (618–906)

H. 26 cm. Musée Guimet, Paris (Michel Calmann Bequest)

The broad and sober handling of this figure wonderfully catches the bovine power of the animal, and it is, therefore, a fine illustration of the small pottery figures of the T'ang.

The glaze is uniformly cream-colored, but this is enhanced by large green splashes, which form irregular flowing rivulets. They are placed quite arbitrarily with no concern for reality.

Exhibitions: Chinese Art, *London, 1935/6, No. 2454.* – Les Arts de la Chine Ancienne, *Orangerie Museum, Paris, 1937, No. 362.*

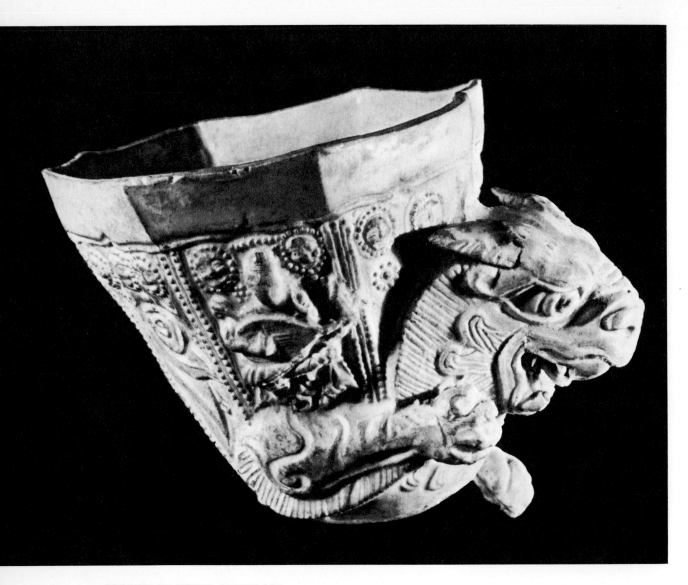

173. RHYTON IN WHITE PORCELAIN
T'ANG DYNASTY (618–906)

L.12.7 cm. Formerly Collection Mrs. Walter Sedgwick, London

The rhyton is a strange shape originating in the Hellenistic
world. There are several variants of it in T'ang ceramics, as
there was a strong taste for the exotic in all branches of art at
that time. The relief work, too, which is found on different
types of ewers and vases is Western in inspiration.

This piece represents a lion modeled in high relief and supporting a kind of octagonal shell. The decoration on each panel is
molded and engraved, and each has a musician or a floral *motif*
framed in ropes of pearls and flanked by medallions with masks.
The stippled decoration has a definite silver prototype.

The body of the piece, a white translucent porcelain, has a
cream glaze.

Exhibition: The Arts of the T'ang Dynasty, *Oriental Ceramic
Society, London, 1955, No. 216.*

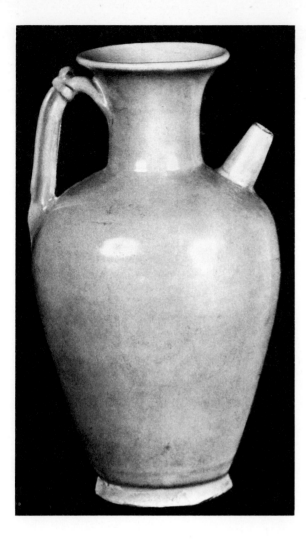

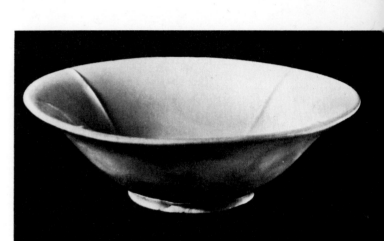

174. EWER IN WHITE PORCELAIN
T'ANG DYNASTY (618–906)

H.20.5 cm. Musée Guimet, Paris (Michel Calmann Bequest)

This small ewer is an example of the earliest porcelain in China, which was first made in the 9th century. It probably belongs to the Hsing-yao group, from Hsing-chou in Hopei (Chihli) Province, which is very highly prized because of its pure white, aptly compared with snow by the early writers.

The body is close-grained and of a clear light buff in tone. The glaze is white with bluish reflections, and under the spout it flows thickly, ending in a greenish pool. Characteristic of the T'ang period are the ovoid shape, flaring neck, short, straight spout, and beveled foot. The handle is tripartite and joined by a knot.

Exhibition: La découverte de l'Asie, *Cernuschi Museum, Paris, 1954, No. 503.*

175. BOWL IN WHITE PORCELAIN
T'ANG DYNASTY (618–906)

D.13 cm. Formerly Collection Mrs. Alfred Clark, Fulmer, Bucks.

The delicate precision of the shape of this precious bowl shows clearly the mastery of material achieved by the T'ang potters. The rim curves gently outwards, while the four incised ribs radiating from the center suggest an opening flower. The clarity and accuracy of the outline was made possible by the quality of the paste which is especially hard and resonant. The white glaze forms quick drops on the outside, foreshadowing the Ting wares of the following Sung period. The small beveled foot perfects the balance of the whole piece.

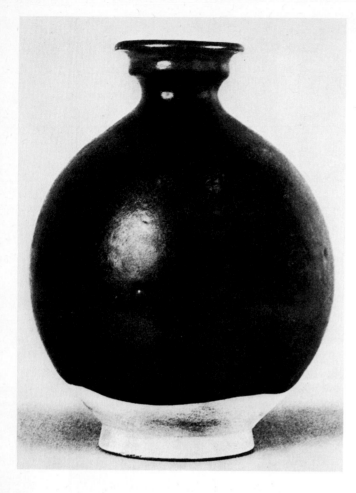

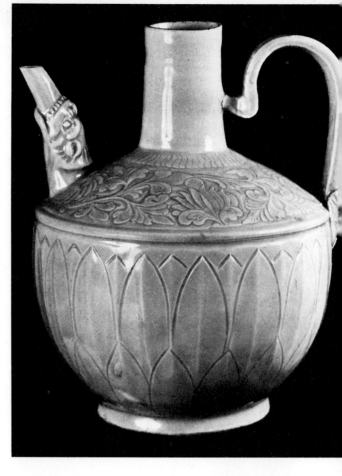

177. EWER OF TING WARE
SUNG DYNASTY (960–1276)

H.18 cm. D.8 cm. Musée Guimet, Paris (Michel Calmann Bequest)

The fascination of Sung white porcelain lies in the warm soft ivory color of the glaze, which never has the cold, crystalline appearance of the later porcelain of Ching-tê Chên. It has been said that, from a technical point of view, the porcelain of Ting Chou is the finest ceramic ware ever to be produced. The most perfect specimens date from the first quarter of the 12th century.

Most of the products found by Koyama on a site near Ting Chou in Hopei Province are bowls and dishes. Pieces like this ewer are much rarer. The elegance of this little vessel, in which the high handle balances the curved spout, is increased by the fine decoration. Remarkable relief masks, and delicate tracery on the belly of the vessel which outlines the lotus petals, seem to represent an opening flower. The floral scrolls on the shoulder are firm but light, and reminiscent of certain Tz'ŭ Chou *motifs*.

Exhibition: Arts de la Chine Ancienne, *Orangerie Museum, Paris 1957, No. 582.*

176. BLACK-GLAZED VASE OF HONAN
STONEWARE. 9TH–10TH CENTURIES

H.23.8 cm. Musée Guimet, Paris (Michel Calmann Bequest)

This beautiful globular vase is still very close to the pottery of the T'ang period. It has the same large belly, clearly molded cup-shaped neck and mouth, and the same beveled base. The body is very close-grained. The glaze, a brownish black, is lightly speckled. It stops well above the foot, contrasting sharply with the body, which is of a light color typical of pieces from Northern China.

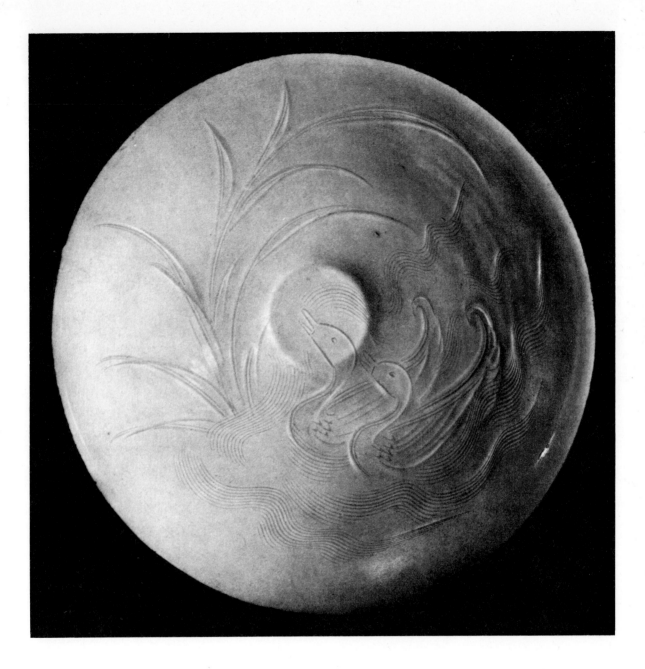

178. BOWL OF TING WARE
SUNG DYNASTY (960–1276)

D. 20 cm. Percival David Foundation of Chinese Art, London

The perfect shape of this bowl, which springs from a very small circular foot, is one of the best examples of the delicate, sensitive taste which is evident in the finest creations of Ting Chou.

The glaze is very pure white of the variety known to the Chinese as *pai-ting*, in contrast to *fên-ting* ("flour" Ting) and *t'u ting* ("earthen" Ting). It is scarcely necessary to stress the quality of the exquisite incised design, curving in harmony with the shape of the bowl.

The decoration of two mandarin ducks swimming through the waves among bent reeds is extremely skillful, and shows incomparable mastery of calligraphic line.

The rim of the bowl is mounted in copper.

Exhibition: Sung Dynasty Wares, *Oriental Ceramic Society, London, 1949, No. 23.*

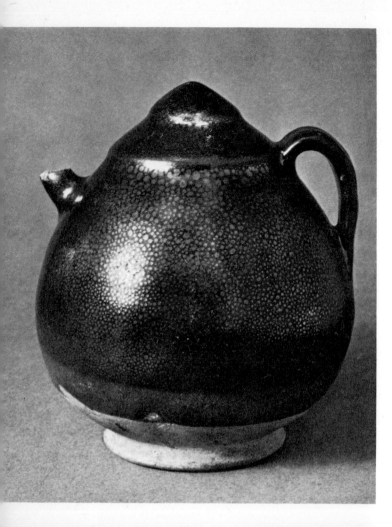

179. SMALL STONEWARE EWER. HONAN
SUNG DYNASTY (960–1276)

H.12.3 cm. Östasiatiska Museet, Stockholm (Formerly Collection H.M. the King Gustave VI Adolphe)

This fine ewer with its stumpy spout was filled from underneath. Its conical top is not detachable.

It belongs to the large group of black-glazed wares made all over Honan Province, supposedly in imitation of the *temmoku* of Fukien. This is one of the most perfect pieces known. A dark brown slip can be seen under the glaze, covering the unglazed foot. The body is a yellowish-gray stoneware.

The glaze has a ferruginous base, and is a fine blackish brown with warm reflections, and small iridescent splashes known as "oil-spots."

Exhibitions: Chinesische Kunst, *Berlin, 1929, No. 547.* – Chinese Art, *London, 1935/6, No. 1218.* – Arte Cinese, *Venice, 1954, No. 502.* – L'Art de la Chine des Song, *Museum Cernuschi, Paris, 1956, No. 84.*

180. STONEWARE BOWL WITH A
TORTOISE-SHELL GLAZE
SUNG DYNASTY (960–1276)

D.11.5 cm. Formerly Collection Mme J. Ramet, Paris

The Japanese name, *temmoku,* is used at present in the East to cover a wide variety of pieces with somber glazes, more particularly bowls coming from the southern province of Fukien. These bowls (Chien-ware) seem to have replaced the white Hsing-yao of the Sung period and the Yüeh bowls used by the T'ang for tea drinking. The Japanese prized them highly for use in the Tea Ceremony *(cha-no-yu),* and gave them this name, derived perhaps from T'ien-mu, a mountain said to be in Chekiang, near the port of Hangchow whence the pieces may have been shipped to Japan.

The *temmoku* wares of Fukien are of blackish stoneware. Pieces such as this with a light-colored body come either from the province of Kiangsi, in the districts of Chi-an or Chi Chou, or from the more northerly Provinces of Honan or Hopei. These were apparently made in imitation of Fukien stoneware, and in such widely differing styles that classification is difficult.

The light gray paste of this bowl, and the irregular glaze which is said by the Chinese to resemble tortoise-shell, make an attribution to North China tenable. The quality of the glaze, with different shades of tortoise-shell streaked on a light brown ground, is altogether remarkable.

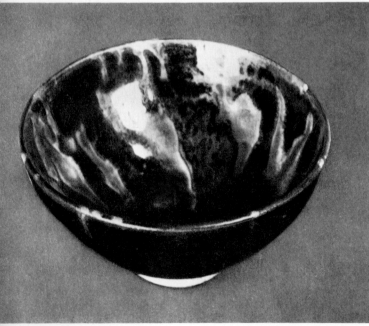

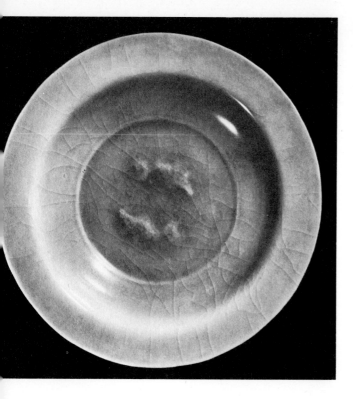 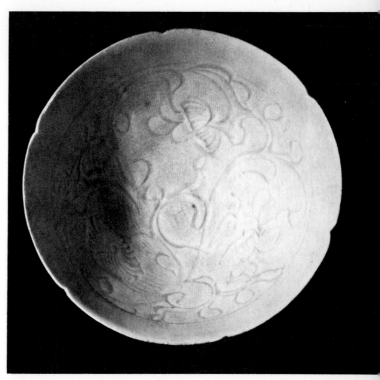

181. CELADON DISH. SUNG DYNASTY. 960–1276

D.23 cm. Formerly Collection Mrs. Alfred Clark, Fulmer, Bucks.

This deep dish, with its broad flat rim, has a relief decoration of fish, and, on the exterior, incised lotus petals. The bluish glaze has a slight crackle, and its dense opacity brilliantly reflects the light. It is a product of the finest period of Lung Ch'üan (Chekiang Province). These studios provided the Court of the Southern Sung with celadons of the greatest refinement during the 12th and 13th centuries. Many of these pieces are undecorated. When they are decorated they have simple, modest *motifs,* such as this one, which accentuate the fine thick glaze, and illustrate the sober, sensitive taste of the period.

Exhibitions: Arts de la Chine Ancienne, *Orangerie Museum, Paris, 1937, No. 440.* – Celadon Wares, *Oriental Ceramic Society, London, 1947, No. 21.* – La découverte de l'Asie, *Cernuschi Museum, Paris, 1954, No. 508.*

182. BOWL IN *ying ch'ing* PORCELAIN
SUNG DYNASTY. 960–1276

D.18 cm. Formerly Collection Mrs. Alfred Clark, Fulmer, Bucks.

The delicate and fragile type of porcelain which we know as *ying ch'ing* (shadowy blue) or *ch'ing pai* (bluish white) seems to have been unappreciated by the ancient Chinese connoisseurs who hardly mention it in the classical texts. They are of very fine workmanship, and generally have a bold and spontaneous decoration which is incised under a brilliant hard glaze which shows bluish tones in the hollows of the incisions. The sensitive floral *motif* decorating this wonderful bowl well illustrates the style of this type of rare porcelain. The impression of a flower is heightened by the indentations on the rim. The ground is delicately covered with a decoration of lightly dotted lines which is peculiar to this class of porcelain.

Exhibition: Sung Dynasty Wares, *Oriental Ceramic Society, London, 1949, No. 168.*

245

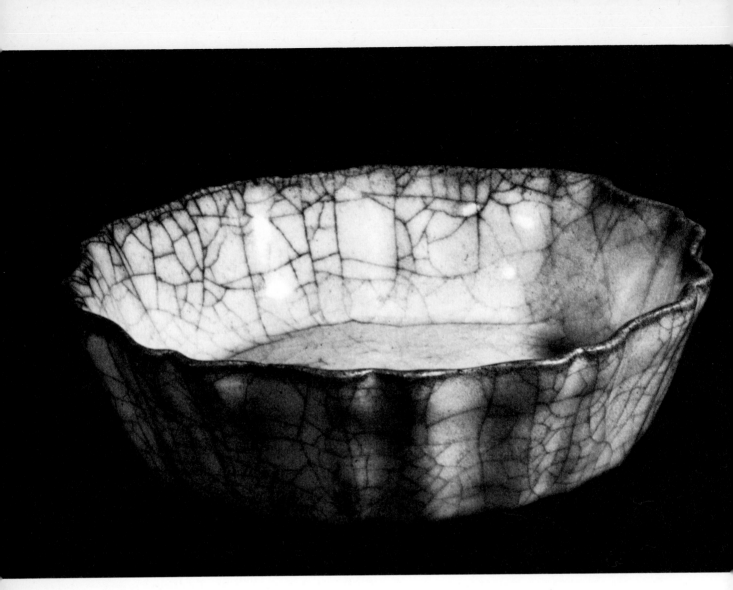

183. KUAN BOWL. SUNG DYNASTY (960–1276)

D.12 cm. (Enlarged). Collection Garner

This bowl with a flat base, intended for use as a brush washer, is one of the finest known examples of Kuan ware from the kilns near the Altar of Heaven, or Ch'iao-tan, at Hangchow. The production of this type of ware started in the 12th century, and must have been considerable, for many fragments have been found on the site of the ancient kilns. The bowl shown here is an Imperial piece, as is testified by the dark, somber body and its technical perfection. The sides are slightly flaring and delicately lobed, while the fine uniform gray glaze has a wonderful crackle of darker gray. The foot, which is also glazed, bears traces of six spur marks.

Exhibitions: Ju and Kuan Wares, *Oriental Ceramic Society, London, 1952, No. 67.* – Arte Cinese, *Venice, 1954, No. 460.*

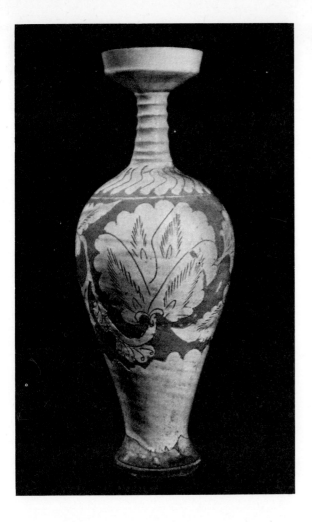

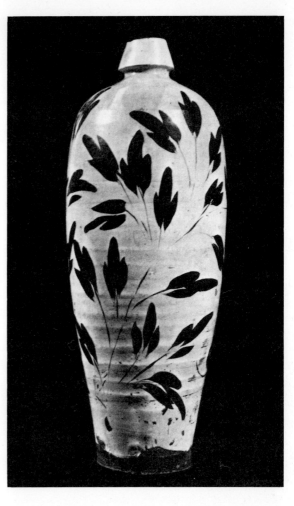

184. TZ'Ŭ CHOU VASE WITH CARVED
DECORATION. SUNG DYNASTY (960–1276 A.D.)

H.36 cm. Private Collection

The production of Tz'ŭ Chou wares probably started after the end of the 10th century. This fine vase seems to belong to the beginning of the dynasty. Indeed, its shape – the long neck ending in a cup-like mouth – remains very close to some T'ang models.

The decoration, peonies, leaves, and swaying branches, is broadly and boldly drawn. The top and bottom are covered with a thick cream slip and the floral *motif* stands out in light relief against the carved ground of gray unglazed stoneware which can also be seen through the incised design (cf. Plate 140).

185. TZ'Ŭ CHOU VASE WITH PAINTED
DECORATION. SUNG DYNASTY (960–1276)

H.38 cm. Collection Eskenazi, London

The shape of this vase is typical of the Sung dynasty; gently curving outlines and pure and simple lines. The small conical neck is also characteristic, and foreshadows the *mei ping* – a classic shape dating from the end of the Sung, and continuing during the Ming period (cf. Plate 146). The vase illustrated is typical of the painted decoration of the Tz'ŭ Chou potters, and is remarkably spontaneous. The leaf *motif* is freely handled, arching gracefully round the vase, and standing out in a strongly contrasting black against the white slip. The whole piece is covered with a transparent glaze.

A very similar vase, but with peonies as well as leaves on the painted branches, is to be seen in the Victoria and Albert Museum, London.

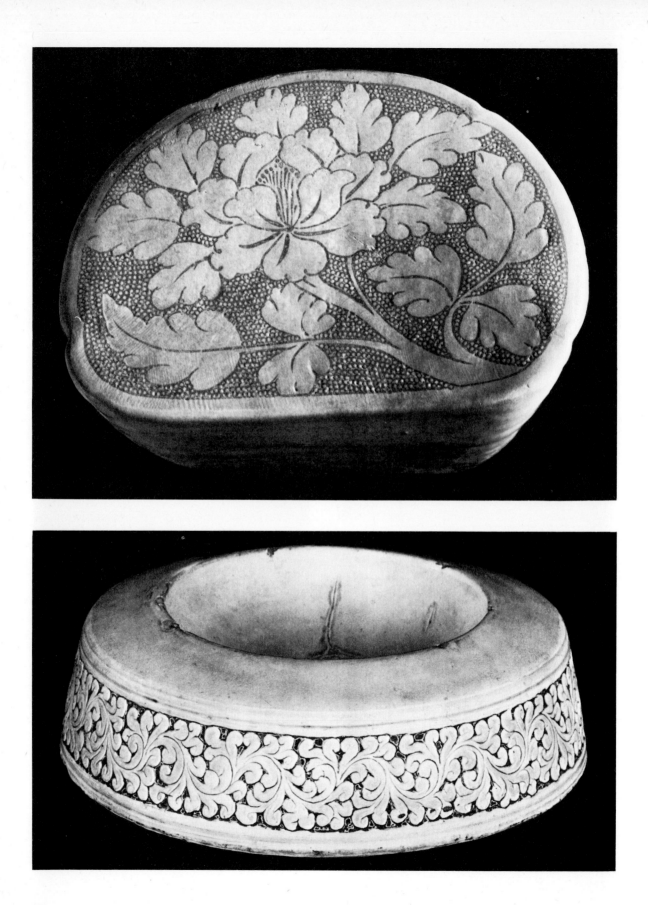

186. TZ'Ǔ CHOU PILLOW. SUNG DYNASTY (960-1276)

L. 22.8 cm. Collection Garner

This heavy stoneware piece illustrates one of the many shapes to be found in pillows of the Sung dynasty. A branch of peonies with spreading leaves fills the whole surface, and this decoration, incised through a thick slip, is filled with brown pigment. Small engraved circles also filled with pigment cover the whole ground. This was a general technique of the Tz'ǔ Chou potters. Professor Koyama has found fragments with similar decoration on kiln-sites at Chia-tso in Northern Honan, not far from Tz'ǔ Chou.

187. STONEWARE MORTAR. TZ'Ǔ CHOU TYPE SUNG DYNASTY (960-1276)

D. of base 21.9 cm. Musée Guimet, Paris (Michel Calmann Bequest)

A very fine example of this type of pottery, and of a rare shape, the piece illustrated was found at Tan-yang in Honan province, and is related to the group of Tz'ǔ Chou wares with carved decoration.
The base in the form of a ring is unglazed; the paste, a pale buff tinged with red. The glaze is grayish-white, thin, and finely crackled.
A continuous scroll of leaves covers the sides with a dense concentrated pattern, incised through the thick slip and standing out in relief against the dark ground.

Exhibition: Arte Cinese, Venice, 1954, No. 520.

188. LARGE CELADON VASE FROM LUNG CH'ÜAN. MING DYNASTY. DATE, 1454

H. 68 cm. Percival David Foundation of Chinese Art, London

Under both the Yüan and the Ming dynasties the Lung Ch'üan kilns were very active. It is known that about twenty kilns were working during this period, whereas there had been only twelve at the time of the Sung. Most of these pieces were intended for export to the Near East, and some were very large, though, in general, they were not so finely potted, and the glaze no longer had the unctuous cloudiness which was the great fascination of the older celadons.
The majestic baluster vase here shown, with its long and flaring neck, is one of the most important dated vases belonging to the David Foundation, which is so rich in inscribed and dated pieces. It belongs to that class of vase known by the Japanese name, *Tenryūji,* after a vase of the same type preserved under this name in the Temple of Kyōtō. In a cartouche on the neck there is a long inscription which places the vase in the fifth year of the reign of Ching T'ai (1454). The incised floral decoration – two large scrolls on the belly of the vase – is typically Ming, and may be compared with some designs in blue-and-white, and also on contemporary *cloisonné* enamel.

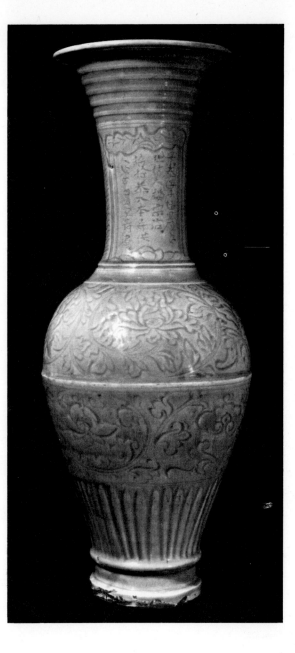

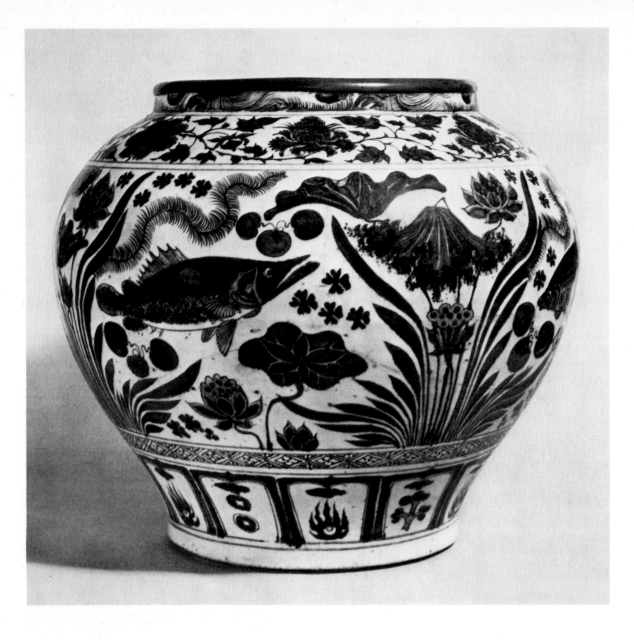

189. WINE JAR. BLUE-AND-WHITE
PORCELAIN. 14TH CENTURY

H. 29.6 cm. Collection Garner

This wine jar is easily recognized from its spreading shape and
wide mouth as one of a group of 14th century blue-and-white
which includes some of the masterpieces of Chinese porcelain.
The decoration is even more revealing than the form – on the
belly a naturalistic theme carried out with faithful observation;
waves encircling the neck (itself lightly ground and mounted
with metal); poppy scrolls on the shoulder; and rectangular
panels with emblems of good fortune – all typical of the repertory of the 14th century artist. These patterns surround the
main design, which was to be repeated frequently in the future,

especially in the 16th century, but never again with this vitality,
realism, and swirling movement, nor with such fidelity.

The pike alone, among the fish swimming in the loosely floating weeds is easy to identify. Every detail of leaves, flowers, and
lotus seeds is depicted with a sense of reality which was to disappear in later years. The intense deep blue stands out through
a thick, bluish, free-flowing glaze. John Pope has recently
published a masterly study of a series of similar wine jars preserved at Istanbul and Teheran. From this we can say that the
jar illustrated here is probably one of a group made for export
to the Near East, and generally thought to date from the
second half of the 14th century. It is not, however, possible to
date them more exactly.

Exhibition: Arte Cinese, Venice, 1954, No. 613.

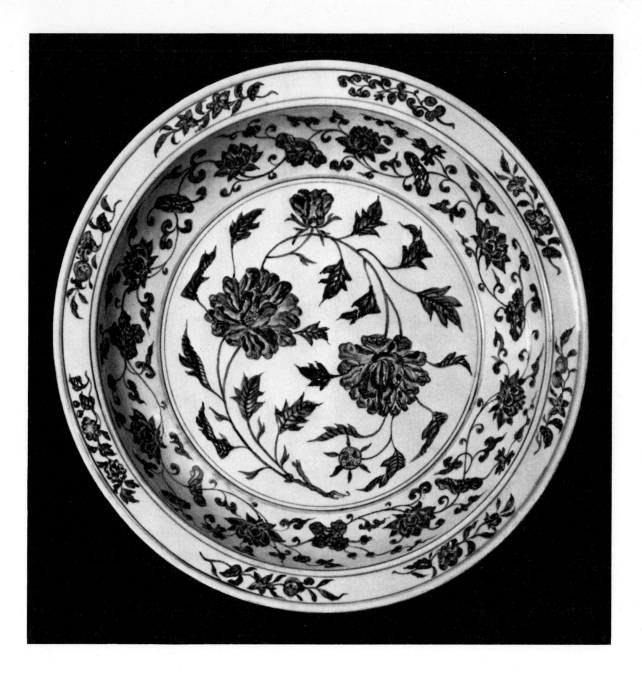

190. LARGE BLUE-AND-WHITE DISH. MING DYNASTY. BEGINNING OF THE 15TH CENTURY

D. 40.2 cm. Calouste Gulbenkian Foundation, Lisbon

Very large dishes of the kind shown here are, in varying form, characteristic of porcelain of the 14th and early 15th centuries. Their perfection is proof of the technical mastery of the Chinese potters of the period.

It is a deep dish, but it has a flat rim after the fashion of Near Eastern metalwork. The base is unglazed, and the body has been fired to a light rose color.

The decoration is in deep blue, skillfully shaded. A freely-handled *motif* of twining peonies with leaves and buds is beautifully painted in the center. The theme is very like those of the 14th century, as are the lotus flowers which decorate the sides. The eight flower *motifs* on the rim are, however, much more conventional in style and more typical of the early 15th century.

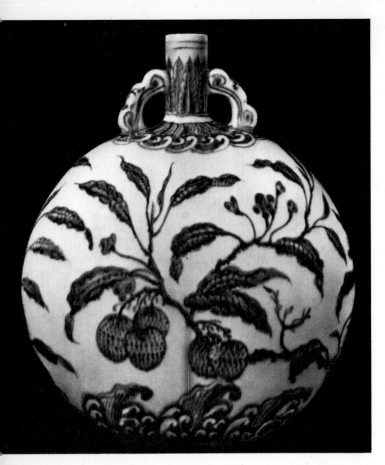

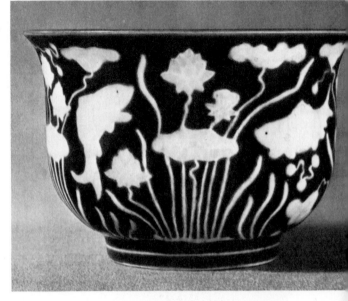

191. PILGRIM FLASK. BLUE-AND-WHITE
PORCELAIN. MING DYNASTY
EARLY 15TH CENTURY

H.24 cm. Formerly Collection Mrs. Alfred Clark, Fulmer, Bucks.

This elliptical bottle with the cylindrical neck supporting two
small handles is an example of the "full moon flasks" typical
of the 15th century. A magnificent piece made early in the
period, it still has the vigor and realism of the blue-and-white
of the preceding century. Lichee branches and fruit decorate the
body, while above and below foaming waves complete the
design. These waves also were taken from the repertory of the
preceding century. Curving leaves twine themselves round the
neck. Strong and shaded in color, the blue is handled freely,
with no firm outlines, and shows blackish spots due to oxy-
dation in the kiln.

Exhibitions: Chinese Art, *London, 1935–36, No. 1470.* – Chinese
Blue-and-white Porcelain, *Oriental Ceramic Society, London,
1953/4, No. 45.* – The Arts of the Ming Dynasty, *Oriental
Ceramic Society, London, 1957, No. 121.*

192. PORCELAIN BOWL WITH BLUE GROUND
MING DYNASTY. REIGN OF HSÜAN-TÊ (1426–35)

H.10.2 cm. Formerly Collection Sir Percival David, London

After the 14th century there was a variation on the blue-and-
white theme, namely a reserved decoration in white on a blue
ground; the opposite, in fact, to the usual method. This technique was still being used at the beginning of the 15th century,
and can be seen in the very deep bowl shown here. The decoration – fish swimming among water plants – is most delicately
executed. As in most cases where this method is adopted, the
white *motifs* are accentuated with a very light tracing of slip
which is finely engraved. The subject is repeated on one panel
of the interior of the bowl.
The piece has the mark of the reign of Hsüan-tê in underglaze
blue on the base.

Exhibition: The Arts of the Ming Dynasty, *Oriental Ceramic
Society, London, 1957, No. 128.*

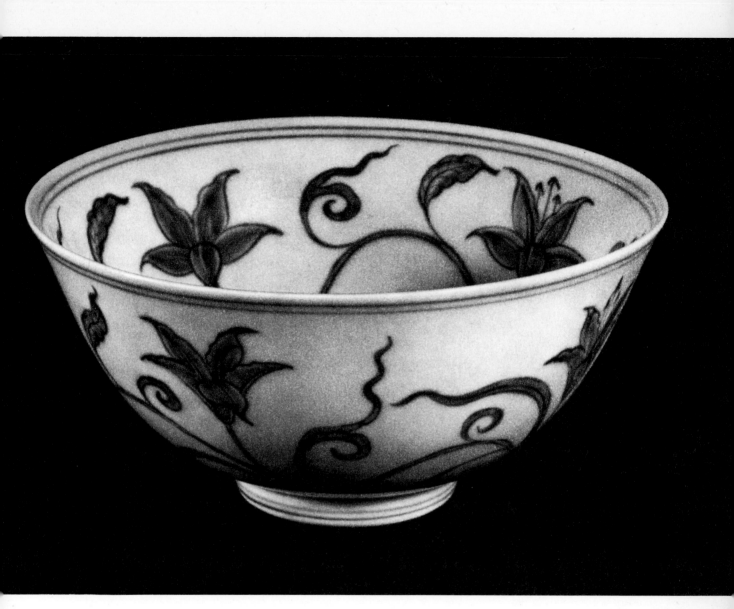

193. SMALL PORCELAIN BOWL DECORATED IN
UNDERGLAZE BLUE. MING DYNASTY
REIGN OF CH'ÊNG HUA (1465–1487)

*D.14.5 cm. Art Council of Great Britain (Formerly Collection
Mrs. C.G.Seligman), London*

This precious little bowl is a good example of the delicate
sensitivity characteristic of the reign of Ch'êng Hua. The almost
silvery nuances of the blue, the lightness of the composition,
the soft outlines of the painting, and the realistic treatment of
the flowers, are equally typical. It is a style which has not lost

any of the beauty, whilst no longer portraying the bold vigor
of the preceding eras.

One of those pieces said to be from the Imperial Collection,
this bowl displays a great refinement. All such examples have
the Imperial reign mark, and are decorated with flower sprays
or with fruit – chrysanthemums, hibiscus, lotus, poppies,
melons, or, as in this case, with lilies.

Exhibition: The Arts of the Ming Dynasty, *Oriental Ceramic
Society, London, 1957, No. 100.*

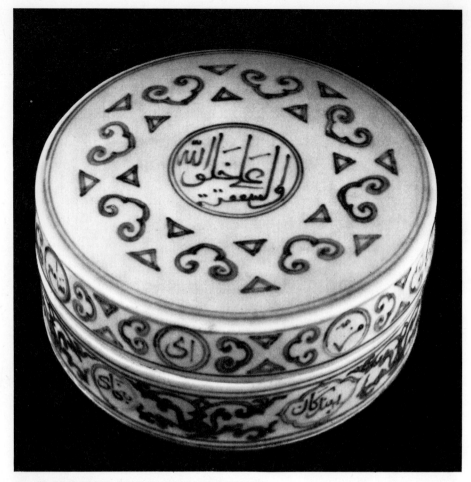

194. CYLINDRICAL BOX IN BLUE-AND-WHITE
PORCELAIN. MING DYNASTY
REIGN OF CHÊNG-TÊ (1506–1521)

*D.16.5 cm. Art Council of Great Britain (Formerly Collection of
Mrs. C.G.Seligmann), London*

The blue-and-white of the reign of Chêng-Tê has several
features peculiar to the period. The porcelain is thick and
heavy, the glaze greenish, and decoration is conventional –
heavily outlined arabesques and medallions with pious inscriptions in Arabic script. These pieces, intended solely for the use
of scribes, were made for the Moslem communities which were
very numerous in China at the time.

The cylindrical box shown here is exceptionally fine. Among
the *motifs* encircling the central inscription are triangles and a
kind of flower-shaped ornament which represent the auspicious
sceptre-heads known as *ju-i* ("which shall fulfill all desires"). The
inscription round the edge of the cover may be translated: "O
Thou who hearest my words, regard now my circumstances."
The other inscriptions are illegible. The mark of Chêng-Tê is
to be seen on the base in six characters.

Exhibitions: Chinese Blue-and-white Porcelain, *Oriental Ceramic
Society, London, 1953/4, No. 138.* – Arte Cinese, *Venice, 1954,
No. 667.*

195. LARGE COVERED JAR. BLUE-AND-WHITE
PORCELAIN. MING DYNASTY
REIGN OF CHIA CHING (1522–1566)

H.45.7 cm. Formerly Collection Mrs. Alfred Clark, Fulmer, Bucks.

The blue-and-white of the period of Chia Ching is characterized by the somber, almost violet color of the blue which, as
here, is often applied in unbroken washes. Among many varying themes, that of children playing *(wa wa)* is often encountered.

This subject is well illustrated here, and in a lively and
humorous way. Stylized clouds fill the empty spaces, the base
is encircled by a frieze of petals, and on the shoulders reserves
with branches of fruit contrast with a checkered ground of
swastikas. The cover has panels with lotus flowers, whilst the
sides have fruit and stylized clouds.

The mark of Chia Ching appears in underglaze blue on the
base.

Exhibitions: Arte Cinese, *Venice, 1954, No. 675.* – The Arts of
the Ming Dynasty, *Oriental Ceramic Society, London, 1957,
No. 139.*

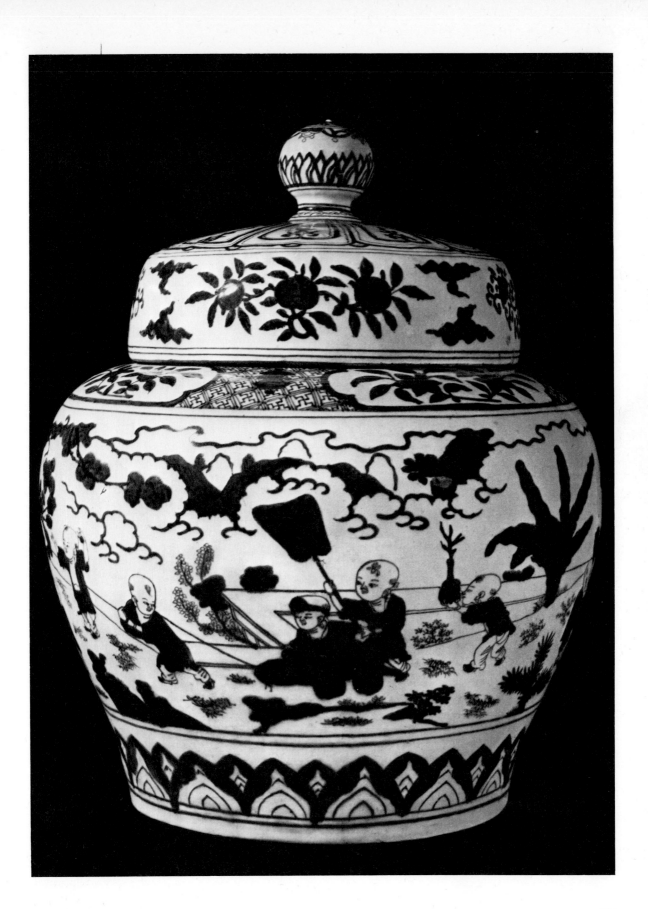

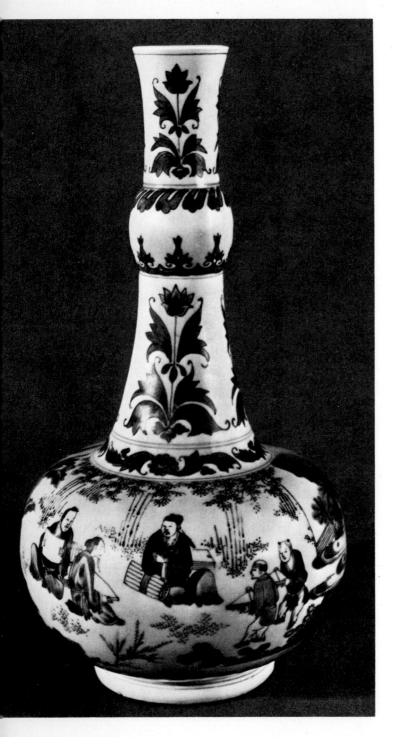

196. LONG-NECKED BOTTLE. MING DYNASTY
PERIOD KNOWN AS TRANSITIONAL
C. 1630–1640

H. 35 cm. Institut Néerlandais, Paris (Collection Fritz Lugt)

The beautiful piece illustrated here is typical of the renaissance
which took place in porcelain about the year 1620. The period
from 1620 to the accession of K'ang Hsi (1662) is remarkable
for a sudden change in style and decoration. At this time the
Imperial Government was undergoing the difficulties which
preceded and followed the fall of the Ming dynasty (1644).
Although for the most part it was made for export to the Near
East and to Europe, the porcelain of the period was, nevertheless, of fine quality as may be seen from the bottle reproduced here. Very often the forms are of foreign inspiration,
while the decoration, very different from the preceding years,
was copied by nearly all the European *faïence* factories, especially
those of Delft and Nevers.

The so-called "tulip" *motif,* seen here on two different parts of
the bottle, is very typical of the style. It was perhaps inspired
by 16th century Turkish *faïence* from Iznik, and in China seems
to be peculiar to the reign of Ch'ung Chêng (1628–1644), the
last Ming Emperor.

The intense blue, the broad sweeping treatment of the different
borders, and the sensitive painting of landscape, are all characteristic of this particular time. This example, like most others
of the same period, has no mark. An almost identical bottle
may be seen in the British Museum in London.

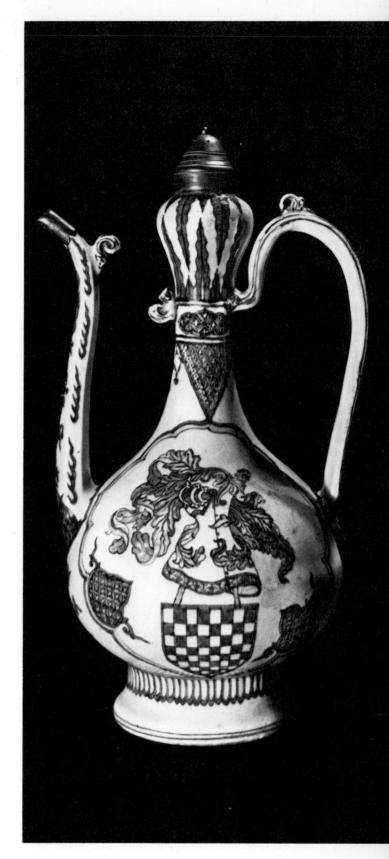

197. ARMORIAL EWER. DECORATION IN UNDERGLAZE BLUE. MING DYNASTY REIGN OF CHIA CHING (1522–1566)

H.33 cm. Collection A. de Medeiros e Almeida, Lisbon

The shape of this ewer, very common in China during the 15th and especially the 16th century, is copied faithfully from a metal ewer made in the Near East. The piece shown here is one of the only two known examples with Portuguese coats of Arms. The other one, which came from the famous Gulland Collection, is in the Victoria and Albert Museum, London. Without their colors the Arms are difficult to identify with certainty, though they may be those of Antonio Peixoto, who is known to have been the co-owner of a ship which went to China in 1542. At that time all trade with the Far East was exclusively carried on by Portugal, and she was, therefore, responsible for bringing the first Chinese porcelain to Europe. Because of her powerful position then, there exists a fair number of 16th century blue-and-white specimens of porcelain decorated with Portuguese coats of Arms, or special Portuguese inscriptions (cf. the bowl, Plate 149). These are the oldest known examples of European decoration on Chinese porcelain, earlier by far than those brought by the East India Companies during the 17th and 18th centuries.

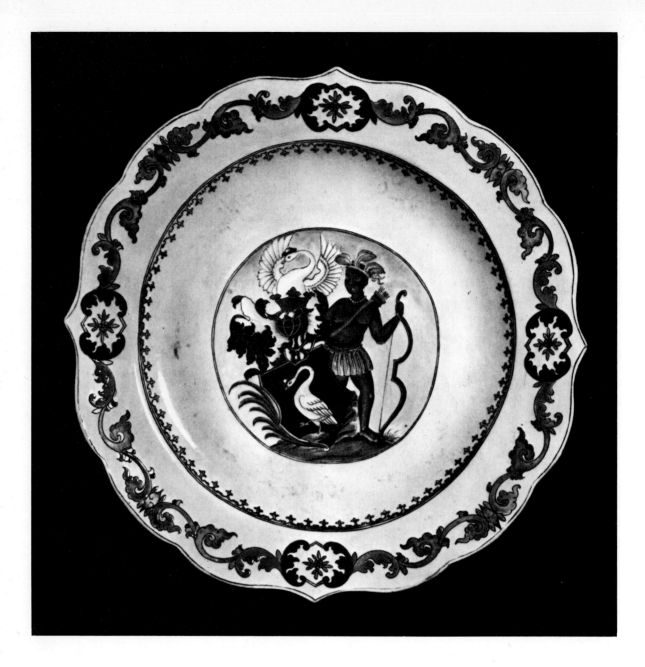

198. PLATE WITH EUROPEAN DECORATION
18TH CENTURY

D. 35 cm. Collection of the Vicomte de Torrão, Lisbon

The festooned border and baroque scrolls of this fine enameled
dish enable us to date it fairly accurately between 1740 and
1750. It is a good example of the exotic taste, and great interest
in distant peoples, which was manifest in so many different
ways during the 18th century in Europe. The central subject
is rare and not easy to identify. Perhaps it represents the Arms
of one of the directors of the Dutch East India Company.

CHRONOLOGY OF THE CHINESE DYNASTIES

Shang dynasty — c. 1500 (?) – 1028 B.C.

    Capital established at An-Yang — 1300 – 1028

Chou dynasty — 1027 – 256

    { Western Chou (Shensi Province) — 1027 – 771

    { Eastern Chou (Honan Province) — 771 – 256

    Period of the Warring States — 481 – 221

Ch'in dynasty (Foundation of the Empire) — 221 – 206

Han dynasty — 206 B.C. – 220 A.D.

    { Western Han (capital Ch'ang-an) — 206 B.C. – 8 A.D.

    { Eastern Han (capital Lo-yang) — 26 A.D. – 220 A.D.

Period of the Three Kingdoms — 220 – 265

Chin dynasty — 265 – 420

Period of the Six dynasties — 420 – 589

In the North
    { Northern Wei — 398 – 534
    { Eastern Wei and Northern Ch'i — 534 – 577
    { Western Wei and Northern Chou — 535 – 581

In the South
    { Sung — 420 – 478
    { Southern Ch'i — 479 – 501
    { Liang — 502 – 556
    { Ch'ên — 557 – 588

Sui dynasty — 589 – 618

T'ang dynasty — 618 – 906

The Five dynasties — 907 – 960

Sung dynasty — 960 – 1276

    { Northern Sung (capital K'ai-fêng) — 960 – 1127

    { Southern Sung (capital Hangchow) — 1127 – 1276

Mongol dynasty of the Yüan — 1276 – 1368

Ming dynasty — 1368 – 1644

Ch'ing or Manchu dynasty — 1644 – 1912

BIBLIOGRAPHY

Abbreviations:

A. A.	Artibus Asiae, Ascona
B. M.	Burlington Magazine, London
B. M. F. E. A.	Bulletin of the Museum of Far Eastern Antiquities, Stockholm
J. R. A. S.	Journal of the Royal Asiatic Society, London
O. A.	Oriental Art, London
O. Z.	Ostasiatische Zeitschrift
R. A. A.	Revue des Arts Asiatiques, Paris
T. O. C. S.	Transactions of the Oriental Ceramic Society, London

HISTORY—RELIGIONS—GENERAL

DE GROOT, J. J. M.: The Religious System of China. Leiden 1910.

GRANET, M.: La Religion des Chinois. Paris 1922.

GRANET, M.: Danses et légendes de la Chine ancienne. 2 vols. Paris 1926.

MASPERO, H.: La Chine Antique. Paris 1927 et 1955.

YETTS, W. P.: The George Eumorfopoulos Collection. Catalogue of the Chinese and Corean Bronzes, Sculpture, Jade, etc. 3 vols. London 1929.

GRANET, M.: La Civilisation chinoise. Paris 1929.

GROUSSET, R.: Sur les traces du Bouddha. Paris 1929.

KÜMMEL, O.: Die Kunst Chinas, Japans und Koreas. Potsdam 1929.

SIRÉN, O.: Histoire des arts anciens de la Chine. 4 vols. Paris 1929–30.

KÜMMEL, O.: Jörg Trubner. Zum Gedächtnis. Berlin 1930.

FRANCKE, O.: Geschichte des chinesischen Reiches. 5 Bde. Berlin-Leipzig 1930–52.

GOLDSCHMIDT, D.: L'Art chinois. Paris 1931.

ASHTON, L. et GRAY, B.: Chinese Art. London 1935.

CREEL, H. L.: The Birth of China. London 1936 and New York 1954.

GROUSSET, R.: Histoire de la Chine. Paris 1942.

ANDERSSON, J. G.: The Prehistory of the Chinese, in: B. M. F. E. A., No. 15, 1943.

SPEISER, W.: Die Kunst Ostasiens. Berlin 1946.

VISSER, H. F. E.: Asiatic Art in Private Collections of Holland and Belgium. Amsterdam 1947.

PALMGREN, N.: Selected Chinese Antiquities from the Collection of Gustav Adolf, Crown Prince of Sweden. Stockholm 1948.

MASPERO, H.: Les Religions chinoises. Paris 1950.

GROUSSET, R.: La Chine et son art. Paris 1951.

DAVID, M.: Arts et Styles de la Chine. Paris 1951.

BUHOT, J.: Arts de la Chine. Paris 1951.

SICKMAN, L. and SOPER, A.: The Art and Architecture of China. Harmondsworth (Middlesex) 1956.

CHENG TE-K'UN: The origin and development of Shang Culture. Asia Major. London 1957.

WILLETTS, W.: Chinese Art. 2 vols. Harmondsworth (Middlesex) 1958.

CONSTEN, E.: Das Alte China. Stuttgart 1958.

Aspects de la Chine. Bibliothèque de Diffusion du Musée Guimet. Paris 1959.

BRONZES

KOOP, A. J.: Early Chinese Bronzes. London 1924.

KARLBECK, O.: Notes on the Archeology of China, in B. M. F. E. A., No. 2, 1930.

ANDERSSON, J. G.: Hunting magic in the Animal style, in: B. M. F. E. A., No. 4, 1932.

SALMONY, A.: Sino-Siberian Art in the Collection of C. T. Loo. Paris 1933.

YETTS, W. P.: The Shang-Yin Dynasty and the Anyang finds, in: J. R. A. S., 1933.

WHITE, W. C.: Tombs of Old Lo-yang. Shanghai 1934.

SALLES, G.: Les Bronzes de Li-yu, in: R. A. A., VIII, 1934.

JANSE, O.: Le Style du Houai et ses affinités, in: R. A. A., VIII, 1934.

ANDERSSON, J. G.: The Goldsmith in Ancient China, in: B. M. F. E. A., No. 7, 1935.

KARLGREN, B.: Yin and Chou in Chinese Bronzes, in: B. M. F. E. A., No. 8, 1936.

PELLIOT, P.: The Royal Tombs of Anyang. London 1936.

UMEHARA, S.: Selected relics from ancient tombs of Chin Ts'un, Lo-yang. Tōkyō 1936.

UMEHARA, S.: Bronzes of the Warring States. Kyōto 1936 (in Japanese).

WU CH'I-CH'ANG: Studies on the dates of bronzes of the Chou dynasty. Shanghai 1936.

LEROI-GOURHAN, A.: Bestiaire du bronze chinois. Paris 1936.

KARLGREN, B.: New Studies in Chinese Bronzes, in B. M. F. E. A., No. 9, 1937.

METROPOLITAN MUSEUM OF ART, NEW YORK: Chinese bronzes of the Shang through the T'ang. New York 1938.

KARLBECK, O.: Catalogue of the collection of Chinese and Korean bronzes at Hallwyl House. Stockholm 1938.

MEISTER, P. W.: Chinesische Bronzemasken, in: O. Z., 1938.

PLENDERLEITH, H. J.: Technical notes on Chinese bronzes, in: T. O. C. S., Vol. 16, 1938–39.

LEMAÎTRE, S.: Les Agrafes chinoises. Paris 1939.

YETTS, W. P.: The Cull Chinese Bronzes. London 1939.

BRANKSTON, A. D.: Chinese bronze mirrors from the district of Yüeh, in: T. O. C. S., Vol. 17, 1939–40.

KARLGREN, B.: Huai and Han, in: B. M. F. E. A., No. 13, 1941.

JUNG KENG: The bronzes of Shang and Chou. Peking 1941.

HENTZE, C.: Die Sakralbronzen und ihre Bedeutung. Anvers 1941–43.

WATERBURY, FLORANCE: Early Chinese Symbols. New York 1942.

KARLGREN, B.: Some Early Chinese Bronze Masters, in: B. M. F. E. A., No. 16, 1944.

LODGE, J. E., WENLEY, A. G. and POPE, J. A.: A descriptive and illustrated catalogue of Chinese Bronzes. Freer Gallery of Art. Washington 1946.

HENTZE, C.: Bronzegerät, Kultbauten, Religion im ältesten China der Shang-Zeit. Anvers 1951.

WATERBURY, FLORANCE: Bird Deities in China, in: A. A., Suppl. X, 1952.

KARLGREN, B.: A Catalogue of the Chinese Bronzes in the A. F. Pillsbury Collection. Minneapolis Institute of Arts. Minneapolis 1952.

LOEHR, M.: The Bronze Styles of the Anyang Period, in: Archives of the Chinese Art Society of America, VII, 1953.

MIZUNO, S.: Bronzes and Jades of Ancient China. Tōkyō 1959.

LAUFER, B.: Jace. A Study in Chinese Archaeology and Religion. Chicago 1912.

GIESELER, G.: Le Jade dans le culte et les rites funéraires, in: Revue Archéologique, Paris 1916.

POPE-HENNESSY, U.: Early Chinese Jades. London 1923.

PELLIOT, P.: Jades Archaïques de Chine. Paris et Bruxelles 1925.

LAUFER, B.: Archaic Chinese Jades. New York 1927.

HENTZE, C.: Les Jades Archaïques en Chine, in: A. A., III, 1929.

KARLGREN, B.: Some Fecundity Symbols in Ancient China, in B.M. F.E.A., No. 2, 1930.

NOTT, S.C.: Chinese Jade. London 1926.

SALMONY, A.: Carved Jade of Ancient China. Berkeley 1938.

KARLBECK, O.: Some Archaic Chinese Jade Pendants and their Dating, in: B.M., 1938.

MICHEL, H.: Les Jades Astronomiques Chinois; une hypothèse sur leur usage, in: Bull. Musées Royaux d'Art et d'Histoire, Bruxelles 1947.

HANSFORD, S.H.: The Disposition of Ritual Jades in Royal Burials of the Chou Dynasty, in: J.R.A.S., 1949.

HANSFORD, S.H.: Chinese Jade Carving. London 1950.

JENYNS, S.: Chinese Archaic Jades in the British Museum. London 1951.

GURE, D.: Notes on the identification of Jade, in: O.A., 1951.

SCULPTURE

CHAVANNES, E.: La sculpture sur pierre en Chine au temps des deux dynasties Han. Paris 1893.

CHAVANNES, E.: Mission archéologique en Chine septentrionale. Paris 1909-15.

SEGALEN, V., DE VOISINS, G. et LARTIGUE, J.: Mission archéologique en Chine. Paris 1923.

LARTIGUE, J.: Le sanctuaire bouddhique du T'ien-long chan, in: R.A.A., 1924.

SIRÉN, O.: Histoire de la sculpture chinoise. Paris 1925-26.

TOKIWA, D. and SEKINO, T.: Buddhist Monuments in China. 6 vols. Tōkyō 1926-38.

SEGALEN, V., DE VOISINS, G. et LARTIGUE, J.: L'Art funéraire à l'époque des Han. Paris 1935.

MASPERO, H., GROUSSET, R. et LION, L.: Les ivoires religieux et médicaux chinois. Paris 1939.

SIRÉN, O.: Chinese Marble Sculpture of the Transition Period, in: B.M.F.E.A., No. 10, 1940.

MIZUNO, S. and NAGAHIRO, T.: A Study of the Buddhist Cave Temples at Lung-men. Tōkyō 1941.

SIRÉN, O.: Chinese Sculpture of the Sung, Liao and Chin Dynasties, in: B.M.F.E.A., No. 14, 1942.

SULLIVAN, M.: Excavation of the Royal Tomb of Wang Chien, in: T.O.C.S., Vol. 23, 1947-48.

FISCHER, O.: Chinesische Plastik. München 1948.

MIZUNO, S.: Chinese Stone Sculpture. Tōkyō 1950.

MIZUNO, S. and NAGAHIRO, T.: Yun-kang, the Buddhist Cave Temples of the Fifth Century A.D. 16 vols. Kyōtō 1950-57.

WILLETTS, W.: Chinese Buddhist Sculptures (P'ing-ling Ssŭ), in: Illustrated London News, February 6, 1954.

CHENG CHEN-TSE: The Stone Caves of Mai-chi shan. Peking 1954.

MIZUNO, S.: Bronze and Stone Sculpture of China, from the Yin to the T'ang Dynasty. Tōkyō 1960.

ZIMMERMANN, E.: Chinesisches Porzellan. Leipzig 1913 (2. Ausg. 1923).

HOBSON, R.L.: Chinese Pottery and Porcelain. London 1915.

MARQUET DE VASSELOT, J.-J. et BALLOT, M.-J.: La céramique chinoise (Musée du Louvre). Paris 1922.

HOBSON, R.L.: The Wares of the Ming Dynasty. London 1922.

KÜMMEL, O.: Ostasiatisches Gerät. Berlin 1925.

REIDEMEISTER, L.: Ming Porzellan. Berlin und Leipzig 1925.

HOBSON, R.L.: The Later Ceramic Wares of China. London 1925.

HOBSON, R.L.: Catalogue of the George Eumorfopoulos Collection. 6 vols. London 1925-28.

HOBSON, R.L.: A Catalogue of Chinese Pottery and Porcelain in the Collection of Sir Percival David, Bt. London 1934.

HOBSON, R.L.: Handbook of the Pottery and Porcelain of the Far East (British Museum). London 1937 (2nd ed. 1945).

BRANKSTON, A.D.: Early Ming Wares of Chingtechen. Peking 1938.

HONEY, W.B.: The Ceramic Art of China and other Countries of the Far East. London 1945.

KOYAMA, F.: The Story of Old Chinese Ceramics. Tōkyō 1949.

JENYNS, S.: Later Chinese Porcelain. London 1951.

POPE, J.A.: Fourteenth Century Blue and White. (A Group of Chinese Porcelains in the Topkapu Sarayi Müzesi, Istanbul.) Washington 1952.

HOCHSTÄDTER, W.: Pottery and Stonewares of Shang, Chou and Han, in: B.M.F.E.A., No. 24, 1952.

YORKE HARDY, S.: Illustrated Catalogue of Tung, Ju, Kuan, Chün, etc. Wares in the Percival David Foundation of Chinese Art. London 1953.

JENYNS, S.: Ming Pottery and Porcelain. London 1953.

GRAY, B.: Early Chinese Pottery and Porcelain. London 1953.

GARNER, SIR HARRY: Oriental Blue and White. London 1954.

DEXEL, Th.: Die Formen Chinesischer Keramik. Tübingen 1955.

POPE, J.A.: Chinese Porcelains from the Ardebil Shrine. Washington 1956.

GOLDSMITH PHILIPPS, J.: China-Trade Porcelain. London 1956.

LION-GOLDSCHMIDT, D.: Les Poteries et Porcelaines chinoises. Paris 1957.

DAVID (Lady): Illustrated Catalogue of Ch'ing Enamelled Wares in the Percival David Foundation of Chinese Art. London 1958.

GOMPERTZ, G.St.G.M.: Chinese Celadon Wares. London 1958.

KOYAMA, F.: Céramique Ancienne de l'Asie. Fribourg 1959.

Photographs by:

Arte e Colore, Milan: 75
Olof Eckverg, Stockholm: 17 24 28 65 73 179
Claudio Emmer, Milan: 50 58
Paul C. Faniel, Brussels: 40 115
Raymund Fortt, London: 120
Hans Hinz, Basel: 2 3 4 5 6 8 13 15 16 20 23 25 26 27 35 36 38 41 43 44 45 46 47 48 51 52 55 56 57 59 60 62 63 64 66 67 74 80 81 86 87 88 90 93 94 95 96 98 99 102 105 106 107 113 119 134 135 137 138 139 140 141 142 143 145 146 147 156 157 159 162 165 171 173 175 178 181 182 183 184 185 186 188 189 191 192 193 194 195
Images et Reflets, Paris: 1 7 9 10 29 34 37 39 49 53 68 70 72 76 77 78 83 84 85 89 91 92 97 101 103 104 111 114 118 121 122 124 125 127 128 129 130 132 133 136 144 153 155 158 160 161 163 164 166 168 169 170 172 174 176 177 180 187
Ken Domon, Tokyo: 117
Jean-Abel Lavaud, Paris: 196
Mario Novaïs, Lisbon: 69 151 152 154 167 190 197 198
André Thevenet, Paris: 14 21 33 54 71 112 116 131 150
Etienne Bertrand Weill, Paris: 11 12 13 30 32 61

Several photographs have been placed at our disposal by:

H.E. M. Giacinto Auriti, Rome: 108 109 110
Freer Gallery, Washington: 18 19 22 42
Mr. Desmund Gure, London: 79 82
Mme Daisy Lion-Goldschmidt, Paris: 148 149
M. J. C. Moreau-Gobard, Paris: 100
Museum van Aziatische Kunst, Amsterdam: 123
Museum of Eastern Art, Oxford (Cliché Larousse): 126

This book was printed in April, 1980 by Orell Füssli Graphic Arts Ltd. Zurich
Filmsetting: Orell Füssli Graphic Arts Ltd. Zurich
Colour lithography: Imprimeries Réunies S.A., Lausanne
Black-and-white lithography: Atesa S.A., Geneva
Binding: Schumacher S.A., Schmitten-Bern
Editorial: Barbara Benson-Perroud
Design and production: Claude Chevalley